D1234676

NILSSON

Nilsson

THE LIFE OF A SINGER-SONGWRITER

Alyn Shipton

OXFORD
UNIVERSITY PRESS

OXFORD
UNIVERSITY PRESS

Oxford University Press is a department of the University of Oxford.
It furthers the University's objective of excellence in research, scholarship,
and education by publishing worldwide.

Oxford   New York
Auckland   Cape Town   Dar es Salaam   Hong Kong   Karachi
Kuala Lumpur   Madrid   Melbourne   Mexico City   Nairobi
New Delhi   Shanghai   Taipei   Toronto

With offices in
Argentina   Austria   Brazil   Chile   Czech Republic   France   Greece
Guatemala   Hungary   Italy   Japan   Poland   Portugal   Singapore
South Korea   Switzerland   Thailand   Turkey   Ukraine   Vietnam

Oxford is a registered trademark of Oxford University Press
in the UK and certain other countries.

Published in the United States of America by
Oxford University Press
198 Madison Avenue, New York, NY 10016

© Alyn Shipton 2013

Library of Congress Cataloging-in-Publication Data
Shipton, Alyn.
Nilsson : the life of a singer-songwriter / Alyn Shipton.
pages ; cm
Includes bibliographical references and index.
ISBN 978-0-19-975657-5 (hardback :alk. paper)   1. Nilsson, Harry.
2. Singers—United States—Biography.   I. Title.
ML420.N6985S45 2013
782.42164092—dc23
[B]
2013003707

9 8 7 6 5 4 3 2 1
Printed in the United States of America
on acid-free paper

To my friend Lee Newman for introducing me to the world of Harry Nilsson.

Contents

Preface

ONCE DESCRIBED BY his producer Richard Perry as "the finest white male singer on the planet,"[1] nobody in popular music is as much of a paradox as Harry Nilsson. He was a major figure in popular culture at a time when stadium rock was in its infancy and huge concerts and festivals were becoming the norm, yet he studiously avoided live performance. This was even more remarkable because he was descended from a show business family—indeed his grandparents' circus act was commemorated in his album *Aerial Ballet*. Nilsson's instrument was the studio, his stage the dubbing booth, and his greatest technical triumphs were masterful examples of studio craft, such as "You Can't Do That," which was a daringly creative montage of Beatles songs.

Many songwriters look to some aspects of their own lives as inspiration for their work, but this was particularly true of Nilsson. He launched his career as a fresh-faced "long-ish...haired blond youth,"[2] whom some critics found had "specialness in his singing."[3] But over time the majority agreed with *Rolling Stone* magazine's verdict that even though "the ways in which he phrases and assembles the songs are clever beyond belief...songwriting is his strongest suit."[4]

In his lyrics, he drew on a well of personal experience, tragedy, and sadness that was at odds with his appearance and cheerful demeanor, and this underpinned a huge number of his songs. He delivered the results in a variety of ways, not least because his range, which spanned three and a half octaves, from light baritone to falsetto, apparently without a break between registers, gave him the attributes of a vocal chameleon. If there were both lead vocals and backups on his albums, the chances were that all the voices belonged to Nilsson. Yet at the heart of all his records was the ability to communicate directly to the listener, cleverly focusing on the emotions of the lyrics.

His first major album, *Pandemonium Shadow Show*, came out in 1967 during a period when pop music on both sides of the Atlantic was developing at an unprecedented rate. For the previous four years, the Beatles had made the running with songs that developed from relatively standard anonymous rock and roll to intense personal statements, drawing on shrewd observations of daily life in Liverpool and beyond. When their former publicist, Derek Taylor, sitting with his children in the parking lot of a Los Angeles superstore, first heard Nilsson singing "1941" from that album, he realized that a new ingredient had been added to the pop vocabulary of the time. He wrote:

> I button-pushed into a 17-bar song snatch and Timothy, eight and bright, said: "Oh, you're smiling now. Why? Oh why?" Why...the song had said: "He met a girl the kind of girl he'd wanted all his life. She was soft and good and kind to him and he took her for his wife. They got a house not far from town and in a little while the girl had seen the doctor and she came home with a smile. And in 1961 the happy father had a son...." Such a fragment of song it was, and from whom? It was new and hardly anything is new! And how could something come so strong and sudden so swiftly to snap the sad and slumbrous Saturday Safeway stupor? Hayes, who rides the discs like Joel McCrae, said, " '1941' folks." Oh yes he said, " '1941' by Nilsson." Nilsson. "Nilsson," he said again, and told us it was good and that is why we smiled.[5]

Hindsight shows how closely that song mirrored Nilsson's desertion by his father during his own childhood and chillingly foretold what would happen to his forthcoming marriage that produced his first son Zak. Yet, at the time, Nilsson strongly denied that this tragicomic ballad of history repeating itself, of love, marriage, and childbirth, leading first to abandonment and then to the pathway to adventure, was in any way directly about himself.

"Experiences are springboards to the imagination," he said. "Since everything you know is what you've experienced, my songs, in that sense, are a product of my experience. But they're not autobiographical."[6]

Even if he publicly denied the autobiographical inspiration behind his songs, Nilsson nevertheless thought deeply about the craft of songwriting, and how it was seldom possible to address major themes such as religion or politics in the three minutes of the 45 rpm single. Love, on the other hand, was universal, and something to which most listeners could immediately relate. Always given to self-deprecation in interviews, Nilsson played down his intentions. "When I started writing '1941,' " he recalled, "I was interested in writing a song about a number. So I thought I'd write a song about a year. First I tried 1944. No. Then I tried 1941. Yes, that's it! Originally it was going to be a war song."[7]

In effect, "1941" is both about numbers and the separation brought about by war. Numbers were a lifelong fascination to Nilsson, who was among the first generation of professional computer operators. He had such mental acuity that he could instantly tell someone the day of the week they had been born just from hearing their birth date. He was so entranced by the numerical symmetry of his son Zak's birth on the 17th of January '71 and his weight of seven pounds, seven ounces that he insisted his son's middle name ought to be a number. (Although it remains a mystery why, with quite so many sevens in the equation, Zak's middle name is 9.)[8] Even more than numbers, however, the Second World War was a key ingredient in shaping the person Nilsson was to become, as a result of his father's departure for the sea and his mother's return to her family to bring up her young son in a deprived area of Brooklyn. His subsequent childhood years in a single-parent family, with a mother who struggled with debt and alcoholism, and an absentee father whom he believed to be dead, not only shaped his personality, but provided a lifelong source of inspiration for the stories behind his lyrics.

Until now, there has been no full-length biography of Nilsson, the closest being an extended article in *Goldmine* magazine in April 1994 by Dawn Eden, based on Nilsson's last interview before his death. In this book, a detailed exploration of his life illuminates many of his songs in a way that has not been possible before, particularly those that combine autobiography with personal pain. Yet even when he was not being autobiographical, he was a songwriter's songwriter, his craft much admired by others, just as he appreciated his peers, including Randy Newman, who willingly played piano when Nilsson recorded an album of his songs.

Nilsson's recordings have become embedded in our consciousness through their use in films and television. Alongside his tour de force in the opening titles of John Schlesinger's *Midnight Cowboy*, many other movies that are constantly shown and reshown, such as *Goodfellas, The Ice Storm, Forrest Gump, Bridget Jones' Diary,* and *Reservoir Dogs,* have Nilsson's voice on their soundtracks. His music has also worked its way into the hearts of a younger generation through the soundtracks of *The Simpsons, The Muppet Show,* and *Beverly Hills 90210.* Other artists, known and not so well-known, have covered his songs, from Ringo Starr and Brian Wilson to Danni Minogue and the Walkmen.

Nilsson himself was concerned that his legacy would be confined to his Grammy-winning performances of two songs he did not write: "Everybody's Talkin'" and "Without You." This book is an attempt to look at the bigger picture and to re-examine a body of work that remains one of the most individual and influential contributions to the music of the 1960s and 1970s, as well as shedding some light on the man who made it.

Acknowledgments

FIRST AND FOREMOST, this book would not have come about were it not for the help and encouragement of Una Nilsson (Harry Nilsson's widow). Equally, it has largely been possible because of the commitment of Lee Blackman, attorney to the Nilsson estate. Both of them have been generous with their time and assiduous in answering every query, no matter how obscure, as well as pointing me to people and documents that vastly enriched my understanding of Nilsson and his world. They have also generously allowed me to quote at length from Nilsson's unfinished autobiography, both in its raw, recorded form, referred to in the notes as the *Oral Autobiography*, and in its semi-edited transcribed form, the "Draft autobiography," on which Nilsson was working at the time of his death in 1994. Anita Blackman has also provided help and support throughout the gestation of the book.

I would also like to single out Harry's son Kief O. Nilsson, who helped me find my way through many boxes of family papers, tracked down obscure music, and kindly ferried me around Los Angeles.

The origins of the book go back to a very pleasant lunch at the Dome on Sunset Boulevard back in 2004. I was working on my biography of Jimmy McHugh (*I Feel a Song Coming On*, Illinois University Press, 2009) and in a break from working on documents, McHugh's great-grandson, Lee Newman, brought me to meet the record producer Richard Perry. Newman had played Oblio in the 1991 Los Angeles revival of *The Point*, and when he discovered my interest in Nilsson's music, he made it his business to bring me into contact with many of those who had known Nilsson. I owe Lee a tremendous debt for being an excellent guide to Nilsson's friends and colleagues, as well as to the locations where he lived and worked, and Richard a similar one for vividly bringing to life the time when he recorded Nilsson's two best-selling albums. I went on to make a documentary biography of Richard for BBC Radio 2, and some of the interviews that have found their way into this volume were originally done at the time of that series. Richard has generously allowed me to quote from my wide-ranging conversations with him, for which I am most grateful.

When I started work on the book, John Scheinfeld was putting the finishing touches on his biographical film *Who Is Harry Nilsson, and Why Is Everybody Talking About Him?* John not only put up with my critical observations on an early cut of the movie, but generously opened up his files. He and Lee Blackman made it possible for me to consult all the unedited interviews for the film, and these have been a tremendous resource. Equally, Stuart Grundy, a BBC colleague, interviewed Nilsson in 1977 on more than one occasion for BBC Radio 1. I have been able to hear those interviews and also a set of others that Stuart did with many of Nilsson's associates for a later series of radio programs on his life. I am grateful to Stuart and the New Unique Broadcasting Company for permission to quote from these.

Rob Santos at RCA Records kindly organized access to the company's archives at the Sony building in New York, as well as finding serviceable prints of some of the photographs in Nilsson's personal files, and my thanks go to him and his colleagues, head of archives, Glenn Korman, and director of archives, Tom Tierney.

Further family information came from Annie Nilsson, Gary Nilsson, Drake Nilsson, and Zak Nilsson.

The website www.fortheloveofharry.com has been a remarkable and consistent source of all things Nilsson.

For interviews, letters, e-mails, and other help, I am indebted to all the following: John Altman, Gerry Beckley, Tim Blackmore, Bob Borgen, Perry Botkin Jr., Henry Diltz, Donna Dolenz, Stanley Dorfman, Ashley and Deborah Dow, Herbie Flowers, Alana Gospodnetich, Jeff Griffin, Anna Harrison, Eric Idle, Samantha Juste, Trevor Lawrence, Jamie Leffler, David Litchfield, Judy McHugh, Mike McNaught, David Nordon-Angus, Michael Palin, May Pang, Chris O'Dell, Van Dyke Parks, Larold Rehbun, Andrea Robinson, Chris Spedding, Frank Stallone, Melissa Van Der Klugt, Klaus Voormann, Cheryl Wadsworth, Jimmy Webb, Tony Wilson, and Fred Wolf.

Gary Brooker was unable to help, but our evening together recalling Procol Harum and the '60s was truly memorable.

I am grateful to Dr. Timothy Jones (deputy principal) and the Research Committee of the Royal Academy of Music in London for help in the transcription of interviews and for assistance toward my research in Los Angeles.

At Oxford, my editor Suzanne Ryan has been tough when it mattered, as well as being her usual supportive self, and her colleagues Caelyn Cobb, Adam Cohen, Amy Rose Perkins, and Madelyn Sutton have all played important parts in the book's progress. Bonnie Kelsey's attention to editorial detail has been vital, as has the calming presence of production editor Molly Morrison.

For permission to quote lyrics from Nilsson's songs, my thanks go to Pat Woods and her team at Warner-Chappell Music, Inc. and Warner-Tamerlane Music Publishing. I am also grateful for similar permission, in respect of the territories that they administer, to Robert Briggs, Marsha Tannenbaum, and Audrey Ashby at EMI Music Publishing.

Alyn Shipton
Oxford, UK
December 2012

NILSSON

Well in 1941 a happy father had a son
And by 1944 the father walked right out
the door
And in '45 the mom and son were still alive
But who could tell in '46 if the two were to
survive.

1

1941

HARRY EDWARD NILSSON was born at Bushwick Hospital in Brooklyn, at 2.15 a.m. on June 15, 1941. His father, also Harry Nilsson and also Brooklyn born, was twenty-four years old, and his occupation was listed on the birth certificate as "painter."[1] Harry Sr. was employed around the Bushwick area, close to his wife and firstborn son, but his livelihood would change dramatically after December of that same year, when Pearl Harbor was attacked. As the United States entered the Second World War, Harry Nilsson Sr., like many of his countrymen, left home to take part. As young Harry was growing up, his mother told him how his father had become a "Seabee," a member of the Naval Construction Battalions, who were recruited from the building trades in the early spring of 1942 to be posted to the Pacific.

The Seabee training after initial enlistment was short and sharp. The men spent three weeks in boot camp, followed up by a posting to Port Hueneme in California, where, after a further six weeks of intensive instruction, they were shipped out to start work. As the years went on, stories would reach the young Harry of his father's duties in operations to clean up the islands that had been held by the Japanese, building temporary airstrips, or constructing and maintaining makeshift bases for the marines.[2] After leaving home well before his son's first birthday, Harry Sr. was away from his family for the best part of two and a half years. On one of his scarce home visits, during which a photograph was taken of father and son together, the infant Harry was dressed in a matching miniature sailor suit. Such opportunities were rare, and consequently Harry grew up deprived of regular contact with the man whose name he bore. So it is not altogether surprising that almost nothing he believed about his father was true. Harry Sr. had indeed gone away to sea, but as an ordinary merchant seaman. He had a busy time during the war years, but his life was a lot more prosaic than the fantasy career as a fighting Seabee that his lonely wife invented for him, in order to convince her son that his absentee father was a hero.[3]

Harry's mother, born Elizabeth Martin, and known by her family as Bette, was a house-wife aged just twenty-one when the baby arrived. She was part of a large Irish-American family, where music and gossip, the *craic* as the Irish call it, were an integral part of every-day life. She was a vibrant woman, full of laughter and tall tales, remembered by her fam-ily as the life and soul of a party. At the time of Harry's birth, she and her husband had moved away from her family home. They were living in a small apartment in a brown-stone at 791 Monroe Street in the Bedford Stuyvesant section of Brooklyn.

In the early 1940s, north Brooklyn was in a state of decline. There were considerable social problems, and these were beginning to be exacerbated by a dramatic shift in the racial and class balance of the area. The prewar Jewish population was moving out, and many African Americans and Latinos from the overcrowded areas of Harlem were mov-ing in, given the availability of plenteous well-built, albeit shabby, housing stock. The entire community, new and old, suffered from poverty and petty crime. In the months leading up to Harry's birth, four Catholic churches in the area canceled their evening services, because of the danger to the congregation making their way to and from church after dark. Residents complained of the "robberies, gambling, assaults and criminal acts of all sorts that take place."[4]

New York's charismatic and active mayor, Fiorello La Guardia, was well aware of the roaming gangs, escalating crime, and social unrest in the area. His reputation had been built on being tough on crime and corruption in the 1930s, but now he was shuttling to and from Washington, having taken on the wartime role of heading the Office of Civilian Defense. Instead of dealing with the problems in Brooklyn as he would most assuredly have done earlier in his mayoral term of office, he entered into a disagreement with the Kings County Grand Jury, which had been convened to report on the problems in Bedford Stuyvesant. The jury accurately pinpointed many of the area's difficulties and possible solutions, but to make political capital, the mayor blamed the problems on "the Negro question," and a stalemate ensued. This did no favors to the population while the city fathers wrangled with one another over the source of the trouble.

Once Harry Sr. was away at sea, it was no longer feasible from either a financial or security point of view for Bette to remain in Monroe Street, so she moved back into her parents' home, a few blocks away in a tenement above a sewing machine shop at the intersection of Jefferson and Patchen Avenues. Today the northeast side of this crossroads has been redeveloped, but the rest of the junction has hardly changed since the Martins lived there during the war. Look upward from the street at the three-story building on the southwest corner, 762 Jefferson, with its brick decorative bands and ornate tiled frieze, and behind the windows of the top-floor six-room apartment, three generations of the family were crowded in together. Nilsson recalled: "We lived with my grandmother, my grandfather, and two uncles."[5]

Unlike Harry's father, his maternal grandfather, Charlie Martin, was a real hero. He had been machine-gunned during the First World War. Outwardly, he had little to show for it, except scars on his legs and a box of medals, but by the early 1940s, his old injuries had worsened, to the extent that he was bedridden, occupying one of the rooms in the apartment. His wounds affected the way the whole family lived their lives. To help give him some respite from his almost constant pain, his wife, Harry's grandmother, known universally as Nana, slept in what was little more than an alcove off the hallway, and everyone else fitted in around the old man's needs. In the largest bedroom lived Harry's aunt, Cissy Martin, and her husband, Fred Hoefer, who was the night manager at the Drake Hotel on Park Avenue in Manhattan. In the next room was Harry's uncle, John Martin, a mechanic who worked in a garage in Brooklyn. When Harry's mother Bette got a job as a waitress on the night shift at the Waldorf Astoria Hotel, also on Park Avenue, she and her brother John operated a "hot-bed" system. As soon as she got in from work, he got up, washed, grabbed a swift breakfast, and left the house, so that she could take over the bed and go to sleep. There was a crib in the corner of the room for Harry.

As the youngest member of the family, Harry heard plenty of lively stories from Nana about Charlie Martin's early life, even though his grouchy grandfather, holed up in bed all day, now bore little resemblance to the man she described. Once upon a time, Charlie had owned Moran's Bar and Grill, a gin mill in the neighborhood, where plenty of Brooklyn's Irish-American population came to be fed and watered, and he had been a well-liked member of the community. Despite the long hours involved in running a tavern, there was a rebel streak in Martin, and as a young man he liked to sneak out at night in search of a good time. It wasn't until, after one escapade too many, Nana poured pounds of sugar into his gas tank—seizing up his car—that Charlie's nocturnal adventures came to an end.

Despite the bravery the old man had shown in winning his medals, including two purple hearts, to young Harry he was an object of fun. The boy gained endless amusement from hiding his grandfather's medicine or dashing in and tickling his feet while he slept. This prank was made easier by the fact that the room had two doors, so that Harry could sneak in by one and out through the other, in time to avoid the swipes of the stout cane that Martin kept at his bedside to assist him in his painful trips to the bathroom.

With his mother and Uncle Fred asleep during the daytime, his grandfather out of commission, and the rest of the family away at work, young Harry spent most of his time with his grandmother. She would play with him when not attending to her reading or knitting. Otherwise, her main occupation was sitting at the window, watching the world go by, and her grandson formed a particularly graphic memory of her. "Her arms were large and flabby, with elbows resembling elephant skin from leaning on the window sill," recalled Nilsson. "She eventually took to using pillows."[6]

Meanwhile, Bette Nilsson, effectively deserted by her husband, living a nocturnal life, and back with the family whom she had sought to escape by getting married, began to drink heavily. She also started what was to be a long-term habit of bouncing checks. When Harry Sr. returned on a visit home in 1944, he confronted Bette about her growing financial and alcoholic problems, and when he went back to sea, they separated for good. In due course, after leaving the merchant marine, Harry Sr. settled in Paterson,

New Jersey, took a job with General Motors, and soon afterward married his second wife Lois. Their daughters Carol and Barbara were born in 1945 and 1946 respectively. A son Keith (who died in infancy) followed in 1951, a second son Gary in 1952, and a third daughter Rainy in 1957.[7]

Despite moving away from the area and starting a new family, it seems that Harry Sr. stayed in contact with Bette, but his young son remained completely unaware of this. Indeed, in the immediate wake of the family split, Bette told her son that his dad had died in the war, bravely fighting for his country. In the opinion of many of those who knew Nilsson, his father's departure (and his presumed death) caused a deep psychological wound that never properly healed. The sense of loss was to influence many of the songs that the adult Harry would write and perform. His songwriting and producing colleague Van Dyke Parks, for example, believes:

> [It] really brought the best out…in Harry, because it was something to overcome.… [In Freudian terms] a father's death is the biggest psychological event of a man's life.…I think it was the case with Harry. He was very mystified by it. To not have had all the conversations with a father that one would want creates quite a longing heart. And he had that, but in a pronounced way.[8]

The songwriter Jimmy Webb, also to be a great friend of Nilsson's, believes that the family breakup was responsible not just for inspiring Nilsson's most profound music but also for many of the character traits of the adult he became:

> I think there was a terrible hunger there, that he needed love so, so badly, and he wanted all of it he could get. And just sucked up as much attention and love [as he could]. It must have been a terrible thing. I can't imagine, because I grew up in this middle-class home.…And he had a father who didn't even stay around to see what he was going to look like. It's got to be a tough thing. We know more about that now than we did then, when we just knew that some people were deeply troubled and disturbed and didn't really know why. I think it's pretty clear that Harry was profoundly disturbed by the fact that he was abandoned by his father.[9]

Yet although Harry Sr. had walked out of his life, young Harry continued to be regaled by Bette with tales of his father and of his paternal family. She took on the single parent role as best she could, given the antisocial hours of her job, and in her former husband's absence, she tended to lionize him. It was from her that Harry learned the romantic legend of his paternal great-grandparents and their acrobatic troupe, Nilsson's Aerial Ballet. He recalled:

> [They] were circus performers, and they had another act called Nilsson's Luminous Butterfly. That was in 1901.…I think my mother…[also] wanted to be in show

business at one time. That sort of rubbed off on me, and I know my grandmother used to play piano in the silent movies. She just played by ear, but she had a good sense, you know? And when I was a little child, they used to put me on the piano and have me sing songs to the adults.[10]

Even if he was not able to spend much time with her during the week, Harry shared the world of his mother's imagination, and songs were a vital part of that world. The vaudeville song "Freckles"—which found its way onto Nilsson's first solo album, *Pandemonium Shadow Show*—was one of the pieces Bette taught her son. He remembered her singing it to the rhythmic click-clack of the windshield wipers as they drove their old automobile around Brooklyn. Pictures from this time show Harry as a street-smart blond-haired little boy, with a winning smile and few hints of the tough life he was experiencing.

During Harry's early childhood, in what little spare time Bette had, she wrote poetry, which sometimes got transformed into songs. In later life Nilsson would record two of her pieces, "Marching Down Broadway" and "Little Cowboy." He liked to recall that Irving Berlin had once offered her $1,000 for the publishing rights to "Marching Down Broadway," but she turned him down.[11]

After his father's departure, as the war reached its closing stages, Harry's childhood memories became more focused. "Army vehicles of all descriptions passed our house," he recalled. "It was like seeing parades all the time, on their way to the Brooklyn Naval Yard."[12] At the same time, the problems of the rough-and-tough neighborhood came a few steps closer to the Martin household. One night, looking out of the window, Harry saw a man being fatally shot with a homemade zip gun. Dripping blood, the victim staggered almost the entire length of the block to a call box on the wall below the apartment, where he fell and died while trying to telephone the police. Other times, members of the gangs that milled about on Jefferson and Patchen would get into fights on the corner below the family house. In 1951, in a bizarre Halloween incident that was neither trick nor treat, Harry and his mother were brutally attacked by a gang of African American girls as they made their way home after dark.

Shortly after the end of the war, John Martin moved out to get married. He and his bride Anna wanted to live closer to the garage where he worked, so Bette entirely took over their room, which she now shared with Harry. "When she would come home, I would wake up to the constant smell of liquor and perfume," he wrote. "Her face felt cold as she would kiss me and lay down next to me. We would talk for a few moments, and then sleep."[13]

Fueled by alcohol and loneliness, Bette, who was still a striking and attractive woman, sought solace in a string of unsuccessful romances. She gave birth to another child, Harry's half-sister Michelle, in 1947. Only a week before, the crib—in which Harry used to sleep—had been commandeered by the Hoefers for their firstborn son Steve. Now, with a new girl in the family, it was handed back to Bette for Michelle. The Nilssons remained squeezed into their room in the apartment until the spring of 1952. Yet it would be a mistake to think of Bette Nilsson as a sad or tragic figure. Harry's second wife, Diane, remembered her fondly as a bright and lively personality:

> She had a terribly hard life, being a single mother in the '40s and being an alcoholic and pulling herself out of that. She was just hysterically funny, an Irish Catholic from Brooklyn, New York. She just was full of stories and jokes. I just adored her. She was one of the funniest people I've ever known. She was warm and loving toward me, toward everyone. She was just over the top proud of Harry.[14]

Yet hand in hand with his mother's love came still more tragedy. One particularly vivid memory that Harry often referred to in later life took place during the winter of 1948, when his adored pet, the family cat, Softie, went outside on a cold winter's evening. A blizzard blew up, and after a couple of nights there was still no sign of the cat. The boy's mother, grandparents, uncles, and aunts reassured the distraught seven-year-old that Softie would be fine, sheltering in a coal bin or a basement, chasing mice. It was only when the snows finally melted, weeks later, that Softie was revealed, frozen solid, trying to scratch his way back in. With the trait that he often used in conversation and in his song lyrics of turning a heartfelt tragic event into a throwaway comic remark, Nilsson made light of his pet's death. "He looked," reported Harry, "like a stuffed attack cat, trying to break into the window. My uncle Fred and Nana had the unpleasant task of breaking him off the windowsill, and disposing of him like an unwanted statue from a distant relative. He had the look of the coyote when outwitted by the road runner."[15]

The offhand, witty story of loss, like the lopsided grin of young Harry in his childhood photographs, conceals pain, much of which was pent up until adulthood. This finally found an outlet in songs that share an insouciant surface charm with deeper emotions beneath. Years later, Harry was to revisit the scene of his childhood with Van Dyke Parks, who said:

> How could you possibly reach any depth, without having had some sorrow? What I'm saying is, Harry had sorrow as a child, an unspeakably harsh childhood. I visited his childhood haunts with him in a stretch limousine [that] took us out to Brooklyn.... And we got lower and lower, through more bridges and tunnels and dank alleys and backstreets and garbage. And finally we got to a place with a sooty brick wall with a sign that said, "Starve a rat. Cover your garbage." And he was shaking and weeping in the car, because this is where he came from. This is what he remembered, and this is what brought acuity to his sense of empathy for other people. And it was that empathy that brought magic and illumination into his work as an artist.[16]

In late 1951, John Martin and his wife Anna decided to escape from the depressing atmosphere of Brooklyn altogether, and they set off to find a better life in California. He found work running a garage in San Bernardino, fifty miles east of downtown Los Angeles. After hearing of the attack on Bette and Harry in October that year, he suggested that she and her family should leave the New York area as well, and move out to join him. So, in early 1952, Bette, Harry, and Michelle set off by Greyhound bus for California. This was an epic five-day journey that involved sleeping on the bus, occasionally disembarking for a few moments at a bus station to catch a sandwich and stretch the legs, but mainly watching the extraordinary panorama of the American landscape roll past. There were plains, mountains, deserts, and towns, large and small, but overall an inexorable sense of constant motion, noise, and poor food left them all exhausted.

Until they found a place of their own, they stayed with John and Anna, and the children were enrolled in local schools. Harry was to attend a Catholic school, but with his Brooklyn sense of street style, he was uneasy. "From what I could see, we had arrived in the land of country, where the mandatory dress code was jeans, and my mother had no money to speak of," he recalled. "I refused to go. My mother took me to a store and managed to buy me a pair of Levis on Monday."[17]

Wearing his jeans with what he described as "relief and pride," he was taken straight from the store to his new school. One of the teaching sisters led him by the hand into the class of twenty-five other children, explaining that he had come from New York and deserved a nice welcome. This was followed by the announcement that as it was his first day, he could be forgiven for not knowing that jeans were forbidden in school.

After a few weeks with her brother, Bette moved her family to downtown Los Angeles, where she thought the prospect of work was more likely than in San Bernardino. For Harry, after briefly enjoying the sunshine and relaxed atmosphere around his uncle's home, the next move was no improvement over life in Brooklyn. He recalled:

We were at a place at Eighth and Catalina. We stayed there a short time, maybe two or three months, at a parent-child boarding house, which I guess is similar to a day-care place today. When people went to work, there was someone to watch over us. There were eight or nine kids living in this house and [one of them] would shit in the bed.... And the house father sort of knew it but, to be fair, he'd have all of us kids line up, turn around, drop their drawers and bend over and he'd look for smeared shit. And of course, he found it on poor Gary. And he beat the crap out of Gary. It would happen day after day after day. And my mother caught on to this cruelty... that's when we moved.[18]

Following this false start, Harry's next year of life in California was generally a success. He was naturally athletic, and he thrived in the sunny climate and the outdoor lifestyle. The photograph of the ten-year-old Nilsson on the front of his album *Harry* (released in 1969) dates from this time, with neatly combed blond hair, a broad-lapelled blazer, and a school tie knotted below his collar. There is nonetheless a hint above his posed smile for the photographer that his eyes have already seen more of life than most boys of his age.

However, living in the West was to give Harry a perspective on his early childhood that would have been impossible had he stayed in Brooklyn. Looking back in 1977, he said:

> Most people are content to fantasize about the way they live. When you're growing up in a shitty neighborhood or something, you just say, well, you don't know it's really a shitty neighborhood, because you're in the middle of growing up in it. And to you, it's just all the good and bad that you know about. You have nothing to compare it to unless you're living in another neighborhood. And the guy living in that other neighborhood has a fantasy about what it's like to live up over there.[19]

From downtown Los Angeles, the family moved to Colton, a small town about five miles away from San Bernardino, where Bette found a job as a waitress at a drive-in restaurant beside the railroad tracks. The work was hard and the pay low, not helped by the fact that this was the local meeting point for the Hells Angels, whose presence kept other customers at bay. Yet the job came with accommodations, and for the next year the Nilssons were happily ensconced in a small silver Airstream trailer tucked into the side of the parking lot. Eleven-year-old Harry began to have adventures, and these blurred into a wistful, semi-mythical account of this first West Coast phase of his childhood. His son Zak said, "You hear a lot of stories about that one, about the move from N.Y. to L.A., Harry telling it three different ways to different people...."[20]

Maybe in response to being uprooted from Brooklyn, Harry recalled that this was the moment when he felt that he might become some kind of performer. He said: "I had a feeling I was going to be some sort of superstar—maybe an actor or something. When I was a kid of ten or eleven, I used to get under the covers and say: 'And now presenting *me* doing the great Al Jolson—"Mammmmmy"'...or 'Humphrey Bogart,' or 'And now presenting *me* spelling the word "Czechoslovakia"!'"[21]

The one ever-present aspect of the family's life in Colton was the bikers. In his memoir of that time, Harry described the lot where the Nilssons lived as the spawning ground for the local Hells Angels chapter:

> [They] would ride up thirty to fifty strong, sometimes only seven or eight. Regardless, they virtually gunned the classic Hogs and a couple of Indians, circled the drive-in two or three times, before leaving their bikes neatly, left to center. Every night, my mother served them, receiving no tips to speak of. It was a little scary and the noise of their rush was deafening. I would always watch them from the window. One of them took a liking to me and asked, "Have you ever been on a motorcycle?"
>
> "No," I answered.
>
> "Hop on the back, put your arms around me, and watch you don't burn yourself on the pipes down there. Okay, let's move!" I've long forgotten his name, but not the ride. Up and onto the railway tracks. He was hot. He jumped over the tracks

onto some gravel, grass, and then the street to the open road at 50 mph. I was stoked. Hells Angels! My friends. Or was I a mascot?[22]

Nilsson never did forget the romance and excitement of that first bike ride when he was just eleven years of age. He also recalled the other initiation of that year, finding out about sex with Mary Anne Schultz, the thirteen-year-old daughter of the diner's manager. When Mr. and Mrs. Schultz and Harry's mother were fully employed at the restaurant, and Michelle had fallen asleep, Mary Anne and Harry would spend their evenings together in the Airstream trailer. They explored one another's bodies with the avid curiosity of all young teenagers, leading to their first fumbling experiences of intercourse. He was besotted with her for six months until the incident of the ducklings, when just as with his cat Softie, something on which he had lavished love and attention was abruptly taken from him.

On an outing to a local fairground with Mary Anne, Harry won a couple of baby ducks by accurately throwing a ping-pong ball into a fishbowl. He had good hand-eye coordination, and this was an easy challenge for him. Back at the parking lot, the ducklings were suitably accommodated, and over the next four months or so, he and Mary Anne raised them into a couple of fine, white adults. One day they disappeared—only to show up on the restaurant menu. "I couldn't believe it," recalled Harry, "as I had been told they ran away."[23] His respect for the Schultz family died with the ducks.

At some point in early 1953, the Nilssons moved on from the Schultz drive-in, and Bette found other work back in the city of Los Angeles itself. From the relatively calm environment of Colton, the family now relocated to a district where the atmosphere was probably as close as it was possible to get to the region of Brooklyn they had left just over a year before. Pico Union had been a white, predominantly Jewish enclave in the 1930s, but now it was becoming a high-crime, multicultural neighborhood, with a majority of Mexican newcomers. Like parts of Brooklyn, it also combined heavy industry and warehouses with residential areas. Nilsson remembered:

We moved in with a woman my mother became friends with, called Mrs. Morey. She was a waitress. They had just bought a small house in Pico Union district.... [After that] we finally went to Sixth and Alvarado, which was not a great place, either. Hookers, gangs, mostly Mexican. And it was just a tough, tough place to grow up. But when you're in it, it doesn't seem as bad as it does when you look back and say, my God, am I lucky to get out of there?[24]

When the family moved to Pico Union, Harry and Michelle resumed their education at the Precious Blood of Christ Elementary School on South Occidental Boulevard. It was co-educational and run by nuns. While there, Harry, still eleven when he started at the school, and not without the urge to continue where he and Mary Anne Schultz had left off, had crushes on several of the many Irish girls who also attended. He was fortunate to have been able to go to the school at all; because of his mother's low income, she had been able to negotiate a special reduced tuition fee of three dollars a month for her children. Despite the poverty and crime all around where they lived, they began to prosper at school.

Not long after Harry started there, the school ran a series of tests, organized for the diocese by trainee priests from the nearby seminary. Nilsson was one of a small group of students selected to take them. He remembered:

> When we got the results back, the Reverend Mother Superior jumped the gun and said to me, in front of my mother, "Do you know arithmetic is easy for you, do you know English is easy for you, spelling is easy for you, science is easy for you? Why don't you apply yourself?" The typical speech. I, of course, didn't know how easy these things were for me.... I hated them, I hated math, I hated science.[25]

Nilsson was showing the first signs of the aptitude and intelligence that later took him into the world of computers, but despite the encouragement of his mother and the teachers, he played down any academic success he had and devoted most of his energy to making the best of life in the area, despite the threats that lurked in the neighborhood. After school, he and his sister usually walked down Occidental to Lafayette Park, where there were games of basketball and softball. One day, as he looked up from the basketball court, Harry saw Michelle walking out of the park, holding an older boy's hand. Nilsson dashed out of the court, picked up a friend's baseball bat on the way, caught up with the pair, and set about the boy. Under his hail of blows, the stranger released his sister, and Harry made her promise never to go off with an unknown boy again.[26] Years of fending for them both while his mother was absent at work had begun to instill a sense of family responsibility in him.

He made several lifelong friends in the area. When the Nilssons first came to Mrs. Morey's house and were squeezed into her attic, Harry befriended a Japanese boy called Bester. They joined in the ballgames in Lafayette Park, but they also shared a love of movies. They discovered that one of the local churches had a cellar where films were shown on Friday night. The two boys found a window that gave a perfect view of the screen, and they could usually just about make out the muffled dialog through the glass. This unofficial weekly viewing was the beginning of Nilsson's encyclopedic knowledge of movies, which was furthered still more when he could scrape together the entrance money for one of the three movie theaters in the area. The love of movies was also the basis of his friendship with Jerry Smith, whom Harry met after he had transferred to the newly opened St. John Vianney School.

At the park, Harry now played basketball with his friends Don and Shreddy from his new school against boys from Belmont High. On the Belmont team was Smith, of whom Nilsson said, "[He became] my dearest and closest friend in life. Jerry and I hit it off right away. We were the best of pals."²⁷ The two boys shared a particular love for Laurel and Hardy, which was to be a passion of Nilsson's until his dying day.

While Nilsson made friends and did better than he would care to admit in school, Bette began drinking again, and in her self-created role of "war widow" rather than divorcée, she was hungry for male attention and affection. Harry remembered a string of "stepfathers" and "uncles," some of whom were kind and gave her money, and others who did not. Her small earnings from waitressing, the cost of booze, and her intention to provide the best for Harry and Michelle gradually drew her back into petty crime. By December 1956, her frequent use of bounced or forged checks was catching up with her, and she decided to leave town to escape her creditors. All the family possessions were piled into a decrepit 1949 Studebaker, and they set off back to the East.

The sunny climate of California did not last long into the journey, and nobody had thought to prepare the car with antifreeze. The block cracked during an overnight stop in the tiny New Mexico settlement of Tucumcari, high up on a mountainside with temperatures well below freezing. The place had originally been built as a construction camp for the Chicago Rock Island and Pacific Railroad, and it was once known as "Six Shooter Siding" owing to the violent fights between the men who were billeted there. By the 1950s, it had turned into a convenient, if impersonal, overnight stop on Route 66, its 2,000 hotel or motel rooms almost exceeding the headcount of its permanent population.

The town's only mechanic specialized in coaxing automobiles back to life after the rigors of crossing the country on that legendary highway. However, he had been blinded in an accident the previous year. Nevertheless, he felt his way expertly around the Studebaker, managed to turn the partially seized engine over a couple of times, and shook his head. He offered a spot payment of $100 cash. Bette took the money, plus what they could carry of their possessions, and she and the children boarded a Greyhound bus for Albuquerque.

One of her recent lovers had been a bookmaker from Bakersfield, known to all and sundry as "Benny the Book." Somehow or other, she had acquired one of his credit cards, and although it had now expired, she managed to use it to cover the cost of the journey. When the family got to Albuquerque she used the card again to provide warm clothes for the children and make the down payment on a set of plane tickets to New York, on the "fly now, pay later" principle. The next day, the family turned up at 211 Bayport Avenue in Bayport, Long Island, the home of Harry's Uncle Fred and Aunt Cissy. For most of the next six months it would also be home to the Nilssons. Bette and Michelle slept in the basement, with Harry in the tiny, cramped, and freezing attic.

In January 1957, Harry started at Bayport High School, where the time he had spent developing his athletic skills in California came to his aid. He made both the basketball and baseball teams. Harry remembered:

I was popular at Bayport High. They couldn't help but notice the work clothes I wore, but I played it up. I gained sympathy votes from the chicks and the guys liked me 'cause I played ball and told exaggerated stories of Hollywood. I was dubbed "the Flash" and "the California Comet." The hottest chick in the school asked me to the Sadie Hawkins Day dance.[28]

After Harry hit a home run in a playoff game for the school, the coach promoted him to the varsity team, and before long he led the league in doubles. However, he was completely eclipsed by another player who played for Bridgehampton and led the league in just about everything else. This remarkable all-rounder could pitch no-hitters; as a left-hander he batted 500, and he was clearly heading for a professional career. On their first meeting, Harry was playing shortstop instead of his usual position of third. When the player in question hit his first pitch like a bullet over Harry's head, he somehow leaped vertically off the ground and caught it. Harry got another double in the game, but despite his own heroics, Bayport lost to Bridgehampton and its most remarkable player, whose name was Carl Yastrzemski. This boy's outstanding playing was no accident. He went on to a professional career in the sport, which took off when "Yaz," as he was known, was signed by the Boston Red Sox in 1958.

Harry's other interest at Bayport was art. He fantasized about painting in the neo-realist style of Norman Rockwell and was trying for an art scholarship. But, he told *L.A. Times* gossip columnist Joyce Haber years later, he was dissuaded by the attitude of his friends, who thought Rockwell was "no good," and by one of the professors who taught him, a professional artist who leafed through his sketchbook and expressed disdain at his efforts. A fleeting thought, prompted by his Irish Catholic grandparents, was to try for the priesthood, but a counselor at Bayport gently talked him out of the idea.[29]

Surprisingly, given his future career, one thing Harry was not closely involved in at this stage in his life was music. He was partly put off it by the efforts of Nana's sister, his great aunt, who was a determined "stage mother," pushing her son and daughter into careers as child singers and actors. She got her son onto the talent contest promoted by poet and songwriter Nick Kenny, who at the time hosted a weekly radio hour. Recalled Harry:

> I remember one time going to see a concert at Madison Square Garden, and he had all these 10,000 Boy Scouts singing, and this stuff, and one of them was my cousin. And I was thinking, wow, he's one of those people doing that. He went on and tried for a professional career and didn't make it, and his sister tried for an acting career and didn't make it. I didn't have eyes for it really in that sense, and I wasn't pushed into it. They had all professional training.[30]

Ultimately, Harry's cousins ended up having nothing to do with performance, one of them selling insurance in Ohio and the other marrying and moving to the West Coast.

In May 1957, just as the school year was coming to an end, the telephone rang at the Hoefer house. It was Bette, the worse for drink, calling from Jamaica, Long Island, to tell Harry that she and Michelle were setting off immediately to go back to California. On the spur of the moment, Harry decided to stay put and try to graduate from high school in Bayport. To tide him over during the summer and make a contribution to his Uncle Fred's household expenses, he got a job as a caddy on a local golf course, carrying bags at the rate of $1.50 for nine holes. By carrying two bags, one on each shoulder and going the full eighteen holes, Harry could make $6.00 a round, and he usually managed two rounds a day as his summer vacation began.

On a blazing hot June afternoon at the golf course, tempers ran short. A scuffle broke out between Harry and one of the other caddies, and as it began to escalate into a fight, the caddy master stepped in and fired Harry. He went home to his aunt and uncle to tell them the bad news. That night at dinner, his Uncle Fred looked him in the eye and, using Harry's childhood nickname from the days of the Martin apartment in Brooklyn, said, "Skeeter, I don't know how to say this gracefully, but I just don't think we can afford you."[31]

There was no time for consideration, no offer to talk things over. In hot blood, tears rising to his eyes, Harry threw down his cutlery and headed up to the attic. It took him a matter of seconds to pack all his worldly goods into a cardboard suitcase, and he walked out of the house. And thus began his own Jack Kerouac adventure, hitching across the United States to find his mother in Bakersfield, California.

Even more than the stories woven around his first stay in the West, this epic road trip became an integral part of the Nilsson legend. He would later embroider the details, but the core of the story never changed.

Initially, he was eager to leave and set out on his great journey. His first ride picked him up in Brooklyn, and the driver immediately sensed that there'd been trouble at home. He asked Harry's destination, and on hearing it was California, dropped him at the edge of Manhattan, pressing a dollar and half a pack of Lucky Strike cigarettes into the boy's hand. Unwilling to risk hitching in the city center, Harry spent part of his dollar using public transport to cross to New Jersey and made his way to a truck stop on the highway heading west. There were stern "No Hitchhiking" signs around the stop, but by asking around, Harry discovered that if he walked a couple of miles up the road, the likelihood was that somebody would stop for him.

That somebody was Shorty Long. Nilsson later described him as a character out of Damon Runyon: stocky, fast-talking, and totally at home on the road. Indeed he was so at home that he was wont to open his driver's door on down gradients, unzip his pants, cross his right leg over his left, and with a twist of his body relieve himself as the rig flew along at seventy miles an hour.

At the end of a long day on the road, they pulled in to a truckers' bunkhouse on the side of the highway. There was food, good company, a safe park for the trucks, and a bunk to sleep in. After a meal, Harry recalled that they sat out beside a fire with some of the men as they passed a bottle around. One asked:

"How old are you, kid?"
"Eighteen," I said.

"Here, let's see you chug-a-lug this."

It was almost a half-pint of scotch. I did it and suddenly became very sick. I staggered to the bunkhouse and stepped on the arm of the man in the lower bunk.

"What the fuck…?" he shouted.

"I'm sorry, I'm sorry, I'm sorry," I said as I jumped into the upper bunk.

He was awake now, and threw his legs over the side of the bunk to the floor, lit a cigarette, and lowered his head into a slouch. At that moment, the room began spinning as I tried to focus with one eye. Then came the inevitable, uncontrollable vomit sickness. I sat up, threw my head out of the bed and managed to puke down the neck of the poor guy in the lower bunk. He must have wondered what he'd done to deserve that, followed by: "What the fuck? I'm going to kill you, you son of a bitch!"

This woke the others who stopped him from grabbing me *and* killing me.[32]

Harry slept fitfully, and he was hardly prepared to be awakened just four hours later by Shorty Long, who was bright, alert, and ready to roll. Barely able to move or see, Harry staggered to the cab and hauled himself into his seat as the truck turned out onto the highway. "Take a couple of these," offered Shorty, and handed him some pills. Assuming they were aspirin, Harry swallowed them down at once. They were actually two tabs of speed. Jerked suddenly alert by the amphetamines, he thought he was capable of anything, even changing the tires of the truck. By the time they actually experienced a blowout that evening, the boy was shaking, tired, weak, and suffering from an almighty headache. It was an inner tire that had burst, and it took all their strength and teamwork to replace it. With the wheel changed, instead of clambering aboard, Harry said he had had enough and needed a rest before carrying on with his journey. Shorty shrugged as Harry hoisted his cardboard suitcase down from the cab. "Here, kid," he said, and pressed a ten-dollar note into Harry's hand. He sounded the horn as the giant rig rumbled off into the night.[33]

Harry found somebody's backyard in which to sleep, but woke to find a huge black dog barking angrily at him. The beast was tethered on a chain, but even five feet away felt too close. Scared and shaking, Harry made a bolt for the road. The dozen or so rides that followed blurred into a long sequence, parts of which he noted in his draft for an autobiography. On some there were laughs and conversations; others passed in silence, and he dozed as the miles rolled by. One man slyly asked Harry to accompany him to the men's room to take a leak together—the boy got off at the next town. This was followed by a middle-aged female schoolteacher who gradually hoisted her skirt higher and higher as she quizzed Harry about whether or not he had a girlfriend. When he made no move to respond to her advances, the conversation changed to how he was doing in his English classes.

Before long, the ten dollars had run out, and Harry had no food. In a small town in Oklahoma, roughly halfway on his journey, he went into a food store to try to steal something to eat. The manager eyed him suspiciously, so he spent his last few cents on a bottle of Coke. Then he struck up a conversation with a shop assistant who was putting fruit on display. The man trimmed the loose grapes from each bunch that went on the stall. "What happens to the loose ones?" Harry asked.

"I make wine or throw them out," chuckled the man.[34] Joining in the joke, Harry persuaded him to hand over a bag of the loose grapes. They were his only source of food. Nilsson recalled:

> It was the second day of grapes when the trots got me, and I wanted to die. I stopped at a fence where, of all things, deer were poised behind it. There was a sign on the fence which read: "Do Not Feed The Animals". I was feeding the animals when I heard the sound of tires on gravel—that unmistakable sound. It was a state vehicle, but from the state I had just left behind. One of the two men got out and tripped a little. I could see he was loaded.
>
> "Hey kid, where's you goin'?"
>
> I said, "California."
>
> He replied, "I'm Joe and that's Jace, and we're headed to Mexico...."
>
> This in a stolen state vehicle, I'm thinking.
>
> "...it's sort of in the direction. You wanna ride?"
>
> I was so relieved to get out of the sun and on the road, I said, "You bet. Thanks."[35]

With Joe and Jace, Harry crossed from Oklahoma into Texas, hurtling along the turnpike in what he later described as "a wild death ride at 90 miles an hour."[36] Leaving the pickup truck in El Paso, the three of them crossed the Rio Grande on foot into Juarez, Mexico, then, as now, one of the roughest cities on the continent. For Harry the visit soon became a blur: one bar after another, then a brothel. Through a drunken haze, he saw Rosie, the hooker he'd just bedded, waving a condom above her head and shouting, "I got his cherry! I got it right here!"

Joe and Jace sprang to the defense of their young friend, as the other drinkers mocked him. In seconds there was an almighty brawl in progress, and Harry fell full length across the record player, the needle screeching wildly across the grooves and coming to a sickening stop. To the background of grunts, groans, and fisticuffs, Harry staggered out through the backdoor and into a cab.

He came to the next morning, with the taxi standing still in a long line of traffic, stuck where part of the roadway had been washed away overnight during a violent storm. Only a few vehicles at a time could pass the rutted track that remained, but now the storm was long gone, and the sun was high in the sky. Members of the driver's family were going through his pockets as the driver himself toweled the remains of a pool of vomit from the seat where Harry had been lying. Once they realized he was awake, the family crowded around Harry asking for money. His requests to take him back to the bar where Joe and Jace would settle up his tab were met with blank incomprehension. In due course, Harry was pulled by his hair from the seat and turned out onto the roadway to walk the five miles or so back to the border in the blazing heat of the day. He staggered past stationary cars, weaving his way alongside squalid huts with dirt floors and naked children, and eventually he reached the bridge back over the river.

The border guard was adamant. The toll to cross back into the United States was two centavos. If Harry did not have the money, he had to stay in Mexico. Walking dejectedly away, he spotted the bar where his adventures with Joe and Jace had begun the previous morning. The bartender recognized him, and remembering how much they had spent, happily gave him the tiny coin. Within a few minutes he was back in El Paso, Texas, and had located the pickup. There was no sign of his fellow travelers, and Harry concluded that they must have been incarcerated for the fray in Juarez. So he broke open the door, lifted his bag out, and set off on the final leg of the journey to California on his own.

When Harry finally reached Bakersfield, where his mother and Michelle were supposed to be, there was no sign of them. But his Uncle John and Aunt Anna, with whom the family had stayed during their last visit west, were now living forty miles or so to the northeast of Bakersfield, farther up the Kern Valley at Wofford Heights. After crossing the United States, it was an easy task for Harry to hitch the few remaining miles to his relatives' new home. There, John Martin was again running a garage and gas station, and he not only offered Harry a place to stay for the time being, but a job in return for his board and lodging, which involved pumping gas and helping with the heavy work on automobiles that were being repaired.

Tall, athletic, and personable, and now with the experience of a seasoned road traveler, Harry made friends easily. Rather than move back in with his mother once he made contact with her, he preferred to stay at his uncle's house, where he had a degree of independence, and where he was not a financial drain on his mother's slender resources. He soon hooked up with some of his former schoolmates from his time in Pico Union. His old buddies Don and Shreddy spent time with him on his days off from the gas station, often walking miles from the closest bus stop to a movie theater. His best friend was still Jerry Smith, and in the late 1950s and early 1960s, they were inseparable. "I had no desire to go anywhere," he remembered. "All we did was play ball, see movies, and hang out. And weekends, we'd go to Jerry's girlfriend's house. Because his girlfriend's name was also Jerri, it got a bit confusing."[37]

In the fall of 1957, Harry's life at the garage was made easier, because his uncle gave him an old 1932 Ford Model B. A customer had left it with John Martin in lieu of payment, and prior to Harry's arrival, his uncle had fixed up the brakes and got it going well, with the intention of selling it. Over its dingy blue paint, Harry proudly painted the word "Sputnik" in silver, in honor of the first Russian space satellite launched that year. It might not have been capable of getting him into orbit, but it certainly allowed him to travel around the local area and as far afield as Los Angeles.

One of the landmarks of the Kern Valley region, not far from the Martins' Wofford Heights home, was a precarious-looking wooden flume built in 1902. This was a raised waterway on trestles that wound its way down for several miles from the mountainous heights above the little town to the hydroelectric power plant in the valley below at Borel. A small nearby settlement had recently been flooded to create Lake Isabella, which consequently became the principal source of water for the power industry in the mid-1950s. But independently of the lake and its brand new dam, the landmark flume still supplied water, which thundered down from the hills, the flimsy structure withstanding leaks and earthquakes to keep the old plant going. Today the original flume is finally gone, and an underground combination of canals and pipes brings water down to a small additional lake, which works as a header tank for the generator. But in 1957, to scramble up the tall trestles of the Borel flume and then plunge into the foaming torrent was a suicidal dare. Harry's friends bet him that he would not do it, so naturally he accepted the challenge. He recalled:

> I jumped in, totally underestimating the current with its fast whitewater. The sides of the flume were too high to grasp. Had I been able to stand still in the current, there were metal spanners across the flume, holding it together. I felt like a speeding, drowning rat. I thought if only I could just push from one side to the other and spring from one of the breakers placed on the bottom, I would be able to grab one of the bars.
>
> It took three attempts but I finally caught hold of one, pulled myself up, and half walked up the side to safety. With my leg over the bar and my hands over the side of the flume, all I had to do was figure out a way to the ground, which was twenty-five feet below. I eventually did it, having traveled over five miles in less than ten minutes. It was scary.[38]

Harry's Uncle John may not have paid him anything much in the way of wages, but the year he spent in the household, between the ages of sixteen and seventeen, was the foundation of his musical career. Late at night, back at the house after work, he would listen to the radio, rotating the dial to hear whatever sounds were being broadcast, but particularly tuning in to Dick Hugg (known as "Huggy Boy") on the local black station that played doo-wop and soul. He heard the Olympics and the Coasters, learned Little Richard's songs and the Everly Brothers' repertoire, but above all Ray Charles was his special favorite: "When I was asleep, if 'I've Got a Woman' came on the radio, no matter how low the volume, I would wake up and listen to it and say, 'Yeah!' " he recalled.[39]

This was also when he began to take an interest in playing instruments. Not far from his uncle's garage was a "Mom and Pop" shop where he would go to play pinball, even though he was convinced the machines were fixed. He consistently lost what little small change he had. One night, in sheer frustration, he savagely kicked one of the machines, and to calm his rage, the woman who owned the place came over and gave him a dusty ukulele. It was, he said, "one of those $1.98 plastic ukuleles with a little chord sheet in it that showed you how to play 'Me and My Banjo.' And I just took it upstairs with a bottle of whisky and started my career. I played by ear. No musical training."⁴⁰ During the weeks that followed, he would drive down to the beach on his days off and start picking out a few more chords on the instrument. Before long he had gotten himself a guitar and was seriously learning how to play it.

He also began picking out piano tunes at this time. He remembered that he pains-takingly worked out how to play "Lady Is a Tramp," some of the current hits by André Previn's jazz trio, and what he described as "songs for piano bars, for any occasion."⁴¹ But the principal inspiration came not from the radio or his attempts to play instruments, but from his family.

"My uncle John could sing like a bird," Harry recalled. "He taught me harmony."⁴² As he worked on engines and transmissions, changing oil and batteries, and rolling tires across the workshop, John Martin sang. And Harry listened and learned from his uncle many of the subtleties of pitch and harmonic nuance that would later surface in his own work. His uncle would have been quite capable of having a professional career. Indeed, when the Nilssons had been in California before, Harry's mother had arranged for an agent to hear her brother, the two of them hiding around the corner of the garage while John sang. The agent was sufficiently impressed with what he heard to offer a contract, which was promptly turned down by John, who was embarrassed that what he regarded as his amateur efforts had been overheard. He subsequently refused to speak to his sister for some time.

At first Harry wondered about whether to pursue his own newfound enthusiasm for music—after all, if his uncle had so much talent yet was too scared to try sing-ing professionally, perhaps Harry was mad to think of it. But the pull of music was strong. He got together with Jerry Smith, and the two of them worked up a passable imitation of the Everly Brothers. Their partnership would last into the 1960s as they played informally and began writing songs together. Yet with the exception of one public appearance with Jerry Smith, Harry was to eschew public performance, and in this respect—despite the success of his records—when it came to singing in front of an audience, he would retain an amateur status similar to his uncle's for almost his entire career.

He might have gone on to learn more from his uncle, but in the summer of 1958, they parted company for good. Increasingly frustrated by the fact that his uncle paid him in board, lodging, and fuel for Sputnik, but no actual money, Harry took to stealing fifty cents a day from the till. One morning his uncle set out as if to drive down to Bakersfield. Harry took the fifty cents and bought himself a drink. Assuming a few customers passed by during the morning, the till would soon have sufficient money in it to disguise the petty pilfering. But on this occasion, suspecting his nephew, John Martin returned almost immediately, before any other customers had arrived. He went straight to the till, counted the money, and confronted Harry: "Did you take fifty cents?"⁴³

Tearfully, Harry admitted his misdemeanor and ran out to Sputnik, setting off to rejoin his mother and sister, who were now settled in Bakersfield. He and his uncle were not to be reunited. "In the end," Harry recalled many years later, "he lived and died in the Mojave Desert, leaving five children, a widow, and five heart attacks."[44]

Up in Wofford Heights, the summer heat had been bearable. Down in Bakersfield at 100 degrees plus, it was not. Yet somehow Bette had found a small, comfortable house with air conditioning, and Harry gratefully settled back in with her. Not long after his arrival, Jerry Smith came over for a week. After spending the first Saturday afternoon in the cool comfort of a local movie theater, they returned home to find a note. On a whim, Bette, Michelle, and their friend Bonnie had gone to Las Vegas. There would be "food in the fridge and credit at the little store."[45]

The week ahead looked as if it would be fun for Jerry and Harry. There was an attractive girl next door, and both boys found that their flirtatious attentions were well received. Until, that is, a passing car ran over her cat. She was inconsolable—the more so because the driver had been a former school pupil of her mother's and was allowed to get off scot-free. Then the air conditioning broke. And far from having credit at the store, as her note suggested, Bette actually owed around forty dollars.

With no food, oppressive heat, and no potential girlfriend, Jerry and Harry put on long coats (ignoring the temperature) and stole from the local supermarket. But after a day or two, even the food they had taken was exhausted. Despite the effect of the grapes on his journey west, Harry once again decided to survive on fruit, and they picked figs from a neighbor's garden. The boys survived on those until they wrought their predictable digestive havoc. Then Bonnie arrived on the doorstep. Bette was in jail, Michelle had been taken into protective custody, and the cops were on their way to the house. With remarkable speed and application, Harry and Jerry pawned all the clocks in the house for ready cash, sold Sputnik for twenty-five dollars, and took the bus to Los Angeles to stay with Jerry's parents.

Harry soon found himself a job as an usher at the Paramount Theatre, at 6th and Hill Streets, just one block west of the main theater district on Broadway in Los Angeles. With 3,387 seats, the Paramount was the largest movie theater in Southern California, and had been built as the Metropolitan in 1923 by Sid Grauman to form part of his empire of local entertainment houses. He had spared no expense. In a hodgepodge of architectural styles, he had commissioned artists to decorate every inch of the building. Although some of the 1920s opulence was gone by 1958, murals, sculpted cornices, decorated pillars, and inventive metalwork could be seen everywhere. The remodeled proscenium arch seemed to be built of chunky stone piano keys, surmounted by a winged head in a style based on native North American designs. One day, Harry, exploring the six stories and two basement levels of the massive building, found a completely hidden mural of cartoon heroes from an earlier era. "Way up behind the rafters," he reported, "I came across a thirty-foot wall covered with beautiful renderings of Smokey Stover and Barney Google, perfect and big as life. I couldn't help but wonder how many people had seen these since 1926."[46]

In 1958, the Paramount was still owned by the studio whose name it bore, as part of its Paramount-Publix chain. It was a first-run house, showing previews and premieres, but it also had a great tradition of presenting live entertainment, stretching back to its early days. In preceding decades, stars such as Fats Waller and Spike Jones had pulled in the crowds. Indeed it was onstage there that Waller is reputed to have coined his catchphrase "All that meat and no potatoes," while describing his ample co-star Kitty Murray. In Harry's time, a potpourri of singers, dancers, comedians, and bands performed between the movies. As a result of working as an usher that summer, he said, "I got to meet a lot of entertainers, and that's when I decided to become a performer."[47]

At a practical level, this mingling with other performers from every style and era of entertainment helped to form Nilsson's wide-ranging tastes. Whether he was hearing swing bands, rock and roll groups, or crooners, they all offered him the opportunity to learn. "There was a piano in the basement," he told *Goldmine*'s Dawn Eden, "and the musicians passing through would show me chords."[48]

He had only been at the Paramount Theatre a matter of days when his mother once again caused him a problem, and had his actions been discovered, he would certainly have lost his job. Bette had been released by the police and had returned from Las Vegas to the Los Angeles area, where she found new lodgings. She contacted Harry while he was staying at the Smiths' house. "Her alcoholism was becoming worse," recalled Harry, "which drove her to take even more risks, although she was doing it for my sister and myself. She was placed on strict probation, part of which called for her to write a list of all the people she had issued bogus checks to. In fact she had forgotten one man, who came to the door one night and demanded payment of sixty dollars or he would turn her over to the Sheriff."[49]

Harry borrowed his mother's beat-up Lincoln and drove to a liquor store in a nearby neighborhood. Holding his finger in his pocket as if it were a gun, he held up the store. The owner backed away from the till, and Harry leaned forward, hit the "No Sale" button, and removed all the bills. Then, behind him, he saw a cop car stopping at the traffic light outside. Time stood still as the car waited for the green light, but the store's owner was petrified and gave no sign, and as soon as the car drove off, Harry lifted the coin drawer, emptied it, wiped the register for prints, and pocketed the cash. He made his getaway in the Lincoln, which had been idling outside with its lights off, unnoticed by the passing cops. In the men's room at work he counted the money. It came to exactly sixty-one dollars.[50] Once his mother's outstanding debt was paid off, Harry devoted himself to work and soon showed that he was exceedingly adept in matters financial.

Before long, now free of his mother's unpredictability and applying himself in a manner he had never managed at school, Nilsson moved from being an usher at the Paramount to working in the box office. In time he was promoted to junior manager, responsible for totaling and banking the takings of the cashiers.

In 1959, he transferred as assistant manager to the equally architecturally remarkable Paramount Theatre in Oakland, in the San Francisco Bay Area. This building survives to the present day with its 110-feet-tall murals on the front wall and a resplendent art deco interior. From Harry's point of view, aside from the splendors of the building itself, the job was doubly important, because not only did it offer him a substantial promotion, but it also gave him a chance, along with the latest movies, to see an even fuller mix of stage shows, which the management ran to keep the place afloat in a competitive market for movie audiences. These additional events included talent contests, prize nights, and standup comedians. Again, there was the chance to learn from all manner of musicians, which Harry did with alacrity, but he also adored the comedy acts. He recalled that this was when he learned many of Lenny Bruce's routines by heart. As Jimmy Webb remembered, "You could sit in a bar with Harry for three days while he did Lenny Bruce. He knew every word of every Lenny Bruce routine that had ever been recorded. He could cough this stuff up verbatim."[51] The end of the 1950s was the very period when Bruce—the recipient of some harsh criticism in New York and Los Angeles—was the darling of the San Francisco press, heartily defended in print by local *Chronicle* columnist Herb Caen in the famous article that began "They call Lenny Bruce a sick comic, and sick he is." Caen went on to point out that Bruce was "sick of the pretentious phoniness of a generation."[52]

Above all, the job was the perfect opportunity for Harry to indulge in his love of films. Building on his early enthusiasm for Laurel and Hardy with Jerry Smith, he now became a serious fan—starting to collect memorabilia associated with the pair. In Oakland, he also took the time to develop a love of Humphrey Bogart, the East Side Kids, and Al Jolson. He also began reading voraciously, and his favorites included J. D. Salinger, James T. Farrell, and Ray Bradbury.[53]

In 1960, Harry was transferred back to Los Angeles, where Paramount-Publix had decided to close down the Paramount Theatre for good. As assistant manager, he oversaw the skeleton crew that kept the giant auditorium running for its final weeks. Two years later it was to be torn down, and for most of the succeeding decades it was a parking lot. Only Grauman's extravagant, and for many years unused, extension of the building onto Broadway survived.

Many of the theater staff, however, found a new line of employment. The majority of the box office cashiers applied for jobs as bank tellers. Their applications were largely successful, as they were used to handling large sums of money accurately and quickly. Given that he had been supervising them, Nilsson thought he might as well try something similar. He lied on his application form that he had graduated from high school and was asked into the bank for an interview. He remembered:

They gave me a test, and then they gave me another test and they said I came out with programming aptitudes. So they sent me to programming school, where I learned how to program. It happened that this was the very first computer bank, the first to use magnetic coding on checks, and they were screening people for their brand-new computer center. Even after I took the course, it was a long time before they let me use the computer. In the meantime I switched to the Security First National Bank in Van Nuys. I was a sorter, then I was head of the sorter room, then computer operator, head computer operator, then I was in charge of the computer operators, and finally, supervisor in charge of the night shift—thirty-two people, three computers.[54]

By the time Nilsson came to supervise the evening operations at the bank, where he was to work for seven years in all, he had developed a way of life that was practically nocturnal. But in his first couple of years on the job, he was at his desk during the daytime. A few months after he started, it was discovered that he had lied about graduating from high school. He immediately made an emotional appeal to his bosses, pointing out that he was doing a good job. He was given six months' probation, following the successful completion of which he was fully confirmed in his post.

This was not least because his timing in applying for the job was fortuitous. The Bank of America had purchased its first computer as recently as 1955, and the upshot was a rapid and widespread conversion to computer technology across the retail banking sector. Daily cash volumes grew exponentially during the period, and this was also the moment when the use of credit cards expanded dramatically. Far from computerization reducing the workforce, as many pundits predicted at the time, banks were having trouble recruiting sufficient financially literate staff to man their quiet white rooms full of softly whirring machinery. The Security First National Bank would have wanted to hold on to an efficient and numerate manager such as Nilsson, because recruiting a replacement from the small skilled labor market was problematic.[55]

While he was working to hold onto his job, musical activities were restricted to evenings and weekends. But increasingly he was trying his hand at writing songs and, either with Jerry Smith or on his own, was preparing to go out and demonstrate them to potential publishers or performers.

In the spring of 1962, Nilsson plucked up the courage to start calling on music publishers during his lunch break. The first of what he described as "big-time companies" that he visited was the local office of Leeds Music, the New York publisher headed by Lou Levy, whose fortune was originally built on songs popularized by Levy's wife, one of the Andrews Sisters. Levy was adept at keeping one step ahead of the game, and in the pop world, his firm would shortly become famous for its exploitation in the North American market of Beatles songs, such as Lennon and McCartney's "I Want to Hold Your Hand."[56]

In May 1962, the Beatles had yet to be published by Leeds, but their Hollywood agent, Lou Stein, was already handling the work of the Canadian-born songwriter Scott Turner. On the day Nilsson chose to visit, Turner was waiting in Stein's outer office, to discuss his Australian royalties. The chance meeting between Turner and Nilsson was to be highly significant for Nilsson.

Turner already had a reputation as a pop Svengali. A former international athlete, Turner had co-written thirteen songs with the teenaged Buddy Holly, had recently toured Australia and New Zealand as the lead guitarist for Tommy Sands and the Raiders, and while there had written a number-one hit for Johnny O'Keefe, "She's My Baby." He recalled his impression of Nilsson:

> In came this tall, blond-haired fellow with a guitar in hand, and we struck up a conversation. I asked him if he was a writer or singer, and he replied, "Oh, a little of both, I guess." Seeing the music room was vacant, I said, "C'mon in here, I'd love to hear you." Reluctantly he picked up the guitar and commenced to sing, and I was absolutely taken with one of the most astounding vocal sounds I had ever heard![57]

Nothing came of the visit to Lou Stein, but Scott Turner was immediately convinced by what he heard that Nilsson had extraordinary talent. Turner took his address and phone number and decided to use him to record demos of a number of songs to be hawked around the local publishers. In later life, Turner went on to be one of the movers and shakers in the country music world, moving to Nashville and becoming a producer and then label boss for the country division of Liberty Records. There he worked with the likes of Slim Whitman, whom he helped guide to four gold records. Throughout his career, his promotional and production methods were the tried and trusted ones of exchanging favors. A little help here could lead to some useful return assistance there. He was soon to be the contact who introduced Nilsson to such songwriting partners as John Marascalco and Phil Spector, but his immediate thought was to work out a way to get Nilsson's voice on tape for the first time.

Turner knew the head of a recording studio with whom he could do a deal. If Turner played session guitar for whoever walked through the door, then he could earn some free overnight studio hours for himself to cut a few demos. Accounts vary as to whether this took place at American Studios or Gold Star Studios,[58] but in May 1962, with the time he had earned, Turner brought in Nilsson to record just over twenty songs.

These first professionally made recordings reveal Nilsson's already broad stylistic range as a vocalist. There are nods in the direction of Buddy Holly on "My Baby's Coming Home," a song co-written by Turner and Holly with additional tweaks from Nilsson, and of the Everly Brothers on Turner's "He Ain't Gonna Get My Girl." Both these are competently performed songs, but the signs of a completely fresh talent are there on "A Man and His Castle," which showcases Nilsson's baritone register, with flawless excursions into his upper range and consistent dynamic control. "Foolish Clock" has a similar range of pitch and dynamics, plus an authentic sounding country music "sob," while "There's Gotta Be a Girl" is a somewhat anonymous but perfectly controlled romantic ballad. On the songwriting front, Nilsson gets co-composer credit for "My Girl," which has an obvious Everly Brothers influence, and "Thank Heaven for Kathy," which has a rather strange echo of Johnny Cash in the low-register repetition of the phrase "poor boy."

None of these songs was so stunningly original as to make an immediate impact on Nilsson's career, but they all demonstrate a singer who had a wide knowledge of contemporary styles and a remarkably adaptable manner of putting them over. In one or two places, and notably on "A Man and His Castle," there are glimpses of the talent that would emerge over the five years that followed. Turner dubbed in backings on some five or so of the tracks at the time, and—many years later—was to add backings to the majority of the rest and issue the set as a Nilsson album. In 1972, the two met again at the Grammy awards, held that year at the Tennessee Theatre in Nashville. Nilsson told Turner he was welcome to use the material any way he wished, and in a subsequent phone call to discuss money, he insisted that because he had received five dollars per track in 1962, he had been paid in full. On the 1995 CD reissue of the material, Turner included an incomplete take of Nilsson learning "In Time." Nilsson is clearly tired as dawn was breaking outside, but the results are proof of his ability to apply himself in the studio and his rapid assimilation and personalization of unfamiliar material. A new talent in pop music might not quite have arrived, but it was certainly on the way.

It's a pleasure to see it's waiting there for me
to keep my hopes alive.
Such a comfort to know it's got no place to go,
it's always there.
It's the one thing I've got, a huge success,
my Good Old Desk.

2

GOOD OLD DESK

THE CHANCE MEETING with Scott Turner in May 1962 eventually had a profound effect on the course of Nilsson's career. Although Nilsson was making progress in his banking job, and would continue to do so for the next five years, Turner gave him the passport to a new creative life beyond the confines of the computer department of the Security First National Bank. This was not, however, something that Nilsson rushed into, because—just about to turn twenty-one—he greatly valued the safety and comfort that had come with stable and relatively well-paid employment. After the rollercoaster of living with (and often without) his mother, it was a welcome change to have a working routine, a regular paycheck, a car, and a premium on his intelligence, which had seldom been allowed to flower at school. Indeed, his second wife Diane believed that the banking regime became a fundamental part of his emotional makeup:

> He liked the bank and I think he felt secure working at the bank. He liked his boss a lot. They were friends. He had [other] friends at the bank and I know part of him wanted to leave, but I think when he actually had the opportunity, it was difficult. His personality just needed that structure of the job and maybe he knew that.... Harry was the most insecure person I've ever known. He just didn't have any self-esteem. So I think that would have to have been part of the reason.[1]

Nilsson himself confirmed this in one of the first interviews he gave after leaving the bank in 1967. "The bank became a womb," he said. "I retreated every time I got stung by the outside world of music."[2] Nevertheless, after making those first discs with Turner, he gave himself five years to make it as a musician. If he had not succeeded by the end of that period, then he resolved to stay on at the bank and keep music as a part-time activity.

When he was transferred to the night shift, the hours became more favorable to the pursuit of his new career. He worked at the bank's office in Van Nuys from five in the evening until one o'clock the next morning. But he needed comparatively little sleep, so in due course he evolved a routine whereby he would sit up at night after work writing songs and spend the daylight hours hawking them around.

At this time, he was living in the low-key neighborhood of Oakwood at 221 North Serrano Avenue, close to its intersection with Beverly Boulevard. This was just a few blocks from the Hollywood Freeway that ran over to the north side of the Hollywood Hills and down into the San Fernando Valley where the bank was located. The apartment was also a short distance from the area where several music publishers had their offices, around the junction of Vine Street and Selma Avenue in Hollywood. Consequently, it was a fairly quick drive in Nilsson's recently acquired Volkswagen Beetle from one area of his life to the other. Like anyone who lives day to day with the traffic in Los Angeles, he became a specialist in using all the back streets and short cuts that would get him to work precisely at five. Wherever he might be, Nilsson recalled, "I would mysteriously disappear at exactly fifteen minutes after four, so I could run out to my Volkswagen, jump in, take the shortcuts I knew through town avoiding the Ventura traffic, tie my tie as I drove, and pop through the door at 5 p.m. when my shift started."[3]

Another reason that Nilsson enjoyed work at the bank, particularly once he had taken on the supervision of other workers, was that it gave him a degree of responsibility that had been absent from much of his earlier life. It went with an intrinsic fascination with numbers that had started to flourish along with his programming career. He approached both technical and managerial problems in much the same way, saying:

> I enjoyed people coming up to me with their problems, and the challenge of coming up with a solution. Like a computer, there's the input, the calculation, and then the output. I enjoy functioning like that.[4]

Nilsson admitted that although he had a huge interest in music when he first started at the bank, "to turn that interest into something I could make a living at was something I didn't know about, and no one was there to tell me."[5]

This was why Scott Turner was so pivotal in Nilsson's career, not only pointing him toward what he needed to find out, but actually providing the first stepping stones for his "very cautious" journey into a new life. Turner had boundless enthusiasm for almost every aspect of Nilsson's music-making, complimenting him on his voice and the quick musical memory that he had demonstrated on several pieces such as "In Time."

"What amazed me more than anything," Turner said, "is that I would sing the song for Harry one time—and I sing like a rusty hinge!—and Harry would sing it right back to me without missing a note."[6] Furthermore, Turner showed Nilsson how to inhabit the world of studios, sessions, singing, and songwriting. As Nilsson put it, "You know somebody who knows somebody who knows somebody who's in the music business, and finally through all of them you get to meet that person. And then you start hanging around the office, you go for coffee, things like that, hoping that some day you can make a demo for somebody."[7]

Turner had connections everywhere. As well as giving Nilsson a co-writer's credit on some of the songs they recorded together in May 1962, he helped to get Nilsson's next group of songs published and recorded. He introduced him to John Marascalco, who would later become a regular writing partner, but meanwhile, Turner also looked out for further chances to work with Nilsson himself.

The first such opportunity came in the early spring of 1963, when Turner ran into an old friend named Randy Sparks. While Turner had been touring Australasia, Sparks had put together a large-scale folk ensemble in Los Angeles that he called the New Christy Minstrels. This had somewhat unexpectedly become a best-selling novelty act. Previously, Sparks and his wife Jackie Miller had led their own folk trio, but by joining forces with a couple of other groups and hiring some of the city's leading session players, they created a new fourteen-voice troupe. They devised a striking and memorable visual image for their group involving stripy blazers and starched petticoats, and made a series of popular live appearances at the Troubadour. Their first album *Presenting the New Christy Minstrels* won a Grammy in 1962 and stayed on the *Billboard* charts for months. It spawned the hit single "This Land Is Your Land," and following this success, Sparks was constantly on the lookout for new songs. He landed contracts to record an ongoing series of live and studio albums, as well as a weekly slot on the Andy Williams television show, for which new material was always required.

Learning of Sparks's urgent need for fresh music, Turner immediately thought of Nilsson. He gave him a call, and they got together around a tape recorder over a weekend to see what they could produce. The song they came up with was called "A Travelin' Man," and like much of Nilsson's subsequent work, it was strongly autobiographical. The lyrics draw on his teenage experience of hitchhiking across the United States and talk of being alone, longing for a home, and always wondering about the next stop along the way.

Having finished the song, according to Turner, "Monday morning, I went by Randy's office and played our home recording. Randy loved it, put it under contract and recorded it on the 'Green Green' album."[8] The song was registered at the Library of Congress by the New Christy Minstrel Company on March 4, 1963, and recorded in April. It was not a significant success, at least when compared with the album's best-known song "Green Green," which became the group's first million seller when it was rushed out as a single. (So ubiquitous was it that the album's official title, *Ramblin'*, is almost forgotten.)

Nonetheless, Nilsson finally had his name on a record label, and in due course, he figured, there would be some income from the album sales to follow up the five-dollar advance that Sparks gave him, and which he spent immediately. It took a while, but eventually a check arrived for his share of the mechanical royalties for the recording. It was worth precisely forty-six cents. Nilsson never banked it.[9] Apparently in due course,

Turner received a slightly bigger check for $41.25, of which he turned the princely sum of $40 over to Nilsson.[10]

While Nilsson and Turner's joint effort for the New Christy Minstrels was being copyrighted on behalf of the troupe's publisher, Nilsson personally registered the lead sheet for a new ballad of his own. For this he had written both the words and music, inspired by a young lady who worked at the bank. "Donna, I Understand" was copyrighted on February 6, 1963, and was to be recorded by Nilsson himself for Mercury a little later the same year.[11]

This recording came about by accident. Nilsson answered an advertisement in the newspaper from an obscure company offering to turn songs into demos. He thought they were looking for someone to sing on demo discs of other people's songs, but it turned out they had been looking for songwriters to provide raw material, which they would then arrange to record. Nevertheless, taken by the logic that they could use a versatile singer as part of this process, they agreed to pay Nilsson five dollars a song for any discs on which he sang for them. From then on he would frequently drop by their office while he was making his daytime rounds of publishers. He made a point of getting to know the secretary, chatting with her about items in the news, and flirting with her so that she would remember him. Only a short time after his first visit, a promoter dashed in looking for a singer to record a new song, and as Nilsson happened to be in the office, his newfound friend the secretary nodded in his direction and said, "What about him?"[12] Nilsson recalled:

> He asked me, "Can you sing?" He played this *awful* song called "Wig Job"—wigs were getting popular again . . . he told me I could put anything I wanted on the other side. This was before I started writing *good* songs. I did "Donna, I Understand." He took it to Mercury records who liked the singer and "Donna" but not the other side. As a result I got signed to Mercury.[13]

The "Wig Job" song was credited to Buddy Lee, a relatively little known country music songwriter who died in 2007.[14] Structurally the song borrows liberally for its chorus from the Everly Brothers' "Bird Dog" of 1958. With a female vocal group chanting "wig job!" and a pedestrian rock and roll arrangement by Jerry B. Long, who subsequently went on to arrange for Berry Gordy Jr. at Motown, it never really takes off. Yet Nilsson himself competently disguises his contempt for the song, and he turns in a convincing performance as a rock and roll singer, helped by an edgy metallic-toned guitar solo that was most likely played by Scott Turner.

The mood on "Donna, I Understand" is a complete contrast. It takes its pace and atmosphere from the kind of teen idol ballad with which Ricky Nelson had been regularly successful on the charts, on songs like "Lonesome Town" or "Sweeter Than You." Again, Long provides girl singers in the arrangement, but the central feature is Nilsson's voice. Pitching higher than Nelson would have done, he not only draws out the name "Donna," hanging on to the second syllable for a couple of measures, but he sings a five-note phrase on the single word "I." His vocal flexibility and precision of pitch are far superior to a run-of-the-mill demo disc, and at this point (before a lifetime of heavy smoking played havoc with it), his effortless breath control is immediately apparent. On the phrase "sometimes bitter, sometimes sweet," he soars into his falsetto register for the second "some." It is clear that while "Wig Job" was thrown together, a lot more care and attention was lavished on Nilsson's own song. At the time, it was common practice when a record label signed any young singer to put them under contract for a year, on the off chance that the results might be successful. Nilsson was excited at first when Mercury gave him such an agreement, but that soon changed to despondency. The 45 rpm single of "Wig Job" and "Donna, I Understand" took ages to come out, and when it did, his composer credit was misspelled as "Harry Nielson," and the company had called him "Johnny Niles," figuring that his real name sounded too much like a "middle-aged Swedish businessman."[15] "Johnny Niles" was never to make another record.

However, the promoter who produced the session—Nilsson recalled his name as Townsend[16]—had no scruples about reissuing the material in virtually identical form on another label. He obviously thought that because Mercury had used a pseudonym for Nilsson and misspelled his composer credit, it was highly likely they would not notice if the same songs came out on a "promotional copy only" issue, designed to hawk around the songwriting talents of Lee and Nilsson. As a result both "Wig Job" and "Donna, I Understand" were issued again within a year of the original release by the obscure Spindle Top label. Nilsson's vocal tracks were virtually unchanged (although a section of John Lennon-like improvising at the end of "Wig Job" is cut out, and his voice is treated to a little more reverb). However, the guitar on "Wig Job" is replaced by a saxophone, and on "Donna" the female vocals are re-recorded, with the saxophone subtly double-tracked into the harmonies.

It may have been a disappointment to Nilsson that "Donna, I Understand" was not released sooner and that it did not do better, but he had at least managed to write, publish, and record an original song from scratch. This gave him some confidence for the future. He realized that he had actually been devising songs for years, but that he was now making the transition from what he described as "a cappella in the car" to a more structured approach to writing. He said:

> When you listen to the radio, you find yourself singing along—a few weeks go by and you're humming a tune that you've forgotten the words to, because most people don't remember the words to anything, and so you make up your own words. Then you hear that record you've been humming six months later and it turns out that the melody was different too, so you find that you've written a song.[17]

From the start of their collaboration on "A Travelin' Man," Scott Turner encouraged Nilsson to use the songwriting method he adopted for most of the rest of his life, to sing and hum his efforts directly into a tape recorder. Thereby nothing was lost, and he saved the time of actually writing the compositions down. As 1964 began, Nilsson started to work in earnest on improving his songwriting.

He was to copyright seven songs in the year. One of them, "I'd Do It All Again," was a further collaboration with Scott Turner. Another, "Pretty Pretty," was a piece he wrote with his school friend Jerry Smith. Nilsson had written his first song with Smith when they were both fifteen, during his original stint in California. It had been called "No Work Blues."[18] Now they got together again to apply some of the lessons learned from Turner, and also to try their hand at performing the material they wrote. Nilsson recalled: "A friend of mine who was my buddy in school decided that we would be the poor man's Everly Brothers for a week. So we went to this office and played them a song we had written. And Johnny Otis used it as a demo."[19]

As the two friends were hawking their wares around the publishers, in one office they ran into a promoter called Hal Ziger. His specialty was putting on variety shows of miscellaneous rock and roll artists, and he was currently touring a package with the Elegants, Don and Dewey, and the Safaris. When Nilsson and Smith met him, Ziger had just been let down by the Safaris, a local white doo-wop quartet that was in the throes of breaking up after failing to recapture the success of its original 1960 hit "Image of a Girl." The group had been booked for the show's appearance the next night in National City near San Diego. So Ziger offered Nilsson and Smith the gig. They could sing anything they wanted for a princely fee of fifteen dollars. They accepted, but decided against performing an original song and opted instead for an old standard, "If I Had a Hammer." For the occasion they kitted themselves out in blue corduroy pants and blue alpaca sweaters—a sartorial style roughly modeled on the clean-cut, fresh-faced Kingston Trio.

They had not reckoned on the fact that they would be playing for an entirely African American audience. As soon as they were picked up in the all-black South Central district of Los Angeles to be driven to the gig, they were mercilessly teased by the bus driver, who spotted that they were the only white faces among the performers, and shouted "back of the bus!" The other performers took pity on them and laughingly explained it was a "Crow Jim" joke. When the two young men eventually went out on stage, they were greeted with shrieks of laughter. But their innocence won over the audience, who eventually howled their approval. After taking their bow, Smith and Nilsson ran out of the theater before the end of the show and took the first bus they could find back to L.A. They arrived to find that the Volkswagen had been completely trashed by the good denizens of South Central. Having spent five dollars on the bus fare, Nilsson handed the other ten dollars back to Ziger, and was therefore always able to claim subsequently that he never broached his amateur status when it came to public performance, even in his early years.[20]

Nilsson and Smith did not tread the boards together again, but they did carry on writing songs and copyrighted further efforts in the years that followed. Although the pair of them looked young and innocent, and Nilsson was holding down a responsible job at the bank, he was not quite so virtuous as the image he projected. He liked to have a few drinks after his long evenings at his desk, and on one such occasion, he told the British writer David Litchfield, he decided to try his luck in the Red Light District:

> I was eighteen years old and it was my second hooker. My first had been in Mexico. Well this girl wanted to do business before we got on with the other business, and I had this check made out to cash, and she said, "What's THAT?" And I said, "It's a check. Don't you remember, I told you in the Volkswagen how I worked in a bank and I'm not allowed to cash bad checks because I'd lose my job." And she screamed, "CHECK SHIT!" And this gorilla beat the door down and pulled out his pearl handled Colt 45. I mean not just a gun. This sucker was REAL! So he hit me with the gun and said, "I'M GOING TO BLOW YOUR MOTHERFUCKING HEAD OFF!" Meanwhile my pants were around my ankles…and I was afraid for my life. So I kept saying, "That's cool, that's cool," and he said, "Get your white honky ass out of here before it's found in some garbage container in Watts and Beverly Hills."…So I left, very fast. The moral of this story is never offer a hooker a check.[21]

Such adventures aside, Nilsson devoted much of his spare time in 1964 to forming a songwriting partnership with John Marascalco that produced almost all the other songs he was to register that year. The two had met when the demos with Scott Turner were recorded in 1962, for which Marascalco had co-written roughly a third of the material.[22]

By 1964, John Marascalco was already a much more well-established and highly successful songwriter, publisher, and talent scout than Scott Turner had so far become. He had written songs for Fats Domino and the Four Seasons, but most notably for Little Richard, penning his hits "Good Golly Miss Molly," "Rip It Up," and "Send Me Some Lovin." He also worked as an artists and repertoire scout for Infinity Records, for whom he had signed Billy Storm and his hit "The Love Theme from El Cid," and he was the publisher of numerous songs including "Wipe Out," which had sold a million copies for the Surfaris. When he and Nilsson started writing together, Marascalco was on the brink of signing an exclusive distribution deal for his own Loa Records company with Atlantic, and he was promoting a band known as the Ric-A-Shays.[23]

Not only did Marascalco subsequently lend Nilsson money when he needed it ("He was the first guy to loan me 300 bucks," Nilsson told *Goldmine*'s Dawn Eden[24]), but as soon as the one-year contract with Mercury came to an end, he financed and produced two ventures for Nilsson in early 1964 that moved his recording career up a step. The first was a single for the Crusader label, called "Baa Baa Blacksheep," that was eventually issued under an apposite new Nilsson pseudonym, "Bo Pete." The second was a promotional single written by Nilsson and Marascalco to be released in time for the Beatles' first full American tour in August 1964, and it featured the added bonus of a cover-mounted eight-millimeter film of the group. This had been shot during their arrival in New York that February, when they appeared on the *Ed Sullivan Show* and played sold-out concerts at Carnegie Hall and the Washington Coliseum. The newsreel scenes of the Beatles waving at several thousand of their fans at the airport and being bundled into limousines were combined with a song called "(All For The Beatles) Stand Up and Holler" by the "Foto-fi Four." There was a rudimentary instruction to play the 45 rpm disc in synch with the movie. All four voices of the "Foto-fi Four" belonged to Nilsson, and it is the first proper example of his love of overdubbing to create ensemble vocal effects, in this case leavened with the sound of screaming girls.

The idea was to anticipate the phenomenon of "Beatlemania." This was already rife in Europe and there were signs of a minor epidemic during the Fab Four's short February visit to the United States.

Ironically, the underlying pattern of "(All For The Beatles) Stand Up and Holler"[25] takes its inspiration not so much from the Beatles, but from the Rolling Stones, whose version of "Not Fade Away" with its insistent "Bo Diddley beat" appeared at the end of February 1964 and was the Stones' first single release in the United States. Although "Not Fade Away" had originally been recorded seven years earlier by its co-composer Buddy Holly, the Stones' version peaked at number three in the U.K. charts and reached forty-eight on the U.S. *Billboard* charts a week or two later. Borrowing unashamedly from it was calculated to put everyone who heard it in mind of the "British invasion." Nilsson and Marascalco took the formula of the repeated "hambone" rhythm and Keith Richards' plangent central guitar solo direct from the Stones' release, and transplanted them into a ditty of anticipation for "John, Paul, George and Ringo, one of them taken but three are single."

Nilsson sings the solo lead vocal of the verse in an Americanized approximation of John Lennon, and then springs into overdubbed Beatles-style close harmony. Once again, the song in itself is not particularly remarkable, but it is a harbinger for Nilsson's subsequent love of all things Beatles, and in particular his aural collage "You Can't Do That" on the 1967 album *Pandemonium Shadow Show*.

It is probable that the screams on the "Foto-fi Four" recording were made by the backing singers from "Baa Baa Blacksheep," whom Nilsson described as follows:

> I was in a little studio one day, hanging around, doing demos, and I heard these teenage girls walk by singing four-part harmony. They called themselves the Beach Girls. They had this quality to them that was so raw and natural, and I thought, "Ooh, that's cool!" So I was working on "Baa Baa Blacksheep," and I said to the girls, "Here, come here a sec," and I started to play the song. I said, "You do the backgrounds, like the Raeletts [*sic*] or something."[26]

What the girls actually contributed to the resulting record of "Baa Baa Blacksheep" was the foregrounds. On the first run through of the old nursery song, they sing a fairly simple four-part harmonization of the tune, while Nilsson's voice darts all around them, almost in the manner of a jazz instrumentalist, creating a verbal commentary on the song and an additional musical layer at the same time. When he takes the lead on the second verse, he never sings the melody itself, always leaving that to his female colleagues. It is not a great record, but it is a good indication of the kind of vocal imagination that Nilsson would bring to his later work, particularly the *Nilsson Sings Newman* album where his own voice provided both the soloist and the backing choir.

"Baa Baa Blacksheep" was credited to Nilsson and registered at the Library of Congress on February 17, 1964. Incredibly, Bo Pete's first outing on record with "Baa Baa Blacksheep" achieved some airplay, and buoyed by its success, Marascalco was able to produce a follow-up by the pseudonymous singer. This was recorded by Nilsson for the obscure Try label and released in August 1964.[27] It featured a Nilsson original on one side, "D'You Wanna (Have Some Fun)?" and a piece they had penned together for Little Richard on the other, an unashamedly similar rewrite of Marascalco's earlier song "Good Golly Miss Molly" called "Groovy Little Suzie."

Actually, both of the new songs for Bo Pete were imitations of earlier Marascalco hits, suggesting that Nilsson was successfully applying his dictum of humming an extant song, adding different words, and then subtly changing the melody. "D'You Wanna (Have Some Fun)?" is based on Buddy Holly's version of "Ready Teddy," although the backing is far less slick. That number was originally written by Marascalco for Little Richard in 1956, and Holly's cover version soon followed. Nilsson's vocal echoes Holly's delivery and has the same insistent repetition of "If you wanna" that the earlier piece achieves with "I'm ready, ready, ready." Judging by the recording quality, Nilsson seems to have cut this Bo Pete single in one take accompanied live by a backing group of organ, guitar, bass, and drums, although on the final chorus, he overdubs a second harmony vocal. An ugly edit on the final word, "scream," suggests that a replacement ending was hurriedly spliced onto the original recording.

There is a similar rough and ready feel about "Groovy Little Suzie" that suggests it was also recorded in one take as a demo, in order to sell the piece to Little Richard, who had just announced his return to rock and roll after three years of recording gospel material. The backing band is virtually the same as for "D'You Wanna," with the addition of a pianist playing the repeated eighth note pattern familiar from many a Little Richard track. The demo was successful in achieving its object, and the song appears on the Vee Jay album *Little Richard Is Back (And There's a Whole Lotta Shakin' Goin' On!)*, which—like Nilsson's version—was released in August 1964. Little Richard's rendition, with his own piano in the foreground, is faster and far more confident than Nilsson's. Little Richard replaces the organ with a sax section, which probably consisted of his regular Vee Jay recording colleagues Buddy Collette, Clyde Johnson, and William Green. Even so, Nilsson recalled that when Little Richard heard "Bo Pete's" version of the song, he complimented him: "My, you sing *good* for a white boy!"[28]

In the second half of 1964, Nilsson also began an association with Tower Records, a new subdivision of Capitol in Los Angeles, named after the parent company's famous headquarters building, which was designed to resemble a stack of discs. Initially, Tower built much of its catalog on British invasion artists, including Freddie and the Dreamers,

Ian Whitcomb, Tom Jones (a few early records prior to his signing with Parrot), and three years later, Pink Floyd. In addition to importing music from the U.K., mainly originating from other parts of the E.M.I. organization, the label also specialized in signing local Southern California artists. Nilsson claimed that "I had T-1, the first contract ever signed on Tower."[29]

He may have been the first artist to sign, but he was not the first act to be issued by the label. That honor belonged to the Sunrays, whose feel-good surf-influenced pairing of "Car Party" and "Outta Gas" came out on Tower 101 in September 1964.

This was swiftly followed by Nilsson's first Tower single, number 103. It featured "Sixteen Tons" backed with "I'm Gonna Lose My Mind." Both these tracks feature the same formula of instrumentation plus backing singers as "Groovy Little Suzie" and "D'You Wanna (Have Some Fun)?" The Hammond organ is once again prominent in the instrumental mix, but the singers are both better arranged and better recorded. Overall, the Tower single is more professionally produced than either of the Marascalco demos. Musically, the two new songs show Nilsson still searching for his own voice. He remains a musical chameleon, although undoubtedly improving many of the skills that would make him a consummate backing singer in the future and showing early signs of the stylistic diversity that made him so hard to categorize in his later career.

"Sixteen Tons" was originally a country and western number, written by Merle Travis. A decade before it had been a success for Tennessee Ernie Ford. From Nilsson it gets a contemporary makeover with a "boogaloo" beat and heavily harmonized backing vocals. It sounds a little like a refugee from a Ray Charles session, except that Nilsson's airy vocals float over the arrangement without really connecting to the meaning of the song. As he creates some lofty a cappella arabesques on the word "soul," soaring into his falsetto register, we never get the feeling that he really owes that soul "to the company store." Meanwhile "I'm Gonna Lose My Mind" written by Johnny Cole, who would later be another productive songwriting partner of Nilsson's, is a piece of lightweight pop that aims to capitalize on the "Twist and Shout" formula. It replaces the Isley Brothers' confident depth and the Beatles' Liverpool edginess with overproduction. The backing singers sound too full, and the arrangement is too busy to create the immediate punchy impact that either of those other groups had with Medley and Russell's song. Consequently, Nilsson's first Tower single did not prosper.

In 1965, Nilsson continued his songwriting partnerships with Marascalco, Scott Turner, and Jerry Smith, as well as composing a number of solo efforts. With Jerry Smith, he also took the opportunity that year to telephone their idol Stan Laurel, whom he had discovered, following the death of Oliver Hardy, was living in a hotel in Santa Monica, where he had his number publicly listed. Nilsson remembered:

There was that familiar voice, "Hello?" Wow, shivers down my timbers. It was a magical moment, my friend Jerry and I were so knocked out. We couldn't think of anything to say. "Well, maybe we can come out to see you and have some tea or

something, and maybe bring a copy of a book you might sign, by John McCabe?"
And he says, "Well I'd love to boys, but I'm not getting around too much now these
days and I like to stay quiet." And we knew then that, for him, it was close to the
end. And it was very sad. I don't know who coined the phrase for Laurel and Hardy,
the fiddler and the bow, but that is about as apt a phrase as you'll find.[30]

Such brushes with his idols apart, there was a hiatus in Nilsson's recording career for the
best part of a year (although his songwriting carried on). This was largely because on
October 24, 1964, at age twenty-three, he married his first wife, Sandi Lee McTaggart.[31]
It appears to have been quite a whirlwind romance. Conforming to the social expectations of his fellow bankers, Nilsson opted for sexual relations within the respectability of
wedlock, rather than pursuing further unsuccessful adventures with hookers. In later life,
when curious fans or family members asked him why he had suddenly gotten married, he
would say, "I just did that to get out of the war."

There was more than a grain of truth in this. Sandi worked at the bank, and Nilsson
described her thus:

She was very pretty. She looked a lot like Kim Novak, and she had an interesting
background. She was from Buffalo, New York, and was a Hells Angels chick, which
at first pissed me off so much. I don't know, I think I hated her for being with all
those guys. Yet I still felt something for her … and we got married. This is right after
I was called up for the draft.[32]

He had successfully avoided being called up for some years. This was largely because quite
early in Nilsson's time at the bank, he took advice from one of his fellow employees, who
had been working day shifts as a recruiting officer for the U.S. Army. Nilsson asked him
how to get out of the draft, and he was advised to drink maple syrup in large quantities
before he attended the call-up medical examination, as it would give the impression of
diabetes in a urine test. Nilsson drank a bottle of the liquid before his morning medical, and when his test results were checked, he was asked to provide a second sample in
the afternoon, once he had eaten a standard army lunch, which would normally correct
any sugar imbalance. Having smuggled in a second bottle of syrup, he drank it with his
lunch and pushed his sugar levels sufficiently high to be graded 4F, unfit for service. As
the Vietnam War progressed, the draft requirements were relaxed. Nilsson's next assessment was 1Y, which still kept him out, but finally, around the time he met Sandi, he was
re-graded to 1A and informed that he had been accepted for the army. The recruitment
officer was firm, he had to report for duty, or he had to agree to see a psychiatrist and sign
up for a six-month course of therapy at U.C.L.A. Nilsson recalled:

He said: "You go see them for the next six months, and if they confirm that you
shouldn't go in the service, I will exempt you. But if not, you're in."

I said, "Thanks a lot."

He says, "Take this paper outside to the lieutenant, and have him sign it."

As it turns out I was planning to get married in maybe three months and as I took the piece of paper outside to the lieutenant, I noticed a date on it.

I said, "Listen, if you just change that two to a six, I'll be out of the draft." This was because at the time Kennedy had said if you were married, you were exempt from the draft. The guy just looked at me for a second and changed it from one number to another. And I never got another call back letter. I was free.[33]

To conform to the forged date on the draft papers, Nilsson and Sandi moved up their wedding day. The marriage was not based on love so much as expediency. It was not to last long, and in later life Nilsson's cousin Doug Hoefer heard him nonchalantly use the stock phrase "I just did it to get out of the war" on numerous occasions. In typical Nilsson fashion, what ultimately came to be a painful episode in his life was reduced to a witty, self-deprecating one-liner. He would seldom say more on the subject.[34] Sandi already had a two-year old son who was called Scotty. Nilsson's family (and particularly his mother) adored him.

At first, Nilsson put some effort into the marriage. Given that his nocturnal hours at the bank could not be altered, his time spent selling his wares to publishers was curtailed so he could spend at least part of each day together with Sandi and Scotty. To make some extra cash, for a short time he took a job for a few hours each morning distributing newspapers, amused that many of his fellow deliverymen were local alcoholics whose attendance was extremely random. Within a few days, Nilsson, suited and smart, was promoted to sit on the truck and hand out the newspapers for the others to throw into front yards and mailboxes. But this did not last long, as he preferred to continue to try his hand at music for his additional income.

Several of the songs he copyrighted during 1965 were not to be recorded until late in 1966 or early 1967, by which time the relationship with Sandi was on the wane. The seeds of this breakup date from the final months of 1965, a year after the wedding, when he gradually resumed his former regime of nighttime writing and daytime salesmanship.

Nilsson's songwriting routine became more fixed when he found himself both an office in which to write and a fixed fee for his wares. In his travels around various publishers' offices, he had gotten to know the arranger George Tipton, who made his main living as a copyist, transcribing orchestral parts from scores, but who was just beginning to make a name for himself by writing and conducting symphonic treatments of "teen-oriented material," as *Billboard* put it.[35] Nilsson's own first memories of Tipton were extremely positive:

The first time I walked into his office, I felt good vibes everywhere. You know, one of those things. It was weird, I played some songs for him and he was just gassed.

Just gassed. And he says, "You're the first guy to walk in here that can sing." I said, "Ah, um." And he said, "Did you write the songs?" It was like a big thing.[36]

Tipton shared office space with a publishing company called Rock Music, Inc., run by Gil Garfield and Perry Botkin Jr., on Vine Street, close to its junction with Selma Avenue. Garfield was a former member of the pop group the Cheers, who had hit the top twenty in 1954 with "(Bazoom) I Need Your Lovin'." Now he worked as a freelance songwriter and publisher, as did Botkin, who had grown up in the business because his father had been a studio guitarist around Hollywood, working with the likes of Bing Crosby and Spike Jones. After starting out as a big band trombonist, Botkin had become a singer, at one point taking Garfield's place in the Cheers. The two men subsequently wrote several songs together, of which the most successful was "Passion Flower." Their own recording of it with the Fraternity Brothers charted at number three in Italy during 1958, and the song was also a chart success in France under the title "Tout L'Amour."

Tipton thought that Nilsson's songs were sufficiently accomplished for Botkin and Garfield to publish them, so he arranged an introduction at the office, as Botkin recalled:

When he walked in, I remember he was not shy. He just opened the door, came in and said, "What are you guys doing in here?" I said something like, "I'm an arranger and we write songs and things," and he said, "So do I."

He was very happy to sit down with his guitar and play. So he started singing one of those early tunes, and I thought "Oh my God! This is unbelievable." A lot of people had walked into that office, but this was unbelievable. I looked at my partner and he looked at me, and we both knew that we weren't supposed to act as we were feeling. Because we both thought, we've gotta sign this guy. So when Harry got done we said, "Well that's very nice, Harry. Would you be interested in signing a contract?" And he said, "Oh yeah, I'm working at the bank down there, and you guys seem to be [okay]." So I believe the deal we had, we paid him $25 a week. He worked at the bank from six at night 'til two in the morning. And then he'd come in after his work at two and he would write up in our office, until I would usually come in about nine, or nine thirty in the morning, and he'd be fast asleep in this big chair we had there. Then we'd go have coffee and he'd go off and promote the tunes and everything. We thought, "This guy's unbelievable!" And each tune's better than the one before. We were so tickled and he was a sweetheart of a guy. We really became good friends.[37]

Soon after he was first employed for twenty-five dollars a week by Botkin and Garfield, they gave him a key to the building. This was not just because he was writing songs for them, but because they were staggered by his energy in not only working at the bank and writing all night, but in starting to clean up the premises and make it more presentable.

Botkin recalled: "He used to climb out on the [ledge] … our offices were on the 3rd floor, and he would climb out the window and wash it once a week.… Oh, yeah, he was the chief window washer up there in that office with George and Gil and I."³⁸

Not even someone with Nilsson's superhuman constitution could keep up a routine like this every night, but Nilsson reckoned he wrote there "two or three times a week." His first song to be copyrighted with Garfield and Botkin was "Headlines," from March 1966, but he had already been using their office for some time when this was deposited at the Library of Congress. He was based nocturnally at Rock Music, Inc., from late 1965 until he became a full-time musician and finally left the bank in 1967.³⁹

The latter half of 1965 saw him record another four songs for Tower. The best of them is Nilsson's own composition "Good Times," the G-minor opening theme of which looks forward to the Monkees' "Last Train To Clarksville" which would be recorded the following year. A honky-tonk piano lick that acts as the hook for each verse also has similarities to the famous guitar figure in the Monkees' song. There the similarity ends, as the echoey chorus is delivered in a quasi-gospel manner by the "New Salvation Singers." This group, which was managed by another agent in Botkin's building, reappears on the flip-side of that original 1965 single, Tower 165, in a song so utterly and completely different that it is hard to imagine that it is by the same artists. Johnny Cole's composition "The Path That Leads to Trouble" has Nilsson singing with a nasal delivery that seems to be aiming to imitate Mick Jagger, with overtones of John Lennon. The boxy guitar backing with an insistent tambourine reinforces this "British invasion" effect, which sits oddly with the gospel overtones of the chorus. An outbreak of random tubular bells toward the end does nothing to help the feeling of transatlantic styles stitched awkwardly together. Nilsson recalled that as a favor to the other agent in Botkin's office building, he did not get a fee for this session, but "sang along with the group for free."⁴⁰

A Nilsson/Marascalco collaboration is the third of these four songs, a simple rocker called "Born in Grenada." The backing is clean and bright, with a well-recorded piano part prominent in the mix that looks forward to the kind of role that Nicky Hopkins or Dr. John would play on Nilsson's future records. There is a perky horn arrangement by George Tipton and some well-integrated backing vocals in the center of the track. It is a beautifully performed piece, but lacks the greater musical sophistication of "Good Times," with its changes of key and two-part structure. It also fails to show Nilsson as a distinctive musical personality. He is just a pleasant-sounding young man who places his phrasing slightly ahead of the beat in order to project a sense of urgency as he hopes to get "back to L.A. before the sun goes down." The flipside has Nilsson singing his own "You Can't Take Your Love (Away from Me)," which is a huge production number with a sumptuous Tipton arrangement, strong backing vocals, and lyrics that—if they weren't delivered with such lighthearted detachment—might be a musical insight into what was going on in Nilsson's life as he experienced his marriage starting to crumble.

The subject of the lyrics is a man who is being publicly put down by his girlfriend, has his picture torn off the wall, and is asked to leave. He doesn't want to go, telling her she can't take away his love for her, and urges her to remember all the good times and not the bad, because:

> When you fall for a girl and then you give your heart
> It's gotta be forever, baby, from the start.

Within less than a couple of years, Nilsson would have found out how to communicate effectively the heartbreak and pain embedded in such lyrics, so that his listeners genuinely shared his emotions. But at this point in 1965, his treatment still sounds superficial.

On a number of songs dating from the beginning of 1966 onward, Nilsson shared writing credits with his office colleagues, particularly Perry Botkin. Their association was to last for several years, extending to record production, and composing a stage musical together in 1979 called *Zapata*. Although with some of his writing partners, Botkin contributed equally to music and lyrics, this was not how he remembered his working routine with Nilsson:

> Harry and I had a basic drill that applied to almost everything we wrote from the early days to the last song. When we'd get together Harry usually had a title, a melody, and almost all the lyrics to the new song. Sometimes he would play the song on the guitar or the piano in a very simplistic manner. I would then sit down at the piano and make a few chord changes if needed and sometimes change the groove a little bit. Sometimes it would inspire Harry to change a lyric and/or a melodic phrase but usually we stayed pretty close to what he walked in with. My job was more as an arranger than an integral part of a song writing team. Harry was so original that if you messed with his basic musical ideas you usually fucked them up.[41]

Although pop music had moved on since the simplicity of the Bill Haley or early Elvis Presley songs of the 1950s—the "Rock Around the Clock" or "Jailhouse Rock" genre—the majority of hits in the mid-1960s were still relatively straightforward constructions over harmonies that were based on the same three-chord system. What Botkin immediately noticed about the songs Nilsson was now beginning to write was that they were inherently far more sophisticated musically. When he performed them, they sounded easy, but it was often hard for other artists to sing them with the same breezy assurance. With Marascalco, Nilsson had learned through imitation how to structure and pace a song. Now he began to impose his own ideas on both words and music. "He brought originality to the era," said Botkin. "No copying anybody. I've worked with some great singers and great people, but he was far and away the most original."[42]

In terms of lyrics, this was because in the wake of "You Can't Take Your Love (Away From Me)" Nilsson now began to look deep into his own life and experience for inspiration. One of the songs he remembered writing in that office was "Without Her," which, like "1941" (also written there), is autobiographical. After jotting down the first draft of the words on the spur of the moment on a napkin,[43] Nilsson came into the office to tighten up the lyrics and add music. The song was copyrighted in January 1967, about ten weeks before Sandi and Nilsson were legally separated on April 6. Perry Botkin recalled: "Sandi was a sweet young girl [but] the relationship fell apart as his career began to take off."[44] Although Nilsson would subsequently reduce any account of his first marriage to the quip about getting "out of the war," the lyrics of "Without Her" show how he was beginning to work his pain into his songs in a highly effective way. The song depicts Nilsson's nightly routine, arriving at the Botkin/Garfield office after, as he put it, "a couple of belts" at a local bar once he had finished at the bank. It runs:

> I spend the night in a chair thinking she'll be there
> But she never comes
> And I wake up and wipe the sleep from my eyes
> And I rise to face another day
> Without her

Nilsson was fond of telling interviewers in later life that he had written "Without Her," "1941," and "Don't Leave Me, Baby" in a single night.[45] Whereas Botkin and his other colleagues recall him coming up with two or three different songs in a sole night's production, it seems unlikely that he did actually create three such well-known songs in one sustained burst. They were copyrighted over the space of fourteen months, and it is improbable that the firm would have waited so long to register songs with such immediate potential. Nevertheless, ultimately "Without Her" was to demonstrate dramatically to Botkin and Garfield the wisdom of their investment in Nilsson. Just before it was registered in January 1967, they sold it to another publisher in the same building for $10,000, so it was actually copyrighted by the rival firm of Ping Music. Then Botkin and Garfield heard that Glen Campbell was recording it for his album *Gentle On My Mind*, so taking swift action before that news reached their rival, they offered to buy the song back. After a bit of haggling, they did so, for $15,000. Within a couple of years, they were to sell their Rock Music, Inc. catalog, including virtually all of Nilsson's early songs for $150,000 to Beechwood, the publishing arm of Capitol Records.[46]

When Nilsson looked back in later life at this stage in his career, he observed that there were two ways of breaking into the music business in the early 1960s in Los Angeles. One was to pound the streets, knocking on doors, whereas "the other way was to be part of the bunch who made records by formula even then. Gold Star was a hip studio then—Phil Spector, Larry Levine and Herb Alpert were all there."[47] Having pounded the streets and knocked on doors since 1962, in early 1966, Nilsson moved briefly from one path to the other, by beginning an association with Spector.

In most interviews and articles, Nilsson recounted his first meeting with Spector as taking place at Gold Star Studios, when he was recording a demo in 1966. Spector happened to hear it and asked who the singer was. He went on to inquire who had written the song, and Perry Botkin Jr., who was in the control room, told him, "He and I wrote it." Spector was impressed and asked Nilsson over to his house so they could write together.[48] In fact, it is likely that Spector had met Nilsson—although without bothering to find out who he was—four years earlier, when he was recording with Scott Turner. Turner's friend Ian McFarlane wrote:

> In the early 1960s Scotty acquired a special guitar called a "lyric harp" which had been designed by a retired L.A. cabinetmaker. The guitar had a very unusual shape and the bracing caused the twelve strings to resonate or cut through without the predominant overtones that most 12-string guitars possess. Phil Spector happened to hear Scotty's "strange" guitar (which Phil later dubbed "The Animal") ringing in the booth of Gold Star Studios as Scotty worked with Harry Nilsson one evening. Phil duly asked Scotty to play on some sessions.[49]

By the time he invited Nilsson to his house in 1966, Phil Spector had become one of the most successful record producers of all time. In 1958, at the age of eighteen, he had written, produced, and played on the chart-topping hit "To Know Him Is To Love Him" by the band he formed with his West Hollywood school friends, the Teddy Bears. He had learned more of his craft in New York with the songwriters Lieber and Stoller, as well as producing discs for Atlantic Records. He had then produced further hits, principally by the Crystals, Bob B. Soxx and the Blue Jeans, and the Ronettes. Although in the months before meeting Nilsson, he briefly took on a role with New York-based Liberty Records as an A&R man, he had now returned to Los Angeles, recording artists at Gold Star Studios for his own Philles Records. Conscious of his status—the writer Tom Wolfe had dubbed him "the first tycoon of teen"[50]—Spector had recently taken the lease on a palatial home in Beverly Hills. The sumptuous mansion at 1200 La Collina Drive was to become part of the Spector legend in the years that followed.

Had they gone on to work together in the studios on a regular basis, Spector might well have become a significant influence on Nilsson's own recording techniques, given his invention of the "wall of sound," in which overdubs and instruments playing in unison were used to create a dense backdrop. "To Know Him Is To Love Him" had been made in half an hour back in 1958, but even then Spector used every second of the time to dub in as many background vocals and instrumental tracks as possible.[51] However, at this point in 1966, it was not a common interest in studio technology, but songwriting that drew them together.

After turning up at Spector's house and being made to wait (as everyone was) over an hour for the producer to make his entrance, Nilsson sat down with him to work on writing ideas. The eventual results were three songs, two predominantly written by Nilsson and one more complete collaboration. The first of them was recorded (but not released on disc at the time) by Spector's current enthusiasm, the Modern Folk Quartet (MFQ).

The other two were fed into the conveyor belt of material that Spector needed for the Ronettes.

The MFQ had originally been formed in Honolulu, but after 1963, it was based in Los Angeles. It had begun, in the words of Spector's biographer Mark Ribowsky, by combining "acoustic folk with modern vocal harmonies,"[52] but following two albums made for Warner Brothers, the group had progressively electrified its sound, so that it mutated into a prototype folk-rock fusion band. Spector took a liking to the MFQ, believing that he could mold them into a rival to the Byrds, whose own brand of folk-rock had burst onto the Los Angeles scene in 1964. He presented them at the Trip, a short-lived Sunset Strip rock club launched by the Whisky A-Go-Go's founder Elmer Valentine, and on one occasion, Spector overcame his own dislike of public performance to sing and play guitar there with the group.

Henry Diltz, later to become one of Hollywood's most celebrated photographers, was a member of the MFQ, and he talked of the "three or four months" that they spent hanging out at Spector's mansion, waiting hours for him to make his appearance each day, before he coached them around the piano as to how he wanted them to harmonize certain songs. Diltz described this as a "musical bootcamp," and he also recalled that to refine his musicianship further, Spector brought him in as an additional member of the "wall of sound" panoply of studio musicians on various sessions for the Righteous Brothers or the Ronettes.[53]

If it had ever been Spector's intention to use the rehearsals at his mansion as the preamble to recording a full album with the MFQ, one way or another, this did not happen. However, in one of the songs that Nilsson played for him at his house, he found what he believed would be an ideal single for the group. The piece "This Could Be The Night," although often claimed as a co-written composition by Spector and Nilsson, was copyrighted in Nilsson's sole name on March 30, 1966.

Performed by Nilsson himself, it was a wondrous song, expressing the heady mixture of hope, desire, and fear experienced when a couple who have been dating for a while are on the point of finally conquering their inhibitions and making love for the first time. Spector added not so much ballast as deadweight to the airy lyrics, with a solid backing of organ, guitars, and drums, over which the MFQ sang a densely harmonized version of the vocal. Yet despite what in this case might be regarded as a prison wall of sound, he managed to retain the air of expectation inherent in the song. He used the recording in the spring of 1966 to run under the main titles of a rock concert film called *The Big T.N.T. Show*, which had been shot the previous November at the Moulin Rouge Club in Los Angeles. With candid pre-concert shots of the performers, such as Joan Baez, Ray Charles, Petula Clarke, and the Lovin' Spoonful, intercut with views of the audience clapping more or less in synch with the beat of the record, it held the viewer's attention through almost four minutes of opening credits. It worked particularly well because Nilsson's highly original harmonic sequence never quite resolves to a tonic chord, but creates a sense of perpetual motion. Those who heard the song never forgot it. The Beach Boys' Brian Wilson, who had been at Gold Star Studios sitting in the booth in a robe and slippers while the song was being recorded, said: " 'This Could Be the Night,' the one Phil Spector recorded with MFQ [is] one of my very favorite records and songs. Well, the idea they've been dating and waiting and finally they made love . . . I love that message."[54]

Although Spector used the song in the film credits, he decided not to release the single at the time, because he was not certain that it would be a sure-fire number-one hit. Nor did a demo mix of the song that he cut with Nilsson himself get released commercially. It featured Nilsson singing over a slightly less solid backing, with a group of female singers harmonizing behind him. Indeed, this version was not known to have survived until a single test pressing turned up on eBay in 2008.[55] The official MFQ single was not released until the Phil Spector *Back to Mono 1958-1969* four-CD collection appeared in 1991. Yet many of those—like Brian Wilson—who heard "This Could Be the Night" in its original version or in the *Big T.N.T.* movie remembered it and deemed it one of Nilsson's very best songs from his entire career. Ironically, apart from a private demo version made when he was selling songs to the Monkees in 1967, Nilsson himself was never to record the song again. Equally, the MFQ was not to make another record at the time, and they broke up later in 1966. There would be reunions in the 1970s and 1980s, as well as in 2003, but in the years to come, Nilsson would keep in contact with just two members of the group, Henry Diltz, who photographed him on a number of occasions, and Chip Douglas, who, after playing bass for the Turtles, was to become a record producer.

With such a fine song lying virtually dormant in Spector's hands, it must have been equally frustrating for Nilsson that the other two songs of his that were recorded by the Ronettes also lay unissued. These also did not appear until the 1990s. In retrospect, there seems to be no good reason for them to have been held back. "Paradise" is a perfectly respectable performance of a song written by Nilsson with contributions from Botkin and Garfield. It is backed by the full Spector paraphernalia of strings, a crowded rhythm section, and dense backing vocals. These feature Estelle Bennett and Nedra Talley over-dubbed many times behind the Ronettes' leader Veronica Bennett. (Veronica, as she was billed, was to become Mrs. Ronnie Spector two years later in 1968.) Some listeners believe that Nilsson's voice may also feature in the backing to "Paradise," but because the recording predates multitracked sessions on which each voice can be identified, it is impossible to verify this from the three track mixes that survive. Botkin had known Spector since the days of the Teddy Bears, and he recalled the way Spector went about recording this song:

My job was pretty much a take-down. Because he said, "We're gonna do 'doom, doom, tchk, tchk, doom, doom." He got that going, and then he sang the string lines, to me, with all the other things that he wanted. He said, "Yeah, then the violins come in going 'dee, dee, da, da, dee," and he sang the string parts.

He pretty much laid out how the whole song was going to be. So I'd come to a session like this with very basic chord charts for everybody. We'd come into Gold Star and I'd run the thing through, and then he'd start the changes. He'd hear something and say, "No, no, no." Then he'd ask for someone else to play a fill there, or something different here. He'd start making or rather mixing the wall of sound. He knew what he was doing, but in order to get there he used the studio like an arranger's tool. He'd build that sound in there, and start the echo going, and the way I'd write an arrangement was so it would work in the context of that massive echo chamber. I assume that's what he always did. And Gold Star Studios was the place, because they had a particularly funky echo chamber that became world-renowned.[56]

Despite the care lavished on "Paradise," "Here I Sit" is a much better song, with all the ingredients of many a Spector hit—a thumping beat, a brilliantly sung lead vocal from Veronica, and a tight arrangement. This is the main songwriting collaboration between Spector and Nilsson. Once "Here I Sit" did appear, it acquired a degree of notoriety, because it exemplifies Nilsson's scatological humor. By 1991, when it came out, his use of expletives and toilet jokes in songs was well-established following *Son of Schmilsson* in 1972. However, had "Here I Sit" been released in 1966, it would have been the earliest issued recording of this element of his writing.

He had taken the inspiration for the lyric from one of the most universal pieces of graffiti, scribbled on the walls of men's rooms in many parts of the country. The stanza runs:

Here I sit, broken hearted
Paid a dime
And only farted.

In Nilsson's lyric, he transforms the second and third lines into a regret that a couple has "parted" because they "couldn't see the writing on the wall."[57] It is an early example of Nilsson embedding private jokes in his songs. Sometimes these were tucked away in the lyrics, as here, and on other occasions they would be purely musical, with apt quotations and thematic borrowings, as happens consistently on his work with Randy Newman.

Because Spector held back the tapes of Nilsson's songs, the two men's collaboration did nothing to advance Nilsson's career, except for the scuttlebutt around Los Angeles that they had been working together. But because Nilsson was virtually unknown, what gossip there was soon faded away. Instead it was up to his colleagues Perry Botkin and George Tipton to try and get their friend and protégé noticed.

After the failure of the Spector experiment, Nilsson felt as hemmed in by his unsuccessful Tower contract as he had been by his one-year flirtation with Mercury. He pleaded with the company to release him from this agreement or record him again. In due course, in mid-1966, Tower offered him one more opportunity, in which four songs were to be recorded. The catch was that they were not prepared to put up any money. So George Tipton drew out his life savings of $2,500 and financed the session himself, on the basis that he would ultimately earn the money back from Tower.[58]

Only one of the four songs that came out of that session is a strong pointer to Nilsson's future potential. "Growin' Up," written by Nilsson, is a delightful evocation of childhood, comparing the toys and imagined games of early life with the maturity of a first love affair. It is tempting to think that Nilsson's sensitive word picture of a little girl in "mummy's shoes and mummy's grown-up necklace" meeting a "restless" little boy harks back to the Airstream trailer in Colton and his puppy love for Mary Anne Schultz. Tipton does him proud with the arrangement, with delicate string writing and subtle countermelodies, arpeggiated guitar figures in the foreground, and a hint of glockenspiel to mirror the childhood images. Nilsson's delivery no longer sounds superficial, but as if he genuinely feels the emotion of the words.

By contrast the soul-inflected treatments of "Do You Believe" and a cover version of Marvin Rainwater's "So You Think You've Got Troubles" are highly competent, but without any personality, while "She's Yours" sounds rather like a hastily cobbled-together fusion of two quite different pieces.

Nevertheless, the arrival of four new Nilsson songs gave Tower the opportunity to collate all their catalog of his work and to release a ten-track LP called *Spotlight on Nilsson*. This was brought out in late 1966 and was his first commercially released album. It was not initially a success, although Tower was to re-release it in the wake of Nilsson's work for RCA the following year. Over time, it went on to sell steadily if modestly. Most important, it established the persona that would be a feature of all Nilsson's future albums, by calling him by his surname alone. Whereas the Tower singles as far back as 1964 had been attributed to "Harry Nilsson," he now dropped his first name, and his publicity was to capitalize on this for years to come: "Nilsson has a first name, but why ruin the mystique by spreading it around?"[59]

Had *Spotlight on Nilsson* really taken off in sales terms, it could have launched his full-time musical career and accelerated his move from the bank. But despite Tipton's generous investment and Botkin's help with production, Nilsson's life carried on much as before. However, changes were on the horizon. After the best part of a couple of years on his twenty-five-dollar-a-week retainer from Perry Botkin and Gil Garfield, the beginning of 1967 saw the arrangement come to an end. "We finally had to let him go, because we were running out of money," said Botkin.[60] This was partly because, in addition to the Tower sessions, Rock Music, Inc. had recorded a number of demos by Nilsson during the time he was on their payroll. In due course, later in the year, Botkin and Garfield would collect these into a limited edition LP called *New Nilsson Songs* to whip up interest in their protégé's compositions.

Most of these songs had been recorded at different points in the two-year-long period of Nilsson's nocturnal writing, and had no doubt been used individually to try and interest producers and bands in buying them. Some featured other singers covering Nilsson's work, such as Jimmie Cross, Robin Ward, and Jean King, but the majority of the demos were by him. Just as his Tower recordings reveal him gradually moving toward finding an authentic voice of his own, capable of wry introspection in his lyrics, and matching this with a delivery that lived the meaning of the song, the Rock Music, Inc. demos—known to collectors as "the Botkin sessions"—do the same. "The La La Song," for example, finds him managing an authentic-sounding imitation of Bob Dylan. This is especially apparent when, to a strummed twelve-string guitar, he part incants, part speaks lines such as:

> There was a day when you would say
> That loving me meant everything
> And there was a night when we shared a kiss and I offered you this
> And I said, "Here, take my ring."

The song mirrors "Without Her" in its sense of loss, its lines focusing on the motif of "and now you're gone," with Nilsson managing what would become his trademark sob on the final "'Cos you're gone." There's also a curious moment in the midst of his Dylan impression when he includes a direct quote from the Beatles' "Yesterday." But despite its amorphous mixture of rock and roll influences, Nilsson is genuinely communicating the emotion of his lyrics, in a way he had never managed in the earlier 1960s.

"The Story of Rock and Roll" is another of these demos that yokes widely different influences into a potted history of the genre, but on a couple of the choruses, Nilsson attempts the kind of "wa-wa-wa" overdubs that would later be a feature of songs such as "1941." And there is more overdubbing on the chorus of "A Boy From the City," a paean of praise to urban living, that "don't find nothing great about the country."

Taken together, the best of the demos and the more recent of the songs on *Spotlight on Nilsson* show the degree to which Nilsson, by early 1967, had largely found a recognizable personal voice, both as singer and songwriter. In quick succession after losing his retainer from Rock Music, Inc., he was to fulfill his ambition to quit the bank by developing first one and then the other strand of his career.

Perry Botkin remembered that "it was weeks, maybe a month" after their financial arrangement ended that "he got connected at RCA, and then all hell broke loose."[61] The catalyst was a young producer at RCA called Rick Jarrard. He had cut his teeth on independent productions at Gold Star Studios, making demos and helping out on other peoples' sessions. Previously, Jarrard had been a music major at the University of Illinois, had played in brass bands, and was classically trained. That background helped him communicate between the rock world in which he now worked and the conservative corporate culture of late 1960s RCA, whose executives' main idea of pop was still beached in the era of Henry Mancini and Perry Como. In late 1966, Jarrard had been entrusted with the second album by Jefferson Airplane, on which he replaced their original producer Tommy Oliver. *Surrealistic Pillow* was a dramatic improvement over the band's first album *Takes Off*, and it yielded the hit single "Somebody to Love," which had also benefited from the input of the album's "Musical and Spiritual Adviser," the Grateful Dead's Jerry Garcia.[62]

At the time Jarrard met Nilsson in January 1967, *Surrealistic Pillow* was just at the point of release, and the hit single had yet to follow, but RCA's confidence in Jarrard was growing. In the relatively small pop music community of Los Angeles, Jarrard had run into Garfield and Botkin, and he also knew George Tipton, whose arranging career was taking off. Through them, he heard the Nilsson demos and was sufficiently impressed to ask the young songwriter into his office at RCA to meet him. Jarrard recalled:

> He was this quirky, skinny little guy that was a bank teller, and came in with his cowlick, and sat down in the chair and we had this conversation.... He started playing songs, and I just liked...some of the quirky things he got into.... The demos weren't anything like we ended up doing. However, I liked his voice, and I wanted to hear more of that. And the only way I could really do that was to have a writer come in and sit right in front of me and play, and look right into their eyes and see if they're real, and see what's going on, because that's important to me.... I think one of my main functions is to help an artist discover who they really are, and to try to bring that out of them. I heard a uniqueness in that voice that I felt we could put in the proper setting, and get him motivated, and work with him, and in addition, do harmonies. And I thought he could really find a niche for himself.[63]

The first meeting led to several more, in which Nilsson played the piano or guitar and sang through his repertoire. Jarrard instinctively seized on the aspects of Nilsson's work that were unique and original. Whereas Turner, Marascalco, Botkin, and even Spector had applied a scattershot approach to Nilsson's writing and singing, rather than systematically helping him to develop, Jarrard saw sufficient potential in the autobiographical lyrics and remarkable voice to create something that he believed to be entirely new on the musical scene. He remembered:

> I said, "Okay, Harry, we've got a deal."
> And when I said, "We've got a deal," I just assumed we had a deal. I went into the West Coast head of RCA and I said, "I just signed an artist."
> And he said, "You're not supposed to be signing artists, you're here to take artists that we assign to you to produce."
> I said, "Well, I've committed to it. I feel honor-bound. I've done it. I love this artist."
> So Harry's deal got okayed. But I certainly overstepped my bounds with that, in their eyes. However, in my eyes, that's what I was there for, to discover and sign new people that I felt had a good shot. And that's what I did.[64]

The contract was signed on January 19, 1967. It was for a one-year term, with a four-percent royalty on U.S. sales, and two percent elsewhere, with no money upfront.

There were various options written in for RCA to pick up, including a possible seven-year term. In the light of his frustrating agreements with Mercury and Tower, both of which had bound him into inactivity for lengthy periods, Nilsson sought legal advice. Through a mutual friend, he had recently met a young attorney named Bruce Grakal, who had gotten his license as a lawyer that very month, but who was also well attuned to the music scene. At that point, Grakal had recently finished working as a tax auditor and was about to join the practice of Kaplan, Livingston in Beverly Hills. Some years later, he would represent numerous high-profile musical artists, including Ringo Starr and Nilsson himself, but at this point, there was no question of representation. Nilsson simply called him and in response, Grakal said, "If you haven't got anything better to do, you might as well sign it, 'cause it's better to have a deal than not have a deal."[65]

Although some accounts of Nilsson's life suggest that, as a condition of his contract, he demanded an office at RCA with a desk, this did not feature in the agreement itself.[66] However, the company readily agreed to his informal request for office space, so that he could continue the nocturnal writing regime he had become accustomed to at Rock Music, Inc. The RCA offices were just a couple of blocks away from the building where Botkin and Garfield were based, so Nilsson felt doubly secure in his routine. In a 1977 interview with the BBC's Stuart Grundy, he said:

> I had this little office with a desk, and a lamp, and then a couple of things on the wall, and a rug. I turned the regular office overhead lights out, and just lit this little lamp, and I was very comfortable there. I'd go there at night, and write, and there was no one in the building. The janitors got to know me, and I'd work, and I'd go in the daytime to just sort of hang out and start planning an album, or get to know the engineers, that sort of thing.[67]

With no money upfront, however, Nilsson could not immediately afford to leave the bank, but he could start work during the daytime with Jarrard, who brought in George Tipton as arranger, with the full resources of RCA behind him. They began making the album that was to become *Pandemonium Shadow Show*.

Work on this was just getting underway when Nilsson had a stroke of financial good fortune. This came along when Chip Douglas (who had recorded "This Could Be the Night" as a member of the MFQ) left the Turtles, for whom he had been bassist and arranger on their hit "Happy Together," to become the new record producer for the Monkees. "I became a fan of Harry's writing when the MFQ worked with Phil Spector," recalled Douglas.[68] "Harry wrote these great tunes [and] he'd come in and play them."

On March 17, 1967, Nilsson met Douglas and members of the Monkees to demonstrate his songs. At this point, the Monkees had just parted company with Don Kirshner, who had been head of music at the production company that made their television show and also produced their first two albums. The band members—who had been hired primarily as actors rather than musicians—were now taking control of their own music and playing their own instruments, as well as singing. (Previously they had sung to backing tracks played by studio musicians.) Douglas had been invited to work with the band by Mike Nesmith, who believed that he and his fellow Monkees would benefit from such a proficient producer.

Fortunately, the entire session at which Nilsson demonstrated his songs was recorded for posterity. Not only does it contain the finest recording he made of "This Could Be the Night," but eight other numbers as well. Of these, "I Live in a World" has Nilsson back in his Dylan mode, as does—to a lesser extent—"Signs." "Hey Little Girl" offers marriage as a route out of a mundane life, maybe a wry comment on Nilsson's own motivations for his first wedding. It is mainly remarkable for the range of Nilsson's voice, being one of the first examples of his full three and a half octave stretch on disc. "Good Times" is a voice and piano remake of the 1965 Tower recording, sounding somewhat like a pastiche of Martha and the Vandellas' "Dancing In The Street," while "Superman" sounds like a promising fragment of an up-tempo boogie number about the Action Comics hero. However, "Counting" brilliantly weaves Nilsson's fascination with numbers into a dainty love song, and it might have made a fine addition to the Monkees' catalog. "The Story of Rock and Roll" also got a remake at this session, and Douglas was ultimately to sell this to the Turtles the following year. However, the outstanding song performed that day, apart from "This Could Be the Night," was a new piece called "Cuddly Toy."

It is clear from the talkback studio intercom conversation between Douglas and Nilsson that both of them already had this in mind for Davy Jones to sing. In Jones's eventual version with the Monkees, particularly in the televised version that dressed the band as an Edwardian music hall act, the double entendre of the song is largely absent. In the raw demo by Nilsson, its multiple layers of meaning are obvious. The song is a heartless rejoinder to a girl who has been dumped by a boyfriend after permitting him to have sex with her. She is "not the only choo choo train to have been left out in the rain, the day after Santa came," and she gave up her "cherry delight," it seems, "without a fight." The boy insinuates that she's not going to tell her mother about him ("the company you keep") and that she must have dreamed the idea that "he loved no other." The brilliance with which Nilsson wraps heartless cruelty into a soft, childlike song is remarkable, and the Monkees recorded it just a few weeks later. According to Nilsson, Mike Nesmith—who had been making the major efforts to get the band to record new and original material in its own right—was blown away by the demo session. "Man where the fuck did you come from," he said. "You just sat down there and blew our minds. We've been looking for songs, and you just sat down and played an *album* for us! Shit!"[69]

In 1967, the Monkees were the closest thing America had to the Beatles. Their tours (performing with a backing band, then increasingly to their own playing) provoked scenes of Beatlemania proportions, and their records sold in colossal quantities. Micky Dolenz remembered the immediate consequence of the Nilsson demo session:

> When Davy Jones said he would record "Cuddly Toy," the music publisher that was there, Lester Sill was the guy's name... walked out into the parking lot [with Harry], and Lester said, "You can quit the bank."[70]

Lester Sill was at that point one of the most powerful figures in the music industry. He was a former colleague of Phil Spector and had now become the vice president and general manager of Colgems Music, the publishing and record production company associated with Screen Gems, who made the Monkees television show.[71] Accounts vary as to how substantial an advance Nilsson was paid for "Cuddly Toy," but it was in the region of $40,000. He told Joyce Haber of the *Los Angeles Times* in July 1968 that his earnings for the previous year had been $75,000 "without turning out a single real musical hit."[72] Despite Nilsson's natural caution and his emotional dependence on retreating to the bank when he felt overcome by the music business, Lester Sill's prediction was correct. Although Nilsson stayed put in his job at first, he finally summoned up the confidence to quit the bank when he heard the Monkees' "Cuddly Toy" being played incessantly on the radio.

He might have tried to stay on longer at his job, had it not been for his immediate boss and friend David Rochele, who was the senior vice president of the Van Nuys branch. As Nilsson's song moved up in the charts, Rochele, a fair-minded man who had been a drill instructor in the Marines and played everything strictly by the book, called Nilsson into his office. He told him he had been passed over for promotion, even though he was the strongest candidate. "You were smarter than the competition," he said, "but I can be sure they'll be here in one or two years, but with you, I can't be sure." As Nilsson recalled, "He laid it out for me, it was time to either shit or put the paper back."[73] So, before the year was out, Nilsson had swapped his desk at the bank for his little office in RCA's building in Hollywood, and his new career was underway.

Well the calendar changed and the pages
fell off,
But the singer remained the same.
And he never grew tired of singing his song,
And the fans still called his name.

3

MR. RICHLAND'S FAVORITE SONG

THE MAKING OF *Pandemonium Shadow Show*, Nilsson's first RCA album, was a long process, which lasted from the initial recording session in February 1967 until its release in October that year. His original intention was to name it *Something Wicked This Way Comes*, borrowing the title from a book by one of his favorite authors, the science fiction novelist Ray Bradbury. In turn, Bradbury had taken his title from a couplet in William Shakespeare's *Macbeth*, in which the witches conjure up the apparitions that prophesize to the Scottish king. Bradbury applied the title to a macabre story of two boys who visit a sinister carnival, with a carousel that changes the ages of those who ride it, culminating in a climactic struggle between good and evil.

However, there was a legal wrangle over the use of Bradbury's title, so instead, Nilsson took his album's name from the traveling carnival in the novel, Cooger and Dark's Pandemonium Shadow Show. Because either working title would have represented the carnival or circus atmosphere, George Tipton went ahead before the issue was settled and produced a set of arrangements that contained plenty of elements borrowed from circus music. The concept came from Rick Jarrard, who had at one time been a cornet player, and who felt that his brass band experience could help shape the overall sound and texture of *Pandemonium Shadow Show*. He recalled, "On the first album, I thought it would be a great chance to use a lot of brass and a lot of percussion, a lot of drums."[1]

Consequently, there are prominent snare drums on several tracks. Amid a heavily featured brass section, frequent passages for valve trombone and either baritone or French horn lend the charts both a sense of the big top and a tinge of melancholy. Indeed, Tipton's close harmony scoring for horns became known henceforth in the trade as "the

Nilsson sound."[2] The carnival setting was to feature strongly in the label's advance publicity for the album that read:

> Nilsson has an inborn sense and feel of the 'sawdust' atmosphere (his grandparents toured Europe about sixty years ago as "Nilsson's Aerial Ballet"), and RCA Victor's *Pandemonium Shadow Show* is a three-ring circus with Nilsson in the center ring. Verbal byplay at the beginning of the album between performer Nilsson and producer Rick Jarrard sets the stage and the big show is under way.[3]

Creating a concept album of this kind was not a new idea in the industry as a whole, but it was a comparative novelty at RCA. A constitutionally conservative company, RCA was used to recording every album in two or three simple three-hour sessions, in which a singer sang standard songs live with a band or orchestra in a succession of complete takes. Jarrard had to fight long and hard for the studio time he knew was necessary to allow complex backgrounds to be built up and to give Nilsson the opportunity for vocal overdubbing.

As the twelve songs for the album were decided upon, each of them went through approximately the same process, once Jarrard and Nilsson had met with Tipton (and sometimes also Perry Botkin Jr.) to work out the basis of the arrangement. "We would first cut basic tracks which would be the brass or the drums or bass or whatever," recalled Jarrard. "Then we would proceed to go and do the lead vocals. And then we would do the harmonies, and lots of times I'd sing with Harry on the harmonies, just for fun."[4]

Nilsson himself valued Jarrard's input, complimenting him on his "marvelous ear" and his ability to "listen to a sound and relate it to someone else." Nilsson was equally fulsome in his praise for the engineer, Dick Bogert, whom he felt was "responsible for getting that sound to come across right."[5] For the first time, Nilsson was recording with colleagues whom he regarded as equals. He was no longer learning his craft as he had been on almost all his previous records. Now he was able to bounce ideas off a producer whose musical sensibilities matched his own and an engineer who understood that Nilsson's love for overdubbing and studio craft was an integral part of the record-making process. Among the first tracks to be finished were Nilsson's original song "Ten Little Indians" and his version of the Beatles' 1964 number "You Can't Do That." The former neatly fused the old children's ditty along the lines of "ten green bottles, sitting on the wall" with the idea of transgressing the Ten Commandments, while the latter not only added inventive harmonies to the vocal line originally sung by John Lennon, but magically wove around it an overdubbed galaxy of additional voices singing a range of clever allusions to other well-known Beatles songs.

On the original opening of side one of the LP, immediately after Nilsson and Jarrard's spoof introduction to the "Shandemanium Shadow Po," the circus drums strike up "Ten Little Indians," with a relentless beat that continues throughout the track. Over this, Michael Melvoin begins a regular, repetitive electric piano pulse, playing a simple repeated chord on each eighth note. This was to be a frequent Nilsson stylistic device in many of his future songs, perhaps influenced by the technical limitations of his own piano playing. Paradoxically, more and more elements are added to the track as the number of Indians gets smaller. It builds to its climax with the disappearance of the final Indian. As the arrangement unfolds, first Nilsson's voice comes in, then one by one the brass section arrives, starting with the trombones and finally the full complement. The technique is not unlike that of Elmer Bernstein's theme for John Sturges's 1963 film *The Great Escape*, where the military drumbeat established in the second chorus keeps going relentlessly as more and more instruments are piled on.

In contrast to the thunderous climax of "Ten Little Indians," the reworking of the Beatles' "You Can't Do That" is subtle and low key, its full effect depending on what appeared to be an encyclopedic knowledge of every album the Fab Four had released up until the early months of 1967. It draws on most phases in the group's work that preceded *Sgt. Pepper's Lonely Hearts Club Band* (which the Beatles were completing during the first few weeks that Nilsson and Jarrard began working on *Pandemonium Shadow Show*.) How Nilsson arrived at the idea was every bit as much a result of his quick-witted craftsmanship as his prior knowledge of the Beatles. He said:

> One time I was just toying with my guitar and I struck this chord, and it seemed to lend itself to a million different songs. I noticed how many Beatle songs could be played with this one chord, so I ran down to Wallach's Music City on Sunset at about midnight, right before it closed, and bought the Beatle songbook, and finished the song that night.[6]

The musical backup to Nilsson's recording is simple, with Dale Anderson's bongos, Milton Holland's drum kit, Lyle Ritz's mobile bass patterns, and some subtle keyboard chording from Melvoin. Over this, Nilsson harmonizes the lead vocal with himself on the left side stereo channel. But on the right, he adds a number of extra overdubbed voices, whose backing vocals paraphrase, copy, or directly quote from (in order) "She's a Woman," "I'm Down," "Drive My Car," "You're Going to Lose That Girl," "Good Day Sunshine," "A Hard Day's Night," "Rain," "I Wanna Hold Your Hand," "Day Tripper," "Paperback Writer," "Nowhere Man," "Do You Want to Know a Secret?" "Norwegian Wood," and "Yesterday." The total effect is a remarkable vocal tour de force, made more effective still by the ingenuity with which each song is briefly introduced. At the time, the publicity talked of the song being crafted from eleven Lennon-McCartney compositions, but there are clearly more present than that. Eager Beatle-spotters have claimed as many as twenty-two direct allusions, although this largely depends on allocating "sha-la-las" to specific songs. However the fourteen listed here are easily identifiable.

RCA Victor did not wait until the whole album was completed before releasing these two new songs individually. Indeed "Ten Little Indians" backed with "You Can't Do That" was tried out in demo form before becoming the first Nilsson single officially released by RCA during the week of August 14, 1967. *Billboard* announced that it was put out "as a result of continued air play by KRLA, Los Angeles."[7] The same article noted that Nilsson's new songs were now to be published by Dunbar Music, the "recently established" publishing arm of RCA, and the effects of writing for a well-networked publishing firm that efficiently marketed his songs were felt almost immediately.

As a result of Dunbar's efforts, Nilsson's single had barely been released when competition arrived, in the form of a rival version of "Ten Little Indians" by the Yardbirds. The song might seem an unusual choice of material for a blues-oriented British band that had previously been fronted first by Eric Clapton and then Jeff Beck. But by mid-1967, touring as a four-piece band led by Jimmy Page, they were making a determined attempt to capture the American popular market. The group's English producer Mickie Most was selecting the repertoire for recording, and in cahoots with Dunbar Music, he decided that "Ten Little Indians" would be an ideal follow-up to their previous release, an inferior cover of Manfred Mann's hit "Ha Ha Said the Clown." The Yardbirds' "intriguing and offbeat" version of Nilsson's song crept into the top 100, reaching ninety-six on the *Billboard* charts and seventy-one on the *Cashbox* listings, before falling back exhausted. The song is now best remembered by Led Zeppelin fans as one of the first examples on record of Jimmy Page using the spacey guitar effect that he termed "backwards echo."[8]

Nilsson's own version of "Ten Little Indians" failed to make the top 100 in the charts, peaking at number 122. However, a Canadian release, timed to coincide with the appearance of the full *Pandemonium Shadow Show* album later in the year, and no doubt benefiting from the attendant publicity, reached number ten in the Canadian charts, thereby making the record Nilsson's first top-ten hit in any territory.

It would be logical to assume that "You Can't Do That," on the reverse side of the single of "Ten Little Indians," would immediately have brought Nilsson to the attention of the Beatles. Yet in most accounts of Nilsson's relationship with the Beatles and Derek Taylor, their erstwhile publicist, the story goes that their mutual enthusiasm for one another actually stemmed from Taylor hearing another song from the album, "1941," on his car radio. This took place in October 1967, after *Pandemonium Shadow Show* had been released. On getting home from the shopping trip during which he heard the track, Taylor verified that it was indeed sung by Nilsson by calling the KRLA disc jockey Johnny Hayes, who had played the song, and promptly ordered twenty-five copies of the album. In due course, he played one of these records to the Beatles, who subsequently adopted Nilsson as their "favorite group." Indeed, Taylor says as much in his notes to Nilsson's second album *Aerial Ballet*, which was released during 1968. He also recalled in his memoirs that he was subsequently introduced to Nilsson by Pat Faralla (an agent who worked for Paul Cooper at A&M Records), and that the two met "for the first time" at the La Brea Inn. Taylor said, "[We were] drinking men both, who couldn't possibly know—but maybe suspected—just how much we would see of each other in the future, how many bottles we would get through together in benders as long and swampy and dangerous as the Amazon."[9]

However, by the time he came to hear "1941" in his car, Taylor already knew all about Harry Nilsson and, albeit briefly, had actually met him a couple of months earlier. This happened in Los Angeles during August 1967 at the very time when the single of "Ten Little Indians" and "You Can't Do That" was released. That month, George Harrison was renting a house on Blue Jay Way, in the area of the Hollywood Hills known as "Birdland." Then as now, the web of streets named for such avian creatures as swallows, robins, mockingbirds, orioles, warblers, and skylarks was home to a galaxy of celebrities. Katharine Hepburn, Spencer Tracy, Vincent Price, and Linda Evans were among those who had settled there, and in this milieu, George Harrison found the ideal hideaway in the 1400 block of the Blue Jay Way cul-de-sac. The house belonged to Peggy Lee's one-time manager, the lawyer Ludwig Gerber. It was a two-story modernistic building with big plate-glass windows, built on three sides of a swimming pool with a clear view southward over the Hollywood skyline.

Soon after he arrived there, sitting at Gerber's Hammond organ, Harrison penned the song "Blue Jay Way" that was to feature on the *Magical Mystery Tour* album, and which describes Derek Taylor getting lost in the warren of tiny streets leading up to the house. At the time, Taylor, after leaving Brian Epstein's British N.E.M.S. company that managed the Beatles, was trying his luck as a freelance publicist in Los Angeles, working, among others, for Paul Revere and for the Beach Boys. While writing newsy, gossipy columns on his main artists and on the rock scene in general for the teenage magazines *Flip*, *Tiger Beat*, *Disc*, and *Teen*, Taylor nevertheless kept his ear to the ground for any new talent that might be suitable for Epstein. Hearing about Nilsson's new single, he invited RCA's latest signing to a reception at Harrison's house. In contrast to Taylor's somewhat chaotic attempts to find the place on his first visit, Nilsson's experience of being brought to meet one of the four most famous musicians in the world seems like a scene from a James Bond movie. He recalled:

> I was met by a car at Martoni's in Hollywood, transferred, and driven to a point in the Beverly Hills area. There I was transferred to another car, and to Blue Jay Way, where we passed the house, turned around and came back, to see if we were followed. I was ushered into this beautiful house with an open main room and a bar. To the right was a large back area with the pool, statuary and so forth.
>
> Not knowing anyone and feeling very nervous and shaky about meeting a Beatle…Derek Taylor took me by the hand and introduced me to his wonderful wife Joan, who was pregnant with Dominic at the time….Derek took my elbow and led me outside. I was looking around wondering, "Where is the man?" Finally I saw him, he was standing at the far end of this long, narrow swimming pool, in a white windblown robe with a beard and long hair, looking like Christ with a camcorder. So there he is!

Derek said, "George, I'd like you to meet the man."

He walked me over and said, "George, this is Harry. Harry Nilsson—George Harrison." George says, "Yeah, right, Harry. Can we get you something, a coke, a coffee or something?" He was looking me over and I thought, "Wow! He's offering me something to eat or drink! This is amazing!"[10]

Nilsson may have been star-struck for an instant, not least through realizing that it was possible to be a Beatle and yet remain sane and normal, but he had made sure that he had with him all the demos for his forthcoming album that were so far completed. Both Derek Taylor and George Harrison listened to the music, and Nilsson recalled Harrison being "very complimentary" about his work. He was struck by the way Harrison was able to pay attention to individuals, making sure their glasses were filled and joining in the conversation, yet remaining aware of everything that was going on. It was Harrison who first took away the songs to play them to the other Beatles, which he did when he and the band reassembled in London to record on August 23.[11]

Taylor, on the other hand, decided then and there to try and poach Nilsson away from RCA Victor. He immediately sent his copies of the demos over to Epstein's lawyer and head of merchandising, the imposing figure of Nat Weiss, who was also in Los Angeles and had been at the reception in Blue Jay Way.[12] Taylor recommended he sign Nilsson on the strength of the sample material. As a result, within a few days of meeting Harrison, Nilsson found himself on August 27 at a poolside cabana at the Beverly Hills Hotel, negotiating a deal with Weiss and his assistant Bob Fitzpatrick. Their opening gambit was to offer Nilsson an advance of $25,000. After a long conversation and several drinks, during which Nilsson said that that was too low a price for his "whole future," the advance and conditions escalated, until an offer was on the table for a quarter of a million dollars and a trip to Canada with "the Beatle of his choice." Weiss set up a signing meeting for the next day and left to draw up an agreement.

That night, Nilsson received a call from Weiss. "Listen, you'll hear this on the news in a couple of hours. Brian Epstein has just killed himself. We'll have to beg off negotiations until the smoke clears and things calm down a bit."[13]

The discussions were never to restart, and Nilsson remained with RCA. Taylor, however, had become an enthusiastic supporter of Nilsson, and was to do everything in his power over the years that followed to promote his career. But when it came to promotion, RCA—possibly alerted to rumors that Nilsson was looking at other possible labels—surprised everyone by putting a huge effort into marketing *Pandemonium Shadow Show*. Key to the campaign was a box of delights, sent to all and sundry in the media. The producer of BBC Radio One's breakfast show in England at the time was Tim Blackmore, who recalled the package that arrived:

A special promo box, which as well as an American pressing of the album and a very flowery biography, included stickers and badges proclaiming Nilsson to be "The

True One", 10" x 8" photos of the man himself, and a sheet notifying us that the LP was also available on "RCA stereo cartridge tape".[14]

The "true one" motif was to dominate the promotion. Full-page advertisements were placed in the music press that read:

> He's the sound of today ... and he sings the total truth. On this album Nilsson delivers the message with such songs as "Ten Little Indians," "You Can't Do That," and "1941." The subject of a big promotion, Nilsson is phasing in as sign of the times listening.[15]

In several of the reviews that followed the release, the lavish press coverage garnered as many column inches as the contents of the album itself. Certainly, few of the reviewers went into much detail on the other ten tracks that made up the remainder of the LP along with "Ten Little Indians" and "You Can't Do That." Yet taken as a whole, this body of material represents a huge step forward from Nilsson's previous work, and under Jarrard's expert guidance, *Pandemonium Shadow Show* is a much more unified album than *Spotlight on Nilsson*.

First, dipping into the Beatle repertoire again, in the wake of "You Can't Do That," Nilsson presents a sensitive version of "She's Leaving Home." This is the ballad written by Lennon and McCartney about the story of seventeen-year-old Melanie Coe who made the British newspaper headlines when she ran away from her parents' home—although the man she ran off with was apparently a croupier, not the member of the "motor trade" described in the lyrics. The song was first released on the Beatles' album *Sgt. Pepper's Lonely Hearts Club Band* on June 1, 1967. Just ten days later, Nilsson cut his version, with George Tipton's mournful brass band backing cleverly evoking the Northern English atmosphere as effectively as Mike Leander's string ensemble does on the original. On the Beatles' recording, McCartney sings the lead vocal, telling Melanie's story, while Lennon sings the underlying chorus looking into the minds of the parents who have sacrificed everything for their daughter and given her all that they could—except fun. The distinctively different voices of the song's co-writers (and tellingly, each sang the section of the lyric he had written himself) enrich the emotional depth of the story and relate it with brilliant clarity. In contrast, on his version, Nilsson sings all the parts, and the similarity of timbre between the two elements of parents and daughter makes it harder to tell them apart. The unintentional effect is to make the parents' commentary seem part of the main narrative, while the "She's—Lea—ving—Home" chorus is reduced to a pretty but ineffectual backing vocal. The clever overdubbing shows off Nilsson's vocal range and dexterity, and the song remains one of the best covers of the Beatles' work by any artist, with the biting social commentary of the original being replaced with something prettier and more wistful.

Nobody would apply either of those adjectives to the blockbuster treatment that Nilsson brought to the Phil Spector song "River Deep Mountain High" that closed the album. Jarrard had been at Gold Star Studios when Spector recorded his original version with Ike and Tina Turner the year before, and he wanted to see if he could go one better. With Nilsson's voice treated to copious amounts of reverb, the backing is a mountainous assembly of "wall of sound" clichés that mimic Spector's own production. The vast backing track actually swamps Nilsson from time to time, and his voice lacks the aggressive punch that Tina Turner delivered. Nevertheless, in terms of showing how cleverly he, Jarrard, and Tipton had assimilated the Spector style, the track is a suitably rousing finish to the LP.

In between "Ten Little Indians" and "River Deep" are several other examples of Nilsson's growing maturity, both as singer and songwriter. Notably his song "Sleep Late, My Lady Friend" is an affectionate ballad, underpinned by the superb jazz bass playing of Ray Brown and featuring the soulful cello obbligato of Jesse Ehrlich. The portrait of a girlfriend sleeping during the morning after the night before takes a sense of contemplative introspection both from the cello and from some deft baritone horn arranging, but it also shows Nilsson's ability to deliver a tender love lyric in a direct and connected way. This was something that had eluded him on most of his earlier recordings. A hint of overdubbing wizardry closes the track, with a stack of Nilsson voices beginning to appear just as it starts to fade.

There is plenty of Nilsson's quirky humor on the album, hinted at by a cover photograph that shows the suited singer standing deadpan in a tented set packed with props that allude (often obliquely) to the songs on the album. A lot of planning went into the final choice of cover image. The RCA files have seven alternative versions of the picture, some with Nilsson standing in different poses, others with him sitting on the box of props, and one with a disembodied conductor's hand and baton. The enigmatic image that was eventually selected chimes best with the music-hall jocularity of such tracks on the disc as Jesse Lee Kincaid's pastiche "She Sang Hymns Out of Tune" and the genuine 1919 vaudeville song "Freckles." Together these embody the circus and carnival atmosphere that Jarrard and Nilsson were seeking for the album, and this is reinforced by the marching rhythm of "It's Been So Long."

This last song is an original composition, which is most remarkable for the overdubbed harmonic choir of Nilsson voices. In this, Dick Bogert achieved a minor technological miracle. He only had four-track machines available to him in the studio, but he hooked up two tape decks to work in synchronization with one another, thereby pioneering eight-track recording.[16] Although the piece is less musically inventive than "You Can't Do That," it is a far more exceptional piece of studio craft, and extremely advanced for 1967.

It was an exhausting process going over and over the same piece of song to create this dense layering of voices, as Rick Jarrard recalled:

I loved harmonies, and Harry and I would work together and sing the parts and work on the songs that way. It was…handcrafted; each cut was handcrafted, really.

I remember the Monkees were in the other studio cutting records at the time. And a lot of times when we worked for eighteen hour days or something, everybody would be going stir crazy. I remember some interesting times of running through the studios late at night with water guns shooting at each other...just to try to get some frustration out because we got crazy. But we would work in there, work on a song, build harmonies, come up with parts.[17]

The RCA ledgers show several "sweetening" sessions for the album, giving details of how Jarrard and Nilsson worked over some sections again and again to arrive at the finished sound they wanted. This was a far cry from RCA's usual practice of the time, but the new working methods are thoroughly vindicated, as the most enduring highlights of the album are the most lovingly handcrafted sections of it. These are Nilsson's own version of "Cuddly Toy," together with "1941" and "Without Her."

His "Cuddly Toy" receives less of a superficial Edwardian music-hall treatment than Davy Jones's interpretation for the Monkees, although it lacks the heartless cruelty that Nilsson managed to inject into his solo demo discussed in the previous chapter. "1941," on the other hand, is the autobiographical centerpiece of the album. It justifies Derek Taylor's paeons of praise because it carries all the emotional punch that is missing from the new version of "Cuddly Toy." It was from the imagery of a fatherless boy running away to join the circus and history repeating itself that Jarrard and Nilsson originally extrapolated the whole "Pandemonium Shadow Show" concept, choosing and arranging the rest of the repertoire to blend with it. Nilsson's wordless scat-singing echoes the brass-heavy circus band that accompanies the track.

The emotional impetus behind the writing of "1941" was Nilsson's stunning discovery that the father he had imagined to be killed during the war was alive and well. The exact moment that this revelation occurred is unclear, but it seems that in late 1966, Bette realized, following the release of *Spotlight on Nilsson*, that it would only be a matter of time before Harry Nilsson Sr. not only found out about his firstborn son's career as a singer, but tried to make contact with him.

She therefore got back in touch with her former husband herself, and they orchestrated telling both sets of children simultaneously. Harry Sr. and his new family had relocated from New Jersey and were now living in Palatka, Florida, a short distance from Jacksonville. Nilsson's half-brother Gary, born in April 1952, was to discover that the photograph on the family mantelshelf of a boy in a sailor suit with his father showed his brother, and not—as he had been led to believe—a distant cousin. Gary recalls that he was still fourteen when he was told and therefore dates this to shortly before April 1967.[18]

The song "1941" was not copyrighted until November 1967, but it was written earlier in the year. The recording session at which the basic vocal track was first laid down was on June 12, suggesting that Nilsson wrote the song within a few weeks of learning the news.[19] Hard on the heels of the emotional trauma of his separation from Sandi, Nilsson now had to come to terms with the fact that his father had not died in action as he had been led to believe by Bette, but had voluntarily abandoned him and apparently made no effort at contact. He had also not been a Seabee, but merely a merchant mariner, "like Ringo," as Nilsson was to point out in later life.[20] The bitterness and pain of this series of discoveries was to emerge in several songs over the forthcoming months, but never so clearly or poignantly as in "1941." As it turned out, the pain went two ways. Gary Nilsson recalls: "The only time I saw my father in tears was when he first heard '1941,' sitting at our kitchen table."

With hindsight, it is easier to see the striking individuality of this song, with its insouciant attitude toward domestic tragedy, compared to the rest of the album, and indeed it offers a contrast to much of the lightweight pop material that was being released by other artists in 1967. At the time, however, it was not "1941" that garnered most attention. The song that did so, particularly in terms of being covered extensively by other artists, was the next most strongly autobiographical piece on the record, "Without Her." *High Fidelity* magazine complained that unlike all the rest of the songs on *Pandemonium Shadow Show*, Nilsson's recording of "Without Her" was at a technical disadvantage. "For reasons best understood by RCA, the track was recorded at an exaggeratedly muted level," it grumbled, nevertheless going on to say that " 'Without Her,' a baroque-rock ballad, shows that Nilsson can be attractive at quiet level when he wishes."[21] Other journalists went further: "He's backed with a big sound on some tracks, probably to diminish the fact that his own sound is very small."[22]

The contrast with the rest of the album was entirely deliberate. Jarrard said, "I heard that song and I wanted it set in a very, very sparse setting." Opening with just the bass of Lyle Ritz and then followed by a cello accompaniment from Jesse Ehrlich that is even more prominent than on "Sleep Late My Lady Friend," the minimal backing creates what Jarrard called "a nice frame for Harry as an artist."[23] The obvious stylistic reference is to George Martin's double string quartet setting for "Eleanor Rigby" on the previous year's Beatles album *Revolver*, with its prominent solo cello part. But where Martin's starting point was apparently Paul McCartney's fondness for Vivaldi, George Tipton—who as Jarrard put it "ended up writing the actual notes" for the Nilsson accompaniment—took J. S. Bach's solo cello suites as inspiration. As the track goes on, a solo flute joins in, but then everything drops back for a reprise of Nilsson's autobiographical lyric about spending the night in his chair. Whereas "1941" is tragicomic in relating an aspect of Nilsson's past, "Without Her" is emotionally direct in its sense of loss, nowhere more so than the final lines of "There's no song without her..." in which the last two words are sung in the falsetto register, with just a hint of an overdubbed backing vocal, suggesting a celestial choir. It is one of many brilliant touches that made this track the album's most immediately influential song at the time, particularly for the other singers who admired it enough to try making their own versions.

"Without Her" (retitled "Without Him") was first covered by Lulu in 1968 with a string quartet backing. Closer to the emotional fragility of Nilsson's version was Astrud

Gilberto, who cut a version in 1969 with a full string orchestra backed by a light bossa arrangement, with acoustic guitar in the fore. It is a very dreamy setting, and the "do-do-do-do-doo" wordless singing is particularly suited to her voice. Al Kooper and Blood Sweat and Tears on *Child Is Father to the Man* (1968) also recorded a bossa treatment, which starts in a low-key way like Nilsson's, but adds jazz piano backing and gradually builds to a big climax on the line "It's ended now...." Perhaps the most unusual version, a long way from Nilsson and Jarrard's vision for the song, is the record that Herb Alpert and the Tijuana Brass made in 1969. The brassy explosions between Alpert's intimate vocals are surprising to say the least.

When *Pandemonium Shadow Show* first appeared, there were high hopes at the record company for Nilsson and the album. Ernest Altschuler, the divisional vice president and executive artists and repertoire producer at RCA Victor in Los Angeles said: "He is one of the truly remarkable writing and performing talents of today and I expect rapid public acceptance of this young man's remarkable versatility."[24] Many journalists picked up on this corporate enthusiasm, including the widely syndicated journalist William D. Laffler:

> Every once in a while a record company feels it has reason to grow ecstatic about the possibilities of a newly signed artist. It happened to RCA Victor when it "discovered" Elvis Presley....Now it believes it has made another discovery with an artist known only as Nilsson, who recently had worked as a computer supervisor for a Van Nuys, California, bank. Nilsson is a singer and composer. He plays both piano and guitar. RCA Victor believes he is symbolic of today's youth even though he is clean shaven, neatly dressed and exactly the opposite of the hippies.[25]

But despite the hype and the high hopes, not to mention some very positive reviews, the album did not sell particularly well, although as *Record World* pointed out, "if it isn't a hit with the public, it's a smash with producers, songwriters, arrangers and other artists."[26] Several of the published reviews are revealing in regard to the competition that it was up against. Obviously the music press assessed the album in context, among other pop and rock releases, but the general papers left Nilsson to sink or swim alongside everything that appeared at the same time and was aimed at the middle-of-the-road market. Consequently, *Pandemonium Shadow Show* garnered slightly lukewarm reviews beside such diverse fare from the same month of release as *Lionel Hampton at Newport, The Big Beat Sound of James Last and the American Patrol, John Gary on Broadway*, Nina Simone's *High Priestess of Soul*, and Hugo Montenegro's omnibus collection of spaghetti Western scores, *Fistful of Dollars, For a Few Dollars More*, and *The Good, the Bad and the Ugly*.[27]

Nilsson was to earn a significant amount from the cover versions of "Without Her"; indeed the following year, *Cashbox* magazine described him as his publishing company Dunbar's "domestic home run" in putting the firm well ahead of its financial forecasts.[28] Yet his royalties from sales of the album itself and its related single issues fell short of expectations. In an effort to focus attention on Nilsson's own versions of "Without Her" and "Cuddly Toy," his publicists at RCA placed an interview in *The Beat*, in which he told interviewer Jacoba Atlas that he far preferred to record his compositions himself than hear other people's versions of them:

> I feel much easier. I guess it's just the songwriter instinct. The songwriter basically knows how he wants a song sung and very few people are capable of transcribing someone else's thoughts in the same way he thought it. So therefore I would rather record them myself.[29]

Equally revealing, he spoke publicly for the first time on the autobiographical element in his work, saying, "I write from personal experience, personal contact. It's like you experience A and B, and then come up with C. Basically they must start from one person, in this case the songwriter, and go to another person, the listener." With such thoughts in mind, the personal element was to be even stronger in the next album he made, *Aerial Ballet*, in which all but one of the songs were originals. For most artists, work on such a follow-up album would wait until plenty of energy had been expended on promoting the current project, but as he was to do throughout his career, Nilsson went about things differently.

Then, as now, the established practice of marketing an album was that after its release the artist engaged in a flurry of promotional activity, ranging from television interviews and guest appearances to full-fledged concert tours. Despite the elaborate "true one" marketing campaign, Nilsson did none of these activities for *Pandemonium Shadow Show*. He decided that if it was at all possible, he was not going to hype his discs through live concerts; indeed, after the experience with Jerry Smith of appearing in public at National City, he intended never again to risk the humiliation of being laughed at by an audience. For this first RCA Victor album, apart from some interviews in the popular music press, Nilsson left the recording to do its own promotional work.

This was not to endear him to RCA's executives. However, Rick Jarrard completely understood Nilsson's reluctance to appear in public. He said:

> He never explained to me, but I don't think he had to. Harry was just self-conscious about being a performer in a public situation. He was much more comfortable in the studio…and that's where he really felt at home. He just was not—at least when we started—cut out to be one of those exhibitionists, or get up onstage and expend a lot of energy performing.[30]

Consequently, that fall, Jarrard found himself defending Nilsson at one of the record company's regular roundtable A&R meetings. With the sales of *Pandemonium Shadow Show* doing little for the company's executives to get excited about, they suggested dropping Nilsson. However, Jarrard managed to convince them that to discard Nilsson so early in his career would be a big mistake. Because of Jarrard's track record with Jefferson Airplane, and one or two of the other bands with whom he was beginning to work, the company agreed to keep Nilsson on its roster. Cannily, Jarrard had already returned to the studio, even before the official October 1967 release of *Pandemonium Shadow Show*, to start work on the next album. Thus—he reasoned—RCA Victor would be keen to go on with the project if only to recoup its investment.

On September 20, Nilsson cut four tracks, of which three eventually made it to the final selection for what *Billboard* called the "suite of detail-dotted anecdotes, sensitively spun" that made up the new album.[31] In keeping with the family circus theme, the title *Aerial Ballet* was decided upon early in the process. Interestingly, the California courts hold records of a Carl E. Nilsson who patented an "aerial ballet machine" in 1896, designed to be "capable of supporting ballet dancers in mid-air, and may be conveniently and easily manipulated, so as to give the aerial dancers the appearance of floating in the air." The coincidence of name and title is too remarkable to avoid the conclusion that this was Nilsson's grandfather's very circus act after which he named the album. Following the court case, a *Los Angeles Times* advertisement from February 28, 1897, shows Nilsson's "Original flying ballet" act in action, with four winged fairies floating in mid-air around another of their kin, who is supporting several long ribbons for a kind of airborne maypole dance. In contrast, the RCA cover design for the new album showed a clown dangling from an elderly biplane, and nothing so exotic as the elder Mr. Nilsson's invention.[32]

The song from that first September recording session that did not make it onto the album was "Miss Butter's Lament" (written with Bob Segarini of the band Family Tree, which Jarrard and Tipton also produced). Maybe Tipton was attempting to show his versatility by producing an arrangement utterly different from the version of the same song that he arranged for the Family Tree album *Miss Butters*. Whereas that version of the song has the drum and brass feel familiar from his *Pandemonium Shadow Show* charts, for Nilsson he recrafted it for strings and flute, with Nilsson's voice overdubbed among plenty of added reverberation. The result is a somewhat over-arranged saga about a single girl that aimed for Beatles-style social realism, but achieved none of the astute awareness of such Lennon and McCartney songs as "She's Leaving Home" or "Eleanor Rigby."

In comparison, Nilsson's melancholy story of "Mr. Tinker," a lonely, embittered tailor whose wife had passed away and whose son had left home, manages a fine balance between the general and the particular, and also between the emotional delivery of the lyrics and George Tipton's subtle arrangement, featuring a prominent woodwind and brass section. The bass clarinet creates a counterpoint to Nilsson's voice, Tipton's trademark valve trombone has the countermelody, and the whole song retains a sense of lightness despite the dark subject. Nilsson's lyrics exemplify his growing ability to give a tragicomic treatment to serious subjects. Just as he dismissed his first marriage as something he did "to get out of the war" in conversations with friends and family, he habitually masked his true feelings with a witty catchphrase whenever the subject got too personal for comfort. And here he cleverly wraps the personal loss of Mr. Tinker into the wider saga of small traders battling massive chain stores. "Who needs Mr. Tinker when all the suits you buy are ready-made?" asks Nilsson, and although we know that Mr. Tinker envied the lives, fun, and colorful clothing of everyone else around him, we suddenly get a sympathetic glimpse of the trap that his life had become.

Even though it was only a few weeks since he had finished work on *Pandemonium Shadow Show*, Nilsson's own writing was showing signs of an even deeper investigation of life and emotion. He successfully returned to metaphors of childhood on *Aerial Ballet* by choosing to include two versions of his own mother's cradle song "Little Cowboy." The wistful evocation of the past from his earlier piece "Growin' Up" is revived here in the form of a brief bedtime story, packed with advice to a little boy to put aside his cowboy clothes and games and get some rest. It works because it is completely without maudlin sentimentality and gets inside the dynamics of a mother/son relationship.

There is a more adult form of autobiography to be heard in "Good Old Desk," which starts out as a piano and tap dance routine, alluding to the album's circus theme, but which quickly settles into Nilsson's reflections on the security provided by his office desk, at least in part looking back at the Botkin/Garfield establishment from the safety of his new cubbyhole in the RCA building. Many commentators have noticed the title is an acronym for "GOD," and even some of Nilsson's closest friends saw this as a piece of conscious religious imagery, comparing the dependability and constant presence of the desk to the role of the Almighty. Nilsson himself was bemused by the fuss, confessing that he had not noticed the significance of the initials until it was pointed out to him after the song had been recorded. However, his sense of fun allowed him to trade on this in the future, and while being interviewed about the album on the television show *Playboy After Dark* in 1969, he solemnly told Hugh Hefner that "the song's meaning was in its initials." For years, those who saw deep significance in the idea used this conversation as vindication of their religious interpretation, but shortly before his death, Nilsson confessed in his final interview with Dawn Eden that "I bullshitted him. I thought it was funny."[33]

The verbal ingenuity of "Good Old Desk" is its strongest aspect, whereas "Don't Leave Me, Baby" is in every respect a neatly constructed pop song, with a gentle opening verse building up to a climactic chorus built around a repetition of the title and an optimistic alternating phrase, "Things are gonna work out fine." This is, however, a false hope, as elsewhere the lyrics make clear that the "happy times, the groovy times" are gone. It was still less than a year after Nilsson's separation from Sandi, and the themes of loss and loneliness surface here and in several more pieces on the album. "Together" is a different take on fragile relationships ("Life isn't easy when two are divided"), and "I Said Goodbye To Me" is an insight into suicidal personal desperation. The old Ink Spots' device of speaking the lyric underneath the sung vocal hints at Nilsson's encyclopedic knowledge of popular music.

Nilsson was beginning to deliver his own songs with increasing conviction and consistency, but the one piece on *Aerial Ballet* that he did not write, "Everybody's Talkin'," gave him the chance to show how he could take someone else's song and make it completely his own. He achieved this so convincingly that the world has long associated this piece with him and not with its actual composer, Fred Neil.

Earlier in the year, Neil, a folk singer and songwriter who had built his reputation in the cafés and bars of New York's Greenwich Village, had released an eponymous album on Capitol. As well as marking the start of what became Neil's lifelong fascination with dolphins in a song of that name, this LP included "Everybody's Talkin'," which was another of his new compositions. Played by his regular backup group that included two other guitars in addition to his own twelve-string instrument, the leisurely delivery of Neil's deep baritone is counterbalanced by the urgency of a country-style guitar figure that continues throughout the piece. His nonchalant vocal is offset by a plangent metallic-sounding solo guitar, which also links the verses. It is a good but by no means great performance. Yet just as Neil's earlier song "Other Side of This Life" had been plucked from his relatively obscure 1965 album *On Bleecker and MacDougal* and given far more successful treatments by Peter Paul and Mary, Lovin' Spoonful, and Jefferson Airplane, Nilsson was to do the same for "Everybody's Talkin'."

Nilsson recalled: "I happened to be at RCA one day and my producer, Rick Jarrard, was listening to a Fred Neil album. He played me a cut which he intended to use with a group called Stone Country. I liked it a lot and we decided to record it."[34]

Nilsson made his version on November 8, 1967, with one of George Tipton's most effective arrangements. The urgent guitar figure remains from Neil's original, but Tipton's masterstroke is to introduce a high, sustained note for the upper string section that remains constant until it moves up a tone on the line "I'm goin' where the sun keeps shinin'." The constancy of this violin part acts as a sheet anchor against the repetitive movement of the guitars and throws Nilsson's vocal into sharp relief. Whereas Neil had been gruff and offhand in his delivery, Nilsson's voice is tender, fragile, and emotionally charged. We believe immediately that he is a dreamer, isolated from a world in which he is surrounded by people going about their daily lives. When Nilsson arrives at his characteristic wordless "wah-wah-wah" vocals, Tipton drops the strings into the cello register, and the singer's voice blends into the dreamy background. The string parts intensify with the reprise of the lyrics, as the fiddles scurry around the vocal line, and gradually overdubs of Nilsson's voice are added until the climactic leap into his falsetto register for "I won't let you *leave* my love behind...." For just over two and a half minutes, the performance enters totally into the escapist world of the lyrics.

More remarkable still was the fact that Nilsson produced the main lead vocal of this exceptional performance almost in real time, with a minimum of retakes. His new girlfriend, Diane Clatworthy, who would later become his second wife, was in the studio in November 1967 during the recording of the vocal track. She recalled:

That was a magical moment. He did that take in I think two or three takes and it was just incredible. You don't see that very often where somebody just nails it, a song like that. And I just feel lucky that I got to see that. Everybody kind of gasped. It was incredible. The music, and the voice, and everything.[35]

"Everybody's Talkin'" was not an immediate success, although Jarrard was sure they had a hit on their hands. He recalled playing it over in the studio at high volume dozens of times, and with each hearing being more convinced that they had between them achieved a perfectly crafted song. His feelings were not shared by the president of RCA or the company's vice president of A&R, who happened to be in Los Angeles at the time and showed scant interest. At first it seemed that they were right, because although the song was one of the first singles to be released from the album, it made little impact outside the Los Angeles area. There it was taken up for its playlist by the radio station KHJ, and according to Jarrard, it sold 40,000 units in the Southern California area on the strength of that exposure alone.[36] But elsewhere in the country there was no similar surge of interest, and the song lay almost dormant for a year following its release in 1968.

Then, Derek Taylor brought it to the attention of the British film director John Schlesinger, who was about to make his American directing debut with *Midnight Cowboy*. Schlesinger and his producer Jerome Hellman had asked John Barry to write the score for the movie, but they wanted to open the picture with a specially commissioned song. They initially approached Paul Simon, who turned them down, but they were successful in persuading Bob Dylan, Randy Newman, and Joni Mitchell to produce original songs for them.[37] As a result of Taylor's enthusiasm, they also contacted Nilsson, who recalled:

I'd come from London and I was stopping in New York for a few days when I was approached by Jerry Hellman and John Schlesinger. They asked if I'd be interested in writing a song for *Midnight Cowboy*—a title song. At the time I knew nothing of either of them, nor the film. Of course I knew of Dustin Hoffman because of *The Graduate*, and I said I'd love to see it. So they showed me four reels of uncut material and I thought "What? This could be the best movie ever made. It's incredible. You bet, you bet!" So I went home and tried to figure out what the story was about, and to me, basically the story seemed to be about a guy who was in Texas who was dissatisfied with his life there so he went to New York for a better one. And he meets a guy in New York who's dissatisfied with his life there, and then they go to Florida looking for a better one. And they're looking for something that isn't there no matter where you go to find it. That's like him, so I thought "The Lord Must Be In New York City."

"Lord's a sort of a Texas word," I thought. I submitted the song. I think I was told that Dylan had written a song for it, "Lay Lady Lay" was written for *Midnight Cowboy*, and also Joni Mitchell wrote something—I can't think of which one—for it. But in favor of the film, they decided to stick with "Everybody's Talkin'," which was not written for the film, but which they had been using as a temporary track until they found a song for it. And they just got used to it. So used to it, that they didn't want to drop it. And they left it in. Thank you very much![38]

One reason for not dropping "Everybody's Talkin'" in favor of Nilsson's newly written song "I Guess The Lord Must Be In New York City" is that by using a slightly extended re-recording of it as his "temporary track," Schlesinger had woven the piece deftly into the nine-minute opening titles and setup sequence of the movie. As Jon Voight's character Joe Buck dresses in full cowboy regalia to leave his dishwashing job in Texas and set off on the bus to New York, the song seems to get inside his head. When characters shout, "Where's Joe Buck?" it is clear he does not "hear a word they're saying," and the flashback sequences to his childhood are accompanied by Nilsson's eerie "wah wah wah" wordless vocals. Although there is an unintended irony that Joe Buck is heading where "the sun keeps shining," when he is actually leaving the sunny South for the cold Northeast, the metaphor of the sunnier life overcomes the literal truth of the lyric. The song's melodic theme comes back repeatedly in the movie, and John Barry recalled that his own music for the film was "orchestrated to fit into the musical language" of "Everybody's Talkin'." He acknowledged borrowing ideas from Tipton's setting, such that in the full score for the rest of the movie "the counter melody is much more important than the melody, in that it's going nowhere—it's just this repetitive thing. Like when you travel around New York and see the homeless and see these people going nowhere. That's where the falling motif for Jon Voight's character comes from."[39]

When the film appeared in 1969, RCA Victor re-released Nilsson's single, and it immediately became a hit, selling over a million copies in all and rising to number two on the *Billboard* "contemporary" chart, as well as reaching number six on the same magazine's "pop single" chart. In due course, Nilsson collected the Grammy award for Best Male Contemporary Vocal Performance of 1969. It was to be this song, above all others, that altered the public perception of him from being a songwriter who sang, to a singer first and foremost.

However, as *Aerial Ballet* was being made, this was all in the future. At the time, the song from the album that achieved most immediate success was "One," which had been recorded a month before "Everybody's Talkin'" on October 6, 1967. It was picked by RCA to be the first single to be released from the album in April 1968,[40] and it drew together several strands of Nilsson's interests and writing, from his fascination with numbers to the use of a repeated chord running all the way through the piece as in "Ten Little Indians." The lyric itself is repetitive, constantly returning to the idea that "One is the loneliest number that you'll ever do." This was a subtle example of Nilsson sending a coded message to his listeners, because those in the know would realize that "doing a number" was smoking a joint.[41] To round off each stanza, the line was subtly altered to "One is the loneliest number that you'll ever know." In a couplet about "making rhymes of yesterday," there is once again a passing allusion to the Beatles' catalog. Nilsson's version of the song is sensitive, introspective, and subtle, and his forays into the falsetto register toward the end include some extremely clever overdubbing. The melancholy aspects of the song are reinforced, in common with Tipton's earlier arrangements, by some solo cello playing from Jesse Ehrlich, and the musical glue that binds the piece together is Michael Melvoin's repeated right-hand chording on the electric piano. This was quite deliberate on Nilsson's part, who explained to BBC listeners in the U.K. that "I wrote 'One' while I was dialing a telephone, and there was a busy signal. In America it goes beep-beep-beep-beep-beep. So I let it stay busy and wrote it while I was on the phone."[42]

Despite RCA pushing the single, Nilsson's own record of "One" failed to chart. However, once again the backing of a strong publishing company led to the song being covered by other artists. Early in 1968, vocalists Danny Hutton, Chuck Negron, and Cory Wells came together in Los Angeles to form a group known as Three Dog Night. (The band's name came from the apocryphal Australian anecdote that, alone in the outback on a cold night, an aborigine would cuddle up with a dingo, a wild dog, to keep warm. If the night was very cold, you needed three dingos.) Their first album, called simply *Three Dog Night*, was made in mid-1968 shortly after keyboardist Jimmy Greenspoon, bassist Joe Schermie, drummer Floyd Sneed, and guitarist Michael Allsup had joined to complete the group's lineup. Most of the material for the disc was written by the band's members; however, they were short a track or two. Consequently, "One" was included in the repertoire for the LP, which was released on October 16. It was promptly forgotten about, as the record company, ABC-Dunhill, focused on the opening cut "Nobody" as the single to be promoted from the album.

But within a few weeks, the phone started to ring on the desk of ABC's Marv Helfer, the executive who looked after A&R, to say that up in Oregon, local radio stations were getting inundated with calls to play "One" from the *Three Dog Night* album. He began calling other radio stations across the country and realized that, whereas "Nobody" had made no impression on the market whatsoever, he had a potential hit on his hands with "One." Briskly, ABC-Dunhill rushed out a single, and it roared to number two on the U.S. pop charts, selling over a million copies in the process and launching the band's career as one of America's best-selling groups of all time.[43]

The Three Dog Night version of "One" has none of the subtle grace of Nilsson's recording, although Chuck Negron's lead vocal, robust as it is, does include a comparable athletic leap into the falsetto register toward the end of the song. But whereas Melvoin's insistent chording captures Nilsson's idea of the telephone "busy" signal, Greenspoon's piano simply acts as a launch pad for a much heavier, rock-inspired backing to the Three Dog Night version. Nilsson's record is whimsical, philosophical, thought-provoking, whereas Three Dog Night transformed the song into a sing-along anthem, pointedly harping on the line "One is the loneliest number" in order to bring chanting audiences to their feet in the huge venues where the band was soon routinely grossing $20,000 to $30,000 a night on its live shows.

Another reason for the song's commercial success is that a level of inner meaning far more profound than the coded messages about marijuana struck a chord with the public. Nilsson himself recognized at the time that "today's music tells stories, has shades of meaning, and pushes philosophy,"[44] and in the decades following Three Dog Night's chart success with his composition, psychologists and counselors, writing about the subject of loneliness, began quoting the lyrics as a sage observation about the human condition, not least that "two can be as bad as one, it's the loneliest number since the number one."[45]

Just as Lennon and McCartney's musings on "all the lonely people, where do they all come from?" captured the public's imagination, it seemed that Nilsson had the ability to ask similarly probing questions on the same subject. As well as writers and intellectuals seizing on the song and its imagery, it also went on to be recorded by numerous other artists, most notably Aimee Mann, who sang it in Jon Brion's arrangement in a Nilsson tribute album in 1994, her version going on to be used in the titles for Paul Thomas Anderson's cult film *Magnolia* in 1999.

It is possible that one reason for Nilsson's own single release of "One" not doing too well was that it was coupled with an even gloomier B-side, "Sister Marie." This song, which was not included in the *Aerial Ballet* album, explores the loss of faith of a nun for whom "life was not easy" and harps back to Nilsson's Foto-fi Four days as it is overdubbed to sound as if he is a four-man vocal group.

Although "Sister Marie" did not get used on *Aerial Ballet*, the overdubbed four-voice technique did. At least, it did on the first pressing of the album, in the form of "Daddy's Song." This portrait of a doting dad who deserts his young family is yet another account of the father figure Nilsson never knew. The lyrics tell of a dad who can banish the pain of a little boy's grazed knee, who was his "mother's biggest fan" and told him "how life would be when I grew up to be a man." It is all delivered in the vo-de-o-do style of a 1920s pastiche, with a suitably rum-ti-tum backing by Tipton, redolent of a British seaside entertainment troupe. And it is against this lighthearted, jokey background that once again the story of Nilsson's desertion by his father unfolds. Images recur from "Cuddly Toy" of playthings left out in the rain. It is not as bittersweet as "1941," but it similarly uses music-hall humor to deaden the pain. But pain there is, with real cries of anguish amid the multifarious overdubbed voices that close the track.

Within a few months of *Aerial Ballet*'s release, a second pressing of the album hit the stores, and "Daddy's Song" had mysteriously been removed. This is because once again Dunbar Music had succeeded in getting a cover version of the song recorded, this time by the Monkees, for the soundtrack of their psychedelic movie *Head*. This film was the turning point in the Monkees' fortunes. Shot during the middle of 1968, the soundtrack album was cut at the same time, and the music was coordinated by the actor Jack Nicholson, who was also co-author of the screenplay and a major investor in the film. When the movie was released in November 1968, its inchoate ramble through the band's rise to Hollywood stardom was incomprehensible to the teenage fans of their television show. Yet it was not sophisticated enough to interest the trendy hippie audience they had hoped to attract. The Monkees were never to regain a mass audience in the numbers they had previously enjoyed.

In the movie, Davy Jones sings "Daddy's Song" as a vaudeville number in part of a sequence that follows a spoof commercial in which the Monkees play flakes of dandruff on a giant scalp—part of the movie's "head" title image. After escaping from a huge vacuum cleaner that is trying to suck up the scurf, Jones steps through a door onto a soundstage and, in a tailed suit that unsettlingly alternates from white to black every few seconds, dances his way through the song. The lyrics were poignant for him as his own father had died shortly before shooting began, but the song seems to have no real place in the movie, and as Jones leaves the studio set, Frank Zappa, who mysteriously appears from time to time in the film and is seen here for no particular reason leading a cow, tells him to spend less time on his dancing and more on his singing.

Not surprisingly, the movie was a box-office disaster, so hopes were pinned on the soundtrack album released by the Colgems joint venture between Columbia Pictures and RCA. To give the Monkees' album every chance of success, the RCA executives decided to pull Nilsson's version of the song from his own album. It did not reappear in its rightful place until a CD reissue of *Aerial Ballet*, six years after Nilsson's death.

The overdubbing on "Daddy's Song" was the most sophisticated on the originally released *Aerial Ballet* album, and Nilsson by this time had his own firm ideas about the method of building up layers of voices to sound like a four-man group or to provide close-harmony backup to his own lead. The technique had come a long way since country singer Patti Page became the first to overdub her voice in 1948 on her single "Confess."[46] He said:

> The singing is [all] mine, but I do alter each background voice to make it sound fuller. If they're too much alike it becomes a double vocal, and any differences have to be imperceptible. I like to think of it as the old Paul McCartney type of thing, rather than the old Patti Page sort of thing, because it's a different medium now. It's changed so much since she did it, since the Beatles started overdubbing. They're using different techniques.[47]

The original release of *Aerial Ballet*—complete with "Daddy's Song"—was scheduled for May 1968, but it eventually took place in July, the final items for it having been recorded and mixed very close to the originally planned date of release. The critics liked what they heard, but with no sense of consistency in their reactions. On the one hand, there were those who discounted Nilsson's talents as a singer, such as Californian reviewer Bill Yaryan: "His voice is fluid but forgettable, and his melodies are conventional. The lyrics and his arrangements are something else. Nilsson, like few other writers, can create a mood that conjures up other worlds and can provide substantial insights."[48] And on the other hand, there were those who—maybe already seeing the potential in "Everybody's Talkin'"—preferred his singing to his writing, such as the anonymous reviewer "M.A." in *High Fidelity*: "The people at RCA are enthusiastic about Nilsson as a songwriter. With the occasional exception, this aspect of his talent is less than spectacular. Anybody could have written these songs. The specialness is in the singing, plus the imaginativeness of the scoring by George Tipton."[49]

In general, the reviews were evenly divided along precisely these lines. Most praised the album, but few agreed as to exactly what Nilsson's special talents were. Faced with a repeat of *Pandemonium Shadow Show*'s disappointing sales, for almost the only time in his career, Nilsson went against his determination to avoid performing in public. He agreed to RCA's requests to do some personal appearances and promotion to support both this and his previous album. "I was advised to have a manager," he recalled ruefully, "and that year I had one."[50]

He began by getting to work on material from his first album, miming to "1941" on a prerecorded edition of the syndicated *Woody Woodbury Show*, a pioneer talk show hosted by a comedian who had made his name telling slightly rude jokes on phonograph records. There was a frisson of daring about this television program, as Woodbury's blue humor, which would now be regarded as tame in the extreme, had succeeded in getting his records banned in several states. Despite his wooden delivery and a total absence of interviewing technique, Woodbury's show was perceived by media and public alike as a suitable, if slightly risqué, place for a pop artist to promote recent songs. After a first airing in New York on May 22, the Nilsson edition of the program was shown at various times across the nation during the following four weeks.[51] As the year went on, Nilsson would make a number of television appearances to promote the two albums, but there was a hiatus during the final lead-up to the release of *Aerial Ballet* in July, because immediately after the Woodbury show, he was preoccupied for three months by quite a different activity. The press reported:

> Nilsson, the sensational young singer-songwriter, has been signed by Otto Preminger to create the score and the title theme for *Skidoo*. The motion picture, which stars Jackie Gleason and Carol Channing, currently is before the cameras in the "millionaires only" haven of Hillsborough, south of San Francisco. The new comedy, a Paramount release, marks Nilsson's first film assignment.[52]

In the annals of 1960s movies, *Skidoo* is rightly regarded as one of the worst films of the decade. Although Preminger had a formidable reputation and had successfully tackled such controversial topics as drug addiction (*The Man with the Golden Arm*, 1955) and rape (*Anatomy of a Murder*, 1959), as well as making a major contribution to screen musicals of the 1950s with *Carmen Jones* and *Porgy and Bess*, by 1968, his career was already in terminal decline. In a flimsy plot about gangland revenge and murder, in which Gleason breaks *into* a prison intending to murder an old criminal associate played by Mickey Rooney, *Skidoo* tackled the contemporary concerns of crime, technology, LSD, and hippies. In doing so, it involved an ingenious score by Nilsson, but overall, Preminger's forte was not light comedy, and much of the movie is leaden and humorless.

Its saving graces are the moments built around Nilsson's music (arranged and conducted by George Tipton with self-evident zest at having a full Hollywood studio orchestra at his disposal). The musical high point of the entire film is a moment when Fred Clark and Nilsson himself, deliberately emulating Laurel and Hardy as a pair of prison guards, look down from their searchlight tower. As a result of inadvertently taking LSD, they see the garbage cans below them dancing a ballet.

Nilsson's song about the "good stuff" with which the average trashcan is filled is one of his most verbally inventive lyrics. A love affair between a banana and a Brussels sprout is to be legitimized by a piece of asparagus "who'll stand up and marry us," and while this is being sung on the soundtrack, silvery garbage cans with dancers hidden inside them do a Busby Berkeley routine bathed in various shades of psychedelic light. There's a similarly inventive moment at the end of the movie when Gleason's character has successfully fled the prison by balloon. At the moment when the titles would usually start to roll, Preminger's voice shouts: "Stop! Before you skidoo, we'd like to introduce our cast and crew." Nilsson then sings the credits, in a long, rolling musical number that is intercut with scenes of the characters being mentioned. However, because of the ingenuity of the lyrics and rhyme scheme, the most memorable names seem to be those of hairdressers and transportation managers, rather than the movie's star actors.

Paramount, who distributed the film, liked the sung credits so much that several parts of the sequence were used in the movie's advertising trailer. And on the subject of advertisements, one almost subliminal moment of ingenuity from Nilsson is the musical backing for a series of television commercials that appears at the very beginning of the picture as Jackie Gleason and Carol Channing argue over the remote controls of their television. While the set jumps from channel to channel, fragments of advertisements flicker past, from overweight girls singing the delights of cola to a brilliant pastiche of a romantic Hollywood love song in which a young couple sing to each other at the tops of their voices: "You need a deodorant!" This was an ironic echo from Nilsson's own past, because during the Marascalco years, he had himself sung the soundtrack to a commercial for Ban deodorant, although that was a far less glitzy affair than Tipton's full-blown orchestral setting for the commercial in *Skidoo*.

At the time, the two sequences from the film that attracted most attention were a scene on a "hippie bus" in which Gleason's screen daughter Darlene (played by Alexandra Hay) strips to her scanty underclothes to have her body painted, and another scene set in Gleason's prison cell where he licks an envelope impregnated with LSD and has a "bad trip." Nilsson had fun with both, using a folksong version of his own "Ten Little Indians" as the soundtrack to the bus scenes and creating a surreal sound collage with bent sitar notes and tabla pulses for "Tony's Trip."

For Nilsson himself, meeting Gleason for the first time—once the cast and crew had finished in Hillsborough and returned to the studio lot in Los Angeles—involved a curious connection with his childhood. By the time *Skidoo* was shot, Gleason had a thirty-year career in movies, television, and music, but he had spent time in the 1940s, when Nilsson was a small child, away from the bright lights, back in his home neighborhood of Brooklyn, honing his stage act. During those years, Gleason not only became a regular at Moran's bar, the gin mill once owned by Nilsson's grandfather, but he perfected his variety routine as the host of the weekly talent contest at the RKO Gates Avenue Theater in Brooklyn. Nilsson recalled:

My mother would grab anyone she could, and talk them into singing with her, or dancing or doing whatever they do, and would form an act for the amateur nights. She lost so many times that Gleason himself actually gave her a trophy. We were introduced and he was loaded. It was about 1:00 am in this bar. Gleason was ready to top dog anyone who had the balls to get in his way and take him on.

"What is it you do?" said the Great One.

"Uh, I'm the music man," I said, shyly, "on the show."

"Yeah, yeah, but what do you do?"

"I write and sing songs."

"Oh, you do? Well, I think you're a clam, you know that?"

I was also drunk, and didn't care. I looked him straight in the eye, "Oh, yeah?"

He said, "If you're a singer, sing us a song."

I said, "You're a comedian. Make me laugh."

And he sort of grunted, "Oh, a wise guy!"

So I said, "All right. A cappella."

As I sang, it was getting late. The waiters, the bartenders were all trying to leave, but they knew the Great One was there. And I sang so sweetly, the song, "Without Her," which I had written recently.

His head snapped to one side, with a big smile, and he said, "You're okay, pally. You're okay. What else you got?" And I had him hooked. So I shocked him by singing one of his songs, which was "Somebody Steps on a Cat."[53]

…His mind was blown, and he started to applaud me, then the waiters applauded, and the leftovers, watching this badminton match between Gleason and a kid.

"How in the hell did you know that song?"

I said, "I liked it a lot."

"What else do you do? Shoot pool?"

"A little, you know. I can do anything that you can do," I said. "Can you play basketball?"

He says, "I can shoot, God dammit. I can shoot."

It was now 3:00 a.m., with a 7:00 call waiting for us. And Gleason actually walked me to the bungalow, patted me on the back, and said, "You're all right, pally." And he gave me a little punch on the shoulder.[54]

The next morning Nilsson, along with the rest of the cast, arrived on set at seven. He felt rough and hungover, but to his surprise he saw Gleason "clean, composed and smooth" looking as fresh as a daisy. Nilsson's mere presence that day was enough to keep him in Preminger's good books, although as time went on, the famously irascible director fueled more than the average number of stories about his eccentricity and bouts of temper during the shooting of *Skidoo*. He had a studio executive removed from the set for talking too loudly; with disastrous results he tested a seesaw that was supposed to lift Frankie Avalon into the air; and he complained volubly about a $50,000 set featuring a bed that was supposed to sink gently into the floor, but which collapsed loudly into a hole in the ground.

The single most bizarre episode, recalled by most of those present on the movie, happened in an abandoned prison outside Los Angeles where much of the location shooting took place. Preminger wanted a long tracking shot in which his camera followed the principal characters down a corridor en route to the prison mess, where dozens of men would be eating their lunch. Instead of a composite of shots, he wanted to do this in one, and spent an entire morning working out an elaborate choreography that had extras dressed as prisoners skillfully dodging the camera dolly and making way for his stars to speak their dialogue as they walked toward a table where Gleason was eating his lunch.

After exhausting rehearsals, the cast tucked into a hearty meal of chicken and ribs. Then it was time for the actual shoot, as Chicagoan journalist Roger Ebert reported from the set:

After lunch, the actors discovered that after getting their plates filled in the prison cafeteria, they were expected to actually eat the food.

"No mouthing," Preminger ordered. "It will not look real on the camera. I want you to actually chew and swallow the food. If you cheat, I will catch you."

And so the performers marched down the corridor, through the cafeteria line and into the lunchroom, sat down, ate and talked. They did it once. Then again. Preminger was still not satisfied. Some of the lines didn't sound right. The cramped space grew hot with the glare of the lights. In all, there were 21 takes before Preminger was satisfied. Many of the actors, having actually eaten 21 helpings of beef stew under Otto's watchful eyes, looked ill.[55]

Halfway through the shooting of the film, in June 1968, Nilsson received a call from Derek Taylor that was to take him away from the set for a long weekend for events that would have a momentous impact on Nilsson's future life.

The background to this was that in the fall of 1967, when *Pandemonium Shadow Show* was released, Derek Taylor had, as mentioned earlier, ordered a box of albums and distributed them to his friends in the U.K. (where the record had yet to be formally released). In his own grandiose prose, Taylor said, "Scattered went the albums by mail and hand across the continents, and in the pockets of humanity bound only by recorded sound, Nilsson was a tiny cult."[56] Although George Harrison had brought "Ten Little Indians" and several other early versions of songs from the disc back to Britain in August 1967, it was Taylor's enthusiasm for the finished album that had really gotten the Beatles interested in the singer who had so effortlessly assimilated their music on "You Can't Do That." Not long after Taylor had handed out the discs, Nilsson was keeping his usual nocturnal hours in his little office at RCA.

One Monday morning about three or four in the morning I get a call and it's John Lennon. I was half asleep. He says, "Hello, Harry. This is John. Man you're too fucking much, you're just great, man. You're fucking fantastic, you know? We've got to get together and do something."

I said, "Who is this?"

"John Lennon."

I said, "Yeah, right, who is this?"

He says, "It's John Lennon. I'm just trying to say you're fantastic, that's all. Have a good night's sleep. Speak to you soon. Goodbye."

Boom.

I thought, "What? Was that a dream?"

The following Monday Paul McCartney called, "Hello Harry. Yeah, this is Paul. Uh, just wanted to say you're great man. John gave me the album. I think it's great, you're terrific. Looking forward to seeing you. How you doing? How's your father?"

And so on and I say [to myself] this is amazing. So the next Monday I got dressed and waited for the four o'clock phone call from Ringo. But no call. And the next Monday no call.[57]

All was then quiet for several weeks. But not long after shooting started on *Skidoo*, Nilsson took a call on May 14, 1968, from Tony Richland, a well-known West Coast freelance song plugger and promoter. Indeed, in return for his enthusiastic support of *Pandemonium Shadow Show*, Nilsson had named one of the tracks on *Aerial Ballet* "Mr. Richland's Favorite Song." The call was somewhat breathless, and Richland kept saying, "You haven't heard yet?"

Nilsson had no clue what Richland meant, but in due course he calmed him down enough to learn that John Lennon and Paul McCartney had just appeared at a press conference in New York to launch their Apple company, and when asked by a newspaperman to name their favorite American artist, Lennon had replied "Nilsson," and the two of them had given the same response when asked to name their favorite group.[58] This was no accident. On the same day, Lennon and McCartney filmed what would turn out to be one of their last joint interviews in the United States with journalist Larry Kane, and when he asked them what they thought about the state of the American pop music business, Lennon immediately replied, "Nilsson, Nilsson for president!"[59] The two Beatles had not long returned to Britain after this event when Taylor, who had returned from his freelancing in Los Angeles to become their press officer at Apple, made his call to the set of *Skidoo*, as Nilsson remembered:

> Derek says, "Hey, the lads, the boys, the Fabs would like you to come over and join them at a session. They're recording at Abbey Road. If you could swing it, please do. They're dying to see you."
>
> I thought, "My Jesus. This is about as good as it gets."
>
> So I went into the office to Otto and said, "Otto, I've just had a call from England inviting me to a Beatles session. Would you give me Friday, Saturday, and Sunday off so I can attend? It means an awful lot of course."
>
> He says, "These are your good friends the Beatles?"
>
> Question mark. Um, well, not good friends. I've never met them. I mean I met George and I spoke on the phone with John and Paul. So I asked Otto one more time, "Please, this means an awful lot to me."
>
> He says, "Sure, if you're such good friends, why don't you ask them to sing a little song in our movie?"
>
> And I said, "But that makes it a business trip! Why don't you pay for it?"
>
> He laughed and said, "You don't think I will? Nat!" And he called the great Nat Rudich [his assistant] to his office once again.
>
> "Get Mr. Nilsson a ticket to London for this weekend. He is going to meet his friends the Beatles and maybe they will sing in our movie!"
>
> Nat laughed so I knew that they both knew that that was out of the question. He says, "All right," and started to walk out of the room when Otto yelled at him, "Nat, make sure the ticket is second class or economy!"[60]

Within a few days of making his request, Nilsson was sitting on a plane crossing the Atlantic en route from the film set, where he had been mingling with Hollywood royalty (Jackie Gleason, Groucho Marx, and Carol Channing), to meet the most famous pop group in the world. Ostensibly this was because Taylor wanted him to be present for some of the recording sessions for *The Beatles*, the double LP known to fans ever since as the "White Album." He was greeted on Friday, June 14, at Heathrow Airport in London by Chris O'Dell, the American-born personal assistant to the Beatles at the newly formed Apple Corps Ltd. Blonde, elegant, and efficient, she nevertheless almost missed him, having taken a bus that was delayed in traffic. To her amazement, as she tracked him down in the arrivals hall, Nilsson was already walking toward a limo, his bags being carried by a uniformed chauffeur. She recalled their first conversation:

"Hey, that was really thoughtful of you to pick me up," Harry said. "It seems that Ringo has kindly left his limo for us. Apparently he and his wife just left for Spain."[61]

They made their way into the luxurious comfort of a big Daimler, and in the early London morning, after his all-night flight, Nilsson took in the sights of the city, with its small cars and distinctive taxicabs seeming to him to be "backwards" as they drove on the left side of the road.

Although he now worked for the Beatles' new company, Derek Taylor's contacts in the industry were legion. On the back of the Beatles' endorsement of Nilsson as their favorite group, he had arranged with RCA that on Nilsson's first morning in Britain, there would be a reception and press launch for *Pandemonium Shadow Show*, marking its official release in the U.K., some nine months after the American version appeared. Nilsson was not an Apple artist, but he felt that he might as well have been when he arrived at the company's offices at 95 Wigmore Street.

I walked through the front door and there's a little tiny lift, an elevator. And there were stickers, posters, and pictures of me plastered all over the elevator on the inside. "Nilsson is here. Nilsson is here!" There were the little stickers that RCA put out with my first album, and it was just covered with them, and "Welcome Harry!"

We went up to the next flight or two and there we opened the gates and there were more of them on the walls, on the desks, and so forth. Then Derek Taylor popped out.

"Welcome, welcome, welcome! I hope you're dressed for the interview."

Of course I was. Also I brought with me, just taking a chance, an amazing amount of marijuana. It was called Keef. It was the best. And I just managed to go straight through customs. They didn't check that stuff then, at least I didn't think so. I just felt safe doing it. So, I did it. I had a whole bunch of it in my arm.

I said, "Well, I did bring this."

And he says, "Oh my God! Do you know what you've brought us? Heaven. Heaven. Did you also bring a bit of music?"

I said, "Yeah, I got the rough on my second album with me."

Instantly Derek snapped it out of my hand and went into a room where there was someone talking on the phone. He says, "What the hell is this? Get out! Don't you know we have our American visitor here? This is Harry Nilsson. Get out of this fucking office. Don't talk to me."

And he threw whoever it was out, slammed the door, and then he apologized.[62]

In the hour or two before the press launch, assisted by Nilsson's herbal gift, Taylor listened intently to the early copy of *Aerial Ballet*. He also ensured that the three Beatles who were still in the country got to hear it during the course of the weekend. As he and Nilsson talked, there were plans to be made and contacts to be sorted out with the Beatles themselves. Nilsson was to spend his first night in Britain at John Lennon's Surrey home "Kenwood," and then he would return to the city to be with Paul McCartney. He would also attend a recording session at EMI's Abbey Road studios before returning to Los Angeles on Monday evening.

After an hour or two at the Apple offices with Taylor, it was time for the press reception, at which, following the pattern set in the United States by his appearance on the *Woody Woodbury Show*, Nilsson was persuaded to sing—or at any rate lip-synch—a song or two from the album. BBC producer Tim Blackmore was there:

> When RCA released Nilsson's *Pandemonium Shadow Show* they really went to town. There was a launch party at a hotel on London's Curzon Street. The reception was a huge success with Nilsson performing and as many eyes on the guests as on the man himself, largely because of the presence of everybody who was anybody including the Beatles themselves, and the much venerated guru of pop Derek Taylor. I was producing the Radio One Breakfast Show at the time and although album tracks formed a small percentage of our running orders, we chose "1941" as the most radio friendly, closely followed by "Cuddly Toy."[63]

Another attendee was Blackmore's colleague, the BBC Radio One DJ Kenny Everett, who presented a Saturday morning show that combined his own tastes in music with carefully crafted moments of comedy delivered in a host of character voices by Everett himself. He immediately became a champion of Nilsson. Within a few weeks, he had recorded his own versions of "Without Her" and "It's Been So Long," from *Pandemonium Shadow Show*, going so far as to describe the latter as "A universal hit, all over the world, number one in every available chart."[64] Everett's gift for mimicry meant that there were moments when his version of "Without Her" sounded remarkably like Nilsson's, albeit with some rather British vowel sounds.

After the press conference, it was back to the Apple office for a few stiff brandies, and then a limo arrived to take Nilsson out to Lennon's home in Weybridge in the Surrey commuter belt, about sixteen miles from central London. "Kenwood" was situated in the exclusive St. George's Hill area, which was fast becoming among the most expensive real estate in England. Lennon and his first wife Cynthia had bought the house back in the summer of 1964, and retaining its half-timbered mock Tudor exterior complete with "arts and crafts" gables and chimneys, they had renovated and remodeled the interior into a contemporary home with the help of Brian Epstein's former designer Ken Partridge.

By June 1968, their marriage was in trouble, and Cynthia had taken off for a holiday in Pesaro on the northeast Italian coast between Rimini and Ancona. As well as working on the White Album, at the time of Nilsson's visit, Lennon was preparing for the premiere of Victor Spinetti's stage production of his book *In His Own Write*, to be held at the Old Vic Theatre on Tuesday, June 18, the day after Nilsson's departure. That was to be one of Yoko Ono's first public appearances in London with Lennon, but they were already inseparable in private, and in Cynthia's absence, she had effectively moved in with Lennon at Weybridge.[65]

When Nilsson arrived, there were various domestic staff bustling about, making tea, arranging the rooms, and so on, but soon they discreetly vanished, leaving Nilsson alone with John and Yoko. He was greeted warmly by Lennon, and a single look between them was the start of a lifelong friendship. Nilsson remembered:

That night we spent the entire night, with a little help from our friends, talking— just sitting and talking all night 'til dawn, 'til seven or eight o'clock in the morning. And Yoko ended up like a kitten at John's feet, curled up never saying a word, listening until finally sleep took her. And John and I are on, and on, and on, about marriage, life, death, divorce, women.

"What's it all about, what are we doing, do you think, Harry? I'm just writing these little songs like you're writing, like, 'Mr. Richland's Favorite Song' from your new album. I wish I had written it. It's great."

And he went on, and I'm thinking, "My God, this is it! This is right. This is truthful. This is good. This is honest. This is exciting. It's inspirational."

And there was I. The next morning, John had a film crew arriving, but John first offered to make some tea. He made a big pot of tea and offered me a cup. And while he was doing that, I looked around the kitchen and there was this coat thing, a ragged looking shaggy coat. It was actually the coat that was used on the cover of *Magical Mystery Tour* turned inside out. The outside of the coat was the famous Indian gold braided jacket with fur trim lining, you'll see it in lots of photos. And I said, "Oh, nice coat."

"If you like it, I want you to have this Harry." And he reached over, took the coat off the thing and said, "Here this is for you."

I said, "Oh, I can't take that. My God that's a famous jacket, John."

He says, "Well, I think it fits you, right?"

John was five-ten, I'm six-two. I tried it on but it's still too short.

I said, "It doesn't fit."

"No," he says. "Harry, I want you to have it. Please take it."

I said, "You bet."

Minutes later a car arrived and the camera crew walked in. John and I hugged. "Good morning."

"Good morning."

And I left, heading for London, to meet with Derek Taylor and then Paul.[66]

Meanwhile, with their camera crew in tow, Lennon and Yoko Ono set off in his Rolls Royce for Coventry Cathedral where they planted two acorns as part of a national sculpture event.

Whereas Lennon was starting his creative and personal partnership with Yoko Ono and was about to launch his debut as a playwright of sorts, McCartney had used the opportunities offered by Apple to flex his muscles as a record producer. His interests were many and varied. He had signed the Black Dyke Mills Band (then the current U.K. brass band championship holders) to play his song "Thingumybob," as well as a version of "Yellow Submarine," and in an entirely different genre, he had signed the young Welsh singer Mary Hopkin.

Hopkin's first single "Those Were the Days" had just been completed. On its release in August, it was to rush up the charts in the U.K. and bump the Beatles' own "Hey Jude" from top position. Originally a Russian song by Boris Fomin, and first recorded as early as 1925, it had new English words by the New York lyricist, playwright, and architecture professor Gene Raskin. These brilliantly captured a sense of lost youth and opportunity, which the innocent-looking Mary Hopkin managed to convert into the feeling that she was bemoaning the passing of the very time in which she lived, losing "our starry notions on the way." McCartney's setting, using a cembalon and banjo to nod in the direction of the song's Russian origins and artfully weaving in strings and brass, not to mention a choir, reinforced the notion that the song simultaneously celebrated and lamented the 1960s.

Although the record had yet to be released when Nilsson was in London, McCartney was already on the hunt for suitable follow-up material for his new star in the making. Shortly after the limo dropped Nilsson at his London hotel, he received a visit from Derek Taylor to say that he'd listened through *Aerial Ballet* and his faith in Nilsson had not been misplaced. Then came a phone call from McCartney: "Hey, Harry, how are you? I'm looking for a song for Mary. D'you think you could rip one out for me?" In Nilsson's suite was a piano, so he set to work to produce a suitable song. He said:

I wrote "The Puppy Song." I wrote it that night and made a tape of it. The next day I was at Apple visiting Derek and I said, "Well, I wrote that song."

He said, "Fantastic."

He listened to it and then he said, "Wonderful. This is exactly what she needs."

And he called Paul. We sent the tape to Paul. In the next few hours, Paul called, and said "Congratulations, Harry. It's perfect. We're trying to get all the best song-writers in the world to write a song for Mary."

And I thought, "Wow, this is amazing!" And then Paul said, "Would you mind if we popped in tonight? What are you doing?"

"What am I doing? Well, I'm doing nothing. Please, pop in."[67]

That evening, at 7:30 sharp, McCartney and his wife-to-be Linda, showed up at Nilsson's room. Either playing his left-handed guitar or sitting at the piano on which Nilsson had worked out "The Puppy Song," McCartney ran through rough versions of several of his newly written songs, including "Blackbird" with its tricky guitar accompaniment, which was to be featured on the White Album. Nilsson sent down for a bottle or two of the best wine on the hotel's room service list, and they carried on singing songs for one another into the small hours. Then came a thunderous banging on the door from the occupants of the room next door: "What the hell do you people think you're doing? Don't you know some people work for a living? Some people have to get up in the morning." Nilsson calmly introduced them to his visitors, and Paul gently apologized. The neighbors were impressed to find that the disturbance had been created by so famous a guest and made no further complaints. The evening ended with McCartney driving Nilsson and Linda around London in his Aston Martin.[68]

Nilsson never established the same really close friendship with McCartney that he was to enjoy with Lennon and later with Ringo Starr, but they struck an immediate chord with one another musically and would work together from time to time in the years that followed. "The Puppy Song," which was another of Nilsson's compositions that got deeply inside the innocent feelings of childhood with its accurate evocation of a child's desperate longing for the companionship of a little dog, was to receive a setting from McCartney that cleverly captured the music-hall or vaudeville atmosphere of George Tipton's earlier arrangements for Nilsson himself. There was a cheerful two-beat rhythm and a trombone obbligato that sounded as if it was on the verge of breaking out into a jazz solo but never quite managed it. Indeed, when Nilsson came to record the song himself later in the year as one of the first pieces for his next album *Harry*, his version owed less to his own back catalog than Hopkin's did. More important for him, the idea that opens the song was to be a central theme in the imagery and ideas of *Harry*.

Dreams are nothing more than wishes
And a wish is just a dream
You wish to come true

Several of the songs he went on to write for his next project further explored dreams, wishes, and themes of childhood, building on the spontaneous lyrics he had created in a single evening in London.

Before Nilsson caught his flight back to Los Angeles and returned to the set of *Skidoo*, carrying an official note from Taylor saying that the Beatles declined the opportunity to sing on the movie soundtrack, there was one more thing to be done in London. This was to look in on proceedings at Abbey Road. There, Nilsson found George Harrison recording the lyrics to "Piggies." Lennon was also there, and in one of the breaks, Nilsson recalled being shown the nude photograph of Lennon and Yoko Ono that they planned to use on the cover of *Two Virgins*, their album of "Unfinished Music no. 1," which they had been recording at Lennon's home studio in Kenwood during Cynthia's absence. Unused to such blatant immodesty, Nilsson was stuck for anything to say when Lennon confronted him with this graphic image, but he blurted out, "It appears as though you masturbate right-handed" (an allusion to the fact that Lennon's penis is pointing determinedly to his left).[69] Lennon dissolved into laughter, and this story was much repeated in their years of friendship that followed.

In Derek Taylor's view, looking back some years after Nilsson had headed off to catch his plane that evening, this visit was immensely important both for him and for the Beatles. It laid the groundwork for future collaborations between Nilsson and all four members of the group. He said:

> Harry and Paul had a relationship, a musical relationship, very quickly, in the sense that [for] "The Puppy Song"…he understood what Paul wanted.…The relationship between John Lennon and Harry Nilsson became intense. These people had something to offer each other. I always thought of him as the Beatle across the water. I liked the phrase. I thought it was a very romantic phrase, "The American Beatle," and I thought that I had some kind of poetic license to use it without permission, and without anyone taking offense, and indeed nobody ever has to this day. No-one's said "That's rubbish." They may have said it was purple prose, but it was true.[70]

For Nilsson himself, the meeting with the Beatles, the chance to see how the most famous band in the world lived their lives and made their music, together with the adulation he had received at the London launch of *Pandemonium Shadow Show*, would make a fundamental change to the direction of his life and career. Although Rick Jarrard was contracted to produce the soundtrack album for Nilsson's songs from *Skidoo*, and was starting work on the basic tracks for several of the projected pieces for *Harry*, Nilsson now came to believe that he could work without a producer as he had seen Lennon and Yoko Ono doing, or at any rate, that he could be his own producer, imitating the way that McCartney was working with his protégés such as Mary Hopkin. He had also seen George Martin at work with George Harrison, showing another seasoned producer's way of managing a studio session that contrasted considerably with his experience of Jarrard. Although Jarrard had been his passport to a degree of success at RCA and had argued for the label to retain him, Nilsson knew that he had outgrown him.

Nilsson had been back for three months when Jarrard received the unpleasant news: "Out of the blue, I got a telegram that said, 'Thanks for nothing. I'm finding another producer.' And basically, that was the end of my and Harry's relationship."[71]

Jarrard received this message following their final session together on September 30, 1968, at which "Open Your Window" and "Mournin' Glory Story" were recorded.[72] RCA acquiesced to Nilsson's desire for a change, and Jarrard never spoke to him again. They did not run across each other professionally, even though Jarrard had produced the future hit "Everybody's Talkin'" and had also done the basic groundwork to get *Harry* underway. In Jarrard's view, Nilsson was a changed man when he came back from meeting the Beatles in London, and the natural, unaffected bank computer manager with the cowlick who had demonstrated his songs barely two years before was gone forever. Before the year was out, Nilsson had formed his own production company, Nilsson House.

Shortly after Nilsson's return from his first trip to Europe, RCA restarted the North American promotion campaign for his albums, and a massive billboard was erected on Sunset Strip with the legend "Nilsson Is Hear" in giant letters.[73] Just as this very public level of recognition was about to take place, he was forced to confront his biggest personal demon, and meet his father face to face. Although Bette had told him of the second family's existence, no direct contact had been made with them. However, while shooting on *Skidoo* was finishing, Paramount received a message from Harry Nilsson Sr., who asked to be put in touch with his son. As a result, Nilsson invited his father to visit him in California. Gary Nilsson recalls that he went along with his parents and one of his sisters, and that during the couple of weeks they stayed in Los Angeles, "Harry spent a lot of time with his Dad, talking alone."[74] Toward the end of the year, when the premiere of *Skidoo* was announced to take place at a big movie theater close to Jackie Gleason's home at Miami Beach, Nilsson was to meet his father again.

Attempts were made to persuade Nilsson to come to Palatka, but a last-minute alteration in his travel plans meant that he was publicly reunited with his father at the movie theater. "We were entertained royally," gushed Nilsson Sr. to his local paper, "The most wonderful thing was seeing my son after all these years."[75] The son in question was not overly impressed. Had he not become famous, he was sure his parents would not have finally colluded to tell him the truth, nor would his father have made contact. Because his father had removed his paternal love for two decades and allowed his son to think he was dead, he did not endear himself to Harry. Nevertheless, preserved in Nilsson's personal files is a collection of press cuttings about him that his father collected over the years and carefully annotated in a distinctive, spiky hand, suggesting a considerable measure of paternal pride, if not love. The second meeting finally moved Nilsson's songwriting focus away from lyrics about lost fathers, but it undoubtedly added to the intensity of those songs on the as-yet-unfinished album *Harry* that deal with nostalgia, dreams, and unfulfilled wishes.

Open your window and take a deep sigh
Think about letting the rest of the world go
fly a kite
Taking it easy, as easy as pie
And holding your hand is such a natural high

4

OPEN YOUR WINDOW

ONCE HE HAD re-encountered his estranged father and gotten over his separation from Sandi, it was time for a little light to enter Nilsson's personal life. When he started work on *Skidoo* in the spring of 1968, he had already become very closely involved with Diane Clatworthy, who had witnessed his recording of "Everybody's Talkin'" the previous November.[1] Slender, blonde, and with a charming smile, she had been introduced to Nilsson by his friend Bob Segarini, of Family Tree, having been that group's fan club secretary. Segarini recalled that "she was so in love with Harry she would cry every time his name came up."[2] Her memory of Nilsson from this period was of a man who was "athletic, trim, slim, cheerful, and fun to be around, but he drank and when he drank he could get very dark and scary."[3]

Although Nilsson liked to drink, he had not yet followed his mother's path into alcoholism, and the "dark and scary" side of his character seems largely to have been kept under control in the early stages of this new relationship. Indeed, in their first years together, Diane recalled him as constantly upbeat, making light of life, and in particular laughing about the problems of his childhood and his gradual transition from banking to music. "I don't remember him really calling them struggles," she recalled. "He made jokes out of them."[4]

By November 1968, when Nilsson made his second trip to Europe to promote *Aerial Ballet* and the movie *Skidoo*, he and Diane were living together, and so she accompanied him. Following on from the media promotion that he had done earlier in the year for the European release of *Pandemonium Shadow Show*, Nilsson was again encouraged to make some personal appearances and to lip-synch to his songs on television. It seems that this time, while he was in England, he actually broke his vow never to appear live in public, albeit only at a semiprivate press reception. Diane remembered:

> In the fall of 1968, we went to London, and did a tour of Europe too. Harry did perform in London in a kind of a hotel function room, for a bunch of people and

the press, with a band. Now, there wasn't a stage, so maybe that helped. He was just on the floor. But he was funny and he was himself and he was doing Stan Laurel faces and things like that and he was fine.... And he did a lot of lip synching on the European tour, but not live performing.[5]

Back in Los Angeles, Nilsson and Diane set up home together in the Hollywood Hills on Woodrow Wilson Drive, not far from its intersection with Mulholland Drive. This was fairly close to Laurel Canyon, where Micky Dolenz and his British wife Samantha Juste had their home. Juste recalled:

> We were the neighbors.... I remember going to his house and listening to him play the piano a lot, and that was very nice. It was quite an English style house, with a country feel. Because Diane was like that, and so was he. He was already a bit of an Anglophile, I think actually. So that's what the house was like, very lovely, very country, cozy.[6]

Nilsson and Dolenz had become close friends since working on "Cuddly Toy" and "Daddy's Song" for the Monkees, not least as a result of the boyish horseplay during their recording sessions in adjoining studios at RCA. By late 1968, they were in and out of each other's houses all the time. They practiced basketball shots together in a nearby park, hiked in the hills (including climbing up to scratch their initials on the "Hollywood" sign), and frequently got together in the recording studio that Dolenz had built in his basement.[7]

If the dark side of Nilsson that Diane described had yet to appear, he nevertheless had the capacity to make things happen around him. Life was a constant adventure, such as the evening soon after his return from Europe when he and Dolenz took Diane and Samantha to dinner at a neighborhood restaurant. Nilsson got talking to the party at the next table and invited them back to Dolenz's house in Laurel Canyon to continue chatting and drinking. The wooden house, a former hunting lodge built in 1900, was set back from the road in a dimly lit cul-de-sac. As Nilsson's newfound friends arrived, their car scraped the side of a neighbor's automobile in the gloom. The neighbor had the reputation of being a tough character and a drug dealer. He ran out of his house swearing volubly at two of the women who had damaged his car. Nilsson retaliated with some choice swearwords of his own. Dolenz takes up the story:

> With that, the crazed long-haired weirdo pulls out a kitchen knife! Suddenly a minor fender bender has become some serious shit. Samantha and Diane quickly disappear inside the house as the knife wielding doper starts to back Harry up the driveway.[8]

Samantha's parents had an apartment at the side of the house, so Dolenz ran up to their door and pounded on it, asking for a pistol that they kept there. Armed with the gun stuck in his waistband, he confronted the neighbor, who now had Nilsson backed into a corner.

"What are you going to do? Shoot me?" asked the man.
"I might," replied Dolenz laconically.[9]

In due course, the gun and knife were put away, and the two sides in the dispute began talking warily. To Nilsson's amazement, his guests actually knew the man whose car they had damaged and after talking for a while longer, they went round to his house for a party. Nilsson was so incensed by what he considered their disloyalty that he threw a rock through the rear window of their car before returning to his own social evening at Dolenz's home.

Samantha Juste was an exceptional hostess. A former model, she had starred on the British television show *Top of the Pops* since 1964, where her duties were to sit decorously alongside the presenter and drop the needle of a phonograph onto the next track to be played. In the days of miming and lip-synching to records, this was completely accepted as normal by the television audience. She had become famous and popular in Britain, and synonymous with all aspects of pop music. She first met Dolenz when the Monkees appeared on the show in January 1967, and after a year of shuttling to and fro across the Atlantic to be together, she eventually gave up her television career to marry him and move to the United States in July 1968. Although Dolenz described their home as "a hippy halfway house decorated by garage sale," she brought a glamorous feminine touch to it, and she also decided that when guests came around to hang out or to party, he could do better than offer them "Red Mountain wine, pretzels, potato chips and onion dip."[10]

She introduced good wine and interesting food and threw sophisticated parties, at which Laurel Canyon neighbors such as Alice Cooper, Timothy Leary, and Jim Morrison mingled with the likes of Jeff Bridges, Jack Nicholson, and Brian Wilson. She also made the place into a real home, rather than the refuge for Dolenz's assorted friends and hangers-on that it had been during the early years of the Monkees. She recalled:

We had a very dark house. It was black carpets, black shag carpets. It was dark, but then it was a night time house really. Except for the kitchen and that area, and outside, where we had lovely terraces, and a pool. But our house itself was pretty big as well. It was built of wood, and wood absorbs all the light. There was a very large main room, which was split-level. They hung out at the bar upstairs, and the living room had a big fireplace. It was a lovely winter house, but you went down another level, and then another level again to the recording studio. And that was where they spent a lot of their time, and of course that was soundproofed.[11]

One reason that Samantha tended to leave Dolenz and his friends to amuse themselves at the bar or in the studio was that she was expecting a baby. Their daughter, Ami Dolenz, was born on January 8, 1969, and Samantha devoted herself to the tasks of motherhood.

She and Diane remained close friends, often visiting one another during Ami's early child-hood, not least because this was when the Monkees were gradually falling apart. In the wake of their successful albums *Headquarters* and *Pisces, Aquarius, Capricorn and Jones, Ltd.*, on which they performed under Chip Douglas's expert guidance, the Monkees' record company had rushed out another album, *The Birds, The Bees and The Monkees*. This was little more than a collection of much earlier offcuts and rejected songs, hur-riedly thrown together to accompany their chart single "Daydream Believer." The band members were incensed, but it emphasized how little real control they had over their lives and work. As they worked on what must have been clear to them would be an even less successful movie than *Head*, namely Jack Gold's *33 1/3 Revolutions Per Monkee*, the band imploded.

In contrast, Nilsson was on a creative roll. Maybe because of his new and settled home life, several of the new songs he was to write as 1968 gave way to 1969 showed a more optimistic outlook.

Professionally, the latter part of 1968 saw Nilsson mainly preoccupied with making plans to complete his album *Harry*. Four tracks had already been finished during the final sessions with Rick Jarrard. Now Nilsson himself, under the banner of his newly formed Nilsson House Productions company, took on the role of producer for the remainder of the songs that he intended to include. He maintained his close connection with George Tipton as contractor, arranger, and conductor, and the two men set up the next studio sessions to begin in January. But as *Billboard* reported in November 1968, he was trying to cram in a lot else too, and some of these activities were to get in the way of the schedule for the projected completion of his new album in the spring:

Pop singer composer Nilsson, praised by the Beatles and missed by the Security First National Bank where he worked as a computer supervisor until last year, returned last week from a promotional tour of Europe to preview the Paramount film *Skidoo* which he scored for RCA. "Spreading myself thin" but evenly over the media, Nilsson has been writing for Mary Hopkin and Glen Campbell, scoring for TV and commercials, on his own Broadway musical, and minding the store for his Nilsson House and Grosvenor Music pubberies [publishers]. The witty and whimsical Californian is also manufacturing (by hand) a wooden box which when open snaps recorded wisecracks. His play, a musical based on the Wright Brothers adventure in aviation is titled typically Nilsson—"How Wright You Are!"[12]

References to the wisecracking box were to turn up in several press releases and inter-views over the next few months. So too would mentions of the Wright Brothers musical. Inspired by the story of the repatriation of the 1903 Kitty Hawk Flyer from London's Science Museum to the Smithsonian Institution in 1948, a substantial draft of this never-to-be-completed musical exists in Nilsson's personal files under the amended title *Orville and Wilbur*. He was fascinated by everything he could find about the brothers and their pioneering work in making the world's first powered flight. He liked to read tales of legal wrangles and controversies, and his imagination was caught by the long-term efforts of the Smithsonian to deny the truth of the Wrights' claim. In the early years of the twentieth century, the Institution's secretary, Samuel P. Langley, exhibited a model of one of his own proposed plane designs, saying that it was "capable" of flight, rather than exhibit the Wright's successful full-size machine. Consequently, an aggrieved Orville Wright sent his aircraft to be exhibited in London instead. It took many years and two world wars for the two sides to bury the hatchet and for the pioneering American aircraft to be brought "home" to the Smithsonian.[13]

There are sketches of the songs for Nilsson's planned show, including "If God had wanted men to fly" and another piece titled simply "French production number" to illustrate the brothers' pioneering trips to France in the early years of the twentieth century.[14] Nilsson first experimented with ideas for these songs in the fall of 1968, and in future years continued to tinker with the concept for the musical. At one point, he saw it as a possible vehicle for Tom and Dick Smothers who were then presenting their popular *Comedy Hour* show on CBS television, but nothing finally came of it. Yet in an interview from the period about *Orville and Wilbur*, it is clear that at least some of the planning he did for an early draft of the show, which closely followed the life of the longer-lived brother Orville, would be incorporated a couple of years later in his animated film musical *The Point*. He said, "It's a science-fiction, horror story musical comedy about a boy, his dog and his airplane."[15]

In contrast, the passing mention in *Billboard* of "scoring for TV" alluded to a forthcoming series that was already well beyond the planning stage and was first announced in the fall of 1968. According to the press:

> Next year Nilsson will be heard in the new ABC TV series, *The Courtship of Eddie's Father* in which he replaces conventional theme music with a stream of vocals, lyrically tuned to the action.[16]

This series, a spin-off from Vincente Minnelli's 1963 movie of the same name, was about a father whose wife had recently died, and whose young son, age six, took an active part in selecting a prospective new bride for him. The film had been based on a novel and stuck fairly closely to the original plotline, but the television producers saw long-running potential in the idea of young Eddie Corbett producing a string of possible partners for his father Tom, with the collusion of the family's efficient Japanese housekeeper, Mrs. Livingston. The director (and originator) of the show was James Komack, who also played the part of Tom Corbett's closest colleague in the magazine publishing office where he worked. The key role of Tom Corbett was played by Bill Bixby. The child actor Brandon Cruz starred as Eddie.

Komack's highly original idea for the music was to have Nilsson sing occasional interludes, in the same way that he had handled the closing credits on *Skidoo*. He could move the story along, comment on the action, or simply set a scene. He and George Tipton tackled this task with alacrity, Nilsson penning short lyrics and fragments of melody, and Tipton turning them into the finished cues with split-second timing to fit the action. Diane Nilsson said of their partnership:

> George Tipton's…arrangements were so much part of the songs that…they just wouldn't be the same without his influence. Harry and George were very close. I think Harry felt really comfortable working with him.[17]

In the early episodes, everything from bringing in a coffee cup to catching the flu prompted a short burst of musical whimsy, and Nilsson also introduced snatches of some of his previous songs, such as "Little Cowboy" from *Aerial Ballet*, which became Eddie's bedtime lullaby. In the event, pinning down a busy musician to record dozens of cues that were often only a few seconds long proved difficult, and after nine episodes or so, Nilsson's interjections were gradually phased out and Tipton handled the majority of the cues instrumentally, with studio singers sometimes dubbing in additional words.

Nilsson's lasting contribution to the series, which ran until 1972, was the jaunty title song "Best Friend," for which the lyrics seemed admirably suited to the unshakable bond between father and son, on which the show depended for its plausibility. They also pulled at the heartstrings, particularly if the listener knew that they came from a songwriter who had never had such a relationship with his own father:

> People let me tell you 'bout my best friend,
> He's a warm-hearted person who'll love me till the end.
> People let me tell you 'bout my best friend,
> He's a one boy cuddly toy, my up, my down, my pride and joy.

In most episodes, the song followed an opening piece of dialog, in which Eddie and his father discussed a weighty matter, or at least a weighty matter for a six-year-old, which would become the underlying theme of that particular show, such as "Why are there rules?" "What do you know about girls?" or "When you dream of Mummy, can I be in your dream?" Then as the opening titles rolled, Bixby and Cruz were filmed in a grainy-textured romantic haze, doing father-son bonding activities such as fishing off Venice Pier, jogging on the beach north of Santa Monica, teeing up golf balls, or going to the park. Accompanying their actions, Nilsson's lighthearted lyrics would begin, preceded by one of Tipton's characteristic baritone horn phrases (in this case borrowed in its entirety from his arrangement of "Daddy's Song" as it was originally conceived for *Aerial Ballet*). The second stanza of the new song cleverly reflected the show's regular snatch of opening dialog:

> People let me tell you 'bout him, he's so much fun
> Whether we're talkin' man to man or whether we're talking son to son.

Yet even though this freshly written lyric and its cross-generational idea of the child becoming the man and the man becoming the child brilliantly encapsulates the very kind of paternal conversation Nilsson had wished for but never experienced, it turns out that almost everything else about "Best Friend" was far from an original contribution to the show. It was a thinly veiled remake of one of Nilsson's final collaborations with Rick Jarrard, originally intended for the *Harry* album. On July 24, 1968, after working on "Rainmaker" (which was included in the eventual album), they had also recorded a song called "Girlfriend."[18] The song opened:

> People let me tell about the girlfriend
> She's a warm-hearted woman who'll love me till the end
> People let me tell about the girlfriend
> She's a one boy cuddly toy, my up, my down, my pride and joy.

This cheery lyric dates from the time Nilsson met Diane. But it seems that when Komack approached him with the concept of doing the incidental music for the series, Nilsson simply dusted off this ready-made song and amended the lyrics accordingly. It would work in his favor once he became his own record producer for *Harry*, because by dropping it, one song fewer from his collaboration with Jarrard would appear on the album. It also gave him the chance to commission a revised arrangement from Tipton, and given that their version of "Daddy's Song" had been dropped from *Aerial Ballet*, the two of them subtly got their own back on RCA by revamping and deftly incorporating the main accompanying riff to run throughout the new TV show's title music. The original version of "Girlfriend" did not appear on record until the *Personal Best* collection was released shortly after Nilsson's death in 1994, by which time no new episode of *The Courtship of Eddie's Father* had been made for twenty-two years. The series originally premiered on September 17, 1969, and Nilsson and Tipton worked on the music concurrently with completing the *Harry* album, which was eventually released during the previous month.

If writing and recording the music for that show was one distraction from finishing the album any sooner, a different television venture also took Nilsson away from the recording studios early in 1969. According to the gossip columns:

> Harry Nilsson, one of the country's hottest new talents on the folk-rock music scene makes his acting debut in an episode of 20th Century Fox Television's *The Ghost and Mrs. Muir*. Nilsson joins series stars Hope Lange and Edward Mulhare as "The Music Maker" in the episode of that name which airs Saturday March 22, at 7.30–8 p.m. KOAM-TV Channel 7 over NBC-TV. For the segment the young composer and RCA Victor recording artist will perform two original numbers destined to become sure hits on the record charts. Nilsson wrote the words and music to "Without Her" and collaborated with *Ghost and Mrs. Muir* story editor Tom August on the song "If Only."[19]

Just as *The Courtship of Eddie's Father* was a television series based on an older movie adapted from a book, so too was *The Ghost and Mrs. Muir*, although in this case the movie was a little more ancient. In 1947, Gene Tierney had starred as the young widow Mrs. Muir and Rex Harrison as the ghostly Captain Daniel Gregg in Joseph L. Mankiewicz's film of the original novel by Josephine Leslie. In September 1968, Lange and Mulhare took on the roles for the first of two six-month runs of weekly television episodes. In a further coincidental connection, Bill Bixby (Eddie's father) played the parapsychologist Paul Wilkie in an early episode of the new series, called "The Ghost Hunter."

The premise of the show was simple. A young widow, Carolyn Muir with her two young children, moves into the haunted Gull Cottage in Schooner Bay, where the ghostly Captain Gregg falls in love with her. As she is mortal and he a ghost, his love can never be requited. Planned immediately after 1967's "summer of love" in the heady climate of sexual liberation, this series deliberately took an opposing stance, stressing old-fashioned values and creating fifty episodes built on unreleased sexual tension. "The thread of the series is the unfulfilled promise of the romance," said Lange at the time. "The fact that Mrs. Muir can never touch the Captain makes it so much more romantic, I feel."[20]

The series writers carefully developed the relationship as the episodes went on, so that the audience shared in the couple's growing fondness for each other, despite the Captain's (literally) stormy temper. Only Mrs. Muir and the Captain's great nephew could see him, and apparently in those early days of television technology, Lange had to master the art of freezing her position on set as Mulhare made his ghostly appearances and disappearances.

The plot of "The Music Maker," the last episode to be aired in the first series of the program, is that the Captain has composed a love poem to Mrs. Muir. But events keep frustrating him from reading it. Nilsson plays the young musician Tim Seagirt, who parks his VW camper van on the nearby beach, where he and his manager play loud music. This coincides with one of the Captain's attempts to read his poem, and the resulting temper tantrum creates a thunderous downpour that maroons Nilsson and his van on the beach. The drenched musician is invited into the Muir household to dry off. He performs "Without Her" to Mrs. Muir, with the ghostly Captain in attendance. The tender lyrics strike such a strong emotional chord in the old seadog that he tricks Nilsson into setting his love poem to music and performing it for Mrs. Muir.

The Captain is expecting a beautiful romantic song, but Nilsson's first attempt is a rock and roll treatment, which he plays in Jerry Lee Lewis style at the piano, only to inspire a further burst of the Captain's meteorological temper. Thunder, lightning, and tempestuous winds slam open the windows, the curtains go flying, and the contents of the house crash about in the squall. However, when the storm calms down and Tim sings the song quietly to his own guitar accompaniment, the Captain glows with pride, exchanging coy glances with his loved one as Mrs. Muir finally receives his message regretfully telling her that he can neither "touch your hand" nor "link your arm" in his.

The lyrics for this song, "If Only," were written by Tom August. They are first heard as a poem declaimed in Mulhare's Shakespearean tones. Originally a stage actor and later to become known to a new generation as the entrepreneurial Devon Miles in the television series *Knight Rider*, Mulhare was an Irishman who specialized in well-spoken English roles. With a piratical beard and his fair hair blackened for the ghostly Captain, he played the part with more than a touch of ham acting, against which Nilsson's understated performance looks far more natural. Nilsson was still, at this stage, the clean-shaven, short-haired young man of the *Pandemonium Shadow Show* cover, and whether dressed in a light blue sweater and white slacks or (after the cloudburst) in his underwear and a blanket, he is a screen presence every bit as effective as that of the show's main stars. In a bit of byplay with the comedy actor Charles Nelson Reilly as the Captain's great-nephew Claymore Gregg in which Nilsson rejects Reilly's offers to become his manager, we get one of the few surviving glimpses of how Nilsson looked and behaved in ordinary conversation, as well as in performance, at this stage in his career. At the time it seemed as if Nilsson's low-key screen presence might appear more regularly on television, because plans were also well advanced for two additional projects in the first half of 1969. As *Billboard* reported, "He stars in the still-pending TV pilot of *Swami* playing an inept musician, while a TV special on the multi-talented musician is tentatively scheduled for July."[21] Neither of these plans came to fruition.

"If Only" was never recorded commercially, but the music for Tom August's lyric was one of a number of Nilsson's collaborations from this period with Bill Martin, a songwriter who was a good friend of Michael Nesmith of the Monkees. Not to be confused with his contemporary and namesake, the Scottish songwriter Bill Martin, who wrote "Puppet on a String" for Sandie Shaw and "Congratulations" for Cliff Richard, William E. Martin (his full name) had written "All Your Toys" and "The Door Into Summer" for the Monkees. He came into Micky Dolenz's social circle at about the same time as Nilsson, and the two of them were regulars at parties in Laurel Canyon and in the upstairs room at Martoni's Italian restaurant near the RCA studios. Martin would later work on planning film and television ideas with Dolenz, but he began writing songs with Nilsson in the middle of 1968, and "Rainmaker" (from the session that produced "Girlfriend") was the first of their joint pieces to be released, appearing as a single that same year. Eventually, alongside it on the album *Harry* were two further songs entirely written by Martin, "Fairfax Rag" and "City Life."

Martin's work spans the two separate groups of studio dates that went into the making of *Harry*. The Jarrard productions (including "Rainmaker") date from between July 24 and September 30, 1968, whereas Nilsson's self-produced part of the album was recorded in a series of intensive sessions between January 27 and 30, 1969, with additional vocal and instrumental parts added in a further burst of creativity in mid-February.

All Jarrard's pieces have his characteristic well-finished sound, and there are conscious echoes of the earlier albums. Thus, Nilsson's moving ballad about a homeless woman, "Mournin' Glory Story," is given a string setting that cleverly evokes both his own songs

"Sleep Late My Lady Friend" and "Without Her." It is also (in keeping with the social message of the subject matter) referencing the Beatles' "Eleanor Rigby," with the mixture of string quartet and vocals. As the press pointed out at the time, the song additionally has some verbal parallels in the line "She wakes up..." with the Beatles' "For No One" from *Revolver.*[22]

As it turns out, the song was based on personal experience, which gave it sufficient emotional depth for Nilsson's voice to draw as much as possible out of the music, helped immeasurably by Tipton's arrangement. Nilsson recalled:

> "Mournin' Glory" is a real person. I was in New York, walking on a street late at night. In a doorway I saw a shadow out of the corner of my eye. It was a woman sleeping in a wheelchair. Behind her was an old man sitting on an apple crate with his hand across the handles of the wheelchair, making a little bridge for himself. I had to go over. I feel embarrassed talking about it. I went over and put some money in her lap. She sensed my presence and started. She saw the money and understood everything—her whole life, my whole life, why we were there. She cried. Writing the song you have to experience it. I copped out, but the song touches my experience.[23]

Every detail of the lyric from the woman's dirty feet to her prayers for "no more sorrow" has the ring of real-life experience. So too does "Open Your Window," but this is totally different in mood and feeling, being an optimistic love ballad, perhaps inspired by Nilsson's courtship of Diane. It gets an unashamedly romantic treatment, with a sophisticated string orchestra backing from Tipton. Few better examples exist of the clarity of Nilsson's upper-register singing, and there are echoes here of the tenderness first apparent in "Sleep Late My Lady Friend." The song itself was a strong piece of writing, aside from Nilsson's own delivery of the lyrics, and it would become a regular part of the jazz singer Ella Fitzgerald's repertoire of torch ballads in the years that followed, after she recorded it for Nilsson's future producer Richard Perry.

"Rainmaker" is notable for the prominent drums of the opening section, but it is also the last example of Nilsson and Jarrard collaborating (as they had so enjoyed doing in the past) on a dense choir of overdubbed voices in the choruses, particularly the final section where Nilsson punches out the lyrics over the "oohs" and "aahs" of his own multilayered voice. In contrast, Bette Nilsson's song, "Marching Down Broadway," although an extremely brief cut lasting not much over a minute, has echoes of the drums and brass of *Pandemonium Shadow Show.* In it, the patriotic post-World War II lyrics that had Irving Berlin reaching for his checkbook are delivered by Nilsson in a more ironic tone, better suited to the fact that the summer of 1968 when it was recorded marked the height of U.S. military involvement in Vietnam, with the Tet Offensive.

The July 1968 sessions with Jarrard marked the final time that Nilsson and the Monkees were working simultaneously at RCA studios, because the Monkees came in to finish the album to accompany their movie *Head,* although little of their work there eventually made it to the issued record. This was largely to be assembled from the actual soundtrack by the film's co-author and producer, the actor Jack Nicholson. It was only a matter of weeks before he got his big break playing the drunken lawyer George Hanson in *Easy Rider*, but Nicholson's stint as a record producer is mainly remembered for his dissatisfaction with the dozens of takes the Monkees did in the studio sessions he supervised.[24] By September, when Nilsson was back in the studios, the group had set off on its final international tour to Japan and Australia, and at the end of the year it became a trio with the departure of Peter Tork.[25] Samantha Juste recalled the final few days when the old order had prevailed at the studios:

> There were some pretty hairy drinking sessions there. It was amazing they could even speak, never mind sing. Of course sometimes they couldn't really sing, they would get really beyond it. Because we'd start the recording session and then we'd go off to Dan Tana's I think it was called. There was an Italian restaurant, Martoni's, very close to RCA and it would stay open late for us and we'd go and eat there and then they'd drink a couple of bottles of wine, and whatever else they were particularly liking that night. And then they'd go back to the recording session again. Total craziness. Those were pretty amazing nights. Actually Harry got into wine at that time, now I think about it. He used to drink some pretty expensive bottles of wine, some very nice wine![26]

Whereas the Jarrard collaborations looked backward both socially and musically, in contrast, the remainder of Nilsson's *Harry* album has a more unified feel and looks forward to new territory. For the most part, it takes its character from the instrumental flavor provided by three musicians who appear throughout the record: Tommy Morgan on harmonica, Bobby Bruce playing a country-style violin, and the sophisticated jazz guitar chording of Howard Roberts. With Tipton's long-term collaborators, Michael Melvoin on keyboards, Larry Knechtel on bass, and David Cohen on both rhythm and Hawaiian guitar, plus the drums of Jim Gordon, the overall effect is far lighter and more spacious than the majority of Jarrard's productions. For a few tracks, a small string section is added, and some others also have brass and saxophones, but the prevailing atmosphere of harmonica, guitar, and fiddle gives the whole disc an inflection of country, bluegrass, and folk music in keeping with the nostalgic content of the lyrics.

The album was to get a critical reception far more favorable than *Pandemonium Shadow Show* or *Aerial Ballet*. *Stereo Review* named it one of the records of the year,[27] and its critic Peter Reilly went on to proclaim: "With this album Nilsson has arrived.... It is a flight of artistic fancy and persistent memory that is, by turns, topical reminiscent, amusing, tough, shrewd, and strangely naïve." Others claimed it as a "conceptual masterpiece," while RCA, again mounting a huge billboard with a blowup of the *Harry* cover on Sunset Strip, promoted him as "the country's most underrated young singer."[28]

"The Puppy Song" that opens the album is taken marginally slower than Mary Hopkin's original recording, and a fifth lower, in the key of C rather than G, which adds a more mournful quality. Instead of the trombone that plays a counterpart to Hopkin's voice on the McCartney production, Tipton adds the discreet wail of a Hawaiian guitar. The vo-de-o-do rhythm is the same, and it is emphasized on the Nilsson recording by gradually bringing in a tuba to double up the down beat with the electric bass. There's no denying the mood of "dreams, wishes come true—and false,"[29] but as Nilsson introduces his vocal overdubs, the effect is remarkably similar to the vaudeville atmosphere of Esther and Abi Ofarim's "Cinderella Rockefella," which had hit the charts in several countries after its release in February 1968. When Nilsson adds a call-and-response repetition of "Your wish will come true" to the closing seconds, it appears to be a deliberate echo of the Ofarims' "You're the lady, the lady who" question-and-answer phrases. Because of this, and the strength of Hopkin's charming recording of the song, Nilsson's version of his own piece sounds more derivative than original.

His originality is at its height in "Nobody Cares About the Railroads Any More," which is one of Nilsson's finest songs from any of his albums. It is beautifully crafted, not least in the close harmony of his own multitracked accompanying vocals, and like "1941" it deals with the passage of time, across three generations of a family. The story focuses on a couple who got married in 1944 and took the Silver Liner from "below Baltimore" to Virginia for their honeymoon. They look back at how they tipped the porter for a private compartment and sent postcards to their parents. Now they are parents themselves, and their daughter—"you ought to see her now"—is about to get married herself, but she will take a plane away from Baltimore, because "nobody cares about the railroads any more." The thrill of hearing "all aboard" and the "oo-ee" train whistle effects, sung in multiple voices by Nilsson, evoke the vanished era of long-distance steam-hauled railroad travel. There is an in-joke too about the prospective son-in-law who "looks just like my gal Sal." This points to Nilsson's encyclopedic knowledge of early film and most likely refers to the 1929 movie short *My Gal Sal* by Red McKenzie and the Mound City Blue Blowers. In a medley of "My Gal Sal" and "I Ain't Got Nobody," this little group of vocals, kazoo, homemade percussion, guitar, and banjo manages just the same loping country-music-meets-bluegrass feel as Tipton evokes on the Nilsson arrangement.

"Fairfax Rag" includes a segment of traditional jazz, which picks up on the 1920s feel, although Martin's song is mainly about embarrassment, wishing that you were "anyplace else but here." Martin's other composition on the album, "City Life," sees the world through the eyes of a down-and-out drifter. Its lyrics resonate with the homelessness theme of "Mournin' Glory Story," and the line "gonna grab me a plane" also links to the son and daughter in "Nobody Cares about the Railroads Anymore." Both Martin's pieces help to unify the various songs on the disc by cleverly integrating with both musical and verbal themes. The same applies to Nilsson's low-key cover of Jerry Jeff Walker's catchy song "Mr. Bojangles," with its nostalgic talk of dancing at "minstrel shows and county fairs" looking back again to the 1920s.

Given that the single release of "Rainmaker" had appeared well before the album, the next track that RCA planned to become a potential hit single from *Harry* was "Maybe." In retrospect, this somewhat anodyne song is one of the weakest on the album. But the choice of the B-side track, "I Guess the Lord Must Be in New York City," also drawn from the album, is what rescued it, and it did so because of the recently reissued single of "Everybody's Talkin'." This, owing to the success of *Midnight Cowboy*, sold the best part of a million copies after its re-release to coincide with the movie in August 1969 and reached number six on the *Billboard* pop chart. As show business reporter Mary Campbell observed:

> The song that Nilsson wrote for the picture, that didn't get used, is "I Guess the Lord Must Be in New York City." It was released in the second week of October as a single, as the B-side to "Maybe." Both are on Nilsson's new album *Harry*. Putting out the single threw Nilsson into a quandary. His first impulse had been to have "Marching Down Broadway" as the B-side to "Maybe."
>
> Since Wayne Newton had put out a single of "I Guess the Lord Must Be in New York City," Nilsson was hoping that Newton could have a hit with that Nilsson song while he might get a hit with a different one. But he was talked into putting "New York City" out with "Maybe." If radio stations turn over "Maybe" and play the B-side instead, he'll be in direct competition with Newton. Even after it was too late to change what was being released as the new single, and before the results were beginning to be felt, Nilsson was still pondering whether he'd done the right thing.[30]

Campbell's article was prescient. Almost unanimously, DJs turned over the single to play the B-side, and as a result, "I Guess the Lord Must Be in New York City" climbed to number thirty-four on the *Billboard* charts in November 1969.

The reasons are not hard to understand. Because it was written at a time when "Everybody's Talkin'" had already been used as the temporary track in the movie, Tipton's arrangement for Nilsson's own composition seeks to recapture as closely as possible the atmosphere they had created for that earlier Fred Neil song. No doubt the intention was to persuade John Schlesinger that this was still the general sound he wanted for his movie, but with lyrics more directly focused on the film's plotline. However, the abstract imagery of Neil's lyrics ultimately fits the movie better than Nilsson's more straightforward lines:

> Say goodbye to all my sorrows
> and by tomorrow I'll be on my way.

Schlesinger stayed with his temporary track. But to the record-buying and listening public, Nilsson's own song was effectively a sequel, another chance to hear the magical recipe that had made "Everybody's Talkin'" so memorable.

The insistent guitar motif that runs underneath "Everybody's Talkin'" is replaced on "I Guess the Lord Must Be in New York City" by a banjo, finger-picking a similar figure, against which a four-note guitar countermelody immediately conjures up the atmosphere of the earlier song. This is helped when the strings again hold a long, sustained high note behind the start of Nilsson's vocal, although there is more movement in their subsequent melody lines than on the comparatively static earlier arrangement. The song lacks Nilsson's characteristic wordless vocals until the end, when long drawn-out vowel sounds replace the lyrics and he moves into his upper register. With some clever overdubbing behind the main verses of the song, this is, if not brother or sister to the hit single, at least a first cousin.

The closing track on *Harry* celebrated Nilsson's growing fascination with the work of Randy Newman. The song was a relatively minimalist cover version of Newman's "Simon Smith and the Amazing Dancing Bear," which had been a hit for the Alan Price Set in Britain in 1967. Price's band, with trumpet, tenor and baritone saxophones, and rhythm section added plenty of ballast to the piece. There were question-and-answer phrases trading between the horns and his vocals, backed by a relatively heavy rhythm-and-blues beat, featuring Price's robust piano playing, which he had honed while in the Animals alongside Eric Burdon. In contrast, Nilsson's version, in Tipton's sparse arrangement, has delicate piano from Michael Melvoin and a few low-key musical comments from Bobby Bruce's violin. Only at the very end of the track do the instrumentalists take over, speeding up the tempo and adding a little spontaneous jazz jamming on violin, guitar, and harmonica. Otherwise the focus is directly on the lyrics, which Nilsson said at the time he greatly admired, following the release of Newman's eponymous debut album in 1968:

> Newman as well as being very articulate has the gift of rhythm and the sensitivity of a blues artist. He has the ability to win people over. You hear that album of his three or four times and you're a fan.[31]

As Nilsson delved deeper into Newman's work, listening through what was then an extensive catalog of songs he had written for other artists, as well as the material for his own album, his admiration grew:

> Randy Newman is special, he's brilliant. One of him comes along when a Beatle comes along, it's one of those. And he will be recognized. It's just a matter of time.... He does his own charts, plays on the dates, and he's an osteopath.[32]

Nilsson's burgeoning interest in Newman was to put an end to his songwriting partnership with Bill Martin, but the two remained firm friends. Nilsson was best man at Martin's wedding, but he so enjoyed the celebrations at a hotel in Las Vegas that he was unwilling to leave the couple alone to have their wedding night. Martin recalled that Nilsson finally abandoned the party at four in the morning when he had to go and throw up in the sink.[33]

Nilsson went on to produce a future album for Martin, his 1970 collection of abstract comedy sketches known as *Concerto for Headphones and Contra-Buffoon in Asia Minor*.[34] This was not a great commercial success, but it was the first example of Nilsson House Productions making albums for other labels, in this case Warner Brothers. (The company had plans to record other artists for Warner, with whom it had a provisional agreement to make four albums a year, including guitarist and singer Randy Marr and singers Nancy Triddy and Scotty Jackson.) As his former songwriting partner, Nilsson had an insider's view of Martin, whom he described at the time of the *Concerto* album as:

> A cross between a Will Rogers and a Lenny Bruce, leaning more towards Rogers than Bruce....Bill is, I don't think, a controversial person, he's very non-offensive...his humor is very general but humorous and intelligent. He has the ability to nail things down, describe something so someone will know exactly what it looks like when he walks in the room.[35]

It would be Martin himself—somewhat unwittingly—who underlined the transition of Nilsson's musical interest to Newman's songs by donning a bear suit for the inside cover photographs of *Harry*. In doing so, Martin bravely did his bit to advertise Simon Smith's dancing accomplice, but, he recalled, it was not easy:

> It was the only bear suit in town, and it was made from an actual bear. You had to be inside the bear and look out through these rows of teeth, and Harry's in a cold-weather type overcoat and a muffler, but it was 103 degrees up in Laurel Canyon. Dean Torrence was doing the photography, and we're both sweating like pigs. Then the bear seemed to return back to life after about 15 minutes. I could see the steam coming out from the bear's mouth. I smelled like bear for three days![36]

Nilsson's unadorned version of "Simon Smith and the Amazing Dancing Bear," in which, as Newman's biographer Kevin Courrier says, his "pristine performance intensified the song's ironic intent,"[37] caught the attention of Newman himself. The two men met and became friends, the somewhat reclusive Newman getting together with Nilsson for the occasional game of Ping-Pong,[38] and before long Nilsson had decided to set aside his own songs and base his next album entirely on Newman's work. He said:

> I did those songs actually because I consciously felt at the time they were the best songs to record....I had like five songs, and instead of doing five of my own, I thought, "Wait a minute, Randy Newman's got a whole bunch of songs." This was in his early days before he was known at all. I thought, "Why not do a unique album, an album of somebody else's songs? That hasn't been done for a while has it?"...And you know the idea was to go in with just him playing piano and me singing, no orchestra.[39]

In September 1969, when they started work on the album, Newman was twenty-five years old, and although his performing career had only recently begun, he had been a professional songwriter for almost a decade. The Fleetwoods, Judy Collins, the Everly Brothers, Irma Thomas, and Jerry Butler were among those who had recorded his material. In Britain, Alan Price had reached number four on the pop charts with "Simon Smith," and Gene Pitney and Cilla Black had also made the top twenty with other examples of his writing.

Newman came from a musical family, with several movie composers among his uncles and cousins. Although he grew up mainly in Los Angeles, he spent part of his childhood in New Orleans, so that a blues and jazz sensibility always ran close to the surface of his writing and playing. But what drew musicians to his work was an ability he shared with Nilsson, to tell quirky stories within the span of a few verses that lured the listener into a world of vivid imagination.

Nilsson was not the first musician to realize that Newman's songs had enormous potential when they were grouped together or made into a central feature on an album. Alan Price had included several Newman compositions on his album *A Price on His Head* in 1967, and Ricky Nelson had also assembled a number of his pieces on *Perspective*, his 1968 bid to move his career forward from his balladeer-cum-rockabilly past by linking disparate songs into an overall narrative structure. On his version of Newman's "Love Story," Nelson had overdubbed effects, such as splashing water, and he had also sung part of the song to the kind of pared-down background that Nilsson envisaged for his own album, first using just a ukulele and later only piano and drums.

Meanwhile, Newman's regular collaborator, Van Dyke Parks, later to be a long-term colleague of Nilsson's, had recently released his debut album *Song Cycle*. An uneven album that sold slowly to start with but eventually reached cult status, Parks opened with Newman's "Vine Street," which reflects on a demo tape of a song that has not "made the grade." To reinforce the point, Parks actually begins with a completely different song altogether, "Black Jack Davey." That is abruptly curtailed to lead into "Vine Street," which then develops a particularly lush orchestral background.

As Kevin Courrier has pointed out, ideas from the albums by both Nelson and Parks found their way onto *Nilsson Sings Newman*. Newman himself did not sing on the record, but only played piano. On the Nilsson album, "Vine Street" would also be the opening cut, but prefaced by a brief excerpt of another Newman song, "Anita." This receives a quasi rock and roll treatment, with electric guitar, maracas, piano, and massively overdubbed Nilsson voices, until it breaks down and Nilsson starts singing:

That's the tape that we made,
But I'm sad to say it never made the grade.

Whereas Van Dyke Parks's voice sits quite low in the mix of the same piece on *Song Cycle*, Nilsson's is immediate, present, and speaking right to the listener. We share his pain as he tells how he has sold his guitar—implying it's the one we've just heard—after making the unsuccessful demo. It is apparent immediately that this is not just an album, but an album about making an album. At times both Newman's and Nilsson's voices can be heard on the studio talkback, making comments or giving instructions.

The record's production was an extremely complex process with multiple overdubs and copious tape editing. In that pre-digital era, this involved first synchronizing several tape decks and, second, precise surgery with a scalpel on quarter- inch tape. "I did a hundred vocal overdubs on it. It was a lot of work," remembered Nilsson, who also confirmed that parts of some songs were spliced from dozens of different takes.[40] Initially Newman was genuinely flattered by Nilsson's interest in him and his writing. He was impressed that Nilsson had a very individual vision of how to present the material that owed little to the prevailing currents in pop music. He said:

> I think that he really admired [my songs]. He was enormously decent, and open-minded about other people's work, which is the case very rarely today. And I think he just wanted to show people my songs. I think it was fairly altruistic. It was a funny time, you know, like we really believed it was an art form.... The records Harry made and the first records I made, it was like we didn't know the Rolling Stones existed.[41]

They began with rehearsals, because Nilsson insisted he needed to learn the songs "inside and out, the way *he* knew them,"[42] and then the two of them went into RCA studios on August 20, 1969, to start recording. In all, there were six sessions at which the basic voice and piano tracks were laid down, between then and September 25, all lasting three hours and often focusing on just one or two songs per session.[43] "Randy was tired of the album before we finished making it," said Nilsson. "Because for him it was just doing piano and voice, piano and voice, over and over and over."[44]

Nilsson listened intently to each take, working out where he could overdub, what would work with what, and where he needed a second, third, or fourth run-through for security to ensure a perfect match of tempo and pitch. He had an idea of how he expected the final album to sound, but for Newman, effectively going over the same ground again and again, the process seemed to be killing the spontaneity that was a key ingredient of his work. He was not to know quite how effortlessly spontaneous Nilsson would eventually make the end result seem to be, but according to Diane Nilsson, this was impossible to discern because for the first time on a full-length album, Nilsson was entirely his own producer. He was not working with Newman the way he had become accustomed to doing with George Tipton, where each acted as a check or balance for the other. Indeed, as Diane recalled, this led Nilsson to seem slightly manic:

> Left on his own in the studio as I witnessed on *Nilsson Sings Newman*, Harry would try to add everything except the kitchen sink to a track. He would have so many layers

that in the end, he would just get confused and not know which sounded best: to leave it on, to take it off, to leave it on, to take it off. I think he really needed a strong producer to work with to keep his excesses in check. And to balance his taste.[45]

There was another reason, according to Diane, why Nilsson's behavior on the Newman sessions acquired such a manic quality:

> Harry was using a lot of cocaine and I never had seen him use cocaine before. Now I don't know if he had used it before those sessions, but that's maybe why he was doing that, why he was adding so many things. Because it's a stimulant. And he just couldn't seem to stop.[46]

If it was manic in the studio during the recording of the basic tracks, it would be more manic still when Nilsson took the master tapes to Wally Heider's studio in San Francisco to mix the final album. This studio was a favorite of Jefferson Airplane and the Youngbloods, and Nilsson knew it had the engineering capability he needed for the extremely complex dubbing and mastering he had in mind. He had to battle hard with RCA to get permission to work anywhere except RCA's "Music Center of the World" in Los Angeles, the use of which was a contractual obligation for most of the label's artists. "We talked it over with the president of the company," said Nilsson, "and after a lot of negotiations the move was OK'd."[47] He worked with four engineers, Steve Barncard, Pat Ieraci, Michael Leary, and Allen Zentz, to assemble the final results from the hours of tape. Accounts tell of their five pairs of hands (Harry's included) working the faders on the sixteen-track mixing desk to combine the different takes of each song.[48] The collective contribution of the studio team was such a vital ingredient of the end result that their photographs were pasted onto the windshield of the 1938 Graham automobile used for the cover shots, to make it look as if they were the drivers on the back of Dean Torrence's design for the LP sleeve. On the front of the album, Nilsson is chauffeuring Newman across an arid landscape in the same car (which had been spotted by Nilsson as it lay parked for years close to Bill Martin's home).

Musically the resulting album is a beautifully balanced gem of intimate performances. Moments of great complexity, such as the three layers of voices on "Yellow Man" with close harmony vocals, a backing chorus of oohs and aahs, and a third set of voices creating a da-da-da rhythm, are offset by the sheer simplicity of "Love Story." On this there are no overdubs, and Nilsson—the "tenor who can sing" of the lyrics—follows the lifecycle of a relationship in a voice that is direct and personal, delivering straight into the microphone with no effects and with no apparent break between his clear middle range and his falsetto voice. The tempo is unhurried and perfectly judged for the song, which dies gently as he sings the words "pass away" at the end.

"Cowboy" starts gently a cappella, but as the piano falls in behind Nilsson for the chorus, he brings the same searing passion to the lines "Can't run, can't hide" as he would to his chart-topping "Without You" a couple of years later. This song neatly links aspects of his two Grammy-winning performances, because as well as prefiguring his future hit, it also finishes by quoting John Barry's theme for *Midnight Cowboy* played by Newman on the harpsichord (apparently at the suggestion of Diane Nilsson). "I'll be Home" and "Yellow Man" both employ a double heartbeat effect, tapped out on the mike. "Dayton, Ohio 1903" (complete with vocal close harmony quotes from Glenn Miller) conjured up the nostalgic atmosphere familiar from Nilsson's previous albums in "a song of long ago." Meanwhile, "Beehive State" briefly recalls the Bob Dylan delivery of some of his earliest discs, on the line "Gotta tell this country 'bout Utah."

When the disc concludes with "So Long Dad," it starkly returns to a familiar theme of Nilsson's, the relationship between father and son. In particular, he manages a remarkable transition from the warmth of "I miss my good old Dad, My but I'm glad to see ya" to the agonizing, desolate, icy news that "No I won't be staying here, Dad." For once on a Nilsson record, it is the son who abandons the father, but maybe because he was singing someone else's lyrics, the sense of pain and loss that he wrings from the song and the exploration of the fractured bond between father and son are the most profound he had yet put on record.

Only one song was specially written for the album, and that is the gentle love ballad "Caroline." In 1997, Newman said:

> I've never recorded it myself. No-one else, I think, has ever recorded it. I didn't think I could sing it and it was his type of thing. It was pretty and it was the type of nonsense: "When…daylight surrounds you, there's no-one around you but me"…that he could make work. I didn't have the type of voice to be like a helden-tenor, a romantic.…That's maybe why it's written like that.…But I mean he could do it. And did. It's one of my favorite things on the album. Damn good.[49]

When *Nilsson Sings Newman* came out in 1970, it was warmly received by those who understood that this music was not coming from the same corner of the pop world as (to take the comparison Newman made in the quotation cited above) the Rolling Stones. This was a comparison often made in the reviews, as Newman had said in interviews about the album that he and Nilsson not only behaved musically as if the band did not exist, but that they were also a "different…branch of homo sapiens"[50] from the Stones. In particular, *Stereo Review*—having already endorsed *Harry* as a record of the year in 1969—now did the same for the new album, its reviewer suggesting that Nilsson "seems to me the best possible choice to sing Newman's songs." After all, he went on, "someone has got to do it, because Newman's voice drives too many people up the wall."[51]

Although George Tipton had only been involved in the *Nilsson Sings Newman* album as an informal adviser, his collaboration with Nilsson continued during a gap in early September 1969 between the first and second sets of Newman sessions. In three days, they recorded, overdubbed, and mixed the title song for the motion picture *Jenny*, scheduled for release in January 1970. The theme of the picture was both socio-realist and topical, involving a pregnant, unmarried girl named Jenny (played by Marlo Thomas) making a marriage of convenience with the film director Delano (played by Alan Alda) who wants to avoid the draft. (The autobiographical parallels with Nilsson's own decision to marry Sandi as a way of avoiding the Vietnam conflict were not lost on him.) The song "Waiting" internalizes Jenny's wish for someone to love and need her at the start of the plotline as she moves to the big city to escape the ignominy of giving birth to an illegitimate child in her small, gossipy hometown. The resulting piece is very much in keeping with the "dreams and wishes" aspect of the *Harry* album, with Nilsson conjuring up a real sense of longing, within a loping, yet optimistic, orchestral setting from Tipton.

In an interview published just a few weeks before this recording was made, Nilsson described his working methods with Tipton:

I play in all the keys and I know all the chords. So I play enough to write songs. I don't write enough to orchestrate songs, to effectively arrange them. If I write a song, it goes like this: I come up with just a sketch, something I can relate to, then put lyrics to it, fill it in, and once that's done I just have a vague concept of how it should be recorded. I have a sound in mind. The job is to get it across to George, then he will add the embellishments.[52]

Maybe because the comfortable Tipton/Nilsson relationship was quite opposite in nature to Nilsson's manic approach to producing the Newman album, the end result of "Waiting" shows their collaborative process at its very best. There are few examples of their work together that have a better balance of songwriting, arranging, and vocal performance.

Once the *Nilsson Sings Newman* album had been mixed and was ready for release, Nilsson could look forward to some time to himself. The unexpected success of "Everybody's Talkin'" and the royalties from other artists' covers of his songs meant that as 1969 drew to a close, he now had a considerable amount of money coming in and could relax his creative schedule somewhat. In the New Year, he would be able to spend a few weeks at home and be with Diane. The couple's impending marriage "around the first of the year" was mentioned in a number of interviews in the fall of 1969, most of which also pointed out that fitting the wedding into November or December was proving difficult given Nilsson's packed calendar.

Coincidentally, one of the unusual musical ventures he had to find time for in December 1969 was to make a recording of Stephen Sondheim's song "Marry Me a Little." The song had been dropped from the composer's most recent musical, *Company*, but he wanted to record it as a present for a friend. To Sondheim, Nilsson seemed the ideal singer for this piece, although when he asked him to record it, he could have had no idea of the likely proximity of Nilsson's own wedding. A handful of privately pressed copies was produced.[53] The performance, arranged and conducted by George Tipton, shows that Nilsson had a natural instinct for delivering a musical theater lyric, and his strong, almost stagey delivery makes a considerable contrast between the intimate vocals of the Newman album and the more standard fare of the Tipton collaboration on "Waiting."[54]

In between this and other diversions, Nilsson told one journalist who asked about the marriage: "There are so many commitments before then. Of course there will always be commitments so unless we make a commitment not to be committed and then commit to each other, we'll never be committed."[55] Eventually on December 31, 1969, they traveled together to Las Vegas to tie the knot.

During their trip to Europe just over a year earlier, he and Diane had started planning their wedding. They shared some unorthodox ideas about how to decorate their house once they were married. Nilsson revealed that they had hatched a special scheme to celebrate having the same surname: "When I was in Sweden in Malmo, a town of about 200,000, there were twenty pages of Nilssons in the telephone book. There are about five in Los Angeles. I ripped the pages out of the telephone book and we're going to use them for wallpaper in the bathroom."[56]

Once the couple returned from Las Vegas to their house on Woodrow Wilson Drive, as well as putting up their personalized wallpaper, Nilsson and Diane became quite a home-based pair. Compared to later years, when Nilsson would spend more and more time out carousing, she described him at the start of their marriage as "more of a family man....He was more interested in doing things together. He didn't drink as much, didn't get drunk as often. He did do drugs sometimes, but it was not as often, it was more tolerable."[57]

Samantha Juste recalls Diane being "a together person" at the time, keeping the house running smoothly despite an erratic pattern of visitors, some of them crazy, drunk, or stoned. Equally, she remembers Nilsson enjoying quiet after-dinner conversations and old-fashioned parlor games when she and Micky Dolenz came to call.

> Harry loved the law. He had these law books. I don't know where he got them from, but we would sit around—these were my favorite nights—and he'd bring up a case. And we'd go through the case, and we'd each one judge it. And it was just riveting. That's what I liked about him most. He had a very high intellectual interest in life. And when he was doing that he was great. But it was the days of charades, too. We loved to play charades.[58]

When he was not at home, Nilsson was in demand on the party circuit in Los Angeles. One single riding high on the charts had done more than his three RCA albums to put him on the social map. In early 1970, he was invited to a party by David Geffen, who was on the point of starting Asylum Records, but was still managing Laura Nyro and Crosby, Stills, and Nash. As Nilsson strolled through the garden toward the pool at Geffen's house, he was introduced to another young songwriter, Jimmy Webb. Immediately Nilsson bristled, because in 1968, Webb had written and produced the album *The Yard*

Went on Forever for the singing actor Richard Harris. On it was a song called "Gayla." In the liner notes, Webb had put the letters "BN" next to the song title with an asterisk. At the bottom of the sleeve, another asterisk carried the note: "Before Nilsson." It was an attempt on Webb's part to make the point that he had come up with the line "skipping like a stone through the garden" before Nilsson had recorded Fred Neil's lyric "skipping over the ocean like a stone." Webb recalled:

> He and I got off to a very rocky start. He was very tough, like a street kid, like a New York kid. He proceeded to grill me for a long, long time about why I had done this, and why I had mentioned his name on an album. And he said, "You know, I didn't even write that song. Fred Neil wrote that song. And you were taking a shot at me."
>
> I said, "No, no, no, no, no. Please don't think I plagiarized this line from Fred Neil's song, or from your album."
>
> And he said, "Well, I think you'd better think about that."
>
> He said, "I think that some introspection is in order. I think you should carefully consider your motives in doing that." And somehow or other, out of that extremely unlikely beginning grew, not only a friendship, but kind of a great love, and we became kind of brothers.[59]

The friendship with Webb would flourish over the years that followed, and it lasted all of Nilsson's life. Webb remembers him at that first meeting looking as if he was not long out of the bank and "as skinny as a rail." But during the early part of 1970 when he was spending more time at home, Nilsson began to change his appearance. He remained relatively skinny—Webb described him as "very much looking the basketball player"—but he grew his hair and a beard.

One reason that, aside from parties, Nilsson was around the house more than usual in the early weeks of 1970 was that for the first time in three years, he was not actively working on a new album of his own, although he was planning a range of different projects. In particular, he was looking for ideas for his company Nilsson House Productions. As well as producing Bill Martin's comedy album and setting up recording sessions for Randy Marr, this was when Nilsson took out his first film option, for a projected feature based on a new short story by Kurt Vonnegut called *The Paradise Hat*. He and his partners in the project (his lawyer Dennis Bond and the future movie producer Larry Gordon) announced that filming would begin on the science fiction drama in "mid-1970."[60] However, like so many movie plans, this one never came to fruition. Yet 1970 was to be the year in which Nilsson created his own animated feature, one of the most enduring parts of his legacy, *The Point*.

The "tale-cum-parable about prejudice" was already taking shape in his mind shortly before his wedding, because he began talking about it in interviews at the end of 1969.[61] At least part of the inspiration for the adventures of the round-headed hero Oblio and his dog Arrow came from Nilsson's domestic life with Diane, as Bill Martin recalled. "Where they lived on Woodrow Wilson, it was sort of a wild area. There was an area of land there where he used to walk their dog, Molly, and this is the evolution of *The Point* and 'Me and My Arrow.' "[62] This hiking area in the Hollywood Hills may well have inspired the characters' foray into the "Pointless Forest," but the most significant aspect of the evolution of *The Point* was that the storyline came to Nilsson when he was high on LSD.[63]

Spending his time at home or at Micky Dolenz's house, Nilsson not only claimed to watch up to forty hours of television a week, but he began to try out various narcotics. Diane may not have remembered him taking much in the way of drugs before their wedding, but he gradually became part of a social circle in which he was encouraged to do so, particularly by the psychologist and writer Timothy Leary who was a prominent member of the Laurel Canyon set. Leary had famously begun a New York press conference in 1966 with the phrase "Turn on, tune in, drop out," and he was a consistent advocate for the recreational use of LSD or "acid." His various publications over the years repeatedly made the case for the LSD experience, which was, as he told *Playboy* at the time, "a confrontation with new forms of wisdom and energy that dwarf and humiliate man's mind."[64] Leary's advocacy of LSD was to have as significant an effect on the Los Angeles music scene as John Riley, George Harrison's dentist, did in Britain when he turned the Beatles on to LSD at a party in Strathearn Place, London, in 1965.[65]

Now that the Monkees had effectively broken up, Micky Dolenz was also at home a lot. "I wallowed in the affluence that the Monkees experience had afforded me," he said, "And I smoked a couple of square miles of Colombia."[66] Nilsson was there as often as ever, and Samantha Juste not only remembers him bringing "mounds" of cocaine, but enthusiastically consuming not only LSD, but whisky, cognac, and anything else on offer:

We had this recording studio, and that was where they spent a lot of their time. Of course that was soundproofed. No light at all in there. So I found it quite oppressive. But that's what they liked, because they wanted to take drugs and be "out there." So it was perfect for them. They had a lot of fun down there making good music, and it wasn't always out of hand. In fact I used to get up and run the board for them, because they couldn't see it. There were so many wonderful things—I don't want to be negative. It was the drugs and the alcohol that were negative. Took possession of them. Became more powerful than them.[67]

Diane Nilsson watched the changes in her husband warily, but at this period in early 1970 he was still mostly good company, funny, and considerate. The dark side of his character was now appearing sporadically, but because he was constantly driven to go on creating and writing, this activity seems to have held his addictive personality in check. In particular, he now went wholeheartedly after his dream of creating *The Point* as a full-length animated movie for television.

He had seen the 1968 Oscar-winning short film *The Box* by the animator Fred Wolf, and he believed that Wolf's charming, scratchy minimalist style might be perfect for his film. Wolf had plenty of conventional experience in making animated commercials, such as the "Tony the Tiger" series for Kelloggs Frosted Flakes and the "Little Green Sprout" advertisements for Green Giant, but he went on to develop a rapid approach to animation as a result of working at the Hanna-Barbera studios on projects such as the weekly *Flintstones* title sequences. In due course, Wolf and his partner Jimmy Murakami developed fast techniques that sidestepped a significant proportion of the huge overheads normally associated with Hollywood animation studios.[68] They avoided the stage known as pencil testing, where a line-drawn version of the movie was created ahead of full color visuals to plot each scene to perfection. Instead, they went straight to color, confident that they would deliver an acceptable finished product. Nilsson's vision of a completely pointed world that had come to him on his acid trip, in which the drug enhanced every spiky visual detail of trees, leaves, rocks, faces, and houses, was one that he felt matched Wolf's approach:

It was just an idea like most things, and the more you walk around thinking about the idea, the more permutations there are. I just realized it was the world's longest pun. And I realized, God! Point of sale! Point of view! Point of...and all those things. I wrote a twenty-two page, what do they call it, treatment, and submitted it to a guy at ABC.[69]

To extend his story into that skeleton screenplay, Nilsson worked with the then virtually unknown writer Carole A. Beers. They were introduced by Fred Wolf, who believed that Beers was potentially a very talented filmmaker. This was indeed the case, and she later went on to work on many episodes of the *Flintstones*, *She-Ra*, and the *Ghostbusters* cartoon series.

The treatment she produced for Nilsson was completed in the early part of 1970, and she was mainly responsible for devising the names of the characters.[70] The hero was Oblio, born into the Pointed Village to pointy-headed parents in a society where everyone and everything had a point. Except Oblio. He does not have a pointed head, although he wears a hat to disguise the fact, and his faithful dog Arrow uses his pointed nose to help Oblio play games and take part in events that his roundness would otherwise prevent him from doing. Oblio's popularity makes the son of the local Count jealous, and after the boy loses a game of "Triangle Toss" to Oblio and Arrow (which as its name suggests involves throwing triangles in the air and catching them), the boy and his father contrive to have Oblio banished.

The weak but benevolent King, who rather likes Oblio, is overruled by the evil purple Count, and banishment is ordered by the court. A dejected Oblio and his dog set off for the Pointless Forest. There, in a series of encounters, they discover that everything they meet, trees, rocks, dancing girls, has a point, much to the irritation of the three-headed

Pointless Man, who is festooned with artificial points. ("A point in every direction is the same as no point at all....") As they get to the end of the forest, a stone finger points their way home, and Oblio receives a hero's welcome as he returns to the Pointed Village. Despite the Count's attempts to throw him out again, the King asks Oblio to tell his tale. As he says that everything has a point, but not necessarily on the outside, it is revealed that he has now grown a point on his head, and at just that moment everyone else magically loses theirs.

It is a charming, whimsical morality tale. Some commentators have seen it as a visualization of Nilsson's own teenage hitch-hiking trip across the United States, and it is certainly tempting to see Oblio's banishment as a parallel to Fred Hoefer's decision that he could not afford to keep young Harry after he had lost his job as a caddy. Wolf, however, is unsure that the story was deliberately autobiographical, although he believes that one reason he and Nilsson worked so well together was because they had both grown up in working-class families in the poorest area of Brooklyn, and that having experienced such a childhood, Nilsson's main purpose was to protest against injustice in all its forms.[71]

Getting the idea sold to the television company, however, was not as straightforward as Nilsson suggested. He might be a million-selling pop artist, but that did not stop Marty Starger, the commissioning editor at ABC, from canceling every meeting that was set up to discuss the project. Starger's immediate boss, the company's vice president Barry Diller, was the man who developed the idea of the ninety-minute "Movie of the Week" on ABC, and Starger was responsible for bringing in new talent for the program. When Starger canceled for the third time in a row because he had been called to an emergency conference in New York, Nilsson saw red. He called every airline flying from LAX to New York, saying that he was confirming Mr. Starger's flight. When one of them responded positively, he reserved the seat next to him, and set off hotfoot for the airport. He boarded the flight and sat down, only to find that Starger was not there. Although the plane had officially closed, Nilsson managed to get off before it took off and dash back into the terminal.

There he rapidly searched for a payphone and called Starger's hotel. Although Starger had checked out hours before, the hotel transferred him to a colleague who gave Nilsson details of a different flight to which the man had transferred. With only minutes to go, Nilsson rebooked onto that plane and dashed off to the gate. Then he realized that he had never met Starger and would not be sure of recognizing him. By sheer chance, as he lined up to board, Starger was talking to a Paramount executive whom Nilsson had met, and they were introduced. Nilsson said: "I'm Harry Nilsson, you've cancelled out of three meetings. You sure are a hard guy to get to know."[72]

The six-hour flight gave him the opportunity to pitch the movie (and a variety of other ideas) in considerable detail, and within a couple of weeks, ABC made a formal offer to screen *The Point*, originally scheduling it for Christmas 1970, but eventually settling on February 2, 1971. As well as agreeing that Fred Wolf would be the director and animator of the film, Nilsson needed a narrator. He recalled: "[When] they bought the idea, I went to Dustin Hoffman and asked if he'd narrate it for nothing, and at the time he was getting a million dollars a movie, right? And he said yes."[73]

Hoffman was in the middle of the final stages of making the movie *Who is Harry Kellerman and Why Is He Saying Those Terrible Things About Me?* In that picture, Hoffman played Georgie Soloway, a writer of pop hit love songs, who was himself incapable of love, but who blamed his failings on the interference of the mysterious—and it appears, largely imaginary—Harry Kellerman. As he began to wrap up his input to that film, offers came in for other work.[74] Perhaps because he had been playing the part of a songwriter who wrote similar material to Nilsson, or maybe just because the idea of voicing an animated feature appealed to him, Hoffman agreed not only to narrate *The Point*, but also to play the part of the animated father who reads the story to his son, hoping to stimulate the boy's imagination. The child is mysteriously able to see the story unfold on the television set above his bed, and Wolf's animation is a visualization of the story as the child sees (or imagines) it.

From the late spring of 1970 when ABC made its commitment, Nilsson got down to work on the project. When he resumed the detailed planning of the screenplay, Carole Beers began trying to take the story into the realm of science fiction, and she was abruptly fired. Instead, Nilsson honed the script with writer Norm Lenzer. In Fred Wolf's opinion, he was the ideal person to turn Nilsson's ideas into a workable—not to say memorable—script:

He was the magic of the show. He was always down to earth, and there was a lot of how to deal with Harry, because Harry [would say he] loved this, but could we make it something else?...Norman brought all the real wit to the story, the writing, the dialogue, everything. He brought the level of sophisticated hipness to it. There was a lot of drinking as the thing trickled out, but we got a script that we all felt was going to work. In order to go forward, you have to have a soundtrack that's been approved and cut to proper length—it all has to be pre-edited.[75]

To kick-start the production process, Wolf started drawing, knowing he would have to create some standalone scenes before having any soundtrack with which to work because of the tight schedule. So he drew the three fat dancing ladies who appear in some of the latter sequences of the movie. Meanwhile, Nilsson began recording the music for the soundtrack at RCA, both for the film and an accompanying album (for which he narrated and provided the character voices himself). He had cut a rough version of one song, "Think About Your Troubles," in December 1969 at the same session as Sondheim's "Marry Me a Little." But he returned to the studio on April 16 with George Tipton and recorded a revised version of that piece and a first version of "Me and My Arrow," which were between them to set the musical tone for the movie. The latter is the jaunty song that recurs throughout the story as Oblio and Arrow trot off on their adventures. The former is a more complex piece, triggering much of the visual imagery of the film and tracing the story of the cycle of life through a teardrop that falls in a teacup. The varied and sharply focused details of an LSD trip hover throughout the lyrics, comparing teardrops to the bubbles that rise when one pours a cup of tea, and with a decomposing whale as a central—if rather unusual—element to the story.

Work on the recordings was interrupted on May 7, 1970, when, at a grand ceremony at the Century Plaza Hotel in Los Angeles, Nilsson was presented with the Grammy award for "Best Male Contemporary Vocalist" of 1969,[76] because of the huge success of "Everybody's Talkin'." (The song was eventually entered into the Grammy Hall of Fame. By 2005, according to BMI, it had been aired on radio or television 6.7 million times.) The follow-up to the award led to a round of interviews and features, and Nilsson did not return to the recording studios for more *Point* sessions until mid-June, when he completed the rest of the music for the film. Naturally, however, the interviews focused not so much on his past Grammy-winning success as his current project. Asked to talk about his method of songwriting, he said:

> Ideas come quickly and…as a matter of fact the best song that I've written I think was written in less than a minute. Many times you write the body of it, the main part, the idea, what it is that appeals to you of all the stuff to choose from…and [then] it will take time developing and expanding it and getting it correct. It is work. And there is design to it and of course it's in search of a certain order of things musically. [The song is] a new one, naturally, it's called "Think About Your Troubles."[77]

This song was placed roughly halfway through the story of *The Point* and took place immediately after Oblio's banishment, giving the viewer (or listener to the album) the opportunity to reflect on the cyclical nature of problems. It offered Wolf the chance to add some highly imaginative images—one of several places in the story where there are free-flowing flights of visual fancy.

The movie is bookended by another of Nilsson's strongest new songs, "Are You Sleeping?" Written as a love song and tackling the fragility of a relationship that might break up at any moment, viewed from the perspective of one of the partners looking at the other sleeping, it also has a note of ambiguity in the movie, introducing the idea of *The Point* being a bedtime story. The opening questions

> Are you sleeping? Can you hear me?
> Do you know if I am by your side?

might well be asked by the father reading the story to his young son. Later, just before Oblio and Arrow leave the Pointless Forest, the song returns as they fall asleep, and it sets the scene for an inventive dream sequence.

Once Nilsson's music was done, the rest of the soundtrack—dialog and incidental music—was recorded, and then the visual images were added. As well as Nilsson's songs and a series of linking sequences arranged by Tipton, the film employed some fine vocal actors. Paul Frees, who was, after Mel Blanc, the most versatile of Hollywood voiceover artists, played the King, the Leaf Man, and various other small parts. He had recently been Santa in the 1969 animated children's classic *Frosty The Snowman*, but the idea of using him appealed to Nilsson as Frees had voiced John Lennon and George Harrison in the television cartoon series *The Beatles* and had written the screenplay and songs for the 1960 cult movie *The Beatniks*. Another familiar voiceover actor, Lenny Weinrib, was cast as the evil Count, assuming a flamboyant English accent modeled closely on that of Terry-Thomas as the caddish Sir Percy Ware-Armitage in *Those Magnificent Men In Their Flying Machines*. It demonstrated Weinrib's versatility, as he was more familiar to children from his friendly laidback Southern drawl as the life-size orange puppet *H. R. Pufnstuf*, the star of a series then in the middle of its three-year run on NBC.

Bill Martin played the Rock Man, his accent veering somewhat alarmingly from African American to Afro-Caribbean, and Jodie Foster's brother, the child actor Buddy Foster, played the Count's evil son. Joan Gerber was Oblio's mother, and the ten-year-old Mike Lookinland took time out from playing Bobby in *The Brady Bunch* to voice both Oblio and Dustin Hoffman's young son. With the Hollywood elements of the dialog in place, Nilsson and Wolf flew to New York to record Hoffman's script. They had asked actor Alan Barzman (who sounded rather like the comedian Jack Benny) to read through a temporary track to help with timing, and when Hoffman heard it, he liked the sound so much that he asked, "What's wrong with that voice?"[78] Overtones of Barzman and Benny remain in Hoffman's own narration.

Once the soundtrack was done, Wolf made the brave, if not foolhardy, commitment that he would animate the entire movie himself. He recalled that once he announced this:

Harry said he would sing the whole thing by himself. I said, "Big freaking deal! You sing, I draw! I'll be drawing for months and months." It did work out, and I did animate it. I was between marriages and I found a place by the beach, to get out of the studio, out of Hollywood. I said, "I'll work by night and sleep by day." I did that for 85% of the production. As for the other delinquencies of that procedure, blame it all on Harry. He used to come out to the beach: "How is it going?"

I'd say, "Fine but I'm going to bed now. Harry, your up all night is different from my up all night." Once in a while I'd have a break, but a break for a weekend with Harry was like a month. If I was out for two days with Harry, I needed three days to recuperate. That was a total of five days out of my production schedule. The numbers were reasonable in the beginning, but they became outrageous because of these "vacations." We had a simple and very direct framework, with none of the discipline that was necessary in a Disney project. Instead, we had a loose, stylistic, simplified way of doing things, which was all according to what our attitudes were. Take it or leave it. It's certainly not the best animation in world, but this was my challenge. I better come through with a style that is going to be consistent for 74 minutes of animation, in other words, a total of 28,000 drawings which I did in 34 weeks. The hand can get numb just thinking of it. The fact that I was doing it all myself dictated a style, which I think was effective.[79]

Just as Norman Lenzer's script added a witty hipness to the dialog, Fred Wolf's drawings captured the spirit of the dawn of the 1970s with a unified visual style that very much went its own way, but simultaneously paid homage to Heinz Edelmann's art direction for the Beatles' animated feature *Yellow Submarine*, the psychedelic "op art" of the British painter Bridget Riley, and the scratch collages and fine pen-and-ink work that Nilsson's future colleague, the bassist Klaus Voormann, had brought to record sleeves such as the Beatles' *Revolver*.

There are moments that vividly evoke Voormann, such as the player of a giant bass brass instrument whose tongue suddenly appears through the bell. Riley's highly stylized graphic work is referenced in the clustered points of the village and the regularity of the saplings en route to the Pointless Forest, whereas the busy citizens of the Pointed Village have a lot in common with the visual language of *Yellow Submarine*, although that movie employed 200 animators rather than one man in a beach house. Wolf also shows he has absorbed much from the style of earlier cartoons. The bouncing words such as "Hello," "Bottom," and "Cold" as echoes in the deep hole into which Arrow nearly falls owe plenty to the fantasy sequences in *Dumbo* and *Fantasia*, and there are more Disney resonances in the masked mice who dance "flying high up in the sky" to the "P.O.V. (Point of View) Waltz."

Mixed into the psychedelic world of the pointed land are elements of Nilsson's own fascination with standup comedy and vintage movies. The entrepreneurial Leaf Man who tries to interest Oblio in "manufacturing leaves" is a comedy routine worthy of Lenny Bruce, while the Rock Man and his "whole family of us folk" looks back on the one hand toward Stepin Fetchit and on the other to Cliff Edwards's voicing of the laconic crows in *Dumbo*. There are art jokes as well, such as the painter who has his picture of a circle thrown out of an exhibition, only to be welcomed back when he repaints it as a triangle. The characters have their personalities reflected in their appearances, so that the indecisive King is pallid and white-haired, while the angry Count is purple with a fine set of orange eyebrows and whiskers.

The Point was the first ever full-length animation made specifically for television's Sunday "Movie of the Week." When it came out, the press and public loved it, and the album (with a special eight-page comic book summary of the story based on Wolf's drawings) spent thirty-two weeks on the charts, climbing as high as number twenty-five, while the single release of "Me and My Arrow" sailed into the top forty. "No other pop performer is nearly as good at portraying innocence without silliness or self-consciousness," declared *Rock* magazine. It continued: "Throughout the fairy tale, the delicate, syncopated and fluid songs continually transcended their context; they were beautiful in a way that very few popular tunes are."[80] It had taken the best part of six months of Nilsson's time to finish *The Point*, but the movie was to go on and develop a life of its own over the years. There would be further television broadcasts, including one narrated by Alan Thicke and later a video release voiced by Ringo Starr. The show would also, in years to come, make a successful transition to the musical stage.

Nilsson was still working on finishing *The Point* in the fall of 1970 when he received a visit from a producer, working for the BBC in London, who wanted to persuade him to appear in a television special.[81] This was the South-African-born painter Stanley Dorfman who had graduated from design and art direction to become one of Britain's leading pop music television producers. He and Johnnie Stewart made the weekly show *Top of the Pops* from Manchester during the years when Samantha Juste starred on the program. He had also produced series for Dusty Springfield and Lulu, the latter including Jimi Hendrix's infamous appearance when he went completely off-message, stopped "Hey Joe" in mid-performance, and launched into an impassioned tribute to Cream.

Dorfman's new project picked up on a couple of successful special shows he had made with Leonard Cohen and Joni Mitchell, in which each of them sang a selection of their own material. The BBC encouraged him to feature more singer/songwriters such as Laura Nyro and Jimmy Webb, but rather than title each show after the name of the singer, as he had done with "Cohen sings Cohen," he came up with the generic title *In Concert*. Dorfman was making his first visit to the United States to recruit the stars for this inaugural full season, which was scheduled to start with an appearance by Randy Newman. The English publisher Terry Oates, who handled the U.K. distribution of Nilsson's songs, suggested him for the series, even though he was sure that the offer would be turned down because of Nilsson's reluctance to perform in front of an audience. Dorfman made his way up to the house on Woodrow Wilson Drive, where Nilsson had installed an editing suite to view the finished sequences of *The Point* with Fred Wolf. He remembered:

I saw Harry, and he said, "There's no way I'm ever going to perform. I don't perform in front of people."

And I said: "Well you don't have to perform in front of people."

He says, "But it's called *In Concert*. Isn't it a concert series?"

I said, "Yes, it is. But we don't have to do it like that. We can make it up as we go along." You see, at the BBC in those days, you could do stuff like that. If it worked, they said, "That was great." If it didn't they said, "You fucked that up." But you didn't have to bother about ratings. You didn't have to bother about advertising. So you just did what you wanted to do, and if it was satisfactory, you'd be left alone to do it.[82]

Nilsson was intrigued by the prospect of making a concert appearance that was not, in reality, a concert. So, remarkably, Nilsson agreed to visit London in 1971 to record the show. Dorfman then used the rest of his stay in Los Angeles to secure visits from various other artists, but he managed to spend much of his leisure time with Nilsson, with whom he struck up an immediate rapport, although early on he learned always to take his own car, as on more than one occasion a simple dinner invitation became a riotous two-day visit to Santa Barbara or San Diego.

In 1971, not only would Nilsson go on to make the BBC television broadcast that most perfectly captured his young singer/songwriter persona for posterity, but it was also the end of an era and the start of another. In the course of the year, his creative focus would move to London and his repertoire would become more rock oriented, with a change of producer at RCA and the most commercially successful album of his life.

There was a time when we could dance until a
quarter to ten,
We never thought it would end then, we never
thought it would end.

5

GOTTA GET UP

THE YEAR 1971 began with the birth of Nilsson and Diane's son Zak, just after the period
when Nilsson had been working at home on his movie. The baby arrived on January 17th,
and weighed in at seven pounds, seven ounces. As part of his lifelong fascination with
numbers, Nilsson wanted the boy's middle name to be a number, and the logical one
given the symmetry of his birth date and weight would seem to be seven. However, after
seeing his son in the hospital for the first time, Nilsson was just leaving when he ran
back to tell Diane, "No, it can't be seven, it has to be nine." Nobody in the family ever
got a clear answer as to why he decided this. In later life, Zak asked his father if he had
been named after Ringo Starr's son Zak Starkey, who was then five years old, but Nilsson
assured him he was not.[1]

Diane Nilsson recalls that "part of [Nilsson] wanted to be a parent, part of him wanted
to be a partner and married, but most of him didn't want to be."[2] For the first months of
1971, however, he continued to center his life around his home and family, although there
was a constant pull between the demands of his home and the fun of going out and drinking tequila with his friends. He had been a stepfather when he was married to Sandi. This
time, perhaps, it would be different, as Zak was his own son.

Nilsson watched the child closely in the first days of his life, marveling at him. He was
so moved by watching Zak sleep that he wrote a letter for him to read when he grew up:

Dear Zak

I stood over you and watched you sleep for thirty minutes this morning.
Someday you will know how I feel as I write these words. You are beautiful. You
moved your feet and toes proportionally to the noise I made. You were on top of
your blanket. An orange blanket with yellow daisies. And your pacifier was an inch
from your mouth. It had obviously been released with sleep.

I love you.
Big Daddy Schmilsson[3]

After the birth of his son, Nilsson got down to making final preparations for the broad-cast of *The Point* in February. With plenty of Fred Wolf's distinctive visuals available as illustrations for the newspapers, Nilsson took on a round of press interviews. He praised Wolf unstintingly, saying, "The film could not have been done under ordinary circum-stances. Wolf put in twelve to sixteen hours a day, turning out the drawings with a staff of five." He also enthused over Dustin Hoffman's contribution, his voice helping to "sustain the flavor of the show."[4] Nor did he forget to write to Marty Starger, saying how happy he was with the outcome of *The Point*. "You're really a good guy," he continued, "I'm glad we flew East together!"[5]

Even before the promotional work on the movie was finished, Nilsson turned his attention back to records. His success with "Everybody's Talkin'" and the significant vol-ume of sales that he had achieved with *Harry* made him realize that there would be a renewed market for his two earliest RCA albums. Instead of reissuing them as they were, he persuaded the company to allow him to remix the best material from those two LPs and reissue the results as a "new" record, *Aerial Pandemonium Ballet*.

At the time, the press hailed it as "new approaches to some of his previous material,"[6] pointing out that he "has dared to inhabit nostalgia and create something new there."[7] The record's sales were a distinct improvement over the combined figures achieved by the two original albums, but essentially this was a piece of fiddling about, stripping back some of Tipton's more elaborate arrangements, cutting out some of Jarrard's more enthu-siastic vocal overdubs, and even altering the playing speed here and there to change the timbre and pitch. With the benefit of hindsight, although *Pandemonium Aerial Ballet* put some money into the bank for Nilsson and RCA, it lacked the freshness and creative originality of the first albums in their previously released form, and the project took his attention away from anything genuinely new. However, working on it did keep him at home for much of Zak's first month or two.

For his next album of completely fresh material, Nilsson had decided to work with a new producer, Richard Perry. Why he made this decision when he did is not obvious, but it seems that during the late stages of the production of *The Point*, all was not well at Nilsson House Productions. In September 1970, he wrote to Derek Taylor to sympa-thize about the restructuring of Apple that had occurred when Allen Klein arrived as chairman, bringing management accounting to the informal chaos that had previously prevailed. He said:

Sorry to hear about the umbrella folding. Historically however, The Apple must be Eaton, I mean eaten. Fucking cunts won't even give it time to ripen any more will they?…Nilsson House has been eaten by the same cunts who ate Apple. However, I managed to slip away with only a bite or two taken.[8]

Evidently, despite the financial acumen that had allowed Nilsson to get *The Point* completed within ABC's budget of $500,000, he had not managed such effective control over his production company, and handing supervision of his records back to a third party seemed a sensible way forward. The working partnership between Nilsson and Perry began in January 1971, but it would take a little time for the two of them to map out a fresh creative direction, partly because of Nilsson's remix of his earlier work and partly because of the arrival of the baby.

Nilsson and Perry had originally met almost by chance a year or so earlier when the singer Tiny Tim had made his Los Angeles debut at the Troubadour. The long-haired, falsetto-voiced vocalist, backed by an eight-piece band, had his audience in hysterics as he romped through such camp classics as "I Enjoy Being a Girl" (sung back to back with "I'm Glad I'm a Boy"), "You are my Sunshine," and his chart hit "Tiptoe Through the Tulips."[9] Afterward, "Mr. Tim," as the press called him, was guest of honor at a party hosted by Phil Spector.[10] With him was Perry, who, after working with an extraordinary range of artists including Captain Beefheart, Ella Fitzgerald, and Fats Domino, had spectacularly transformed Tiny Tim's career, taking him from being an unknown busker in Cambridge, Massachusetts, to become an internationally successful recording artist. Perry recalled that Nilsson introduced himself during the evening, expressing enthusiasm for the Tiny Tim album. In return, Perry told Nilsson that he had liked *Pandemonium Shadow Show*, and on the back of this discussion, a friendship began. In due course, Nilsson decided to move the relationship beyond friendship to a professional association. He went over to Perry's house in Laurel Canyon with the specific aim of enlisting him as his producer. Perry remembers that he told him, "I would love to, under one or two conditions: that he had to trust me and let me call the shots, which he agreed to, for the time being, and that was mainly it."[11]

In between working on *The Point* and remixing his earlier albums, Nilsson had not had the time to write any new songs. Nevertheless, on January 12, 1971, just days before Zak's arrival, he returned briefly to RCA's studios with Richard Perry to cut "Early in the Morning," the first piece for the potential new album on which they would collaborate. This tune was not a Nilsson original, but it comes quite close in feel to the loose, relaxed sound of the demos that he made earlier in his career for the Monkees. Twenty-five years earlier, the song had been recorded as a straight-ahead rhythm-and-blues number by its co-author, the saxophonist and singer Louis Jordan. Nilsson's version retains the basic twelve-bar blues structure, but at the same time takes a few liberties with it. He accompanies himself on the organ and occasionally stretches the chord sequence to accommodate a slight lengthening of the lyric, or phrase repetitions, or an excursion into his higher register to imitate the voice of a waitress, who tells him, "Harry, you sure look beat!" The simplicity of the track and its clear ties in terms of vocal delivery and storytelling to the Ray Charles influence that Nilsson had long acknowledged, but seldom demonstrated so graphically, pointed the way toward a sound that was more earthy and more connected to rock, soul, and blues than anything on the previous albums.

Looking back on this first session with Perry, Nilsson told reporter Dawn Eden, "Richard was thinking the same thing I was thinking. Let's go to work and do some rock and roll, and get down!"[12]

A month later, after Zak's birth and the television premiere of the movie, Nilsson and Perry were back at RCA to cut a George Tipton arrangement of a new Nilsson song, "I'll Never Leave You." Despite some interesting doubling of lower strings and tuba in the arrangement and a strange effect that seems to be an echo of Anton Karas's zither from the *Third Man* theme, the performance is uncharacteristically lame. Nilsson's voice seems as fettered by the arrangement as it had been freed by the organ accompaniment on "Early in the Morning." This was to be the last time that Nilsson cut an album track with Tipton. The partnership and friendship that had underpinned so much of Nilsson's success from the Tower records days to *The Point* came to an abrupt end, as Nilsson and Perry jointly realized they needed to move in a different direction to capitalize on the bluesy potential of "Early in the Morning."

Just as had been the case with Rick Jarrard, there was little advance warning for Tipton that Nilsson would make such a radical move. As recently as June 1970, Nilsson had produced (through Nilsson House Productions) an instrumental album of his own compositions, entirely featuring Tipton's arrangements, called *Nilsson by Tipton*, involving such stalwarts of their previous recording sessions as guitarists Howard Roberts and Dennis Budimer. This "fine album of mainstream music,"[13] as one of the reviewers called it, seemed to cement their creative partnership even more firmly than before. Yet only eight months later, the collaboration was over. It was an emotional parting for Tipton as Diane Nilsson observed:

> When Harry...went off into that rock direction, I think George probably would've been disappointed, just because George loved Harry's work so much and loved what he did. I just imagine he might've been...hurt and maybe, maybe couldn't go back.[14]

Tipton has generally declined to talk about his work with Nilsson ever since they went their separate ways, although he did admit in a letter to Lee Newman (who played Oblio in the 1991 stage production of *The Point*) that he was proud of what they had achieved together. He said: "1964 through 1971 were wonderful years for all of us who were fortunate enough to be part of the recording industry at that time. Everything imaginable was possible and able to be done. We did it, while we could, and then moved on.... We could get our feet 'on the sunny side of the street,'... Harry and I sure walked there for a while."[15]

The main reason that Tipton could not go back to the kind of relationship he had previously enjoyed with Nilsson was the totally different way in which Perry worked. As a staff producer, Rick Jarrard had been very much one of the team when it came to studio work with Nilsson and Tipton, and he saw himself as the liaison point in both directions between the bosses at RCA and Nilsson. After his departure, Tipton had become the sounding board for Nilsson's ideas, and a degree of commercial success had given Nilsson the ability to call at least some of the shots directly with his record company. But quite apart from the problems at Nilsson House, he was aware of his shortcomings as his own producer, as had become evident during the Newman sessions.

Richard Perry functioned differently from the way either a staff producer or an artist-producer worked. As *New York* magazine, who described his appearance as "shirt open to the waist, major hair, etc." explained it at the time:

[He] is one of a new breed of cat that has come onto the record scene in the past few years. Perry is a record producer who works not for a company, but as a freelance agent. He works with artists, planning, arranging and directing a complete record-package, and turns the resultant product over to a record company, which then presses and distributes that product.[16]

Nilsson already had a contract with RCA, but when Perry took over as his producer, he asked for and was granted control over almost every other aspect of making each album. He had not only created Tiny Tim's successful records and concerts, but he was in the process of reviving Barbra Streisand's career, and when he began work with Nilsson, Perry had just completed her *Stoney End* album, which restored her to the top ten on the pop charts after an absence of five years.

He had a reputation for bringing artists together with unusual or interesting repertoire, including persuading Ella Fitzgerald to sing Nilsson's song "Open Your Window" and getting Streisand to sing his ballad "Maybe." Perry had produced Fats Domino's successful version of the Beatles' "Lady Madonna," even though he was sure that the New Orleans pianist and singer never entirely understood the words. If there was one underlying principle in all of Perry's work, whether it was with Tiny Tim, Captain Beefheart, Carly Simon, or Streisand, it was that he framed an artistic vision for each of them and then did his best to realize that vision on record. When it came to Nilsson, he was absolutely sure what was needed. Both men were immense Beatles fans, and Perry believed that Nilsson had the promise to be "his" Beatles:

I knew that he had the ability, certainly the vocal ability, as well as the songwriting ability, to do something that could take him to another level than he had been to. He was quite well respected, and he would sell an average of 75,000, maybe even 100,000 records per LP, but when we did the *Nilsson Schmilsson* album I would think it probably sold in excess of five million.

I knew that the one thing missing from the equation in terms of truly making him as close to an American Beatles as possible was to do the album in the UK. Because at this point, having digested the L.A. music scene for a number of years, I knew that the real center of creative recording was in London—the technology, the way they trained their engineers and arrangers was completely exemplary and much more to my taste than their American counterparts.[17]

Another producer had tipped off Perry that the engineer he should aim to work with, in order to get the sound he was after, was Robin Geoffrey Cable, who was based at Trident Studios and who had worked on several early albums by Elton John.[18] It took a few months following the sessions at RCA's L.A. studios in February 1971 to make the arrangements to transfer the entire production of Nilsson's album to London. Nilsson also wanted to wait until Zak was old enough for Diane to travel with him. In due course, everything was sorted out and Trident Studios was booked for a number of successive sessions in June. This was not as easy as it might seem, because the very popularity of this studio, despite it being in operation twenty-four hours a day, made it difficult to book the sizable block of time that Perry knew he needed. In the end, he had to settle for some sessions between 2 and 8 a.m. But most were scheduled to run from 7 p.m. to 2 a.m. The studio itself was a long room with a control box reached by a flight of stairs that overlooked the playing area. Musicians had mixed feelings about it; some guitarists, for example, disliked the fact that to get good separation in the room, their amplifiers would be covered in baffles, making it hard to hear their own playing. All of the players who had heavy gear to lug into the studios rued the fact that Trident, located in St. Anne's Court, was in the heart of Soho, which was (and still is) a nightmare for parking. Once a precious space had been found, there would be constant breaks in the sessions as one player after another sneaked out to feed coins into the parking meters. After the narrow alleyway to the door had been negotiated, the studio itself was several levels up in Trident House, reached by an old-fashioned elevator.[19]

Perry had already made some records at other studios in London including the Ella Fitzgerald album for Reprise, so he had a good idea of the capabilities of London-based session players. For Nilsson's album, he booked the American drummer Jim Gordon, who had recently finished touring with Eric Clapton, as well as doing tours with Joe Cocker and Traffic. Another American musician, Jim Keltner, later to be associated with many of George Harrison's projects, was also booked on drums. On bass and guitar was Berlin-born Klaus Voormann, who had recently finished a stint with Manfred Mann, as well as designing many an album cover. Herbie Flowers, soon to be famous as the bassist on Lou Reed's "Walk on the Wild Side" came in for some tracks, as did jazz-meets-punk guitarist Chris Spedding, who was at the time a member of Ian Carr's rock fusion group Nucleus. Nilsson himself would play piano, organ, and electric piano, although Gary Wright and Jim Webb handled additional keyboard duties. On a couple of tracks, the virtuoso American brass player Jim Price multitracked his own arrangements on trumpet and trombone, with saxophone parts handled by his long-term session colleague Bobby Keys. For the one piece to feature a string orchestra, arranger Paul Buckmaster, a veteran of many Elton John sessions, as well as a recording colleague of David Bowie, was brought in.

This one track was the song that Perry and Nilsson both agreed when they arrived in London was essential to be recorded (alongside the two already cut in Los Angeles). It was a song that Nilsson had heard at a party in Laurel Canyon. At first he thought it was an obscure Beatles track, and he began scouring the record stores to try and find it. In due course, he discovered that the number he had heard was called "Without You," and it had been written by Tom Evans and Pete Ham, members of the British rock band Badfinger, who had recently been signed to Apple.[20] It appeared on their newly released third album *No Dice*, but had been passed over as a possible single release in favor of "No Matter What," another Ham composition that became a U.K. top-ten hit.

It took a certain amount of insight to see the potential of "Without You," because although the Badfinger version does make a small degree of contrast between the verse and the "Can't live, if living is without you" line of the chorus, it is otherwise a rather undistinguished rock number, loping along at medium tempo with the occasional guitar solo. Nilsson, however, had exactly the instincts necessary to see what could be done with the song, and almost as soon as he arrived in London, he cut an emotionally charged demo version of it, backed only by his own piano accompaniment. Even though he crashes into some seriously wrong keyboard chords as he wrings every drop of passion from the "Can't live…" line, he does the one thing that Badfinger failed to do, which is to inhabit the song with total conviction. Within just a few bars, we know that this is someone whose fragile emotions are laid bare, and who really does sound incapable of going on without the person he "had to let go." Although he is singing about a departed lover, he could just as well be pouring out his personal anguish at being deserted by his father. Nilsson was greatly enthused by his performance on the demo and by the way his personal pain had been captured in this spontaneous recording, especially on the line "I can't live, if living is without you." It took all of Perry's powers of persuasion to convince Nilsson that he could not release the raw demo, but he needed to try and record a properly backed studio version, without surrendering the conviction and passion of his solo version.[21]

As a result, the first backing track to be put down in London, with guitarist John Uribe, pianist Gary Wright, plus Voormann and Keltner, was for "Without You." Once a guide version of the vocal was in place, Paul Buckmaster then wrote the string parts, which he conducted for the recording.[22] Everything was going well except, as the sessions progressed, Nilsson started to go off the idea of using the song. Richard Perry was not amused, because as they put down each take and called the musicians in to listen to a play-back, Nilsson would start saying how terrible he thought the song was. In particular, he disliked the apparent non sequitur of being unable to forget the evening or his lover's face as she was leaving, followed up with "That's just the way the story goes." Perry, sensitive to the fact that as soon as musicians sense any disquiet about a performance, they stop giving their best, tried hard to dissuade Nilsson from voicing his criticisms. Perry said:

It may have been that he was still fighting for the demo to be the record. But, like two proper gentlemen, we decided to have a meeting over high tea at the Dorchester

Hotel to discuss what we were going to do. And I said, "Harry, you do remember that when you came to me and asked me to produce you, my only condition was that I have control, creative control?"

And he looks at me dead in the face and says, "Well I lied!" And then with that, we both looked at our watches and realized that we were late for the session where he was supposed to do his vocal on "Without You." Without another word, we jumped into a taxi down to the studio. He ran right out and sang the vocal that you hear on the record."[23]

Derek Taylor was the first to hear the results. He had by this time moved from Apple to WEA, the British division of Warner Brothers, where as director of special projects he was a mixture of producer, talent scout, and publicist. His own roster of artists included the veteran British blues singer George Melly, and he had also taken on the promotion of the up-and-coming Bette Midler, then starring in the Who's *Tommy*, who was about to make her debut album *The Divine Miss M.* Taylor was closely involved in the distribution deal for the newly formed Rolling Stones Records, and he remained on good terms with the Beatles, so consequently he was totally immersed in every aspect of the current music scene. He had barely arrived in his office when Nilsson and Perry turned up to play him a rough mix of the finished track, which they had finally put together at an all-night session at Trident, running until eight in the morning. He had vivid memories of Nilsson's visit:

> He took that Badfinger song, Ham and Evans's "Without You," and made such a success of it. Really it's breathtaking. The perfectionism of Harry and Richard Perry made that possible. They'd... made a very good demo, which to me was sufficient to be a hit. But they wanted to get more power, more power on the top notes, so they went away with it and did what was necessary. Harry burst into terrifically unpleasant hemorrhoids on that top note. Whenever I hear it I always think of the hemorrhoids. It somehow doesn't spoil it—though it should.[24]

Perry was convinced they had a hit on their hands, and so it would eventually prove to be, as the song went on to sell a million copies, topping the charts in Britain and America and winning Nilsson his second Grammy award. The raw passion of the piano and voice demo is slightly diminished, but Perry's decision to record the track properly and add a tasteful amount of orchestral backing is spectacularly vindicated. The untutored feel of Nilsson's opening piano chords remains from the demo, but his voice is anything but untutored, in what ranks as one of his most vocally perfect performances. The smoothness and innocence of the opening verse gradually give way to greater passion, helped by the low-key way the strings slide in behind the line "No, I can't forget tomorrow...." On the following line beginning "And now it's only fair...," Nilsson is double-tracked with himself, his back-up vocal mirroring perfectly the nuances of his original melodic line.

The reprise of the "Can't live…" line thrillingly opens up to much of the intensity that Nilsson had put into the demo, and Buckmaster's backing arrangement catches that mood exactly. In the same way that Tipton's subtle use of strings had moved Nilsson's "Everybody's Talkin'" a quantum leap forward from Fred Neil's original, this record makes the Badfinger original sound like the roughest of pencil sketches for a full color painting. During the final mixing at Island Studios in London, Perry discovered that Badfinger was recording in an adjacent studio. According to writer Curtis Armstrong, "Harry and Richard invited them in, poured them a little champagne, and then played back the song at top volume. Pete Evans and Tom Ham, the song's co-writers, were reportedly speechless."[25] Perry's decision to record in London and achieve a different feel from both the accompanying musicians and the studio sound gives the performance a far more contemporary edge than anything Nilsson had ever achieved with Tipton.

The contrast with his earlier work goes further than this, because the sessions in London also involved a remake of a song that Nilsson had originally recorded with Tipton in March 1968, but which had failed to be included on either the *Aerial Ballet* or *Harry* albums. This was his own composition "Gotta Get Up." In Tipton's setting, it is upbeat and cheery, propelled forward at just too quick a tempo by an insistent tambourine and with a prominent brass section that plays call and response with Nilsson's double-tracked vocal in the lines "We never thought it would end, we used to carry on and drink and do the rock and roll."

Perry's production of the song is altogether darker and less buoyant, an atmosphere helped by Chris Spedding's scratchy guitar chords at the start, which finally dissolve toward anarchy at the end as the band follows Nilsson's upwardly spiraling piano into chaos. "We had to do so many takes," recalled Spedding, "that we got cabin fever and started messing around, and Harry decided to incorporate the craziness into the song."[26] In the central part of the piece, after the spiky chords of Nilsson's piano introduction, the vocal seems less throwaway and superficial than on the Tipton version. Indeed the new performance highlights one of Nilsson's main autobiographical themes, as he tells us of the sailor who would "come to town and he would pound her for a couple of days, and then he'd sail across the bubbly waves." Whether merchant marine or Seabee, there is little doubt that this is Nilsson Sr., as seen from the perspective of Bette Martin, a woman who could no longer stay out all hours dancing as if the fun would "never end." There are also overtones of Nilsson's days at the bank, having to phone to "let the people know I'm gonna be late." Whereas Tipton's production was tight and well organized, Perry's is looser, quite accommodating to the occasional wheezing utterance from Henry Krein's accordion or Jim Price's jazzy brass interjections, which now seem like an ironic commentary on the lyrics, rather than a central part of a pretty arrangement. By making this the lead-off track, it announced that *Nilsson Schmilsson* was going to be a very different and more mature album than its predecessors.

When this was finished, Perry and Nilsson had two tracks from January in the can, this remake of "Gotta Get Up" and a likely hit in the form of "Without You." They had the musicians and the studio booked, but they had only a set of unfinished demos to provide material for the rest of the album. These were cut during the first couple of days at Trident, before the other band members were brought in, when Nilsson recorded segments of various of his own songs at the same time as he made his piano and voice version of "Without You." Perry said:

> He hadn't really written any new songs. He only had bits and pieces of things that had been written lying around for some time. He wasn't particularly enthusiastic about them because they were "old songs." So we were walking down Oxford Street the day before the sessions meeting with different publishers hoping to find an outside song at the last minute that we could incorporate into the sessions.[27]

Nothing came from this search that made the grade. However, the album was ultimately to include one additional older song, the 1956 top-twenty hit "Let the Good Times Roll" by Shirley and Lee. They decided to do this "on the spur of the moment in the studio," according to Perry,[28] and it takes on an atmosphere that is deliberately more rock and roll in flavor than Nilsson's earlier albums, with a heavy backbeat from Jim Keltner, Nilsson's piano pounding out the beat, and some anarchic guitar from Spedding. Nilsson takes an atmospheric and bluesy harmonica solo on an instrument he picked up on a whim from a shelf in the studio during the recording, but the track's main strength is some dramatic vocal overdubbing. Instead of the angelic choirs of a Rick Jarrard production, however, this is a far more rock-inflected vocal. The peerless clarity of Nilsson's voice on the opening to "Without You" is replaced by a harder edge and some Everly Brothers' style harmonies on the catchline "C'mon baby." Yet this atmosphere was achieved at a price, according to Chris Spedding:

> People might imagine, knowing Harry Nilsson's lifestyle, that his recording sessions were a wild party, but they were all very serious, and the work ethic was the thing. And one of the things I do remember was take after take after take on some of the songs. On "Let the Good Times Roll," I remember, he was playing piano on that and all day we were doing that. There were about fifty takes on two-inch tape.[29] I have a memory of going home exhausted, having lost all objectivity and spontaneity on the music. Arriving at the studio the next morning I had the impression—reinforced by the fug in the studio and the overflowing ashtrays at 10 a.m.—that Harry, Richard and an engineer had been there all night listening to all the takes, trying to decide. When Richard realized that we were assembling again for the next day's work, I have a distinct memory of him saying, "OK, let's go for take three." Take three out of fifty. None of the musicians thought this was a good way to work, as it was wasteful of energy and resources.[30]

Richard Perry, on the other hand, was a firm believer in going for as many takes as possible. He was sensitive to minute changes in balance or to whether the sound was right from everyone in the band in order to achieve the perspective that he wanted to hear. He was usually specific about what he was looking for, although this might not have affected every musician in the band, so some would seem to be redoing the same thing over and over as he made minute adjustments to other parts. "I would do lots of takes in the Nilsson period," he said, "because I guess I had a sixth sense about what might still be missing from making it the perfect take. Hopefully I've been right more often than wrong, and although some musicians felt I was pushing them too hard, they always came back to work with me again." In retrospect, he also believed that he knew when asking for too many takes was beginning to lose the "feel" that he was after.[31]

The most overtly rock and roll feel on the album is on "Jump Into The Fire," the track that was sequenced to follow "Let the Good Times Roll." It kicks off with a punchy bass riff from Herbie Flowers, who recalled: "There was only Harry at the piano, with Jim Gordon in the drum booth, and Chris Spedding on guitar. The directive was: 'lots of tom-toms, a bass riff in D major.' That's what we did, with Harry singing little bits, like verse and chorus."[32] Flowers's pulsating bass line sets the pace, and late in the number he slackens off the strings, creating a remarkable effect by detuning the instrument after a thudding drum solo from Jim Gordon.

"I remember thinking that we're two-thirds through a really good take and now Herbie decides to start clowning around and Richard's going to make us do yet another take," remembered Chris Spedding. "But Herbie had judged his moment perfectly. That take was the keeper."[33] As it happened, Flowers himself had no intention of doing anything unusual; he really was just clowning around: "The fade went on a bit, and normally the engineer would say 'thank-*yew*!' through the headset and then we'd stop. But as it happened, the order to stop never came, so for a laugh I slowly detuned the bottom string until it was flapping about. A bit silly really—just the sort of thing us musos would do at that time. No real reaction from those up in the control tower, but ever since, forums, discussion groups, bass magazines, keep contacting me for inside information."[34] On the finished track, there is a wild guitar solo from John Uribe, backed up by Spedding, with some extra rhythm guitar playing added by Klaus Voormann. Spedding continued: "Uribe was hanging around the studio waiting for us to record the track so he could do his overdubs. He never played on the backing tracks with us."[35]

In its extended album form, the song is a rock jam, lasting a full seven minutes. But the most remarkable thing about the track is Nilsson's vocal. Instead of the angelic choral perfection of his early efforts with Jarrard, this is a shattered chandelier of sound, fragments of voice darting in every direction, like an aural kaleidoscope turning at speed. Syllables of the relatively simplistic lyric are picked up and echoed, and the cries of "Wooo-a" are split apart in a forest of delayed overdubs.

A three-and-a-half-minute single version of the song was released by RCA, with the jam session elements curtailed and a reprise of the vocal leading into the final fade. Despite its dramatic difference from "Without You," it duly climbed to number twenty-seven in the U.S. charts. When asked to comment on the contrast, Nilsson said, "My earlier stuff had more soul, only it was more subtle."[36]

The remainder of the London sessions was devoted to four more Nilsson originals, which were among the demos he had cut in very rough form. Some were more complete than others, but in most cases they were fragments of a minute or so. However, because their trawl of music publishers had drawn a blank, Perry was forced to try to make something of Nilsson's own writing, however sketchy. One of Perry's talents has always been to construct beautifully finished performances from recorded fragments, and it is a technique he has used with various singers over the years with considerable success. Yet to rely on this for such a high proportion of an album was risky, even for him. In some cases, there was a verse and no chorus. In others, maybe a chorus section with no bridge. Nevertheless, Perry set to, and with the backing musicians, he created instrumental tracks that added structure and form to Nilsson's ideas. He recalled:

I'd cut every track as if it were a full-blown song, And finally, when it came time for him to do the vocals, well, we had one slight problem. No lyrics. And then he lay down on the floor of the studio propping himself up on his elbow with his head resting on his hand, and a sheet of paper on the floor and started to just write the lyrics. And so in fifteen minutes he had lyrics. He had no alternative. He was forced to do it. We had to do the vocals and we had to move on. So that's how most of the songs for that album came about. It's just one of those things that you never know when the magic can suddenly appear.[37]

Even before Nilsson could cut his lyrics, he had had to teach the songs to the band. Chris Spedding described the process: "Harry would play us the tune we were to work with on the piano, sometimes singing so we'd get an idea of the song. No charts. Rhythm section only—no horns. Once we'd got the so-called 'perfect take' there was usually no overdubbing or dropping in."[38] It was these rhythm section backing tracks that Perry then extended into more conventional song structures for Nilsson's new lyrics, although the most complete of the songs, "Coconut," already existed as an almost finished set of lyrics on the demo. The new version added a few more repetitions of the line "Put the lime in the coconut and drink them both up," but in essence the song remained the same, with Nilsson impersonating the three voices of the narrator, the woman who drinks the mixture, and the doctor who gives her advice. Originally he had intended to sing the whole piece with just his own voice, but Perry persuaded him while he was cutting the demo to try the contrasting impersonations, and this was so successful that it carried through onto the final record.[39]

He and Diane had been on a short holiday in Hawaii the previous year, and he had scribbled down the word "coconut" on a matchbook, thinking that it would be a great word to use in a lyric. On returning home, he recalled:

I was in L.A. driving along the Freeway when I picked up the matches. I started writing the song in the car. Then I made it like the cause is the cure. You put a lime in a coconut, it makes you sick, you call the doctor and he tells you, "Well, put a lime in a coconut and call me in the morning."[40]

The idea was one that Nilsson had toyed with for some time. His papers include a collection of miscellaneous "Quotes, quips and observations," and among various similar sketches from this period are the lines:

Whisky makes you sick when you are well.
Whisky when you're sick makes you well.[41]

"Coconut" encapsulated the same idea, and in Perry's imaginative production, the somewhat two-dimensional demo sprang into life. Replacing Nilsson's finger-picked acoustic guitar on the demo was the electric guitar of Caleb Quaye (son of the famous entertainer and singer Cab Kaye), and joining him on acoustic guitar was Ian Duck. Both these musicians were in the band Hookfoot, which had grown out of Elton John's accompanying band from the late 1960s. Backed by Jim Gordon and Herbie Flowers, the subtle interplay between the two guitars builds up an intense backing track, allowing Nilsson to extend his vocal pyrotechnics toward the end, as the woman's screams to her doctor become more extreme. According to Flowers, this was an example of Perry's patient assembly of the perfect track from several takes:

We ran "Coconut" over and over, like you do on RP [Richard Perry] sessions. A bit of a roast-up really, in a funny key [the entire song is just on a C7 chord], and not a lot of room for anything other than a repetitive bass part. I found it, and still do, quite difficult not adding little twiddly bits. So, amongst all the takes, RP edited the best bits together, and then at a later date got other players in to overdub their bits, then redid the voice, and Bob's your uncle, another masterpiece.[42]

This was to be the third single from the album, and it climbed to number eight on the U.S. charts in 1972.[43]

Much more work was needed to transform the two sketchy verses of "Driving Along" into a full-scale song, and here the Perry/Nilsson collaboration functioned at its best. There is one startling chord change in Nilsson's original verse, where the song moves a tone up from its home key of C to D major. A new bridge section introduced by Perry deliberately creates the reverse effect by dropping the home key a tone to B flat for eight bars before returning gradually to C. This serves to create a momentary pause, a dreamy reflection on all the people jamming the freeways in their cars and increasingly alienated from one another. Nilsson's hastily sketched-out hallucinogenic linking lines about driving at "fifty seven thousand miles an hour" and the Zen-like "Look at all those people standing on the petals of a flower" leading to a "petal to the metal" pun catches the mood of this new musical section perfectly, before a guitar solo relaunches the original vocal.

A final chorus built out of earlier lines from the song reconstructed into the repetitive "They seem to say nothing / They seem to go nowhere" adds a dynamic closing section. Few better examples exist of their intuitive understanding of one another, Perry taking the chance to create new musical sections of a song, and Nilsson reacting spontaneously with witty verses that extend and deepen his original message. The partnership with Tipton had seen many of Nilsson's sketchy ideas develop into finished songs, but always more deliberately and less spontaneously than this.

The new lyrics added to "The Moonbeam Song" actually amounted to no words at all. But Perry tweaked the structure of the song, and he needed a new linking verse to fit between the reprise of the two main stanzas, in the same way that the verse "On a fence with bits of crap around its bottom" does the first time around. As a result, Nilsson provided a glorious chorus of multitracked "ooohs" and "aaahs" that slide in during the repeat of the main "Have you ever watched a moonbeam" section and then become an abstract musical collage of linking tissue. Perry commented:

> To this day, I have no idea what it's about, but that sometimes happens with some of Harry's songs. But even if you don't know what it's about, all you have to do is listen to the blending of the vocals. His vocal prowess was extraordinary. He could do things that even Lennon and McCartney didn't do.[44]

The backing track for the next piece they worked on, "Down," is a ballsy, bluesy contrast to the "Moonbeam Song." Anchored by Nilsson's rocking piano, it is propelled by the drums of both Keltner and Gordon, Voormann's bass, and Spedding's guitar, plus a few snatches of organ. But it really starts to rock with the overdubbed brass of Jim Price. In contrast to the minimalism of "Early in the Morning," although the main section is also a twelve-bar blues, this song mirrors the feel of Ray Charles's backing band rather than his vocal delivery. Price had recently been on the road playing in the brass section for the Rolling Stones and also with Eric Clapton. At this point in 1971, he was well on his way to being one of the top session players in the world. Here his contribution lifts the track into something exceptional. Not much was added to the words except for one line: "You've gotta give love, or love will walk away." The addition of this brought an extra level of meaning to the lyric, which otherwise might be interpreted only as a somewhat guilt-ridden description of oral sex. ("You gotta have soap to wash your sins away....")

"Down" was the final track to be included on the album. Perry's next task was to decide on an order for the music. In the LP era, he felt this was a very different process from more recent times. He liked the concept of a vinyl record having two acts, in a theatrical sense, in which each side or act had a deliberate sequence. It was something he had really begun to think about in his work with Tiny Tim, and by the time he came to make *Nilsson Schmilsson*, the order of songs and the opening and closing of each side had become important, in a way that is hard for present-day listeners to conceive now that CDs are produced in a single long sequence of tracks.[45]

The two acts of *Nilsson Schmilsson* were carefully arranged. Perry had already decided that "The Moonbeam Song" would lead into "Down" as the closer for side one, and he preceded it with "Gotta Get Up" as the opener, followed by "Driving Along," still alert but with a touch of whimsicality, and then "Early in the Morning." The second side was opened by "Without You" and concluded with Tipton's "I'll Never Leave You." In between, the tension was gradually increased with "Coconut," "Let the Good Times Roll," and "Jump Into The Fire." This proved a winning formula, and the album spent the best part of a year on the album charts, its highest weekly position at number three.

Success with the public did not necessarily mean success with the critics, particularly those who had enjoyed Nilsson's earlier albums and some of his more introspective lyrics. The widely syndicated music writer David Proctor, who had been a strong supporter of Nilsson, wrote:

> I think that if I were to take a stab at what's different about this album it would be that it is less intellectual. The immaculate production by Richard Perry is there. The top session men are there. Nilsson's delicate multi-tracked voice is there. And the album is fun to listen to. But is that all? In this case I think it is.[46]

But he was in a minority, and although the wide range of styles on the record made it harder to categorize Nilsson than ever before, there was definitely a sense that he had moved firmly from gentle country-meets-folk-meets-rock territory to being a rock and roll singer, with the added bonus that "Without You" was a ballad performance of which any popular singer in any genre would have been proud. "When we did 'Without You,'" said Perry, "I would say that at that point he was arguably the finest white male singer on the planet."[47] Whereas Nilsson had addressed the turmoil in particular aspects of his own life directly on his previous albums in songs such as "1941," "Without Her," and "Daddy's Song," *Nilsson Schmilsson* was altogether a more complex psychological mix. *Rolling Stone*'s Bud Scoppa accurately observed: "He continues to develop a performing personality that is at once ambiguous—some would say schizophrenic—maddening, wide-ranging and remarkably engaging. With the child-like openness of some of his songs, there is about Nilsson a mysterious core."[48]

If there was one slight hint in the album that this might be a turning point in Nilsson's career, it was in the cover photography, which was once again by Dean Torrence. On the back was an open refrigerator, packed with food and drink. This would be the basis of an imaginative advertising campaign by RCA, which used the design to promote the singles drawn from the album, suggesting that each would be the next item to be taken from Nilsson's fridge.[49]

But on the front, instead of the clean-cut, suited Nilsson of *Pandemonium Shadow Show* or the boyish images of *Aerial Ballet* and *Harry*, a disheveled, bearded Nilsson dressed in a brown robe and holding a pipe looks slightly away from the camera. Shifting his music into rock and roll territory also mirrored the fact that he was increasingly embracing the rock and roll lifestyle. Diane Nilsson recalled that the moment they arrived in London for the *Nilsson Schmilsson* sessions, "we were immediately given uppers and downers by people I'd never met."[50]

Nilsson's use of cocaine had, according to Diane, also increased after the Newman sessions. But as well as the pills and the hard drugs, he was introduced to the alcohol-fueled lifestyle of the London music scene. If they were not playing on record sessions at all hours of the day and night, one or two of the musicians with whom Nilsson recorded would be hanging out close to Trident in Soho. The majority of the British players, particularly those who had families, went home. "There was no hanging out," remembered Chris Spedding. "It was back home or on to another session."[51] Flowers, who noted that the rate for a three-hour session in 1971 was a princely twelve pounds, said that although he had been lucky enough to be on successful records with Blue Mink and Elton John, he was just one of the city's pool of dozens of similar players. Many of them were, like him, "leftover jazzers" from the previous decade when Soho had offered plenty of jobs to traditional and modern jazz players, and all of them were "terribly busy, sober, family types.... I packed my gear up, shook hands with Harry and Jim, waved to Richard and the engineer and went home."[52]

However, some of the others who played on the *Nilsson Schmilsson* sessions, particularly American visitors to London such as Bobby Keys, might stroll a couple of blocks to Ronnie Scott's jazz club on Frith Street, which was open until 3.30 a.m., or they might see what was happening a few paces in the other direction at the Marquee, where, during June 1971, Keef Hartley, Mungo Jerry, and Amazing Blondel were among the bands appearing.[53] Both these clubs had recently acquired late-night licenses to sell alcohol, and virtually any session player would be welcome at the bar. It was an eye-opener for Diane Nilsson:

> I'd never seen anything like that in L.A. It seemed like the musicians over there could just drink Harry under the table. I never saw musicians in L.A. go around with bottles of stuff, you know, like some of them over there did. So maybe they did and I just didn't see it, but I saw it in London. They were heavy, heavy, heavy drinking guys, like Bobby Keys.[54]

At the end of June, Nilsson and Diane returned from Britain to Los Angeles. The late-night London lifestyle gave way to carousing on home ground, the British beer and Scotch whisky replaced by wine and tequila. Samantha Juste saw a change in Nilsson when he returned from the U.K. She recalled him being "on a destructive course," in contrast to Diane.

> She was very lovely, very patient, and very calm, Diane. She could handle it very well. She had a little baby at that time. Well, we both did. But she was pretty amazing I think. She wasn't a big drug taker either. I never remember her being out of control ever. But it obviously took its toll on her, because this was not her normal

mode of operation. She was much more a together person. I think she was good for him, but he just went so off the wall. There was a big change in Harry and it wasn't for the better. Harry was destructive to himself and he knew it was destructive. There was something tragic in his soul, and that came from the background he had really. He talked to me a lot about it and it was terribly touching.[55]

Nilsson had not been back in America for long when a call came from Stanley Dorfman in London reminding him of his commitment to make a television special for the BBC. Again, Nilsson demurred, saying that he did not want to do a live performance for the BBC or anyone else. But, according to Nilsson, Dorfman was as convincing as he had been when he visited the singer's house the previous year: "[In] a gentle, persuasive way [he] said we could do the first *In Concert* without an audience. That I found appealing and attractive. And a first-class ride back to my favorite city, London."[56]

The *In Concert* series was taped at the Television Theatre in Shepherd's Bush, West London, a former Stoll theater built in 1903 that was bought by the BBC specifically because it was close to the Television Centre studio complex. Unlike the corporation's own studios, it was capable of holding a sizable audience of up to 2,000. For the Nilsson show, Stanley Dorfman manufactured an audience by taking clips of audiences filmed there for other shows and cutting them in. Between his songs, Nilsson did suitable bows and acknowledgments as if there was a real crowd present, except that from time to time Dorfman shut off the applause like a faucet, and it is obvious that the sound is canned.

For the majority of the concert, Nilsson either sat at the piano, playing and singing, or accompanied himself on the guitar, with a selection of songs from all of his previous albums including *Nilsson Schmilsson*. A small television monitor atop the piano introduces a couple of clips from *The Point*, but there are also two places in the show where Nilsson and Dorfman pushed technology to the limit. On a version of the Everly Brothers' "Walk Right Back," Nilsson appears sitting next to himself at the piano singing a close-harmony second part and showing in the process that he could deliver the lyrics more beautifully than the famous brothers. After the first chorus, a third Nilsson appears on the right of the screen, with only his head visible above the piano, and interpolates the lyrics from another Everly Brothers song, "Cathy's Clown." These continue as an underlying harmony while Nilssons one and two continue with the original song. Nilssons two and three also contribute a brief harmonica duet, and whereas the central Nilsson is dressed in a blue sweater, the outer Nilssons wear fawn-colored jackets. The three Nilssons conclude the medley with "Let the Good Times Roll." Since 1971, television technology has advanced considerably, but at the time, using the technique of shooting against a blue background to superimpose images, as Stanley Dorfman pointed out, had never been done on a pop music program before:

The three Harrys was the first time we'd used blue screen actually, which was something the BBC news department did. But we'd never attempted to do anything like that. So that was great fun. The Television Theatre wasn't actually set up to do blue screen, so we put it in. We took great pains to do one take, and then you had to roll the tape back. You couldn't do it in editing, you had to do it live. Roll the tape back and do the next one, and then roll the tape back again to do the last one.[57]

The idea was entirely Nilsson's, but it was up to Dorfman and the technical team to make it work, even if the central Harry seems to fade somewhat as the third and final version of himself appears. In setting up these routines, they were nodding in the direction of the experimental American comedian Ernie Kovacs, who had died just seven years before in an accident. In particular, the reaction shots of the audience, whom Nilsson quells with a single hand gesture before launching into the piano introduction to "Walk Right Back," and the final cut to a sleeping audience (made up of members of the crew) with a solitary Nilsson applauding himself, are typical of Kovacs's desire to break down barriers between artist and audience on screen. Just as Nilsson admired Laurel and Hardy (the third Nilsson in the superimposed sequence ends his appearance with a Stan Laurel head scratch), he was a great Kovacs fan, especially his all-gorilla version of *Swan Lake*. So, in a further tribute, Nilsson donned a gorilla suit and was again shot as three separate characters, one playing piano, one guitar, and one percussion for "Coconut."

"What we forgot to do at the end of it," said Dorfman, "was to reveal who he was, and take the heads off, so the audience could see they were all Harry. They just could have been three actors. It didn't really matter because we made it all up."[58]

The audience walks out before the end, which was just the beginning of what Nilsson conceived as a self-deprecating conclusion to the show. Dorfman felt that he should build himself up as a star, but for live-performance-hating Nilsson, this was not what he had in mind.

We ended the first show with something that was absolutely his idea. He said, "There's a scene in Orson Welles' *Citizen Kane* where the lady's singing on stage." She was supposed to be an opera singer. "And there's a slow pan up from the singing up into the rafters. And there are two scene men standing on the gantry, and one holds his nose. If only we could get that! At the end of my show, let's do that!"

I said, "Why would you want to put yourself down like that?"

He said, "It'd be fun!"

I said, "How are we going to get that? The copyright will be a fortune."

But we found that the BBC had a copy of it. So we just used it without telling anybody, and we never told anybody. I've never admitted it to this day! So there's this scene from *Citizen Kane*, and then at the end of it, Harry said, "Do you think we can get a cream pie? At the end of this thing, smash me in the face with a cream pie!"

I said, "What are you doing? This is absurd. We're trying to sell you. Nobody knows you, and you're trying to be a clown."

"No," he said, "I'd really like to do that."

So at the end we smashed him in the face with a cream pie with my name on it.[59]

The "Music of Harry Nilsson" edition of *In Concert* was broadcast by the BBC on January 1, 1972,[60] immediately after midnight on New Year's Eve, making it the first television show of the year. In contrast to the disheveled figure on the *Nilsson Schmilsson* cover, it showed a youthful, slender Nilsson with a neatly trimmed beard and a shortish haircut, clearly identifiable as the young man who had appeared in *The Ghost and Mrs. Muir* or who had lip-synched his way through tracks from *Pandemonium Shadow Show* and *Aerial Ballet* on his second visit to London in 1968. It remains the only extended portrait of Nilsson actually performing (rather than miming) a sizable cross-section of his early work, and it suggests that he would have been a very effective live performer had he chosen to follow that route. Indeed, Stanley Dorfman recalls that during the time Nilsson was in London recording and editing the show, he was very happy to be the warm-up man for live music programs such as *Top of the Pops*. He would come on, sing songs, tell gags, do his Stan Laurel impression, and work the audience into a good mood, just as long as he was never required to do the same thing in front of the cameras.[61]

In Concert was recorded several months ahead of its transmission, and by the time it was shown, *Nilsson Schmilsson* had been released for almost three months. It had come out in the United States in October as part of RCA's "New For Yule" promotion, along with *Bark* by Jefferson Airplane, *Hunky Dory* by David Bowie, and *Aerie* by John Denver.[62] Nilsson and Richard Perry had become firm friends during the making of the album. Immediately after the recording had been finished in London, they went on holiday together. And on their return to Los Angeles, they continued the friendship. "We were best pals," recalled Perry. "We hung out together all the time. We traveled together. We had a blast. We partied together. There wasn't anything we didn't do together. And we worked together and I was looking forward to a lifetime of hits."[63]

Both men presented the album to RCA's top executives in the early fall ahead of the release, and at that meeting Perry insisted that "Without You" be the first single to be released. It was backed with "Gotta Get Up," and Perry was horrified when he discovered that in the run-up to the key Christmas holiday sales period, the company was promoting the B-side harder than the main song because it was "easier to get on the radio."[64] Eventually, as RCA threw its marketing muscle behind the right song, "Without You"—reviewed by *Billboard*[65] as "by far his most driving rock ballad in some time"—went to number one on the U.S. pop charts on February 13, 1972. It was Nilsson's first number-one hit.

The success of the track meant that RCA began to put a lot of additional weight behind both the single and the album. By mid-March, the song was also number one in the U.K. In an effort to push its sales farther afield, Nilsson and Perry were flown to Japan early in 1972. While they were there, Perry found himself standing next to the company's vice president, Rocco Laginestra. Was there anything he wanted or needed for the next album that he and Nilsson would make, the vice president wanted to know. Perry joked about a raise in his percentage, but the next day he decided to ask if the making of the album could be filmed. RCA agreed.[66]

The date for recording the second LP, eventually to be entitled *Son of Schmilsson*, was set for a four-week period in March and April 1972, nine months after Perry and Nilsson's first London sessions. Again they were to return to Trident. Playing with a film crew in attendance was going to make working in the studio more difficult, and Perry was anxious to avoid the whole exercise being somewhat self-conscious. However, he convinced himself that *Nilsson Schmilsson* was just a stepping stone toward greater things, and that they could repeat its considerable commercial and artistic success with a promotional movie as part of the bargain. Those feelings were reinforced when "Without You" won a Grammy for best male vocal and in the same round of Grammies was nominated for record of the year. *Nilsson Schmilsson* was also nominated as album of the year, only to be narrowly beaten by George Harrison's *A Concert for Bangladesh*.

But Perry had not anticipated a dramatic transformation in Nilsson. Fueled by his increasing intake of alcohol and narcotics, he was becoming a changed man. Diane Nilsson saw the gradual alteration in his personality firsthand:

I don't think Harry handled success well. I think that the more successful he became, the more he drank. And when *Nilsson Schmilsson* became his biggest hit, he had everything he wanted. [There was] the Grammy it got, and he just went really downhill then. By 1972 he was a snarly, angry, person, and he didn't look healthy. He looked bloated. He was just really drinking a lot. I look back at pictures and even in '71 he looked good. He didn't look good in '72.[67]

When they got to London, Nilsson was drinking a bottle of brandy a day. Diane had been shocked when she saw the amounts the session players drank the previous year. Now she was appalled that her husband's intake exceeded theirs, and she felt even more aghast on one isolated occasion when Nilsson and Derek Taylor snorted heroin in front of her. Soon he was staying away after the sessions, preferring to hang out and drink with the musicians or other friends than to be with his family. As the sessions continued, Diane remained the loyal wife, sending out for Chinese food during the recordings, laughing with everyone about his eccentric habit of wearing an odd pair of baseball shoes (one striped and one plain), and hosting visits from pressmen such as Keith Altham of *New Musical Express*. He described her as "an attractive lady with long hair and nice teeth, a whole lot smarter than her all-purpose smile might suggest."[68]

Behind her all-purpose smile, their marriage was falling apart, and immediately after the recordings were done, Diane packed her bags and took Zak back to Los Angeles, leaving Nilsson for good. Thirty years after the events described in "1941," Nilsson's wife had "walked right out the door." They separated on July 1, 1972, and Nilsson eventually filed for divorce on July 25 the following year.[69]

At the time, Nilsson was well aware that his marriage was on the rocks, but instead of modifying his behavior in London, he carried on drinking and taking whatever drugs came his way. In the company of his fellow musicians, and above all his producer, instead of making light of his pain with a quip as he had so often done in the past, he fell apart emotionally. Perry was surprised:

I had the greatest expectations for the *Son of Schmilsson* album. Unfortunately, that's when Harry hit, or started to approach, a low point in his life. He was just separating from his wife, Diane. And it hit him really hard. I don't quite understand to this day why it hit him so hard. Because it wasn't like he was heartbroken. So, I felt like saying, "What's your problem? Let's live and let live. It didn't work out. It happens to everybody." But he…maybe interpreted it as some failure in him. I don't know. I tried to talk to him about it. But unfortunately the way he would respond to it was to begin what was a downward spiral for the rest of his life. It was the beginning of the end. He would show up to the studio with a half bottle of cognac, the first half had already been consumed that afternoon.[70]

The excessive alcohol and the emotional upheaval of his wife and son's departure played on the insecure side of Nilsson's character. Instead of exuding confidence from his success, he became withdrawn and uncooperative. What started out as an even-handed collaboration with Perry, similar to that of the previous album, became increasingly uneven, as Nilsson refused to do vocal retakes and was unwilling to think about restructuring any of his songs. Whereas a year earlier, Perry might have suggested a new bridge or a reshaped verse, all his suggestions were flatly refused. He tried subtle persuasion, reiterating that they were a team and that their best work came from collaboration not confrontation, but it was to no avail.[71]

Despite all Perry's goading, Nilsson did not alter his behavior. His idea of the potential single from the album was his angry, brutal song "You're Breakin' My Heart." The lyrics are generally interpreted as pouring out his distress at Diane's departure, but also at his own responsibility for what happened. So that while his wife is blamed for stepping on his ass, breaking his glasses, and driving his car, he makes it plain that:

All I want to do
Is have a good time…
I'm goin' insane
There's no-one to blame.

So far it was saleable, but in 1972, there was barely a radio station in the world that would play a song with the chorus:

> You're breakin' my heart
> You're tearing it apart
> So fuck you.

The overwrought atmosphere in the studio when this was recorded comes across in the documentary film of the session that (thanks to Rocco Laginestra's agreement) was shot at the time and never officially released, called *Did Somebody Drop His Mouse?* Having cut the backing track (with Beatle George Harrison in the lineup on slide guitar), Nilsson and the horn section of Price, Keys, and Klaus Voormann (playing tenor saxophone) work on a drunken dance routine for the camera. As the horns sway in step like a throwback to the Jimmie Lunceford Orchestra, Nilsson swings an old radio microphone that pivots on its stand as if it were some kind of slender saxophone. As Nilsson admits in the soundtrack (dubbed a year later by himself and Perry), the final version of the dance—at the end of which Voormann imitates a dying saxophonist, collapsing on the floor—was done after four bottles of brandy.

Most commentators have focused on "You're Breakin' My Heart" as the one song that expressed Nilsson's emotional torment about Diane's departure. However, there is another interpretation, which was that it represented his first quarrel with the Beatle (and occasional member of the backing group on this album) with whom he would eventually have the longest, closest relationship, namely Ringo Starr. There are coded references to Starr and their social life together, notably in the lines:

> You wanna boogaloo
> Run down to Tramps
> Have a dance or two.

The reference to the Beatles' "Drive My Car" is another clue to this possible interpretation. Yet it was clear that the split from Diane was the major event in his emotional life at the time, and more than any other album in his entire catalogue, the collected songs on *Son of Schmilsson* laid bare his soul, from the angst of this marital split to his troubled upbringing, his earlier relationships, and even his anxieties about the future and old age. This emotional range was not readily apparent at the time, at least not to commentators such as *Rolling Stone*'s critic Stephen Holden, who, used to the whimsical air of Nilsson's earlier work, commented: "Life is just a silly, meaningless jumble of dreams and memories, OK—but where is the hurt and disappointment that infuses such a vision?" He saw the entire album as an essay in deadpan humor, to which it was difficult to relate on a more than superficial level. In a somewhat unintentional direct hit on one of Nilsson's emotional wounds by playing on the "Son of..." in the album title, he concluded: "Stop trying to impress 'daddy' by playing childish practical jokes."[72] Nilsson had always hidden his true feelings behind humor to some extent, but all five songs on the first side of the album in one way or other vividly express rejection, misunderstanding, or nostalgia for good times lost.

The opener, "Take 54" (its title an ironic reference to Perry's habit of recording plenty of takes, compounded by a moment in the film of the session where he says "I think we'll pick take 49"), was almost as musically strong a song as "You're Breakin' My Heart," but its prospects as a hit were equally hampered by its lyrics. It is an old-fashioned rock and roll piece with gutsy sax from Bobby Keys, propulsive drumming from Ringo Starr (under the pseudonym "Richie Snare"), and some outstanding piano from Nicky Hopkins. Nilsson's lyric—set in a recording studio—implores "Baby, baby come back, I need you to make a good track." Even if the idea of trying one's best to make a good take in a studio was not normal lyrical subject matter, the same streak of anti-commercialism and crude content, as in "You're Breaking My Heart," surfaces again, as if to destroy any real chance of commercial success with the song. It starts with Nilsson eyeing a girl and thinking

If I wanted to get in it
Then I'd have to get on it.
I sang my balls off for you baby
I worked my fingers to the bone.

An audience that had fallen in love with Nilsson's romantic voice on "Without You" was not necessarily going to be enchanted by this. Yet it is not hard to see the entire lyric as an exhortation to Diane to stay with him in the studio and help him make a better album. When he reaches the final high note, he wakes up to find he is alone and that the whole experience has been a dream.

"Remember (Christmas)," the second track on the album, is in the vein of Nilsson's much earlier exercises in nostalgic reminiscence, from "Growin' Up" to "Without Her." In the documentary film of the sessions, he can be seen recording this while sitting side by side with Nicky Hopkins at the piano, experiencing the unusual sensation of another pianist playing for him with no backing band. According to Keith Altham who was present in the studio, it took twenty-five attempts to arrive at "a really beautiful take, which is not going to be bettered."[73] Yet they went on, trying again and again, including a version that had "the kind of vocal gymnastics that leave most people gasping for breath, he hits impossible notes." Clearly, this intense way of working and the added strain of the cameras made it a difficult job for Nilsson, and he comments on the movie soundtrack that he and Hopkins would anticipate one another or hang back, giving even the finally issued version of the song a rather unusual ebb and flow. The lyrics, however, pick up directly on the concept from "Take 54" of love being a dream, and the listener is urged to remember that "life is just a memory." Again, there is a sense of loss and regret for not attaining "all that life can be."

It is, however, beautifully sung, with Nilsson using all his range. The seasoned string arranger Del Newman supplied some subtle string quartet backing, which Perry added after the original duo recording, and there is also some delicate bouzouki playing from Chris Spedding, who recalled: "I think I must've had the bouzouki with me in the studio one day and I was tinkering around with it and Richard thought he could find some use for it!"[74] It was eventually released as the second single from the album and climbed somewhat disappointingly to number fifty-three on the U.S. pop charts.[75]

In total contrast, the next song is "Joy," a tongue-in-cheek country-and-western parody that Nilsson delivers just seriously enough to be convincing. Part of the lyric is spoken in a deep Johnny Cash-like voice, and the chorus is sung by two Nilssons in close harmony (complete with authentic sobs), with yet another lyric about the loss of a girlfriend:

Joy to the world was a beautiful girl
But to me Joy meant only sorrow.

In due course, Nilsson persuaded RCA to let him release this song as an additional single on its country music list under the pseudonym "Buck Earl." This was an in-joke because John Voight's character in *Midnight Cowboy* was "Joe Buck," the song had a cowboy feel, and the B-side was an unmodified "I Guess the Lord Must Be in New York City."

The prequel to "You're Breaking My Heart" is a gentle Nilsson composition called "Turn on Your Radio," which is on the surface an open letter to a former girlfriend whom he has left, beginning:

I don't know where I'm going
Now that I am gone.

Given the circumstances of Nilsson's separation from Diane, it becomes a plea from a musician who wants his ex-lover to hear him on the radio or on her record player, as his life soon "will be gone." The low-key setting has a simple repetitive figure played delicately by Klaus Voormann and the twenty-two-year-old guitarist Peter Frampton, who had already collaborated with George Harrison and been in the band Humble Pie. "It was the first time I'd met Peter," said Chris Spedding. "I always thought him overlooked and underrated as a guitarist and a solid musician."[76] Nicky Hopkins provided some minimal piano, and some subtle brass playing was added in when Perry returned to Hollywood, under the expert direction of Kirby Johnson.[77]

The second side of the album moved a little away from the recurring theme of separation and loss, although "The Lottery Song" is a series of speculations about how a young couple might spend their winnings if they were they to have a lucky ticket. It is tempting to think of this being Nilsson's wish for another chance in love, given that "life is just a gamble." In the movie of the session, Nilsson explains that he wrote the tune the day before it was recorded, and he is seen teaching the piece to the backing musicians, clearly inhibited by the camera and "the band just looking at me."[78] Yet when he came to record it, Nilsson's voice on the main vocal was as clear and precise as on "Remember (Christmas)" and "Turn on Your Radio." In addition, the song has some of Nilsson's most ambitious vocal overdubs of the album. Percussionist Ray Cooper, who had been introduced to Nilsson by George Harrison a year or two earlier, was playing on the track. He remembered vividly the moment that Nilsson put down the vocal:

The voice was extraordinary and clear, a boy's choir voice in a man. Absolutely beautiful—a surgical instrument because it would heal you. You felt an overwhelming wave of warmth. You would work on the backing tracks, and as soon as Harry would go into the booth (we used to record almost live in those days), you had your headphones on and that voice would come through and you almost couldn't play, it was so beautiful, seriously beautiful.[79]

It is hard to disagree with Cooper about the quality of Nilsson's voice, although one or two of the backing harmonies might have benefited from a retake, as there are odd moments when Nilsson's usually faultless sense of pitch wavered slightly. But this was the least of Richard Perry's problems. By now he was searching for potential hits on the album and not finding anything that had the clear winning formula of "Without You."

He was determined to do things the way *he* wanted to, on that album, although even his worst songs had a lot of charm about them. He had a song on there called "The Lottery Song," which was a lovely little ditty, but, [I said to him] "Come on, this isn't where we should be. We shouldn't be recording 'The Lottery Song.'" Even though it could be fine if it was the 11th or 12th track on the album. But there weren't the killer songs, and the killer tracks on there that there should have been.[80]

Perry believed that the song that they selected as the closing piece for the album had huge potential as a hit. "The Most Beautiful World in the World" is mainly a love song to the planet, but as Nilsson had written it, the romantic element of the song was preceded by a quasi-comic reggae parody. Perry's instincts told him to separate the two. He knew that in a three-minute pop record, if the opening half of the song is a Jamaican send-up, *that* would *be* the song in most people's minds. Perry argued with Nilsson to make the cut, but he would have none of it:

The first half of it didn't do anything for me, but the second half made me swoon. And he refused to drop the first half. It's vintage Harry, creating circumstances to shoot himself in the foot. If he's determined that this song has to have this sort of Reggae type first half, it's like two different songs. But "The Most Beautiful World in the World," is some of the finest lyrics and melody that he's ever written. It's just gorgeous.[81]

As well as being unable to give this song the shape he felt it deserved, Perry also had to go along with Nilsson's farewell lines of the song:

Tell her she's beautiful
Roll the world over
And give her a kiss and a feel.

The effect of the crude final line after a lush, beautifully produced orchestral ballad, coupled with the split personality of the piece, made this into another loser as a hit. In the movie shot at the time, Nilsson delivers the closing words wearing a top hat and tails above the waist and only his underwear below—an unintentionally apt comment on the punch line, which is surrounded by the harps and choirs of the closing titles of a Hollywood love story. Yet Perry put all he could into the recording, transferring production to the larger CTS Studio in London and bringing in a symphony orchestra to surround Nilsson, who wore the bathrobe from the *Nilsson Schmilsson* cover and smoked a cigarette held elegantly in the air as he crooned into the microphone. The forty-piece orchestra and twenty-four singers were contracted by string arranger Del Newman, who rehearsed them in a morning session and then conducted the first part of the afternoon before Perry took over the baton, as he had done for Tiny Tim's concerts in London's Royal Albert Hall (which Nilsson had attended). The arrival of the film crew delayed the final recording until the closing minutes of the afternoon, but the results show exactly why Perry was so keen on this romantic second element of the song.[82] Although in the months that followed Perry would be firmly against the idea of giving a similar orchestral treatment to standard songs, in many respects this track prefigures the following year's *A Little Touch of Schmilsson in the Night*, with a symphony orchestra directed by Gordon Jenkins, that was made after Perry and Nilsson had gone their separate ways.

The next most complex piece of production after "The Most Beautiful World in the World" was "I'd Rather Be Dead." The song is a rage against old age, about never wanting to attain the state of decrepitude that goes along with bedwetting and the inability to tie one's tie in the morning. "You will be tempted to laugh when you first hear it," wrote critic David Proctor, "but it suddenly becomes sobering."[83] The reason for the sudden sobriety is that it is sung not only by Nilsson, but by a sizable choir of fifty-five senior citizens aged between sixty and ninety drawn from a couple of clubs in the outer London suburbs of Pinner and Stepney. Encouraging a choir of elderly people to sing "I'd rather be dead than wet my bed" might be regarded as a colossal exercise in bad taste. However, partly because (as documented in a running series of scenes in *Did Somebody Drop His Mouse?*) the pensioners had a jolly day out with a coach trip to the studio, and partly because Nilsson then turned the recording itself into a party, the final effect is of cheating death and making the most of one's final years. Everyone was given a paper hat, a badge, and a liberal helping of sherry, so that when Nilsson (in a new suit and kipper tie) turned up, there was an impromptu chorus of "Everyone's Wild About Harry."[84]

The track as it appeared on the record has the atmosphere of a club social evening, with Nilsson as an entertainer leading a community sing-along. The effect is compounded by the deliberately simplistic accompaniment, with accordionist Henry Krein prominently featured in a quartet that also included Klaus Voormann on bass and an elegantly attired and buttonholed Richard Perry on piano. (Some discreet brass chords were added to the ending by Kirby Johnson during post-production in Hollywood.) As a tragicomic set piece for the never-to-be-issued movie of the sessions, the number is a triumph. But it is not the hit that Perry was looking for. This left four other possibilities, a loping, bluesy song called "What's Your Sign?" (which featured prominently in the movie), a remake of the 1955 doo-wop hit for the El Dorados, "At My Front Door," an antiwar song called "Ambush," and finally a new Nilsson piece called "Spaceman."

In retrospect, "What's Your Sign?" (which Nilsson eventually remade in an otiose arrangement by Perry Botkin for his 1975 album *Duit On Mon Dei*) would seem to have been an obvious candidate for the charts. It has a slightly sinister (and what would more recently be considered very sexist) lyric, in which Nilsson approaches a girl at a dance and makes out with her, because "they say you never made it with a Gemini." The light but effective backing is built around Nicky Hopkins's agile piano and also features Peter Frampton on guitar, Barry Morgan on drums, Klaus Voormann on bass, and Ray Cooper on percussion.[85] Clearly this was a track on which Perry worked hard to try and arrive at "the perfect take," as he also commissioned some additional brass and reeds from Kirby Johnson that were added in Hollywood the next month, but in the final mix these were stripped out again. For reasons that are not entirely clear, it was not included in the final album and never issued until it came out as a bonus track on the 2006 edition of *Son of Schmilsson*.

"At My Front Door" is an old-fashioned rocker included in this album in much the same way as "Let the Good Times Roll" made it onto *Nilsson Schmilsson*. Whatever tiff might have occurred between them, on this track, Ringo Starr's drumming is exemplary, with Voormann, Frampton, and Spedding laying down a solid backing for Nilsson's vocal, John Uribe's lead guitar, and some fine brass and reed work from Price and Keys. It works as an excellent anchor for the middle of side two of the album, but it was also not destined to be a single release. Nor was "Ambush," a curious song about a platoon of soldiers who sing as they approach the theater of war. Attacked by the enemy, they don't feel like singing any longer. Over a backing, rather different from anything else on the album, that includes a jazz-inflected trumpet solo, Nilsson delivers a vocal that—like the backing—seems to contrast with the music around it and owes most to the dispassionate monotone storytelling of David Bowie on songs such as his 1969 "Space Oddity."

Perry knew that Nilsson's chameleon-like tendencies and the widely contrasting sound of his voice from one track to another might be a liability. So, even as the album was still being made, he began to present this to journalists as an asset, putting a positive spin on the lack of stylistic unity. He told *Record Mirror*:

> Harry sounds different on each track, more so than any other artist except McCartney, who can also do it. He does things out of the ordinary. He doesn't just like doing typical things and this natural quality is what makes him a great artist. It makes his music odd. He does the unexpected and he's an eccentric person, but it's all very subtle and never intrudes on the original concept.[86]

This interview was given as Perry and Nilsson were recording the final song for the album, which both of them decided stood the greatest chance of being a hit. "Spaceman" looked at the pointlessness of being in orbit, going "round and around and around and around." It had a dramatic opening on the repeated line "Bang bang shoot 'em up" and an orchestral backing provided by Paul Buckmaster who had worked such miracles on "Without You." Furthermore, Nilsson sang the song in something approaching his "normal" voice. In other words, if one heard the track by chance, it was probable that the voice might be recognized as belonging to the same singer as on "Everybody's Talkin'" or "Without You." Clearly, journalist Lon Goddard thought so as he witnessed Nilsson recording the final vocal track:

> The tremendous talent of the singer was overpowering. His command of voice and unique ideas stayed on a brilliant level. He knew what he wanted and how to do it, and Richard Perry knew how to produce it. . . . I can safely guarantee that this album will soar instantly to number one when it's released and that this pair who work together so beautifully will go on to do more exceptional work.[87]

Goddard and other journalists watched Nilsson and Perry at work, and in particular they were impressed with Perry's control of what looked like quite unruly sessions. Despite the forest of empty lager bottles on the piano and the smoked cigarettes standing on their filters on the window ledges and shelves of the studio; despite the comings and goings of different musicians, the Chinese meals, the uppers, downers, lines of coke, brandies, and reefers, Perry—as one report described him—"embodied the essential qualities of a diplomat in the studio with an overall objectivity."[88]

To all those who saw it being made, it seemed that "Spaceman" was going to be the killer track. And with "You're Breakin' My Heart," complete with its "fuck you" lyric, on the flipside, it was released as a single and rose to number twenty-three in the U.S. top forty. It might well have climbed higher, but unbeknown to Perry and Nilsson, Elton John had recorded a song on his new album *Honky Chateau* that covered almost exactly the same subject, the astronaut whose job—once seen as heroic—has become routine. "Rocket Man" roared past

"Spaceman" and reached number three in the United States and number two on the U.K. pop charts.

Even though it lacked a major hit song, the new album fared reasonably well. There had been some discussion about its title. Ideas that were bandied around included "Bushwick Bomber" (after Nilsson's childhood neighborhood); "Ha-Ha-Harry," (after Perry's occasional stammer when excited); and "Buy My Album" (after a single Nilsson had recorded a year or two before). But the eventual title *Son of Schmilsson* was intimately tied up with the wife and son who had left him, and to whom Nilsson signed his letters "Daddy Schmilsson." The marital separation triggered a latent self-destruction mechanism in Nilsson. The album uncomfortably mirrored what had gone on in his personal life, and the writing was on the wall for the partnership with Richard Perry.

I wandered around, and finally found
The somebody who could make me be true.

6

IT HAD TO BE YOU

ALTHOUGH THERE HAD been much carousing during the making of *Son of Schmilsson*, and his relationship with Diane had foundered, Nilsson nevertheless cemented some close friendships at that time, which effectively made London into his second home. Primarily, he renewed his association with Derek Taylor and his family, often visiting their house in Sunningdale, Berkshire, some twenty-five miles west of London. Somehow, Taylor had managed to do what Nilsson failed to achieve, namely to live a rock and roll lifestyle, frequently indulging in drugs and alcohol but establishing a stable and secure home and raising a family of six children.

Taylor's wife Joan recalled that there was, nevertheless, a cost in terms of her relationship with Derek when Nilsson dropped in: "He'd come over and see us at the house, and he was probably the person that was interested in the kids most, apart from George Harrison...it was just a joy to be around him. The downside was that he took my husband away, far too often. They wanted to go out and play."[1] Undoubtedly, a lot of playing went on during the making of the *Son of Schmilsson* album, but Nilsson and Taylor's friendship endured for the rest of Nilsson's life and was, on balance, always productive. It led in 1973 to one of his most celebrated records, *A Little Touch of Schmilsson in the Night*. It is also tempting to think of Taylor's large family as a role model for Nilsson's subsequent third marriage, to Una O'Keeffe.

In 1972, Nilsson also became particularly close to two of the musicians who played on *Son of Schmilsson*. The first of these was percussionist Ray Cooper, who recalled:

At the studio in Soho...once the backing was done, people would go home. But as a percussionist there were lots of overdubs and this meant it was Harry and myself. These were wonderful moments in the early hours of the morning, tapping things in the kitchen. Harry became, as the evening went on, more and more alive, more and more adventurous. As most people were falling asleep, the engineer was

144

saying, "Okay, I've got this." Time was going by and we were talking about all sorts of things.... Harry was very sweet, he'd put his coat over his shoulders and we'd leave the studio and find a bar somewhere. That was the wonderful thing. It gave me the privilege of this close association with Harry, when everyone else had gone home.[2]

In these late-night conversations, Cooper and Nilsson would talk about anything and everything, and Nilsson became a frequent visitor to Cooper's London apartment overlooking the River Thames. In future years, they would always meet up when their paths crossed in London or when Cooper's touring itinerary brought him to Los Angeles.

The other friendship, soon to be one of the cornerstones of Nilsson's life, and which really blossomed in the latter half of 1972, was with the drummer credited on *Son of Schmilsson* as "Richie Snare," better known as Ringo Starr.

"Ringo and I spent a thousand hours laughing," said Nilsson. "All the things we'd do...some were friend-like, some Laurel and Hardy-like."[3] Ringo, often sporting mirror sunglasses that disguised the effects of the night before, was at the heart of a social set that enjoyed late nights, exclusive bars, nightclubs, and brandy. Along with Nilsson and Ringo, there would be Marc Bolan of T. Rex, The Who's drummer Keith Moon, and Graham Chapman, of *Monty Python's Flying Circus*. They would frequently meet in the afternoon, drinking brandy and swapping yarns, each new arrival dropping in with the catch phrase: "I hope I'm not interrupting anything?" Nilsson recalled:

We would drink until 9 p.m. That's six hours of brandy. Then between 9 and 10, we would usually end up at Tramp, the most uproarious, exclusive disco-restaurant in the world. Royalty, movie stars, world champions, all frequented there. It was really a ride meeting these luminaries and having total blow-outs almost every night.[4]

When Nilsson decided to purchase an apartment of his own in London that summer, Ringo was to be closely involved. The apartment was a two-bedroom top-floor flat in a tall eighteenth-century house at 9 Curzon Place, a short stroll from Shepherd's Market on the southern fringes of Mayfair. The building was constructed of dark London bricks with an off-white stucco bay window extension on the front. A formal doorway with a Georgian fanlight led in off the street, and at some time after World War II, the interior had been gutted and transformed with a central elevator shaft that had apartments leading from it on every floor. Flat 12 was unusual, in that being above the bay window extension, it had open-air balconies on both sides of the building, from one of which it was possible to see the clock face of Big Ben over the Houses of Parliament at Westminster, while the other offered a good view of the "bunny" girls coming and going to work at the nearby Playboy Club. When Nilsson first found the place, he felt it was in need of a makeover. He discussed this with Ringo, who had recently set up a design partnership with the sculptor and furniture-maker Robin Cruickshank that they called "ROR," or "Ringo Or Robin." Nilsson recalled:

> When I bought the flat I said, "Why don't we let you and Robin run wild?" Robin made this great, amazing pad. It was...all glass and chrome and felt and velvet. And the price had doubled from the quote, and then Mr. R. Starkey [Ringo Starr] picked up the difference, or most of it. The first day I entered the flat it was completely finished. I had just come from America and I was shocked. I didn't know what to think. And then I thought for a second, and I loved it. As a little gift, Ringo and Robin had made these special mirrors for the two-sinked bathroom. They were done in etched glass. One was a picture of an oak tree. But on the other, there was etched a hangman's noose. It bothered me, the joke from Robin was made with good intent, but each time you woke up and brushed your teeth, you would look into the mirror and be hanged, and I didn't like it. So I called Ringo and told him and he didn't like it either. The next day, it was replaced by an apple tree.[5]

The dark symbolism of the hangman's noose would return to haunt the apartment in future days, but the flat was to become Nilsson's home for roughly six months each year until 1978. While the apartment was getting its makeover from Robin Cruickshank, Nilsson got involved in a project with Ringo to make a movie, *Son of Dracula*, which was no doubt much more fun to make than it is to see. Although George Harrison would later be the Beatle most involved in the movie industry, forming HandMade Films in 1978 to finance Monty Python's *Life of Brian*, it was Ringo who originally took the initiative, first as an actor and later as the main producer for the film division of Apple.

In 1968, his first non-Beatle film venture had been a cameo role as a gardener in Christian Marquand's update of Voltaire's *Candide*, renamed *Candy*. This screenplay was partly based on a story by Terry Southern, and later that same year, Ringo took a more prominent role in another Southern screen adaptation, *The Magic Christian*, playing a major part opposite Peter Sellers. In 1971, he appeared in Frank Zappa's *200 Motels*, as well as the Spaghetti Western *Blindman*, and this increasingly regular screen experience led him to undertake the production and direction of *Born to Boogie*, an occasionally surrealistic picture that focused on the music of Marc Bolan and T. Rex. For this, Starr filmed much of the footage himself, principally from the photographers' pit immediately below the stage during a T. Rex concert in Wembley on March 18, 1972.

The movie has some bizarre moments, including long shots of Bolan being driven across an airfield, wearing a top hat and confronting a mischievous dwarf who eats the side mirrors of automobiles, not to mention an outdoor tea party with a string quartet, nuns, and a butler. This latter segment of the film borrows heavily from Jonathan Miller's 1966 BBC Television adaptation of *Alice in Wonderland*, which made a significant impression at the time because of its surrealistic treatment of the Mad Hatter's tea party. However, it is the accomplished treatment of the music that holds the entire enterprise together.

Throughout *Born to Boogie*, Starr showed a sure directorial touch. His insistence on pacing the editing to suit the music, with cleverly intercut audience scenes, and his deft handling of some eccentric studio performances shot at John Lennon's house at Tittenhurst, including Bolan singing from inside Elton John's piano, suggested he had the credentials successfully to underpin a full-length dramatic movie. But whereas his intuitive understanding of how to present the excitement of a live band on screen has left us with some of the finest seventies rock coverage ever shot, this instinct largely deserted him when it came to his new venture.

Nevertheless, as soon as word got out about the project, the press immediately got excited about the Starr/Nilsson collaboration:

> Nilsson, who appears on his album cover *Son of Schmilsson* in Dracula form, will play the title role in an upcoming film *Countdown*. The film put out by Apple is an updated version of Dracula. Ringo Starr will also be in this one as a wizard.[6]

Ironically, the invitation to Nilsson to take part in the role of Count Downe, the son of the murdered Dracula, was extended well before Starr realized that Nilsson had been photographed as a vampire on the sleeve of *Son of Schmilsson*.[7] In the eventual movie, there is a jokey visual reference to this when Count Downe is strolling through the West End of London at night and pauses in front of a record store where, in the window display, Nilsson glimpses himself in similar garb on his own album cover.

The London-at-night scenes have some stylistic similarities with the Bolan movie, in that there is a beautifully edited dramatic and colorful montage of the neon signs of the theaters, clubs, and bars of the West End, focused around Piccadilly Circus. And there is also a comparable central concert sequence shot at the Surrey Docks in East London during August 1972. This comprises a highly atmospheric set of scenes in which the vampire-costumed Nilsson and an all-star band mime to his recent recordings of several songs including "At My Front Door," "Remember," and "Jump Into the Fire." Astute Nilsson spotters will recognize Bobby Keys, Jim Price, Peter Frampton, and Klaus Voormann reprising their recently shot studio sequences in *Did Somebody Drop His Mouse?* But added bonuses here are a white-suited Keith Moon hammering the drums on "Jump Into the Fire" and John Bonham of Led Zeppelin taking a similar role on the other songs after Moon had to leave the film set early in order to rejoin The Who in Europe.

The concert and London location scenes apart, *Son of Dracula* was burdened from the outset by a poor script by Jay Fairbank and wooden direction by Freddie Francis, a seasoned director of low-budget horror movies for Hammer Films. In an attempt to draft in some heavyweight acting talent, Francis recommended that Starr should recruit two of Britain's most popular television actors of the time. These were Freddie Jones, who had dazzled the critics with his offbeat performance as Claudius in BBC television's classical drama *The Caesars*, and Dennis Price, known to millions as Bertie Wooster's suave butler Jeeves from the BBC's adaptations of P. G. Wodehouse's famous novels. However, Jones could not resist camping it up and playing Baron Frankenstein as an outrageously theatrical, psychopathic would-be murderer, whereas Price, always a low-key actor who specialized in understatement, was even more relaxed than usual, playing Van Helsing entirely from a wheelchair. Add to that Starr's robotic performance in a vast grey wig and beard outfit as Merlin, together with the pneumatic but otherwise stilted Suzanna Leigh as Count Downe's love interest Amber, and the odds were stacked against any producer being able to salvage the results.

On the practical front, this was in no way due to lack of effort on Starr's part. He allegedly sank $800,000 of his own money into the movie, and he assumed the lion's share of the work himself: "I went through everything," he recalled, "casting, meetings with actors, electricians. The lot. I wanted to make the film in England because it's easier to learn at home."[8] One lesson that came early in the shoot was that filming a regular movie with normal working-shift patterns was a very different matter from hiring a crew to cover a live T. Rex concert. Down at Surrey Docks, just as the musicians really started to make sense of the musical scenes, it was time for the sound and camera crew to pack up. Starr, somewhat puzzled, reported:

> [It was] such a headache. Everyone shouts at you. I didn't know that if you didn't get the crew home and in their beds by midnight, you couldn't work them the next day, because you see, I'm a musician. If we start working and it starts to cook, we'll keep it rolling for three days if necessary.[9]

Maybe it was for this reason that on many evenings, Starr and Nilsson took themselves off to the new Apple offices on St. James Street after shooting was over. There, Chris O'Dell and Pattie Boyd (George Harrison's wife) chanced to find them one night. O'Dell remembered: "Music was playing, the lamps were lit, and the coke was laid out in lines on the desk."[10]

In the final released version of the movie, despite having to spend almost the entire film clad in black evening wear and a red-lined cape, Nilsson acquits himself well. His lines are quite naturalistically delivered, in contrast to the thespian tones of some of the more seasoned actors around him, and his tall figure has a strong screen presence. He took no fee for appearing in the movie, but in exchange for playing the lead role, Ringo paid for him to have cosmetic dentistry to straighten his front teeth. There are several close-ups of Nilsson's mouth in the film, and when his prosthetic fangs are "surgically removed" by Dennis Price, in contrast to the uneven teeth visible in all previous photographs of him, he now has a neatly even set.

Some of Nilsson's closest friends believed that self-consciousness about his crooked teeth had been a significant factor in his decision not to appear in live concerts, and also explained why on all his album covers he had adopted a degree of disguise so that he would barely be recognized in the street from the images they presented of him. Samantha Juste, for example, said:

He didn't have great teeth. I remember when he had his teeth fixed, it did a lot for him. In the early days he didn't smile really. Those teeth made a big difference to him, and to his confidence. [Before] he wasn't outgoing, really at all, I don't think. So he began to have confidence.[11]

By the time the movie was eventually released, with a premiere in Atlanta, Georgia, on April 19, 1974, Nilsson's new facial appearance had become well established. But the film that had helped him to achieve it was soon destined to disappear almost without trace in the United States, and was deemed so bad by British distributors that it was not released in England at all.

Because Nilsson's albums were still being produced by Richard Perry, the soundtrack record for *Son of Dracula* (eventually released in 1974 by RCA in association with Apple Films as the only ever release on the "Rapple" label) was handed over to Perry to assemble in late 1972. With the help of the "Without You" string arranger Paul Buckmaster, who had composed the background score for the movie itself, Perry pulled together a set of tracks to be interspersed with snatches of Ringo's dialogue and the original versions of Nilsson's songs that were included in the film. Screenwriter Jay Fairbank took a co-composer's credit on the new incidental music, mainly for suggesting such titles as "It is he who will be king" and "Perhaps this is all a dream," but the actual music—some of it quite atmospheric—is all Buckmaster's, apart from the backing to the curious scene in which Count Downe is made mortal in an impromptu operating theater set up on a billiard table. The music for this, entitled "The Count's Vulnerability," was written by the up-and-coming classical composer John Tavener, who had been signed to Apple in 1970 for his albums *The Whale* and *Celtic Reunion*.

Although Nilsson's working relationship with Richard Perry had been put under some strain during *Son of Schmilsson*, they remained good friends, not least by again going on holiday together after completing the album. As the year passed, Perry remained convinced that Nilsson potentially had sufficient talent, songwriting and singing ability to create another album of hits as potent as *Nilsson Schmilsson*, and he continued to urge Nilsson to write new material in the hope that such an album would be their next project together. In the interim, to prove that their partnership was still as active as ever, shortly after shooting finished on the Dracula movie, Perry called Nilsson into Trident Studios in London during September 1972. This was to add some backing vocals to an album he was producing with a young singer named Carly Simon.

The album was to be called *No Secrets*, and the standout song, which would top the charts in January 1973, was one that Simon had written, entitled "You're So Vain." Perry had made two previous attempts to record the song, but neither had achieved the buildup of tension he was after. Now, again based at the same London studio at which he had recorded both Nilsson albums, he had another try.[12]

Simon herself had not been keen to record this song for a third time, but on hearing the playbacks at Trident, she immediately recognized that Perry had finally found the successful formula that had previously eluded him. A day or two after the basic tracks were laid down, Nilsson came in to add his backing vocals. As it turned out, another star unexpectedly happened to be there, namely Mick Jagger, adding his distinctive voice to the multitracked chorus of "You're So Vain." As a result, after singing through his own harmonies a couple of times, Nilsson discreetly dropped out of the session to leave Jagger and Carly Simon to continue layering the vocals, giving rise in the years that followed to the rumor that Jagger himself was the subject of the song's enigmatic lyrics.[13]

The fall of 1972 saw much roistering with Ringo, as Nilsson remained in London and finally moved into his apartment in Curzon Place. In October, Ringo began work as an actor on another movie, playing the part of Mike Menarry in Claude Whatham's film *That'll Be the Day*. As a barman and amusement ride operator, with much of his dialogue improvised, Starr produced a totally convincing screen role in stark contrast to his performance as Merlin. The whole movie was shot in October and November at a Butlin's camp on the Isle of Wight, the stars shivering in their tee shirts as they tried to give the impression that the chilly autumnal British coastal climate was actually the height of summer.

As he had in *Son of Dracula*, Keith Moon (who had urged co-producer David Puttnam to get Ray Connolly's holiday camp story filmed and had helped choose the soundtrack repertoire with Apple's Neil Aspinall) landed a small supporting role in the picture. Again he played a drummer, this time in Billy Fury's backing band—a character named J. D. Clover. There was no way that Moon and Starr were going to be at work on a movie a couple of hours' travel away from Curzon Place without their carousing colleague Nilsson showing up on the set. After Moon had made his spectacular entrance to the proceedings by arriving in a helicopter and landing on the roof of the Shanklin hotel at which the cast was staying, there were some riotous parties and late-night music sessions. Nilsson was there for several of them and memorably joined in one spontaneous jam with the film's star David Essex, Starr, Moon, and saxophonist Graham Bond that kept the hotel residents awake until 4 a.m.[14]

Back in London, Moon, when he was not flitting to Los Angeles, opening car rallies in Wales, on brief jaunts to the Mediterranean, or—on a couple of occasions—being given emergency hospital treatment for accidental drug overdoses, would get together with Nilsson to hang out.

One night in early 1973, Moon stayed over at Nilsson's apartment. They had been out on the town the evening before and woke up, as Nilsson recalled with "a Saturday hangover only ice can cool." As they came to, they groggily went through their shared repertoire of Laurel and Hardy gags and then walked the short distance to the Inn on the Park. Nilsson continued:

> We had a great breakfast of sausages, eggs, coffee, croissants and were about to order brandy for the coffee. I stopped and said: "This is nuts, you know, All we ever do is this. What's it like to be sober? I swear I can't remember the last time I was sober."
> Keith listened, joked appropriately and then got real.
> "Let's be civilians and see if we can get through the weekend. What do you say?" I asked.
> "Done, here's my hand," he replied. And he meant it as I did. Around noon we decided to see a movie, like real people do. See a movie on Saturday. We walked to Leicester Square, purchased our tickets and went in.... We hit the daylight about 2 p.m. "Now what?" "I don't fuckin' know!" "What about another movie?" "Right." With that we walked across the Square and took in another film.[15]

After emerging from the second cinema, Nilsson and Moon headed back to Curzon Place. As they were walking close to the shops on Lower Regent Street, a blonde girl ran toward them. Behind her was a man driving a car, who mounted the curb, apparently trying to kill her. She, Nilsson, and Moon jumped clear as both car and driver headed for a store window. Within minutes, shocked and with all vows of sobriety behind them, Nilsson and Moon were in a nearby pub downing brandies, until they realized that having earlier gone to the Inn on the Park on Nilsson's tab and then paying for two rounds of cinema tickets, they had no actual money left. Moon offered the barman his mink coat as collateral, but he recognized him, saying, "Aren't you Keith Moon?" and before long the drinks were flowing on the house and from other customers keen to spend time with the celebrities.

After many brandies, they staggered back to the Inn on the Park, where they were welcomed by the management, who told them that because it was the opening night of a new disco in the former banqueting room, the hotel would treat them as "honored guests" and take care of their drinks, food, and so on. As they made their way upstairs to the new room, the bell captain explained that the hotel's other honored guests included Neil Sedaka. Keen to display Nilsson and Moon to its paying clientele, the hotel gave them a bottle of Remy Martin and placed them at a front table right next to the DJ's speakers, which got louder and louder once the operator recognized Moon. Nilsson recalled:

> Keith was great to be with anytime, except...when he got into his second bottle. About halfway, something would happen. He would snap. This was added to the DJ playing a medley of non-stop songs including "Staying Alive." Keith stiffened. I began to get worried and thought, "Uh oh, here we go." At that moment Keith stood up and shouted over the music, "Enough! Enough!" He picked up the bottle

by the throwing end and threw it like a bullet directly over the head of the DJ. The bottle bounced back miraculously, and landed on the turntable, screeching, followed by silence. "Enough is fucking enough!" Suddenly there were waiters and bartenders rushing our table. Keith tried to throw a punch at someone, but they pounced on him like cats on a mouse. The table was knocked over. I reached out from under it, grabbed somebody's leg and shouted, "It's okay, it's okay, cool it!" Just then, lying on my back I looked up to see Keith being carried out literally over the heads of six waiters. It looked something like the flag-raising at Iwo Jima, or a Kafka cockroach on its back with arms and legs flailing, screaming at the top of his lungs: "Charge this to Neil Sedaka!"[16]

Nilsson extracted himself from under the table and calmly sought out the bell captain, offering to pay for the damage. Reaching into his pocket for a tip, he recalled he had no money and ended up borrowing twenty pounds from the man, who smiled at the irony, but knew Nilsson to be a regular and high-spending customer. He pointed Nilsson in the direction of a large reception room, where Moon was lying wrapped in the mink coat, flat on his back in the middle of the floor, surrounded by stacked chairs in the dim light of the emergency exit signs. "Keith, they've called the police and I figure we have about forty seconds to get the fuck out of here," Nilsson told the recumbent figure. With that, Moon sprang unsteadily to his feet, and arm in arm they marched down the main stairway, leaving through the front door just before the police pulled up. They made it back to Curzon Place without further incident.

Between carousing with Moon and Ringo, Nilsson was beginning to discuss ideas for his next album with Richard Perry. Hoping that the Carly Simon experience would make Nilsson keen to try for a more commercial album than *Son of Schmilsson*, Perry ensured that they met regularly in London to discuss plans, and in early 1973, they worked closely together on editing the footage and recording the voiceovers for the film *Did Somebody Drop His Mouse?* When the next album finally came to be talked about in detail, Perry was not happy with Nilsson's idea that he should make an album of standards. To Perry, it seemed that Nilsson's talent was in being the ideal fusion of singer and songwriter, and that he had it in him to craft original songs as brilliant as his work on his two Grammy-winning singles by Fred Neil and Badfinger. The more Perry tried to persuade him to do something new and original, the more Nilsson clung to the idea of exploring the great American songbook. In the end, Perry wished him good luck and walked away from being his producer.[17]

As Nilsson's plans coalesced to make his record of established standards from Broadway and Hollywood (with a few British additions), he turned to his friend Derek Taylor, who, although he worked on the staff at WEA, agreed to produce it for RCA. Although it seemed as if this would end his working relationship with Richard Perry, in the weeks before Nilsson went into CTS Studios in London with Taylor and a symphony orchestra to record the songs from a bygone era, he was cajoled into working with Perry and Ringo on a solo album featuring the former Beatles drummer.

Ironically, given his steadfast opposition to Nilsson's project, Perry had worked three years before on Ringo's own album of standards, producing and arranging the title track "Sentimental Journey." It had done modestly well on the album charts on both sides of the Atlantic, but peaking at number twenty-two in the United States, it tended to support Perry's theory that a standards album would not sell in similar quantities to *Nilsson Schmilsson*. However, when they finished "Sentimental Journey," Perry had offered his services to Ringo, should he ever want to abandon George Martin as his overall producer and work with someone different. Then fate took a hand when the organizers of the 1973 Grammy awards wanted to get Nilsson to present one of the awards, because he had been nominated in several categories for *Nilsson Schmilsson*. Perry—knowing of Nilsson's close friendship with Ringo—suggested that they ask Starr as well, as a sure way of getting the two men to agree. His instincts were right, and both said they would be presenters. At which point, Ringo called Perry and said that if he was going to be in the United States anyway, it might be a good moment for them to try to record some material together. They went into the studio for five days immediately after the Grammys.[18]

The award ceremony on March 3 was a mixed blessing for Nilsson. Despite his range of nominations, he only won for Best Male Vocal Performance on "Without You." His acceptance speech was a brief "Thank you." But his appearance with Ringo to present the award for Best R&B Performance (won by Billy Paul for "Me and Mrs. Jones") was something of a comic tour de force, the two of them walking onstage in synchronized steps and then speaking in unison, except when the odd giggle interrupted their flow. It is clear that there was a great personal bond between the two of them, and this was to manifest itself when they got together at Sunset Sound in Los Angeles on March 5 immediately after the awards to record "You're Sixteen."

Perry had assembled a backing band similar to the one on *Son of Schmilsson*, with Nicky Hopkins, Klaus Voormann, and Jim Keltner, plus guitarists Jimmy Calvert and Vini Poncia. An imitation saxophone solo was later added in London by Paul McCartney, but the Los Angeles sessions yielded the basic track, a vibrant update of Johnny Burnette's 1960 hit version of the song by Robert and Richard Sherman. Whereas that original record featured an orchestral backing, Perry's production was built around Hopkins's jangly piano and Nilsson's multitracked backing vocals. Of all the many-layered vocal backing tracks on Nilsson's own albums, none came close to the perfection of this number. Not only does he sing multipart harmonies, but there are subtle vocal interjections of the "Mine, all mine" line, and even behind McCartney's kazoo-ish solo, there is a splendid vocal choir, followed on the next chorus with some deep bass notes at the very bottom of Nilsson's range. If Nilsson could not fashion his own "killer song" for Perry, he was at least able to bring his talents to help Ringo create one, and the resulting single topped the American charts in late 1973 and sold over two million copies worldwide. It is also a great tribute to Nilsson's studio discipline, which could still be applied when it really mattered. In contrast, a duo version of "Love Hurts" recorded in London late the previous year with Jimmy Webb was never issued at the time, because Nilsson's vocal additions were considered to be too melodramatic. With Ringo, his audacious professionalism as a backing vocalist remains unsurpassed.

Nilsson knew that in this period of early 1973 his voice was still in perfect condition to record a collection of standard songs. He was also aware that his increasingly hedonistic lifestyle might mean that time was running out to demonstrate just how well he could sing. Before he undertook the Grammy awards visit to the United States, he and Derek Taylor identified Gordon Jenkins as the right man to arrange and conduct the standards sessions in London, and they brought him across the Atlantic to discuss the project. Looking back on it in 1988, Nilsson said: "The choir boy thing [was] gone. I knew it then. I told both Derek and Gordon, this is the last of it. That incredible, flexible, rubber-band-like voice—I barely just snuck in that album under the gun."[19]

Jenkins was, along with Nelson Riddle, the most celebrated orchestral arranger in the United States at the time, with a career stretching back to the 1930s. His positive first impressions and his agreement to participate in Nilsson's project were formed at least in part by the lavish style in which Taylor received him, with a television crew at the airport, limousines to and from his hotel, a Steinway in the suite, and whisky in the refrigerator. As a man who had made best-selling records with Louis Armstrong, Billy Eckstine, Ella Fitzgerald, Judy Garland, Dick Haymes, and Frank Sinatra, Jenkins combined integrity and taste with a flair for the popular. Yet he was not known as a great enthusiast for contemporary pop music. His son had been surprised to see Nilsson's album *The Point* on the music desk of Jenkins's piano, and although Jenkins felt that Nilsson's voice was not in the class of some of the artists with whom he had worked, he took the trouble to listen to his albums and decreed "he had good pitch and feeling, and he was willing to work."[20]

At those early London meetings, the repertoire was planned out, and Jenkins immediately threw out plans to include "Hey Jude" and "Auld Lang Syne." At the same time, Nilsson rejected "Smoke Gets In Your Eyes." This meant that when Jenkins returned to London at the end of March, he had sufficient time to produce full symphonic arrangements of the selected songs, and Nilsson also had the time necessary to learn them. This he did, during endless sessions with Jenkins's regular rehearsal pianist Charlie LaVere. Given that Taylor had always worked as a publicist and had never produced an album before, there was a lot at stake. He said:

We boldly went where really no amateur producer like me had gone before.... So we got Gordon over, put him up in good accommodation, swamped him with enthusiasm, and love, and we had enough knowledge of the genre to be *bona fide*. We were all, in other words, believers in standards, and yet not be thought old hat. Yet again, it just worked out. We brought in Phil MacDonald, who'd engineered *Abbey Road*, as our engineer, and he was in his twenties, Harry was in his thirties, I was in my forties, the orchestra were in their fifties, and Gordon was in his sixties. This was the way we rationalized it—did we have it covered? And we all liked a drink, so we chose CTS Studios at Wembley, which had a 24 hour bar, and the finest orchestra was chosen, because Gordon's experience really went back all the way to Isham Jones and Al Jolson. He knew what he wanted, everyone had heard of him.[21]

The sessions were the antithesis of a Richard Perry album. Instead of putting down multiple takes of a backing track and then painstakingly adding detail as Perry was wont to do, the Wembley tracks were recorded in the traditional style of orchestral records, with Nilsson singing live in a makeshift booth of screens, surrounded by the symphony musicians. *New Musical Express* sent its reporter Danny Holloway along, who wrote:

> Even though he appeared to consume a substantial amount of booze when working, Nilsson was diligent and sensitive to the slightest musical error. His sincere appreciation for the songs was demonstrated by his strong effort to create a mood fully complementing each tune. During the afternoon, he concentrated solely on vocals while the band played live.[22]

Another British pop magazine, *Record Mirror*, also reported on the sessions the same day and noted how Nilsson would break off immediately if he felt a note had gone awry.[23] There were many takes of some songs, and Phil MacDonald would be required to do both tape surgery and overdubbing to achieve the finished result, but Taylor had boundless confidence in the combination of artist, arranger, orchestra, and engineer. Nilsson also had to get used to Jenkins's direction, which was so sensitive it followed every nuance of his delivery. If he pulled back the tempo, Jenkins took the orchestra with him, exactly as he would have done for Sinatra or Fitzgerald, and initially this was an unusual sensation for Nilsson, as he had become used to working with predetermined backing tracks that did not allow for any subsequent ebb and flow. Nevertheless, Derek Taylor was delighted with the way the sessions went:

> It was done live, in a little booth, with the orchestra, with a whisky and whatever it was he drank, sometimes whisky and milk. Gordon was whisky and milk, and Harry would be whisky and whisky, probably. And a lot of cigarettes. His breathing was terrible. I claim credit for taking the breaths off this record. Phil and I took out all of them.... We took out some real gulps for air, because Harry was such a smoker and in rock it doesn't matter, you can do all kinds of breathing. But there was an immediacy in the album which I think we can claim some credit for, because of the honesty of what we were doing, namely the singing live, which was an old art, by then much abandoned, I think. But anyway there's an honesty in the performance and there's also this refinement of taking out the heavy breathing, which makes it seamless.[24]

The original twelve tracks of the album were artfully linked together by Jenkins's witty scoring, with the closing track "As Time Goes By" prefigured at the very start of the record as its opening verse gradually transforms into the relatively obscure song "Lazy Moon." Later when the arrangement for "Makin' Whoopee" begins, the "As Time Goes By" theme drifts back into our consciousness for a few measures at the start. Even the penultimate track "This Is All I Ask," by Jenkins himself, is prefigured by the "A kiss is just a kiss" phrase from "As Time Goes By." Looking back on the sessions, Derek Taylor recalled Jenkins's elegant scores, every detail written out in fountain pen and with a slight cant to the left accounted for by his left-handedness.[25] It is clear from the fully integrated musical texture of the album that Jenkins and Taylor planned the exact sequence of material and the links between tracks with a degree of artfulness that probably bypassed all but the most keen-eared of listeners. Nilsson appreciated Taylor's wholehearted commitment to the project, not least because Perry had been so dismissive of it. He told interviewers at the time that Taylor "has a way of defending what he believes in." Taylor's staunch advocacy for the record, his deliberations with Nilsson over the choice of repertoire, and his ability to pull as seasoned a campaigner as Jenkins into full engagement with the project, prevented Nilsson from doing what he might otherwise have done when slightly insecure and treating it all as a tongue-in-cheek joke.[26]

Nilsson's view that his voice was at its best at this time is borne out at several points on the originally issued record (a further set of tracks, recorded in 1973, but not issued at the time was added in 1988 to the re-released album under the title *A Touch More Schmilsson In The Night*). Nilsson's falsetto register is beautifully demonstrated on Irving Berlin's "What'll I Do?" and his whole three-and-a-half-octave range can be heard on the Kalmar/Ruby song "Nevertheless." His most assured and balanced performances are on "It Had to Be You" and the closing "As Time Goes By."

The seven additional tracks released in 1988 also have their moments, from the slightly other-worldly quality of "I'm Always Chasing Rainbows" to the wistful "Thanks for the Memory." Yet all these additional tracks have tiny flaws—a momentary catch in the opening to "It's Only a Paper Moon," a slight wobble on "Make Believe," and a split second hesitation on "Trust In Me." The original album and its carefully sequenced tracks for each side of the LP were as carefully matched an "act one" and "act two" as Richard Perry's earlier records had been.

The title of the album came from a quote that Taylor dredged up from his schoolboy memories of Shakespeare's *Henry V*, namely the chorus speech at the beginning of Act IV as the young king steels his troops just as the sun is about to come up before the battle of Agincourt:

A largesse universal, like the sun,
His liberal eye doth give to every one,
Thawing cold fear, that mean and gentle all
Behold, as may unworthiness define,
A little touch of Harry in the night.

Hearing this, Stanley Dorfman, who was at the Wembley sessions, suggested they substitute "Schmilsson" for "Harry," and the title was born. Watching the recording in progress, Dorfman realized that he was witnessing a potentially highly successful BBC broadcast. He worked quickly to persuade Nilsson, Jenkins, and Taylor to recreate the album as a television special:

> We did it in the Television Theatre, whereas the album was done at Wembley Studios. Harry sat in the middle of the orchestra, as opposed to being in a booth or something. He had no ego about this at all. He took instruction from Gordon about phrasing, and things like that, which Gordon was helping him with, because these were unfamiliar songs. Well, they were familiar songs, but it wasn't current then for a rock and roll star to sing those standards. And we literally took the orchestra from Wembley and put it on the stage of the Television Theatre. And just shot it as if it were a studio. And we just shot it in one take. We let it all go, including false starts. At one stage I was taking a shot, through the drummer on one side and the bass player on the other, and in between the songs, one of them handed a joint to the other one, across the lens of the camera. Why would anybody be smoking in the middle of a concert anyway? But we left it in. Nobody bothered.[27]

The resulting television special was Nilsson's second full-length collaboration with Dorfman, and it was broadcast by the BBC to coincide with the release of the album that fall. Just as their previous work together had captured the young, innocent Nilsson as singer/songwriter, this was to remain the best visual document of his prowess as a mature vocalist. The album would receive many warm, affectionate reviews, as did the single release of "As Time Goes By," which as one paper pointed out, "caught on surprisingly well with young people who weren't even born until about 20 years after it was a hit."[28]

After spending several months in London, Nilsson returned briefly to the United States in May, when he, Derek Taylor, and Phil MacDonald traveled to New York to dub in a few words of replacement vocal on the album's penultimate song "This is All I Ask." He had been unhappy with one line, and RCA paid for the three men to come over for a week and stay at the Algonquin Hotel while the patch was recorded and put in place. Taylor recalled they were "careening around New York like men demented," drinking and on one occasion narrowly avoiding a drug bust, when they were discovered snorting coke in the RCA building by a group of cops who turned out to be corrupt and absconded with the drugs. Looking back on the adventure, all to replace a single mispronunciation, Taylor wrote: "That one word cost about $20,000 in drinking time."[29]

Nilsson traveled to Los Angeles in the summer of 1973, filing for his divorce from Diane on July 25. At the end of July, Dorfman came back to Los Angeles himself to recruit more musicians for his BBC *In Concert* series. As before, he spent a considerable amount of time with Nilsson. When the time came for Dorfman to fly home to England,

Nilsson said, "Why don't we just drive across the country? And you can get your plane from New York."[30]

With no real idea of quite how big the United States actually is, Dorfman agreed. At first, Nilsson tried to rent a car for the trip, but the rental company would not let him take the car out of the state. So instead, the would-be adventurers turned to Jimmy Webb. He had a brand new burgundy-colored Jaguar XJ6, and he was not particularly perturbed when Nilsson appeared on his doorstep and said: "I'd like to borrow your car for the afternoon." Webb said, "Okay, here's the keys. Take it guys. Have some fun."[31]

Nilsson made sure that they were well-prepared for the trip:

We loaded up on spirits, food and drugs (acid, coke, pills and reefers)...and headed across country toward New York, in a slight storm.... We hit the highway fearless, laughing and calculating our time at various stops. What we might see. What an adventure! It began well, but the rain became heavier out of L.A. as we headed East. It was still raining through Vegas, but the open road and the Jag encouraged me to respond up to 95 m.p.h. in the storm. What I did not realize was that storms travel East at approximately 34 m.p.h. which was our average speed, what with the acid dropped. I asked Stan if we could pull over. He didn't take any of the drugs and had no concept of what Derek Taylor called, "A dollop of the dreaded heaven and hell" meant. Stan remained cool, although he did comment later that he'd rather have walked through Beirut in a yarmulke. Or something to that effect.[32]

In his memoir of the trip, Nilsson failed to mention that in Las Vegas he and Dorfman had lost all their money. But, to Nilsson, this was just a minor setback, according to Dorfman:

Yes, we lost all our money. All the cash we had on us. So he called [the lawyer] Bruce Grakal, who wired money to Salt Lake City where we were going next. We made our way to Salt Lake City and picked up the money. And Harry needed a drink, but you couldn't drink in Salt Lake City. It's a dry town. And we stayed in a Howard Johnson, which was just awful. We couldn't find a drink anywhere, so we quickly left Salt Lake City. But before we went he had a haircut. When we'd left from Los Angeles, he had long hair. As we drove out of Salt Lake City he had short hair. He seemed to be one of the first rock and roll guys to cut his hair.[33]

They headed north from Salt Lake City, taking them slightly off their route along Interstate 80, to the small town of Logan, Utah, which Nilsson thought would make a good stop for a few hours to recover from their dreadful night. He wrote:

The mountains surrounded us on three sides in a beautiful wide-street town with many clean, old buildings, two colleges and a population of 25,000. There were wooden Indians, a barber shop with the *Police Gazette* (I swear) and best of all, since we were killing time, the tavern, complete with punch cards—a thick cardboard playing size card with about fifty holes, covered with membrane paper. You place a peg in a hole to win a drink. I won three straight away and, for some unknown reason, when the manager shook hands with us, in mine he placed a neatly rolled joint. One never knows![34]

Driving through Utah and Nevada involved areas of desert, and the first time they pulled over to take a nap at the side of the road, the temperature in the car quickly rose to over 100 degrees. Nilsson suggested they drive a little further on the grounds that, wherever there is a desert, there is likely to be an oasis. And sure enough on a bend in the road, they found one—a group of shade-giving trees, a huge sign advertising cool drinks, and the whole place surrounded by bizarre plaster statuary, with giant flamingos, swans, animals, and saints. Nilsson became particularly enamored of a two-foot-high figure of Venus, which he decided to buy for Rocco Laginestra, who was a senior vice president of RCA. However, no sooner had the statue been bought and paid for, than the owner started acting oddly. "He seemed apprehensive when he saw me stalking the mementos," recalled Nilsson. "I was grinning from ear to ear. It was the acid, of course. It's amazing what you see when you stop and look."[35] The man picked up a knife, and the two of them ran to the car, carrying the bulky statue, and drove off. Dorfman takes up the story:

> We were still in the desert, and Harry was getting higher and higher as we went along. We stopped for a rest. We'd also decided to switch drivers every hundred miles. No matter where we were. So we stopped, and it was hot. God knows how hot it was. And we lay in the car talking, and then we got out of the car. And he found a nest of ants that were eating a dead rabbit. Those were red ants. Then we found another nest, this time of black ants. So we decided to have a war, and we put the rabbit between the two nests. We watched them fight, and bet one another as to whose ants would kill more of the others.[36]

Nilsson's account of this incident is that he was "flying" to the extent he had to get out of the car so as not to frighten Dorfman with the "Mr. Hyde" side of his personality. Seeing the ants triggered the more rational "Dr. Jekyll," and through the filter of the LSD, he watched what he described as "a fantastic scene from a science-fiction nature show."

From there they headed east, and somewhere near Chicago, Nilsson took Dorfman to his first American football game. Gradually they made their way toward New York State. By this time, the car looked as if it had been driven across some of the roughest territory in the world. The hood latch had broken, and lacking any kind of normal garage on the road, a local blacksmith had forged a makeshift lock, welded in ungainly fashion to the nose of the car. Furthermore, the speedometer had stopped working, which presented some problems, given the effects of the drugs on Nilsson's perception. But ironically, it was not Nilsson who got caught out by the speedometer, but Dorfman:

It was my turn to drive when we were stopped by the police. We had no idea how fast we were going. The cop said we were going at something like 98 miles per hour. He said, "You're going to have to come with me, get in the car." I told him I had to get back to England. He said, "You were going so fast you'll have to go before the court." Harry offered to follow him, but the cop told him to stay where he was. He put me in the police car and he took me to a place called Brutus. It was like something out of a movie. We went there and went into the judge's house. He was eating lunch. He said to the cop: "Hi, Jim, how's it going?" and the cop said, "Doing well. I'll be bringing you quite a few people today."[37]

In due course, the fine was paid and Dorfman rejoined Nilsson, but not before he noticed that the next miscreant to be brought in was paying his fine in chickens. Back at the Jaguar, Nilsson was sitting a short distance from the car, a pile of joints concealed close by in the long grass. He had, however, buried some of the other drugs in case the cop returned and started sniffing around, and it took the pair quite a while to locate everything so they could set off again. Just as they neared Manhattan, Nilsson asked Dorfman if he had ever seen Niagara Falls. The inevitable negative answer led to another interesting diversion on the director's homeward journey, but finally, a day or so later, he was delivered to the airport for his flight back to London.

Nilsson took the Venus statue to RCA, attended a couple of meetings, and then arranged to ship Jimmy Webb's Jaguar back to California. Webb was not terribly pleased:

He sent it back to me on a flatcar, and he called me and said, "Your car will be arriving on such and such train at 3 p.m. on Friday." And I thought, "Well I'd really like to get my car back." It was a real pain in the behind. So I went down to Union Station, and I went to the freight yard. I found the train. I found the brakeman and had all the guys helping me find the particular car that my car was on. And it had been staked down, chained down, to a flatcar, and it had crossed the country in the open. It wasn't covered, and it looked like it had been driven in a round-the-world rally. It was disgraceful looking. It was just the joke of the thing, is all it was. It was just for the fun of it. And then I hasten to add that he put the car back into perfect condition. I mean, he redid the whole car. He had the interior redone. He put a nicer stereo in. And when he got finished with it, it was nicer than it was when he took it.[38]

The day after Nilsson returned the automobile was a Sunday. He had checked in to the Park Lane Hotel, and in the evening he was wandering around Manhattan with a rolled-up newspaper in one pocket and a flask of brandy in the other, feeling slightly drunk and suddenly rather lonely after the companionship of his epic road trip. As he strolled back to the Park Lane, he passed the neighboring Hotel St. Moritz, where there was an ice cream parlor called Rumpelmeyer's on the ground floor. On an impulse, he went in and sat down at a table.

There were two young Irish waitresses standing together chatting by the counter as they waited for customers to arrive. One came over, and Nilsson ordered a brandy and an ice cream. Then the other one arrived with his order. She was a nineteen-year-old student, and her name was Una O'Keeffe. She and her friend Grainne were on a two-month summer work experience program in the United States before going to college. Their two months were almost up, and it had been a quiet evening until Nilsson came in and gradually joined in their conversation. She was quite unprepared for what happened next:

He looked at me and he said, "You have the most beautiful eyes I've ever seen, Will you marry me?" Both my friend and I were at a very happy time in our life. We were 19 years old. We loved America, we loved Americans, we were having a great time. And we just sort of made a joke out of it. Banter back and forth. Obviously, no one had ever said anything like that to me before, but it was very special. Then he said, "No, really, what can I do to prove my intent?" And we said, "Well, we like flowers and we like melons." Now you might think that's a very odd thing to say, but I'd never eaten a honeydew melon and this was a new thing for us in New York. So, he said, "I'm probably the most eligible bachelor you'll ever meet!" Anyway, we went back to work and a little bit later he was gone.[39]

Imagining it was just banter, and that their customer was not serious, Una and Grainne assumed that they would never see him again. At the end of the evening they were counting up their tips when the manager came over and said, "There's a man waiting for you outside the kitchen." Right by the back door of the restaurant on 58th Street was a huge black limo, and on the sidewalk beside it were baskets of flowers, piles of melons, and soft toys. Leaning nonchalantly against the car was Nilsson.

In the couple of hours since his visit, Nilsson had returned to the Park Lane, showered, sobered up, and changed. He had hired a limo, and gone first to Smiler's Deli on Madison and 54th Street for melons. Finding flowers was more of a problem at 11 p.m. on a Sunday evening. Heading first for the docks, Nilsson chanced on a florist who was preparing for a funeral the following morning. "At first he said no," recalled Nilsson, "I pointed out the limousine and flashed a $100 bill. He succumbed and opened the door...."[40]

The two girls had run out of the back door, giggling and laughing. They stopped, mouths agape at the scene of the car, the gifts, and Nilsson. "They hugged and hugged me," he said. "The sweetest hugs I've ever had. I knew then that I would marry Una."[41]

In the summertime
By the poolside
While the fireflies
Are all around you
I'll miss you when I'm lonely

7

DON'T FORGET ME

UNA O'KEEFFE HAD not intended to be in America for very long. The Students' Union organization that had set up her visit provided little more than a pre-visit briefing, a round-trip air ticket, and a couple of nights in a New York hotel, with an orientation meeting to allow students to get their bearings. Then it was up to them to find a job for two months before heading home for the autumn term. Many Irish students opted for summer camps up in the Catskills, working with younger children in the area's open-air resorts. Una and Grainne had decided quite spontaneously to go to New York City itself when they attended a presentation at their college. She recalled:

> I asked my parents, "Would it be okay if I went to New York for the summer?" My father is a very quiet man, but he really believed in travel. So he thought it was a good idea. He had no worries about it, but my mother told me later that they were doing the dishes that night, and she said to my father, "I don't know about this. It's very far away, and she'll probably marry a Yank. And we'll never see her again." So I did marry a Yank—but they did see me again![1]

Despite Nilsson's proposal, it was some three years before they were married, and Una was to spend much of the intervening time in Ireland completing her studies. But, as she reached the end of her job at the ice cream parlor, she had been planning a week of travel in North America. So, in place of her original plans, Nilsson suggested that he take her back with him across the country—effectively retracing part of the route he had just traveled with Stanley Dorfman in reverse—but this time traveling in private planes or chauffeured cars. Finally, she would fly home from Los Angeles. He started in true romantic fashion by taking Una on a nighttime tour of Central Park in a horse-drawn cab.

Two days later, Nilsson and Una arrived in Washington, D.C., so that he could attend a hearing of the U.S. Senate Watergate Committee. The hearings, investigating the break-in to Democratic Party headquarters by burglars acting on behalf of President Nixon's reelection campaign, had begun in May 1973 and by August they had become something of a media circus attraction. Many leading figures from the entertainment world attended the hearings as the weeks rolled by and further damning evidence was uncovered by the committee. Ultimately, the process led to Nixon's impeachment and resignation. Nilsson was fascinated by the story. Indeed, one of his lapel buttons on the cover photograph for *A Little Touch of Schmilsson in the Night* shows Frank Wills, the African American security guard who discovered the break-in.

Nilsson's attendance had been arranged by the controversial left-of-center senator from Connecticut, Lowell P. Weiker, who was one of the three Republicans on the committee. Tickets were in short supply, and Weiker could obtain only two for Nilsson, who was joined at the committee rooms by Erik Preminger, the son of the director of *Skidoo*, who had become a firm friend of Nilsson's during the filming of that movie.

Nilsson and Una stayed at the Watergate Hotel itself—the scene of the break-in—in a suite overlooking the Potomac River, a fittingly romantic setting for the start of their journey across the nation. They began by driving west across Virginia and then hopped by plane and car over the country until they arrived in Las Vegas by private jet, landing in the nick of time before the airport was closed by a violent sandstorm. Trying to book a hotel from the airport, Nilsson was told that every room in town was taken because of the storm. Fortunately, Liza Minnelli, whom Nilsson knew from Los Angeles, was appearing at the Flamingo, doing her "Judy and Liza Concert" with Jim Bailey. When Nilsson called her, she immediately arranged rooms for them there. Their pilot, who swiftly consumed several drinks after his epic dust-storm landing, tagged along as well, particularly when he heard that Minnelli had offered ringside seats for her midnight show. Nilsson recalled:

> After a bite to eat, showers and a change of clothes, we were ready to head downstairs with our now *gonzo* pilot, who kept slurring unintelligible stories of his barnstorming days. There we were, Una, myself and "Gonzo," and at the same table a new future friend, Tony Martin Jr. and next to him sat Desi Arnaz Jr. and Dean Martin Jr. all of us watching Judy Garland Jr. Afterwards we went back to Liza's bungalow and had a nice time, and fortunately we lost "Gonzo" somewhere along the way, which suited us fine.[2]

Una had gone in a week from working as a lowly ice cream waitress to socializing with the stars at one of Las Vegas's most prestigious nightclubs. The next day, she and Nilsson drove to Los Angeles and settled in at his penthouse apartment at the Fountain Building, close to the intersection of La Cienega Boulevard and Fountain Avenue, where he had moved after separating from Diane. After recovering there from the rigors of the trip, Una eventually set off back to Ireland to continue her education.

Nilsson agreed to meet her at Christmas in Ireland, followed by a visit to London, but in the interim, his day-to-day routine in Los Angeles changed dramatically with John Lennon's arrival in the city in the fall of 1973 at the start of the chaotic eighteen months generally referred to as the ex-Beatle's "lost weekend." Ever since their time together at Lennon's home during the recording of the White Album, there had been a strong bond of friendship between Lennon and Nilsson. However, unlike the camaraderie he enjoyed with Ringo, Nilsson always slightly hero-worshipped Lennon, and there was an explosive personal chemistry between them that shared a love of the outrageous. This could, and often did, prove to be a destructive force.

It was a crossroads in Lennon's life. His album *Mind Games* was about to be released in October to indifferent reviews, not least because during the sessions for the album in June he had split from his wife Yoko Ono, and some of his personal turmoil is reflected in what *Rolling Stone* referred to as "his worst writing yet… underrating his audience's intelligence."[3] Bringing little more than a couple of suitcases from New York, he and Ono's former personal assistant, May Pang, eloped to the West Coast, where Lennon planned to make an album of rock and roll classics. It was to be produced by Phil Spector.

Although Lennon was upbeat about the project and told journalists such as the *Melody Maker*'s Chris Charlesworth that "Phil and I have been threatening to do this for years…[to] sing 'ooh-ee-baby' type songs that are meaningless,"[4] there was a commercial imperative to make this record, as he had just lost a legal action against the music publisher Morris Levy. In an out-of-court settlement for plagiarizing Chuck Berry's "You Can't Catch Me" in "Come Together" from the Beatles' *Abbey Road* album, Lennon had agreed to record three songs controlled by Levy's firm and include them on his next album to be released.[5] This more or less restricted him to the rock and roll era, as much of the rest of Levy's catalogue consisted of jazz standards quite inappropriate for Lennon to sing. The project was nicknamed "Oldies but Goldies," although because that title had been used for a Beatles hits collection in 1966, Lennon himself was prone to refer to it as "Oldies but Mouldies," which hardly augured well for the end results.

Almost as soon as the sessions started, it became apparent that they would not go smoothly. In the years since he had previously worked with Nilsson, Spector had become more of a recluse. He was in the midst of a messy divorce from Ronnie, and although he had worked with Lennon before, this time the unwise decision was made to hand complete control over to him. Given Lennon's normal insistence on taking a role in his own productions, this was surprising, especially because Spector had not made any attempt to move with the times. He still intended to revert to his "wall of sound" approach, imposing the equivalent of a symphonic background over what—in Lennon's mind—were simple rocking hits from the days of his first school rock and roll band, the Quarrymen.

If the impending clash of musical personalities was not enough to spell doom for the project, both Lennon and Spector were drinking heavily, and Spector further altered his already fragile personality by taking "poppers"—amyl nitrate capsules that were "popped" and inhaled to give a sudden rush of pleasure as his muscles relaxed and his blood pressure went up. They smelled, according to May Pang, like boys' dirty socks.[6] Lennon's drinking had been under control in New York, but in Los Angeles, away from Yoko Ono, it increased dramatically, not least because immediately when he arrived in town, he began socializing regularly with Nilsson, who then took to turning up at the studio during the sessions. As she watched Lennon trying to match Nilsson's impressive intake of brandy, aided by the more than occasional snort of coke, May Pang felt she was powerless to help:

> [Nilsson] had charm. He had the gift of gab. He could get to anyone; he could get in anywhere. We love him—we did love him. I still have many fond memories of him. But it was almost self-destructive, the things he would [do]. He would take it to the nth degree. There wasn't [any] moderate. He went to extremes, and that was where the danger was. That's where it would all lie, in that extreme part. That [was] Harry.[7]

There was one unexpected outcome of the Spector sessions, which was that Nilsson ended up recording a single with Cher, who dropped in to see how the *Rock and Roll* album was coming along. That particular day, Lennon had left the studio feeling unwell. Spector wanted him to learn a song called "A Love Like Yours (Don't Come Knocking Every Day)," which he had previously recorded with Tina Turner. He suggested to Cher that she could sing it as a demo for Lennon. As Nilsson was also in the studio, he was corralled into singing as well, and on the finished song, their voices blend eerily amid the echo-ridden ambience in which Spector recorded the track. It appears not to have been used for its original purpose, and in due course, Spector released it through Warner Brothers in 1975.[8]

According to Spector, Nilsson was otherwise something of a hindrance to the sessions, and one of his more extreme pranks involved suggesting holding up a 7-Eleven store where the musicians had dropped in to get coffee and groceries during a break in recording. Of course, according to Nilsson, Spector was no less outrageous. He started arriving at the studio dressed up in various costumes, first as a doctor, then a karate instructor, and finally a cowboy, complete with loaded revolver. Given the tragic turn that Spector's life was later to take, regarding the misuse of loaded weapons, he might have taken some warning from Lennon's shocked reaction when, trying to assert his authority in the studio, Spector fired the gun into the air. In the confined space, the report was deafening, and Lennon covered his ears with his hands to dull the impact of the intense pain. Eventually he quipped, "Listen Phil, if you're goin' to kill me, kill me. But don't fuck with me ears, I need 'em."[9]

This incident accelerated the inherent conflict between them, not helped by a regrettable morning in a Los Angeles courtroom in November 1973, where Lennon had been called as a character witness in Spector's divorce hearings, only to watch as Spector launched into an uncontrolled tirade against his wife. By December, the recording sessions had staggered to an untimely end.

Paradoxically, Lennon, despite the drinking and the wild nights with Nilsson, was a stickler for using studio time productively. As May Pang observed, "A lot of people don't realize he was a real workaholic in the studio. If it was a seven o'clock call it was a seven o'clock call. He didn't want seven thirty or eight o'clock. He was very strict about it and he had a strong work ethic."[10] In contrast, Spector was habitually hours late and instead of relying on advance preparation, used his studio time to react to what he heard, endlessly fiddling with the result to add a little here or take away a little there, in order to achieve the sound he imagined in his head. Numerous tracks were started, but virtually none had been finished. Lennon ultimately decided that only four of them could be rescued,[11] and asked for the master tapes. Spector refused and retired to his mansion, taking the tapes with him. It took six months for Capitol Records to retrieve them, by which time it was reckoned that the studio costs had escalated to a hefty $90,000, and this sum was paid over to Spector in exchange for the tapes.

Once the sessions broke down, Lennon was adrift in Los Angeles without a project to occupy him. Even though he was living with May Pang, he spent more and more time with Nilsson, who introduced Lennon to all his nocturnal haunts. This included the Rainbow Bar and Grill in Hollywood, where the upstairs room still has a plaque on the wall commemorating the late-night drinking club, the "Hollywood Vampires." The "Vampires' Lair" would often play host to Lennon and Nilsson along with Micky Dolenz, Keith Moon, and Alice Cooper.[12] Lennon and Nilsson also started to be seen together at various other nightclubs at this time, notably the Troubadour. They were photographed there at Thanksgiving and again a few days later for the opening of the early December season by "Capitol's Canadian songbird" Anne Murray.[13]

In those days, Nilsson owned a Volkswagen Kurierwagen, a small military-style jeep based on the VW Beetle and similar to the wartime Kübelwagen used by Rommel in the desert. It was known as the "Thing" and in between bursts of carousing, he chauffeured Lennon around the city in this strange vehicle. Nilsson recalled:

We were singing somewhere, playing piano and talking. It was almost dawn and John said, "I'd love to get some girls and some acid and fuck 'em."

I said, "Yeah, I know what you mean. I bet I can arrange that in one phone call."

John said, "You're so full of shit, Harry."

I called a girl I knew and apologized for calling so late, but she said it was okay. "Well, look, a friend and I have a bet going. What are you doing?"

She answered, "I was just going to take a shower. A girl friend of mine is coming over and we were going to drop some acid, it's such a beautiful day."

I couldn't believe it and said, "I'll be there in twenty-five minutes with a surprise for you. Goodbye."

I looked at John and said, "Done."

"You're so full of shit Harry."

So we got into the little Thing, we drove to her place, walked in and there were the two of them, with everything prepared, plus a little tea. They were nice and clean, in bathrobes. John's eyes were bugging out and he was rubbing his hands together. It went on for almost two days—that was the real "lost weekend"—we didn't even know where the hell we were after the first day. We just kept doing it. At one point it got stupid—sucking our toes, massages, music in the background, cool water, and I'm laughing. John was on a roll, and we were laughing uncontrollably. Neither of us could stop laughing, and finally I said, "I can't take any more pleasure, John. I can't take any more pleasure. Stop! It's gotta stop!"

He said, "Yeah, yeah, yeah."

Just then the phone rang, and John picked it up. "Yeah? Yeah. No. Yeah. Yeah. Sure, cheese, cheese."

"Who was that?"

John said, "I don't know. A foreigner." [14]

It was around the time of this adventure in hedonism that British jazz and blues singer George Melly was rudely awakened by Nilsson, Lennon, and Derek Taylor bursting into his bungalow at the Chateau Marmont Hotel during the early hours of the morning in a wild state. Taylor was trying to get Warner Brothers to book Melly and his band the Feetwarmers on an American tour to cash in on their cult success in Britain, which Taylor had stage-managed. Naturally, Taylor had taken time out in Hollywood to get together with his old friends, but by the time they returned to the hotel, Lennon was in a particularly ugly and aggressive mood.

Melly recalled: "I wouldn't guarantee what substances were involved in creating his condition, but certainly drink was a contributory one." [15] In previous encounters, Lennon had aggressively blamed Melly and his jazz colleagues for holding up the Beatles' path to fame by continuing to be booked at the Cavern in Liverpool long after traditional jazz had passed out of fashion, so Melly feared the worst. But fortunately, Lennon's sentimental side emerged when the ever-charming Melly, a fellow Liverpudlian, chanced to mention that Lennon's condition reminded him of Dirty Jackie Pye, an old wrestler from their hometown, and the confrontation rapidly descended into hysterical laughter.

Like Lennon, Nilsson had no recording project to work on in the final weeks of 1973, although he had been toying with the idea of recording a set of songs by Allen Toussaint, in a manner comparable to his earlier Newman project. Those who knew him recognized that despite all the positive enthusiasm that had been kindled in New York when he had met Una O'Keeffe in August, the self-destruct button was being pressed again. Samantha Juste, for example, came to dread Nilsson's arrival at the Dolenz household:

I remember him getting crazier. And then it was depressing because I was seeing Micky going down the same path too. They were getting too crazy, and all the people around them. John Lennon, he was there too. But he seemed to be able to handle it I think.[16]

Lennon managed to control himself, in public at least, that December. Then, he and Nilsson took a much-needed break from each other at Christmas when Nilsson headed for Ireland and Una, who was back at her family home in the Blackrock area of Dublin. Despite the distractions of Lennon's presence in Los Angeles, they had been writing to one another regularly during the fall. Nilsson's letters, their envelopes sometimes inscribed "Fast Please!" under the air mail logo, are an outpouring of his love, and it is clear that her letters to him reciprocated. "I picture you pausing for words to really get through to me," he wrote, "and you do, you really do!" He told her how difficult he found it to write when he had "a million thoughts for every word."[17] However, even with this regular contact, he became so nervous about the visit to Ireland that he invited Micky Dolenz and Samantha Juste to come along and offer moral support when he asked Una's father for her hand in marriage. Una recalled:

He hadn't met my parents until that time. It was exciting. Micky and Samantha and Harry stayed at the Shelbourne Hotel on St. Stephen's Green in Dublin and they invited my parents to dinner. They loved him. You had to—he was an incredibly charming person. And he was so sweet. He said such nice things and flattered my mother. So they all felt good about it. And it was really, really funny, the fact that he wanted Micky and Samantha to be there. It was very charming—he wanted their support, because I think he was a little bit nervous. I know one of my brothers, my brother Paul, was a little bit wary of who this character was, and they had a conversation. Harry was saying, "Well, I love your sister." And Paul was saying, "We love her, too!"[18]

When she arrived in Dublin, Samantha Juste was pleased to see how enthusiastic Nilsson was about Una, and she genuinely hoped this would help him out of the negative spiral he had gotten into with Lennon.

I loved Una. She was a clean living lovely girl, and I went to Ireland and met her parents. He wanted me to go, because he said. "If they meet you, they'll let her go!" He wanted me to be a sort of chaperone, so I met the parents. And he was going to be different, and everything was going to be wonderful. I thought it was going to be a great chance for Harry. He'd get clean and he was going to do this for this girl[19]

After a few days in Ireland, Nilsson took Una to London to spend a week or so at Curzon Place. They celebrated Christmas with Joe Cocker and his friends at Joe's London home. Then Nilsson returned to Los Angeles, and Una went back to college. Far from his earnest statements to Samatha Juste that he was going to reform his character on account of Una, it was just a matter of days before Nilsson and Lennon were hanging out together again.

At some point in 1973, Nilsson—a fan of standup comedy since his days working in the Paramount Theatre—had dropped into a club in Georgetown to see the comic Tom Smothers working through a new set of material before being reunited with his brother Dick. On that occasion, through sheer nerves, Tom romped through his act too fast, and Nilsson came to his aid with some witty heckling that gave the comedian the chance to engage the crowd with one-liner ripostes and complete his set at the proper time.[20]

Not long after Nilsson's return to Los Angeles, the Smothers Brothers opened their new joint act at the Troubadour on March 13, 1974, and Nilsson took Lennon along to see them. During Nilsson's absence, Lennon had been out on the town a few times, and his drinking had escalated, including one occasion when—in a seriously inebriated state—he had attached a sanitary napkin to his forehead in a restaurant and kept it in place for a visit to the Troubadour. When one of the club's world-weary waitresses studiously ignored him, he asked her if she knew who he was, and she replied, "Yes, some asshole with a Kotex on his forehead."[21] This was hushed up at the time, and any possible bad press was avoided, but when Lennon returned to the club with Nilsson for the Smothers Brothers' midnight show, he proceeded to get equally drunk again, slurping down Brandy Alexanders (a potent mixture of cognac, crème de cacao, and cream) as if there was no tomorrow. On the way to the Troubadour, Nilsson had regaled Lennon with the story of how he had heckled Tommy the previous year, and he went so far as to suggest that the brothers might benefit from a little enthusiastic audience participation. But Nilsson cannot have been prepared for what followed. The press reported the next day:

> Customers in the jammed nightclub complained that Lennon made sarcastic comments and shouted obscenities during the comedians' second show. Said the Smothers' manager, Ken Fritz, "I went over and asked Harry to try to shut up Lennon. Harry said, 'I'm trying—don't blame me!' When Lennon continued, I told him to keep quiet. He swung and hit me in the jaw. I hit him back and the first thing I heard was the breaking of glass."[22]

The club bouncers had Lennon out of the place within seconds, and by 12:20, he was on the sidewalk, his entire visit having lasted little over half an hour. A female photographer, Brenda Mary Perkins, tried to snap him with a Polaroid camera, but the enraged Lennon took a swing at her and his fist allegedly connected with her right eye. She filed charges at the sheriff's office a short while later.

By his actions, Lennon had put himself at great risk of being deported from the United States. The Nixon administration had devoted considerable efforts to getting him returned to Britain because of an ancient drug charge for possession of marijuana, and it was clear that if Lennon left the country, he would not be allowed back in. One criminal misdemeanor attached to his record would have been enough to have him sent home. As a result, Lennon immediately launched a press campaign to say that although he admitted being drunk, he had not gone near the photographer.

Nilsson, who had followed Lennon out into the street after the fray, realized he would have to mobilize himself and his friends to protect Lennon's name. His thoughts immediately turned to Jimmy Webb, who said:

> I remember it very well, because they came over to my house the next morning. And Harry again—it was one of those—when Harry wakes you up at nine o'clock in the morning, you know there's trouble. There's something up. He's either gonna steal your car, or something untoward is going to happen. He woke me up at nine o'clock and he says "What're you doin'? I need you to go with me right now."
>
> I said, "Are you crazy? What's going on?"
>
> He said, "I've got John Lennon in the car." He said, "C'mon, c'mon!" I went downstairs and sure enough he had a limousine, and in the back of the limousine was Mr. Lennon. And he says, "You've gotta go with us downtown, John's gotta give a deposition in front of an attorney." I said, "Why on earth do I need to go?" He said, "Because you were at the Troubadour last night, with us, and you saw the whole thing. And John never laid the glove on anybody. Got that?" So here I am in the back of a limo, going downtown to the attorney with John and Harry and I'm going, "Let's see, what's my story again?" Terrifying because I am going to perjure myself. But you see, there was a code. An inflexible, unbreakable code. And it was power and a strength that came along with Harry…anyone who loved him and was his friend did whatever he wanted them to do. Whenever he wanted them to do it.[23]

In an effort to placate the Smothers Brothers and the club owner Doug Weston, Lennon and Nilsson sent them apologetic notes attached to bunches of carnations and chrysanthemums.[24] Eventually, after a two-week investigation, Robert Immerman, the deputy district attorney, dropped the charges against Lennon on the basis of insufficient evidence.[25] He would be able to remain in the United States a little longer, while his appeal against his proposed deportation and his request for a green card continued their snail-like progress though the immigration service.

Nilsson, who was considerably less overcome by the effects of Brandy Alexanders than Lennon, expressed his surprise that following his participation in the affair, the press began to label him as a hell-raiser. He later told the BBC:

> I don't know when it happened. It just sort of happened. "Raising hell with Harry" became the catchphrase of the month. I think it was probably during the period with John when he was bounced out of the Troubadour for being a naughty boy and blaming it all on me, because I wasn't as famous as him, the bum! I was associated then with drinking and carousing, because I think Keith Moon was a friend,

Ringo was a friend, and we had good times, and people assume you're raising hell if you're having a good time. I promise you folks—we don't raise hell, but we do have a good time![26]

In the aftermath of the Troubadour incident, Lennon and Nilsson agreed that they had to do something more positive than spend all their time going out on wild benders. In due course, it was settled that Nilsson would start to record his next album for RCA and that Lennon would produce it. This was not an entirely new idea, because Lennon had announced somewhat garrulously to Phil Spector and a room full of spectators at the *Rock and Roll* sessions the previous fall that he wanted to produce a record by Nilsson. After that evening with Lennon and Spector, Nilsson thought, "Oh, he's drunk, he'll forget about it."[27] But the idea refused to go away, as May Pang recalled: "John and I used to talk about what a magnificent voice he had. When John said, 'I want to produce you, Harry,' he didn't think in a million years that John was going to do it. Then he got really nervous."[28]

Perhaps somewhat foolishly, they decided that they and the principal musicians involved should rent a beach house close to Santa Monica, where their creative juices would flow, and the tracks for the album could be worked on during the daytime before heading for the studio each evening to record.

The house was an elegant two-story villa facing the ocean, with white walls and a terracotta tiled roof. A tall hedge and trees screened its yard and pool from passersby on the beach. Behind it ran the highway to Malibu, and across the road were tall brown cliffs leading back up to Santa Monica. It had been built for the film mogul Louis B. Mayer and was later owned by Peter Lawford. (Ironically, Lawford had been seated at an adjacent table to Lennon and Nilsson during the infamous Troubadour evening and had urged the ex-Beatle to be quiet.) Lawford had often loaned the house to his brothers-in-law, Robert and John F. Kennedy, and it was allegedly where the president had some of his secret trysts with Marilyn Monroe. As Lennon installed himself and Pang in the master bedroom, he cast his eyes around and remarked nonchalantly, "So this is where they did it!"[29]

Lennon took over the property on March 22, and before long, Keith Moon, Ringo, Klaus Voorman, and Nilsson were installed there, along with Ringo's business manager Hilary Gerrard. "We had the wildest assemblage of that part of history in that house," said Nilsson, "it makes the round table look like a toadstool."[30]

The sessions for the album were booked to start at the Record Plant in Hollywood on March 28, the day after Lennon's final court hearing for the Troubadour incident, and the studio was reserved from around 5:30 each evening until midnight. During the week leading up to the recording, a pattern was set that continued with little alteration once the music-making had actually begun. Ferried around by a fleet of limousines, the residents of the house went out on the town from midnight until the small hours, and then sat up drinking and taking drugs when they got home. They awoke in the late morning and recovered from hangovers or worse around the pool during the afternoon, before either playing through songs at the house or—once recording had started—heading to the studio in the evening. May Pang was astonished at the quantity of pharmaceuticals Moon had brought with him and was also aghast at the state he was in most mornings, frequently in the company of a different girl.[31]

Despite the pleasurable diversions available, Lennon and Nilsson did manage to cobble together a list of music to be recorded for the album, which would eventually be titled *Pussy Cats*. On the one hand, because the classic rock and roll repertoire on which Lennon had been working with Spector was still fresh in their minds, they settled on Dylan's "Subterranean Homesick Blues," Jimmy Cliff's "Many Rivers to Cross," Doc Pomus and Mort Shuman's "Save The Last Dance For Me," plus the jam session favorites "Loop De Loop" and "Rock Around The Clock."

Meanwhile, on the other hand, Nilsson had his usual collection of original song ideas that were in various stages of completion. "Black Sails in the Moonlight" had been written a few months earlier as a song for the soundtrack of a pirate movie being made by a friend of Derek Taylor's. Nilsson described it as "a zany, wacky, wonderful kind of yucko song—a sort of blues blood ballad."[32] When it was dropped from the movie, it became an immediate candidate for the album. Its lyrics draw jointly on at least a couple of earlier songs, first in a direct quote from Ira Kosloff and Maurice Mysel's 1956 hit for Elvis Presley, "I Want You, I Need You, I Love You," and second (in some wordplay about a treasure map being imprinted in the veins of a woman's legs) in an allusion to the Carly Simon song on which Nilsson contributed backup vocals, with the line "You're so veiny you probably think this map belongs to you."

He and Lennon jointly came up with "Mucho Mungo / Mt. Elga," in a process which Nilsson described as "He had half of a song, and I had half of a thing I ripped off from an old calypso song I'd heard as a kid. We put 'em together because they fit."[33] The other three Nilsson songs "Don't Forget Me," "All My Life," and "Old Forgotten Soldier" were all hastily finished for the sessions and contain more than a touch of autobiography. The first, "Don't Forget Me," looks back at a failed marriage from "beside the poolside." "All My Life" adds a note of regret for "Shootin' them up / Drinkin' 'em down / Takin' them pills / Foolin' around," which pretty accurately described another aspect of life in the Santa Monica beach house, while "Old Forgotten Soldier" looked back further into Nilsson's past and reverted to his habitual themes of faded glories "left out in the rain" like an "old forgotten railroad." Another song on which a huge amount of energy was expended, but which never made it to the final album, was the "Flying Saucer Song," in which Nilsson speaks the parts of three men at a bar having a conversation about the sighting of a UFO, interspersed with some overdubbed singing.

One reason this song was omitted from the album is that Nilsson's speech is so slurred that at times it is unintelligible, and because his singing voice simply is not up to the challenge of the falsetto overdubs. Indeed, the constant late nights, the drink, and the drugs were taking their toll on him physically, and the beautiful transparent sound of his upper register voice on Ringo's "You're Sixteen" from the previous year was no longer there. When the *Pussy Cats* sessions began, he was still, as he had been when he started his career, in awe of Lennon. So, instead of admitting he was in danger of seriously damaging his vocal cords, Nilsson carried on both with the recordings and the party lifestyle, never telling Lennon as the sessions progressed, that his throat was becoming a painful, bleeding mess. May Pang witnessed Lennon adopting his habitual work ethic as the studio sessions began, in stark contrast to Nilsson:

> Harry really couldn't understand that he did have a problem. I've seen him over the years and he always had a problem with drinking and drugs. And when we were doing his album, it was hard because he didn't tell [us]. John was almost sober during that whole time, and Harry wasn't. He hid from John the fact that he was still drinking and that he hemorrhaged in his vocal cords. He sounded so horrible. The majority of the vocals were redone in New York, because they were unusable. And Harry, during the day would go and get acupuncture done, and at night he was doing coke and drinking brandy. Now you tell me what happens there, you know! His voice just was shot. He didn't tell us he hemorrhaged, nothing.[34]

There is no obvious sign of damage to Nilsson's voice on the first track to be recorded, "Subterranean Homesick Blues," which was cut on Thursday, March 28, and features him in the heavy rocker mode of "Jump Into The Fire" from *Nilsson Schmilsson*. The session sheets show that Jim Keltner was nominally the musician who contracted the players for the date, although Nilsson's Santa Monica housemates Ringo Starr and Klaus Voormann (who can both be heard prominently on the track) are absent from the listing in the RCA archive (although they are mentioned in the liner credits for most issues). Nilsson's vocal is double-tracked, no doubt to give it some strength and projection over the deep, dark sounds of the backing band, anchored by Voormann's urgent bass and the massed drums of Starr and Keltner.

However, this track exemplifies one of the mysteries of the *Pussy Cats* sessions, which is that the quadraphonic mix is entirely different from the originally issued stereo version. As a general rule, Nilsson's voice is more prominent and in better fettle on the tracks used for the quad issue, but on "Subterranean Homesick Blues," there is also a radical adjustment in balance between the bass and drums. The quad album reduces the drum echo and pushes the bass more into the foreground. Nilsson enthusiasts have tended to argue that because his voice is better on the quadraphonic mixes, these vocal tracks must have been recorded first, before he damaged his vocal cords. But there is no evidence for this, and in any event in late March, there would have been no backing tracks for Nilsson to sing over, as these were constructed, roughly at the rate of one a day, up until April 10 when Lennon moved out of the beach house with May Pang and called an end to the recordings. He and Pang then flew back to New York and booked time during the following two months at the East Coast branch of the Record Plant to finish the mixing and re-dub the majority of the vocals.

Days two and three of the L.A. sessions, Friday, March 29, and Monday, April 1, were officially devoted to "Many Rivers to Cross" and the "Flying Saucer Song," and Nilsson's voice degraded rapidly over this weekend. This was partly because around midnight on Thursday, March 28, just as the first session was wrapping up, Paul McCartney suddenly appeared in the studio, along with Stevie Wonder and the producer Ed Freeman. After some slightly prickly banter between the two ex-Beatles, it was suggested that Paul might play something, and he and Wonder joined Keltner, Nilsson, Lennon, Bobby Keys, and Jesse Ed Davis on a few rambling informal tracks. Lennon was passing cocaine around, and his offer of a "toot" to Stevie Wonder gave the bootleg album containing these tracks its title, *A Toot and a Snore in '74*. Singing more than he should have done to preserve his voice, Nilsson contributes an enthusiastic, shouty vocal to "Stand By Me" alongside Lennon's more restrained voice, before Stevie Wonder adds his inimitable singing as well. The thrill of vocalizing alongside Lennon, McCartney, and Wonder on "Chain Gang" also drew more hoarse singing from Nilsson. It was the last time the two former Beatles ever played and sang together in a studio, although McCartney spent much of the following Sunday afternoon at the beach house, informally jamming with Lennon while Nilsson, Moon, and Ringo were out.

A Toot and a Snore was not the only extracurricular session that was made during the *Pussy Cats* recordings. Nilsson also lent some harsh backing vocals to "Too Many Cooks (Spoil The Soup)," a single track that Lennon produced for Mick Jagger, who had been staying at the Beverly Wilshire along with Moon, Lennon, and Ringo during the week or so before they moved to the beach house. In the backing band for Jagger were Bobby Keys, Danny Kortchmar (a.k.a. Danny Kootch), Jesse Ed Davis, and Jim Keltner, all of whom were working on *Pussy Cats*, plus Al Kooper and Jack Bruce. It seems as if this simple rocking track with a magisterial solo from Keys and some growly singing from Jagger came as light relief on April 2, after most of the same musicians had spent the earlier part of the evening wrestling with the "Flying Saucer Song." Nilsson enthusiasts have often tended to date this track to late 1973, but former Apple assistant Chris O'Dell was in the Record Plant studio for the recording and helpfully recorded the date in her diary.[35]

Also in the studio for that after-hours recording was Richard Perry, who had dropped by earlier in the evening to see how things were going with Lennon and Nilsson. Watching Lennon working on this completely unofficial track gave him an insight into the total concentration that Lennon brought to record-making, however wild his life had been outside the studio walls. "They had to know," Perry said, "that there was no way of Mick and John persuading their respective record companies to go along with it and release it. But John treated it as if it was the most important track of his life. He was just totally absorbed in the studio. I suggested an edit that might help them improve some aspect of it, and we did that, but just seeing his passion for a track which might never be released, I realized he had just as much passion for that as he did for the next track on Harry's album which they would be cutting the next day."[36]

The first two tracks recorded for *Pussy Cats*, "Subterranean Homesick Blues" and "Many Rivers to Cross" are the best of the cover versions on the album in terms of Nilsson's singing. His husky voice is painful to hear on "Save the Last Dance for Me," and it sounds worn out on "Loop De Loop," becoming virtually a monotonous rumble on "Rock Around the Clock." However, that track is enlivened by the honking saxophones of Bobby Keys, Trevor Lawrence, and Jim Horn, plus a searing guitar solo from Jesse Ed Davis.

Nilsson's own songs fare better and include two originals that might have been highly successful hits in the hands of a more experienced producer, such as Richard Perry. On the first of them, "Don't Forget Me," Nilsson sings to his own homespun piano, with a brilliant and subtle string arrangement added by Ken Ascher. Just as Nilsson's somewhat clunky piano playing was a vital ingredient of "Without You," it is an integral component here, his slight variations in tempo and the odd hesitation adding to the charm of this wistful, poignant song. It is also the one song on the album that displays something of the tone, clarity, and range of his former voice, and this was dubbed in during May or June in New York, when his vocal cords had had time to recover from the ravages of early April.

A demo version of "Don't Forget Me" that survives from early in the Record Plant West sessions is taken at a faster tempo and has some frenetic drumming from Keltner and Starr, as well as a bass line from Voormann. Lennon wisely stripped away this accompaniment altogether and used the string section to underline the dramatic movement between the two sections of the tune. But compared to the polish of a Perry or Jarrard/Tipton production, the track still seems slightly unfinished. The quad mix has the cleaner-sounding vocal of the two issued versions, and in particular, a throaty catch on the line "Make it easy on me" is avoided. Some subtle double-tracking of Nilsson's voice on the verse beginning "In the summer time" recalls the choruses of "Without You" and, as the song subsides into its sad final reflections about old age and cancer, Nilsson deliberately allows a momentary huskiness to appear. His voice on the original stereo mix has not got quite such a clean sound as the quad version, but it carries more emotional punch, and the song deserves reappraisal both as one of his best compositions and because it is unquestionably the finest performance on this album.

"All My Life" is a creatively catchy piece, and its loping accompaniment with some snarling bass notes from Voormann and pelting woodblock from Keith Moon over the rattling snare drums of Keltner and Starr creates a bed for Nilsson's patter vocal. There are parallels here with "Gotta Get Up," both in Nilsson's delivery—again his voice sounds more like his old self—and in the host of tiny details paced into the fast-moving words. But what lets the piece down is the string arrangement. Almost every note is arrived at via a scooping glissando that slides up into pitch. The end result is akin to trying to stand upright on the deck of a rolling ship, or perhaps more accurately trying to see the world straight after "drinkin' 'em down" and "takin' them pills." The song lacks a credible second section to give it some real development or any respite from this uncomfortable pitching. Again, Perry's instinct for song structure would have come in handy here, although given the overall chaos of producing the album, Lennon must have been grateful to have even a halfway serviceable track.

There were further reports of craziness as the West Coast sessions progressed, some of which were done at Burbank Studios. There are tales of Lennon and Nilsson riding motorcycles around, and epic nights of drinking and merrymaking. At one point Nilsson lost his voice more or less completely. So he went to see a doctor who specialized in treating throat complaints. Klaus Voormann remembers:

> He was worried about going there, so he said to all of us in the band, "Why don't you come along?" So we did. I remember the doctor's name was Kantor, and as Harry was sitting in the chair with the doctor looking down his throat, we were all standing in the surgery [doctor's office], staring over his shoulder at what was going on. There was John Lennon, Jesse Ed, Van Dyke and myself. The doctor said sternly to Nilsson, "You are not going to talk for two weeks. And you are not going to sing. If you have anything to say, write it down." Of course, Nilsson didn't keep to that, or at least not for long. But for a day or two, having gone to the store and got these little blocks of paper, we all kept quiet and wrote notes to each other. Harry wrote some very funny things, but the most amusing event was when we all went with him to buy a pair of trousers. The sales people thought we were completely nuts, because we did the whole thing entirely by using notes on these little pieces of paper, nobody actually said a word to each other from the moment we went into the store to the moment we left![37]

At the end of two weeks of similar high jinks, Lennon's self-preservation instincts kicked in. As May Pang recalled:

> In L.A., they had more of a lax attitude when making records. That's what I found. It was a tough situation. Harry would do one thing to make his vocals great or get his voice back, and at night he'd be out there drinking again, and it would undo everything. And this was a cycle. Finally John said, "We can't do it here. We'll have to redo all the vocals back in New York. I can't be in L.A. any longer."[38]

Lennon also had plans to make a further album of his own, given the ongoing debacle with Spector over the tapes for *Rock and Roll*. He and his engineer Roy Cicala, who had been with him in Los Angeles, retreated to the Record Plant East and the safety of its cutting room in Manhattan. As well as setting out to repair what he could of *Pussy Cats*, Lennon started planning what would become his *Walls and Bridges* album, which he began rehearsing on July 13.[39] He reflected in an interview at the time:

> In L.A. you either have to be down at the beach or you become part of that never-ending show business party circuit. That scene makes me nervous, and when I get

nervous I have to have a drink and when I drink I get aggressive. So I prefer to stay in New York. I try not to drink at all here.[40]

Looking back from the comparative calm of New York on the actual business of recording, Lennon was astute in his observations about Nilsson's behavior in L.A. He said, "I think it was psychosomatic. I think he was nervous because *I* was producing him. You know he was an old Beatle fan when he was in the bank....But I was committed to the thing, the band was there and the guy had no voice, so we made the best of it."[41] Lennon also observed in more than one interview that he would end up taking the blame from both the fans and the media for it being a poor album (which he did) and for trying to make Nilsson sound like Lennon himself. He was particularly stung by the last comment, because he felt that even despite the screaming yelp toward the end of "Many Rivers to Cross," which has its Lennon-like aspects, the whole reason he had wanted to record Nilsson in the first place was because of Nilsson's very individual sound.

When Lennon arrived back in New York toward the end of April, Nilsson did not share the journey, because Una had recently arrived from Ireland to join him in L.A. They then flew to Atlanta with Ringo for the premiere of *Son of Dracula* on April 19. Despite a slightly halfhearted publicity campaign involving hearses, hot-air balloons, and even a ghoulish makeup competition, the press was not kind, pointing out, "They premiered it in Atlanta because nobody else would take it."[42] One reviewer said that without the mystique of its two main stars, Nilsson and Starr, the film had "about as much appeal as a dubbed Mexican monster movie on television."[43] There were one or two more provincial showings, and then after a flicker of interest in Manhattan, it faded away forever. Nilsson's co-star Suzanna Leigh said that when the New York reviews finally appeared, they were "the worst reviews ever."[44]

After the premiere, Una returned to Ireland for her final term of school, but before Nilsson went to New York to work further on *Pussy Cats*, he had one more attempt at feature filmmaking with Ringo. The idea was to document their nocturnal Los Angeles social life in a multimedia movie. Part animation, part live action, it was provisionally entitled *Harry and Ringo's Night Out*. Recording entrepreneur Mike Viner, who had recently done a deal with Atlantic to distribute his Pride Records imprint, agreed to finance the venture, and his ideas were extremely visionary for 1974. He budgeted $1.5 million for the movie, but began shooting a pilot in mid-April which, he told the press, would "test some different techniques like 3-D and quadrasonic sound." The pilot alone cost $25,000, and a sample was scheduled to be screened at the Beverly Hills Theater on June 17, before invited guests from the music industry, whom Viner hoped would put further funds into the project. It seems that this was not successful, and the movie went no further, but Viner did briefly strike up a publishing partnership with Nilsson and bought the rights to some material he had written with Perry Botkin Jr.[45]

In New York, Lennon's main thought was to make as serviceable a job as possible of finishing the album. But he immediately discovered that they had been operating on very shaky ground in L.A., because the seven-year option on Nilsson's 1967 contract with RCA had actually expired, and although a replacement had been drafted, it had never been signed. This would not have been a problem had Rocco Laginestra still been the head of RCA's records division, because he remained a strong supporter of Nilsson. But at the end of 1973, he had moved to the parent company to oversee a corporate restructure, and Kenneth Glancy had been appointed in his place.[46]

Media pundits predicted that Glancy would make sweeping changes to the records division, which would include dispensing with artists whose success was marginal or unpredictable. Had Nilsson managed a repeat of the commercial triumph of *Nilsson Schmilsson*, his position would have been unassailable, but the controversial lyrics and lack of a hit single on *Son of Schmilsson*, followed by a standards album that—despite being decades ahead of its time—was not a strong seller, had put him in jeopardy.

Within a couple of days of Nilsson arriving in New York toward the end of April, Lennon decided that the two of them should pay Glancy a visit at the RCA Tower at Rockefeller Center. For over three months, Nilsson's requests to have his contract signed had been ignored or sidestepped, but Lennon figured that if he appeared in person with Nilsson and hinted that he might be prepared to sign his solo albums to RCA, then Glancy could not ignore them. After a wild night out, during which neither Nilsson nor Lennon had been to sleep, they arrived at the RCA building at 10 a.m. wearing hats and shades and demanded to see Glancy. They were immediately ushered into his office and offered cigars and brandy. Lennon turned on his considerable powers of persuasion, saying that RCA really only had two artists of any stature, Elvis Presley and Nilsson. For the money they proposed to pay Nilsson, he, Lennon, would be prepared to sign with the company. At that, Glancy asked for the Nilsson contract to be brought in, and he signed it then and there. In various accounts, including his long interview with Dawn Eden for *Goldmine*, Nilsson said the deal was worth five million dollars.[47] In fact, it was worth somewhat less, namely a total of four and a half million, on the basis of an advance against royalties of $562,500 to be paid on delivery for each of eight albums. Glancy signed it on April 26, 1974.[48] In future years, Nilsson would say that he owed everything to Lennon for that negotiation, even though he did not collect the entire $4,500,000. This was because (despite some accounts to the contrary) the costs of recording were deducted from the advance payable on each album. Furthermore, ultimately, he only delivered five of the eight albums specified in the agreement, starting with *Pussy Cats*.[49]

With the contract signed, Nilsson's confidence and voice began to return. He, Lennon, and Cicala installed themselves in Studio C on the tenth floor of the Manhattan Record Plant, and set about mixing the album, finalizing arrangements, overdubbing some instrumental parts, and adding less husky vocals. Cicala, a veteran of Lennon's previous four albums, observed at the time, "They were serious, having a good time, but mostly they just came in and did the work."[50]

In New York, Lennon assumed a different personality from the man Nilsson had come to know in California. Nilsson noticed immediately that he could simply fade anonymously into the bustling city: "He could turn invisible. He'd take off his hat, wear different glasses, and adopt another persona. He'd walk slowly and he was no longer John Lennon."⁵¹ This was the very kind of anonymity that Nilsson loved about his own life in Los Angeles, where by never having given live concerts and using a variety of disguises on his album covers, he could pass by the majority of the population unrecognized and unobserved. Nilsson and Lennon were staying at the Pierre Hotel, and as the mixing and dubbing went on, they decorated the walls of Lennon's room with images and slogans that might be used for the album cover art and title. Despite sharing a house in Santa Monica and spending hours together on both sides of the continent, Nilsson was still discovering aspects of Lennon's personality, and one night as they had been laughing at some ideas for titles, Lennon sneezed. He then just walked over to the expensive brocade drapes by the window and blew his nose on them. Nilsson was appalled. "Harry," said Lennon, "what the fuck? It's just going to turn into dust in a little while. It's nothing."⁵² Nilsson was also taken aback by Lennon's habit of relieving himself whenever he felt the need, and not necessarily seeking any privacy to do so.

Once the overdubs were finished, Lennon and Cicala focused on the mix. "I became an extra arm, an unnecessary ear," said Nilsson. "I busied myself in New York, working on the cover, the title and the inside stuff, plus locating Derek Taylor for the liner notes."⁵³

One day in a pharmacy close to the Pierre, Nilsson found a child's postcard of two anthropomorphic cats dressed up in dainty dresses and fixing one another's hair, and he immediately realized this would solve their search for the new album's cover art, especially if his and Lennon's heads were superimposed over the feline ones. RCA vetoed the original proposal for the album to be called *Strange Pussies*, but went along with *Pussy Cats*, although their marketing department failed to notice the coded addition to the design of the children's letter blocks "D" and "S." These were placed on each side of the kittens' rug, thereby spelling out "d-rug-s." Before the album itself was released on August 19, two singles appeared. "Many Rivers to Cross" came out in mid-July. This was closely followed by "Subterranean Homesick Blues." Both Lennon's and Dylan's names were prominently featured in the press advertisements for the latter. Neither single did particularly well, and *Pussy Cats* only crept to number sixty on the top 200 album chart.

As Lennon finished work on *Pussy Cats* and started on *Walls and Bridges*, he continued to spend much of his spare time with Nilsson. Even though he professed to be aiming at greater sobriety than in L.A. and was working a nine-to-five routine from Monday to Friday, there were nevertheless some wild evenings on the weekends. At the time, Derek Taylor was in town, staying at the Algonquin Hotel while George Melly and his band appeared at Michael's Pub. Indeed, somewhat incongruously, Taylor brought the entire Melly entourage of rotund middle-aged English jazz musicians into the Record Plant to watch Nilsson redoing the vocal for "Save the Last Dance For Me," only to be hushed and hurried from the studio by Lennon. "Actually, we hadn't said a bloody word," remarked Taylor, "Hardly dared to breathe or strike a match, any of us."⁵⁴ Yet Lennon showed no comparable restraint when he appeared with Nilsson in the small hours a couple of nights later at Taylor's hotel suite, intent on smashing the chandeliers. Expelled by Taylor, Lennon called Melly's female publicist who was also staying in the hotel and demanded sex with her. "She replied, 'I'm asleep, go away,' " reported a somewhat intrigued Melly. "I couldn't help reflecting when I heard about it the next morning on the number of girls round the world who would have received that phone call from John Lennon with a certain enthusiasm."[55]

Nilsson remained in New York beyond the finishing of his own album to add some lyrics and a background vocal to "Old Dirt Road" on Lennon's *Walls and Bridges*, spontaneously drawing together verbal pictures of rural Americana in lines such as "trying to shovel smoke with a pitchfork in the wind." But then he returned to Los Angeles, where Una joined him, and the two of them set off for a short vacation in Hawaii.[56] When they returned, Una moved in with him for good, having finished her studies in Ireland.

That August he would team up with Ringo Starr and Richard Perry to take part in Ringo's *Goodnight Vienna* album and, by coincidence, he once again found himself working with Lennon on that disc, albeit slightly at arm's length. This was because, in July, Lennon took time out from finishing *Walls and Bridges* to help Ringo by making demos of his contributions, as May Pang recalled:

> John had already written the song "Goodnight Vienna" for Ringo. So just before we started the *Walls and Bridges* album, John told the band, "Listen, I've got one song. Let's make a demo; it's going to be sent down to Ringo." It has a lot of different changes and so he wanted Richard [Perry] to be prepared when we arrived in L.A. to do the track [itself].... Then what happened was Ringo was one song short for the album and they didn't know what to do, so John goes, "I'm going to give you a song that I was going to do [for the *Rock and Roll* album]. And I know you can do it because we can make it in your key. It's called 'Only You.' " It was the old Platters tune. He already had the arrangement, so he sat around, with all the musicians, and he played out the arrangement, and he showed them how he wanted it done. The guide vocal track was John's. John sang the song with Ringo and Jim Keltner playing drums. And then later on Ringo did the final vocals.[57]

In Nilsson's contributions to the *Goodnight Vienna* album, which were recorded at Sunset Sound during August, his voice had recovered remarkably from the ravages of *Pussy Cats*. He is first in evidence on Hoyt Axton's "No No Song," which carries an extended—if ironic—anti-drugs and alcohol message. The song opens with a chorus of Nilsson oohs and aahs, and as the track progresses, Nilsson brilliantly shadows Ringo's vocal through each "no no no no" chorus, as well as providing "aay, aay, aay" links between verses. The difference in production values between Lennon's work and Perry's is immediately obvious, however passionate and committed Lennon may have been in the studio. Here, as well as meticulously balanced vocals, Voormann's bass line is etched in sharp relief against Nicky Hopkins's discreet electric piano and the brilliantly detailed guitar interpolations from Jesse Ed Davis. The horn parts from Trevor Lawrence and Bobby Keys are low key and effective. The cast list is almost identical to several tracks on *Pussy Cats*, but the difference lies in the discipline of Perry's rigorous and painstaking efforts to achieve as perfect a take as possible in the studio. The song was to chart at number three the following year.

On "Only You," Ringo having based his slightly tentative lead vocal on the demo recorded by Lennon in New York, Nilsson again added a quantity of backing vocals as he had done the previous year on "You're Sixteen." His range is more restricted, but the tone is mellow and the control admirable. As Ringo speaks a basso profundo version of the lyric, Ink Spots style, Nilsson provides an impressive array of harmonic oohs and aahs. Ringo was charmed, saying at the time, "Harry is the only backing vocal on it. He's like a man of a thousand voices, Harry, he's amazing what he can do."[58] The song was released prior to the album and reached number six on the pop singles charts.

It might seem that Ringo's voice was not ideally suited to a romantic ballad, but that is what Nilsson provided for him to sing on this album, in the form of the words and music for the song "Easy for Me." There are moments when it sounds almost as if Ringo is doing an impression of Nilsson, but Richard Perry worked hard to avoid this track descending into pastiche, as it is an excellent piece of ballad writing, featuring Nilsson's typical elisions of the lyric line and slightly unexpected verse structure. In creating the backing for the track, Perry replaced Nilsson's own piano playing with the suave concert style of the session musician (and subsequently Gershwin specialist) Lincoln Mayorga. Ringo introduced the piece to British radio listeners as follows:

> Nilsson wrote this next track and it's the only one on the album with full orchestra. It's piano, my voice and orchestra. We did the basic track just with piano, and then we overdubbed the orchestra. Trevor Lawrence and Vini Poncia arranged the strings on this one and Richard Perry conducted it. It's a nice slow ballad, and I thank Harry very much for writing it for me, because it's so beautiful.[59]

The *Goodnight Vienna* album with Lennon's bouncy contributions to the title song, plus guest appearances from Elton John, Stax guitarist Steve Cropper, and Dr. John, as well as Nilsson, reached number eight on the American album charts. It showed Nilsson still on good terms with Perry, who was able to conjure performances from him that seemed almost impossible, given what had happened to his voice. And again, Perry proved that his methods could create chart hits, both at album and single levels, whereas Nilsson and Lennon had failed to do this, despite no less suitable raw material, on *Pussy Cats*.

Ringo's record also gave Nilsson the opportunity to work again with Stanley Dorfman. In 1974, Dorfman was no longer working full-time for the BBC. Having pioneered several aspects of the music video for the *Top of the Pops* show in Britain, he was increasingly making promotional films for albums, and he was engaged to film a commercial for *Goodnight Vienna*. The album cover showed Ringo as the alien Klaafu, adapted from the movie poster for *The Day the Earth Stood Still*. Consequently, the flying saucer theme was continued into the commercial, which featured a voiceover from John Lennon ("Is that Ringo Starr advertising his new album…") as a spacecraft lands next to a suitably futuristic building and Ringo clambers into it before taking off over the city. The building chosen was the headquarters of Capitol Records in Hollywood, the white tower that had been designed to look from a distance like a stack of discs. Ringo, Nilsson, and Keith Moon were among the cast assembled on top of the structure. Dorfman recalled:

> We shot on the roof of the Capitol building, and the roof slopes. It slopes from the middle downwards, so everybody was terrified of falling off. They were drinking, and getting a little far-gone, staggering around a bit. I was really terrified that one of them was going to fall. And we had a helicopter, which we got permission for. Insane permission. I don't know how we got it, but we took off from the car park, and went up, found them on camera, and then just went up and up and up. It was very exciting. They were dancing on there, leaping about all over the place, which was actually terrifying. I was directing from the roof, but I was behind them in some little building thing, a little structure up there. So we did that. And then we had a marching band. It was one of the very earliest music videos, I suppose. There wasn't any MTV at that point, so I guess it aired as a commercial.[60]

Nilsson was highly amused by the video shoot. Assembled on top of the building at various times were the flying saucer (a lightweight construction that Dorfman's helicopter towed into the air for the action shots), plus a forty-foot robot called Gort, Ringo in a spacesuit, and a rocking chair. Nilsson sat in the chair wearing his brown robe, reading that morning's *Los Angeles Times*, with a front-page photo showing Ringo in his space costume. Prancing around below them at ground level were a marching band clad in dazzling orange, as Dorfman mentioned, and forty midgets, most of whom were former Munchkins from the *Wizard of Oz*. Dorfman had arranged lasers to shoot beams of light from an adjacent building onto Ringo's breastplate. The complications of filming all this action, preventing Nilsson's rocking chair from sliding over the edge of the building, and getting the lighting and lasers right for the helicopter-mounted camera took all day. Between takes, Keith Moon, who was happily taunting his fellow performers with witty quips during filming, was on the floor below the roof, surrounded by increasingly intoxicated Munchkins, serving drinks. "It was brandy, brandy, brandy at every opportunity," remembered Nilsson. "Keith was in his element, in fact we all seemed to be, finally drunk, and about to have fun, knocking over the precarious rocking chair and dancing with Ringo. Stan managed to get it all somehow, but I don't know how he did it!"[61]

In the final cut for the one-minute television commercial, the footage with Nilsson and the rocking chair was not used; nor do the Munchkins or Keith Moon appear. But a world-weary horse and a vintage Rolls-Royce add to the curiosities on display as Ringo's spacecraft lands bumpily in the Capitol car park and then takes off again, amid clouds of dry ice.

For the time being, the film commercial for *Goodnight Vienna* marked the end of Nilsson's close association with various ex-Beatles. The following year, Ringo would return the favor and appear in a promotional movie for Nilsson, but with his voice returning and his new contract in hand, Nilsson returned to the studio to produce his own next album, *Duit On Mon Dei*. With less need to worry financially about how long this took, after preliminary sessions in July 1974, he was to spend all of September and part of October back at RCA's Hollywood studios with a vast cast of musicians and extras.

8

TURN OUT THE LIGHT

On Tuesday, July 30, 1974, the day before the first official session for the album that became *Duit On Mon Dei* was scheduled to take place at RCA in Los Angeles, Hilary Gerrard telephoned Nilsson with an urgent message. He had just received a call from London to say that the singer "Mama" Cass Elliot had been found dead the previous night in Nilsson's Curzon Place apartment. Little more than a month earlier, Nilsson had been her guest for dinner in Los Angeles, where she told him that she was about to go to Britain for two weeks of concerts at the London Palladium. He recalled:

> I mentioned to her it seemed silly to pay for hotels in London, and suggested she stay at Number 9. "You can house-sit." She was happy and we parted with a kiss. I gave her the key from my pocket.[1]

The fourteen performances went extremely well for Elliot, who had successfully reinvented herself as a solo artist after coming to fame as a member of the Mamas and the Papas. After many months of battling with a weight problem that had threatened to end her career, although she was still heavy and needed to pace herself carefully throughout the shows, she knew she had a strong act to offer the British public. Her run at the Palladium sold out, and there were nightly standing ovations. Her manager Allan Carr said that she was happier than he had ever seen her, and before celebrating after the curtain fell on her final show, she told him, "I have never felt better about anything I have ever done professionally."[2]

The celebrations over, she returned to Curzon Place feeling very tired on Sunday night. The following day, her assistant Dot McLeod and singer Joe Croyle who had also been in the Palladium show tiptoed around the apartment trying not to disturb Elliot, as she was never an early riser. Then at 6:30 that Monday evening, thinking that it was late even for a nocturnal being like Elliot, McLeod went into the bedroom and found her dead: "slightly propped up in her double bed. A ham sandwich and a soft drink were beside her on the pillow, and the TV set was on."[3] In the public's imagination, the food was to take the blame for her death, because prior to a postmortem examination, her doctor, Anthony Greenburg, told the media "the singer probably choked to death on the ham sandwich."[4] This report was flashed around the world and seemed to be confirmed when the pathologist, Professor Keith Simpson, told *The Times* in London that she might not have died from natural causes and that further tests were needed. The paper repeated the sandwich story in the next paragraph of its report.[5]

Because of the doubts about the cause of Elliot's death, there was an inquest. When this finally ruled a week later that she had died of natural causes, from "fatty myocardial degeneration" as the result of being morbidly obese, it was tucked away in the news columns and barely noticed by her fans, many of whom believe to this day that she was killed by a sandwich. Rather, it was because she stood five feet, five inches tall and weighed (even after her diet regime) 238 pounds. Being so overweight had led, according to the grisly details given to the coroner by Professor Simpson, to "fatty degeneration of the heart muscle fibre."[6]

Nilsson thought back to the hangman's noose that had been etched on the bathroom mirror in his apartment. But arrangements were swiftly made to clear the flat of Cass Elliot's effects, and he was forced to put the tragedy out of his mind as he went to work on his new album.

In many ways, *Duit On Mon Dei* was to be an extension of the methods he had used for his own compositions on *Pussy Cats*, with songs worked out collectively in the studio from little more than fragments of lyrics or melody. Several of the same musicians were present, although Nilsson himself replaced Lennon as producer, with the engineer Richie Schmitt as his deputy. His voice had recovered considerably from the ravages of earlier in the year, and as he had now done several times, he took some unfinished or unsatisfactory material from earlier records and revamped it for the present project. Yet it was an all-new song that he brought into the studio on July 31.

The resulting piece became Nilsson's "Easy for Me," and his first action was to give the recording to Ringo as a demo for *Goodnight Vienna*. For his own version of the song, subtly retitled (with a typical Nilsson in-joke) "Easier For Me," he gave the same July demo to another old colleague, the brass player Jim Price, who helped out with a completely different arrangement. Ultimately, Price's score was recorded with strings on September 14, along with a new vocal track. Although Nilsson's voice no longer has the luster of *A Little Touch of Schmilsson in the Night*, and he is a shade hoarse on the high notes, he demonstrates what potential the song had for a singer a little more accomplished than Ringo. Price's string arrangement is much sparser than Trevor Lawrence and Vini Poncia's for *Goodnight Vienna*. Without a piano (or the somewhat hyperactive harp that Perry had added), the majority of the track draws the listener's attention to the balance between the delicate orchestral texture and Nilsson's voice. In terms of space and musicality, it shows just how much Nilsson had learned from working with Gordon Jenkins.

Yet to those who had known the glories of Nilsson's voice in its heyday, even this fine song was a letdown. For some of the more ambitious pieces on the album, Nilsson called on his old friend Perry Botkin Jr., who accepted with alacrity the opportunity to work with him again as arranger and musical director. Nevertheless, Botkin felt that Lennon's influence, the "lost weekend," and the saga of the making of *Pussy Cats* had all but ruined Nilsson's status as one of the finest white male singers on the planet:

> That was the beginning of the end. They were a friendship made in hell, as far as I'm concerned. John had his troubles. Harry had his troubles. And they got together and really that was when Harry totally blew his voice, I mean to the point where he was bleeding, and he just destroyed his voice. And those albums—and from *Pussy Cats* on, I worked on several—that wasn't Harry. You listen to them now compared to the earlier things; and he was trying to adjust. He was becoming funkier by that time…to get more soul in his voice and all this kind of thing. Well, it wasn't that he was trying to get more soul. He was trying to sing around his problems, and he couldn't, and he never really did pull it off. I mean it just broke my heart, because I was there when he really sang good. But we do what we do. He still laughed, and he still had funny jokes.[7]

The first two tracks on which Botkin worked, starting on September 10, were a revised version of "What's Your Sign" (which had been dropped from *Son of Schmilsson*, despite the ravishing unissued performance produced by Richard Perry from those sessions) and another recent song called "Down By the Sea." Indeed, all the songs on the new album were written by Nilsson (or in the case of "Salmon Falls," co-written by Nilsson and Klaus Voormann). Whereas the earlier London version of "What's Your Sign" is light and frothy and has some clever overdubs of Nilsson's effortless falsetto register, offset by some characteristically bluesy piano from Nicky Hopkins, the new version sounds rather like a clunky throwback to a 1950s party record. There is a prominent tambourine and a reed section built around a honking baritone sax. Nilsson's attempts at high register vocals, backed by the fulsome voices of the Zodiac Singers, are self-conscious, and the whole effect is stagey, almost like a film set of a party. As it turned out, flush with the generous terms of his new contract, Nilsson had transformed the recording session itself into a five-week party. "He wanted everybody in the studio to be happy," recalled Una, who was there for the earlier part of several evenings before she went home to bed, leaving Nilsson and the others to work into the small hours. "If people weren't happy," she said, "what was the point of recording a song? There were no hysterics, or anything like that. He worked very hard."[8] But according to Botkin, it was something of a miracle that any serious work got done at all:

> First of all, Harry had a full bar set up in the studio, with hors d'oeuvres. I mean with everything, from corned beef to bagels, and bottles of booze, any drink you could possibly want. And, let's say, the orchestra got very loose after about the first

hour. It took an enormous amount of time to get something done. And of course it was fun, we were all in the bag and laughing and carrying on. But it certainly was a silly way to make records.[9]

Nilsson had also decided to attempt to record as much of the album as possible by singing live with the backing musicians, as he had done with Jenkins in London. But this presented some problems for Botkin and for the other musical director who arranged the majority of the tracks and played piano on most of the album, Van Dyke Parks. In the case of some songs, Nilsson had complete lyrics written out, but for others, there would be part of a lyric and further ideas scrawled on anything that was at hand. And although he might have taped fragments of a melody or have a tune in his head, extricating it and communicating it to a studio filled with increasingly inebriated musicians was never going to be easy. Botkin felt this was very similar to the process he had experienced with Phil Spector over a decade before:

> When we were laying out the songs, [Nilsson] would come in with these little bits and pieces, and then I would sit down there and say, "Well what do you think of this?" and play him some ideas. "We'll bring the strings in here." "Oh, yeah," and that's the way I worked with most of the artists that I worked with. But in this particular case, there was a lot more sweeping up, and extending. The ideas were getting shorter and if I could extend them, then right on the spot, he might come up with a line or something. That's the way we worked. I'd say, "That's great. Let's leave that in and we'll do that." And we ended up getting at least thirty minutes of music out of it.[10]

Botkin's second contribution to the album, "Down By the Sea," recorded the day after "What's Your Sign," is in some respects the track that sets the mood for the whole record. A trial version of the song had been cut during the *Pussy Cats* sessions in April, but it was rejected because Nilsson's voice was so lacking in power, it barely cut through the energetic background. Botkin's version picks up several elements of the demo, principally a light Caribbean feel, largely from the inspired steel-drum playing of the Trinidadian maestro Robert Greenidge, who had been introduced to Nilsson by Van Dyke Parks. Born in 1950, Greenidge had been a member of a multiple award-winning band, the Desperadoes, on his home island before studying music in New York and moving to California to join the Music Makers Steel Orchestra in Los Angeles. Nilsson described him as "the best steel-drum player alive,"[11] and it is clear that his rhythmically precise and melodically inventive presence enlivens much of the album. Nilsson said at the time that "it adds another dimension to the music. It adds color to it. And it seemed to fit all the songs, because the songs are kinda light, and the steel drums brought out a lot of the goodness from them."[12] Indeed, the first reviews picked this up immediately, saying that it was "a tribute and study into the variety of ways reggae music can be used."[13] Yet not all the critics agreed, some lambasting what was described as a "frail attempt at calypso."[14] Nilsson was scathing in his response, saying, "Those assholes! They're used to hearing one instrument all the time like the piano. Then they don't think anything of it. If I used one guitar, they wouldn't call it a guitar album. But I use one steel drum and they call it a calypso album. Does that make sense?"[15]

Greenidge takes his most impressive improvised solo at the start of Botkin's third major contribution to the album, the orchestral setting for the powerful song "Salmon Falls," the music for which was composed by Voormann. Establishing itself over sinister, sustained lower notes from the orchestra and then elbowing its way through a string countermelody in the opening section before trading phrases with Jane Getz's piano, Greenidge's lightning-fast steel-pan playing justifies Van Dyke Parks's assessment of him, saying "if head-to-hand accuracy and velocity are criteria for virtuosity, he truly qualifies."[16] The song has a strong lyric in Nilsson's most reflective mood, not just addressing issues of lost childhood, but life and death itself, in the story of "a salmon travelin' upstream to its final destination." A falling raindrop metaphor picks up and develops ideas from Nilsson's "bubbles in a tea-cup" imagery from "Think About your Troubles" in *The Point*. The whole thing appears to be a masterly example of disciplined writing and performance, with Nilsson's voice using its huskier elements to convey pain and raw emotion. And yet the session at which it was recorded on October 2, 1974, had none of the feeling of strong control and artistic vision that is apparent from the final mix. Jimmy Webb dropped in on the recording:

> "Salmon Falls." I remember the night I heard that song, I was shaken by the power of that thing. But this particular night it was chaos. There were steel drums all over the place, and a bunch of saxophone players, because he didn't appear to have a clue as to what they were supposed to be doing. Somewhere in the back of the studio Brian Wilson was noodling on a B3, apparently trying to sing "Da Doo Ron Ron," in counterpoint to whatever else was going on, and I don't know what Danny Hutton [of Three Dog Night] and Micky Dolenz were doing. So this jolly crew is going at it hammers and tongs as I walk into the studio. And I am amazed as I sit down, mouth slightly agape, and watch this for about fifteen or twenty minutes as Van Dyke Parks is trying to hum the parts of the orchestration to the players, and keep them all organized. I finally turned to Harry, who was sitting next to me, and said: "Harry, why don't you write this down?" And he turned at me with a look of sublime contempt and said, "You would say that!"[17]

The feeling of chaos in the studio was apparent to one of the song's composers as well. Voormann had originally intended that Nilsson's vocals would begin over the first part of the piece, where Greenidge's solo can be heard on the final version. "I'd written a long melody with difficult chords, and Harry was supposed to sing it from the start," recalled Voormann. "But Harry had been drinking and carrying on and he couldn't get it together. So in the end he sang it over the fade, and that's what we used on the record."[18] Yet the end result is undeniably an artistic success and one of the strongest performances in Nilsson's later catalog.

Botkin handled the arrangements and conducting for the tracks on the album that employed the largest forces, "What's Your Sign?" "Salmon Falls," and "Down By the Sea," but the job of working on Nilsson's fragmentary ideas for the bulk of the remainder of the record fell to Van Dyke Parks. He had made a name for himself as an aficionado of Caribbean music during the years since completing his 1967 album *Song Cycle* (which included his very different take from Nilsson's on Randy Newman's *Vine Street*). Parks's *Discover America*, released by Warner Brothers in 1972, had revived several lesser-known songs of mainly Trinidad and Tobago origin, and he had continued the process with *Clang of the Yankee Reaper*, which had been recorded just before *Duit On Mon Dei*. Parks was the ideal collaborator to realize Nilsson's idea that his new album should tap into West Indian culture and a general Caribbean feeling, and as Parks explained, it was a partnership that worked well for both of them:

I think he was really impressed with the intelligent design of Caribbean music as I was.... Once we were past the point of introduction I became his sort of musical secretary. We developed a situation of mutual need. I needed him because I had quit a job at Warner Brothers, I had no other real employment. So for him to commend me for my ability in the studio was a very big thing. That's what we did. We went into the studio and we tried things. I say musical secretary because he might write an idea on a matchbook, and sit at a bar until five minutes before the time the session was due to start, then he'd take the matchbook from the bar—Martoni's—walk the block or two over to RCA studios, and want to get it done.[19]

Even if, in Parks's view, Nilsson's "perfect instrument," his falsetto voice, was irreparably damaged, he recognized that Nilsson's formidable ability to imitate vocal sounds in other registers was undimmed, and that he could easily assimilate the Trinidadian atmosphere from Parks's recent recording projects. This was further helped by the fact that both Nilsson and Parks had been working with many of the same session players during the course of the year, including Jesse Ed Davis, Jim Keltner, Bobby Keys, and Klaus Voormann. "He was really comfortable with the musicians. He'd worked with all of them, and the arrangements were fashioned on the spot," said Parks.[20] Fortunately, Parks was a veteran of the spontaneous session, of using the studio as a blank canvas for creating music with a group of sympathetic colleagues, particularly when he had worked with Brian Wilson on the controversial but ultimately aborted 1966–67 Beach Boys project *Smile*.[21] So, given Nilsson's generous hosting of the musicians in a convivial atmosphere, with food and drink on tap and a fairly leisurely production schedule, Parks was undaunted by the scale of the task:

I'd seen unparalleled experimentation and extemporaneous approach to music. In terms of the song structure, I'd never seen it so unpremeditated as with Harry, but when you saw these veteran studio musicians adjust to that, there was absolutely no fear in the situation. Competition was put aside. All sense of propriety was lost, but a very companionable atmosphere took over the sessions when Harry Nilsson had a date.[22]

The first session on which Parks worked as musical director was on September 12 for "Turn Out the Light," and he achieved a relaxed Caribbean feel, far more effective than a raw demo of the song that had been cut at the time of *Pussy Cats*. Before coming back to the studio, Nilsson had thought long and hard about how this and other rejected songs from *Pussy Cats* could be revitalized. As Una Nilsson later recalled: "He'd come home...with a cassette and listen to it over and over and over again. So, if we were driving somewhere in the car, that's what we were listening to. I think that was a very important part of the creative process for him. Listening over and over again."[23]

The orchestrations for this remake of the song were by the classically trained Fredric Myrow, who had film scores to his credit, but who was also a former composer in residence with Leonard Bernstein at the New York Philharmonic. Doubling steel pans and cymbalon is an inspired idea, but Myrow's use of bass trombone smears doubled with baritone sax pedal notes adds a slightly unsteady gait to the swagger of the piece. Nevertheless, it is one of Nilsson's best and most consistent vocal performances on the album, and much of the texture of his younger voice is still present. In common with "Salmon Falls," the lyrics explore an autobiographical idea that first surfaced in *The Point*, only in this case, the theme of lovers lying side by side that is picked up and developed comes from "Are You Sleeping?" However, Nilsson's life with Una brought with it a security that is reflected in the words. Banishing fear of the dark allows them to enjoy lying side by side and to dream, whereas in the earlier song—written during the Diane era—the lovers have the threat of breakup hanging over them.

According to Parks, once Nilsson had finished revising his older songs and gotten down to working on new material, an even more symbiotic process between him and the other musicians was established:

Things would take a general tone in the studio. [For] a month, maybe, the personnel would be stable. It would be an ensemble. Harry developed an ensemble situation, so that everybody knew everybody, so by the time he got to... "It's a Jungle Out There" [it was] great.

Tarzan and the vine. Only Harry would do that. Get Tarzan and Jane talking about the vine. There would be about seven things that blow—maybe that would be four saxes, two trumpets, and a 'bone, or something. And then there'd be a rhythm section—a sit-down drummer, or two, maybe Jim Keltner and Ringo Starr together. So you've got a lot of rumble —record them in maybe a room with a lot of wood in it—and get a bassist, and a pianist, and maybe an organist, too.... And it...all seemed so proper to me at the time. It really did. The results would never have been the same in an "un-extemporaneous" environment, and they wouldn't have been so good.[24]

Harry in
Brooklyn,
circa 1946

Bette Nilsson

Harry
with John
and Anna
Martin

Nilsson—publicity
photograph for
*Pandemonium Shadow
Show*

Harry—billboard
on Sunset

Nilsson and Richard
Perry at RCA in New
York (photo by R.
Brenner)

Harry Nilsson Sr.
and Nilsson

Zak Nilsson
in 1975

Dr. John and Nilsson,
mid-1970s

Nilsson and
Keith Moon

Having a drink or
two in London

Ringo Starr and Nilsson, Santa Monica
beach house, during the *Pussy Cats* sessions

Polaroid of Nilsson and John Lennon, recording *Pussy Cats*

Ringo Starr as Klaafu with Nilsson on Capitol Records tower, filming for *Goodnight Vienna*

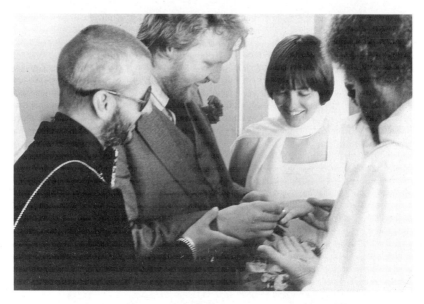

Nilsson's wedding to Una O'Keeffe, with best man Ringo Starr (left)

Conducting the boys of St. Paul's Cathedral choir for *Knnillssonn*

Polaroid of writer Jules Feiffer and Nilsson on the set of *Popeye*, 1979

Nilsson lobbying Philadelphia mayor William Green on gun control, October 1981

The Nilsson family at Upper Nyack, 1985: (l to r) Una, Olivia, Beau, Ben, Annie, Nilsson, Kief

Nilsson and Terry Gilliam, recording for *The Fisher King*

Turn Out The Light | 191

Not everyone felt quite so upbeat about this process, especially musicians who had worked with Nilsson back in the Richard Perry days, when he had been more focused and generally somewhat better prepared for the studio work. Klaus Voormann, for example, said: "We'd get started around seven [in the evening], and we'd be set up and ready to go, that's myself, Danny Kortchmar, Dr. John, Van Dyke, Jim Keltner, but with Harry's generous hospitality—and he paid for every penny of the cost of the bar and the food and the drugs—it often got to ten o'clock and not a note had been played. I listen back and think that really I was playing very well, but I hated all the hanging around. Also Harry would get very particular as he got half-drunk, and he'd start calling for another take and another take, to the point of getting obnoxious."²⁵

Nevertheless, however long-drawn-out the business of finishing a track became, it did produce results. As well as "It's a Jungle Out There," the new songs that were fully developed for the album were "Home," "Kojak Columbo," and "Good For God." The first, in Van Dyke Parks's view, was part of Nilsson's continual re-exploration of the themes of his childhood home, his divorce from Diane, and what home meant to an adult—especially a millionaire adult. The second is a lively love song to the television set, buoyed up by an energetic New Orleans funk beat developed at two pianos by Parks and Dr. John. "I can remember doing some tapes with Dr. John when the two of us would play, one thing or another," said Parks. "This was from a matchbook cover, okay, or a couple of napkins.... So there was nothing kosher about this process."²⁶ The third was a song built out of a phrase that casually came up in conversation, allied to the music from an unused demo from the *Nilsson Schmilsson* days called "How Can I Be Sure of You?"

Parks recalled, "Something happened and I said, 'Good for God,' and he said, 'Can I use it?' And I said, 'Take it.' Whatever that meant. I thought he was kidding."²⁷

Nilsson's immediate response to the phrase was, "Good for God, I bet he's got a very hard job looking after all this nonsense."²⁸ Using the melodic bones of his older song, he worked out some new lyrics, in which he developed some of the ideas from "The Most Beautiful World in the World," about the crying rivers and the deep blue seas. Soon the song had become a piece of sidelong admiration for God, who "goes and makes the planet blue... who knows each time a sparrow falls, but who can answer all His calls?"

Having created this number and placed it at the end of the album, Nilsson decided to bookend the record with another song that had religious links—in its title at least—namely "Jesus Christ You're Tall." The version used on this album was a rough demo, albeit one with plenty of spirit, played and sung by Nilsson alone at the piano. The lyric is a clever one, using the idea of a very tall child as a prototype basketball player and teasing out images from the game by way of some effective puns: "We could dribble our way down a courtship.... I would shoot a little love inside your basket, mama." The song would later get the full Van Dyke Parks treatment on Nilsson's subsequent album *Sandman*, but the curtain-raising demo version and the closing "Good For God" suggested a suitable title to Nilsson for the present disc. He told BBC interviewer Stuart Grundy that he had the perfect name for it:

> *God's Greatest Hits*, which I thought was a great title. Some people thought other people…might be offended, you know? So we compromised and, on the outside cover…if someone might be offended in Utah, because it says *God's Greatest Hits*, because they think it's pretentious or something…. I had to change the title, and we already had the artwork, so it changed to *Duit On Mon Dei*…which I stole from the Ringo logo, and we compromised with putting another cover on the inside, which said, "Formerly *God's Greatest Hits*," you know? Which worked out, I think better.[29]

The logo Nilsson mentioned is to be found on the front cover art for the solo album *Ringo*, where, above Tom Bruckner's painting of the crowd of participating musicians, there hovers a board surrounded by the theatrical masks of tragedy and comedy. Lettering on it reads "Duit On Mon Dei." The words are ranged below a giant apple, in the form of the motto of a coat of arms. And indeed, they are a pun on the arms of the British royal family, "Dieu et mon Droit," or "God and my right (shall me defend)." Nilsson enjoyed the surreptitious connection with *Ringo*, although because the cover art for his album had already been created before RCA insisted on the title change, the twenty passport-size photos of Nilsson, each with a golden halo, that adorned the back of the record sleeve had nothing to do with *Duit On Mon Dei* and everything to do with *God's Greatest Hits*.

The final recordings for *Duit On Mon Dei* took place in early October 1974. Almost as soon as he had finished in the studio, Nilsson and Ringo Starr (who had played on "Kojak Columbo" during one of the last sessions on October 7) got together to make a low-budget promotional film for the album. It was a return favor for Nilsson's work on Starr's space-ship film for *Goodnight Vienna*, and although it was made for a fraction of the cost of that ambitious production, it once again involved Stanley Dorfman. The commercial would pick up the basketball imagery of "Jesus Christ You're Tall." Nilsson recalled:

> I had a bet with RCA that I could produce the cheapest video in their history, for $5,000. In exchange, if they didn't feel it was the best they had ever seen, the bet would be off. However, if it turned out to be the best, RCA would triple their TV time for the new single "Kojak Columbo." Now I needed to come up with something for $5,000. On a hunch I called the Los Angeles Forum, home of the Lakers and Kings, and asked what it cost to rent the Forum when it was not in use. The pleasant lady inquired what I wanted it for. I explained that I wanted to shoot a basketball from behind half court and film it for a record album. After some thought, she asked who it was for, so I told her about the bet. She said, "How about $800 for three hours?" I couldn't believe my ears. When I called Stan he just about fainted too. This price included the lighting, plug-in systems, use of the scoreboard, message board etc.[30]

Nilsson's idea was to resuscitate his own teenage talent for ballgames and attempt to place an accurate scoring shot from midway down the court. The only member of the audience would be a thinly disguised Ringo Starr, sitting high in the bleachers, who agreed to applaud if Nilsson succeeded in putting the ball in the basket. On a midweek morning, when the vast Forum stadium in the Inglewood area was not in use, Nilsson made his way there straight from the studio where he had been working all night on the final adjustments to the album.[31] Meanwhile, Dorfman turned up with a truck full of lights, camera equipment, and crew. He managed to do the whole thing for $3,000, keeping the enterprise well within budget. Once the gear had been set up, Ringo, sitting in his lofty seat in the empty auditorium, called across to the makeshift control booth to be sure they filmed the first shot, knowing that Nilsson was lucky at this kind of impromptu display. Dorfman called for "Action!" Nilsson continued:

I placed an NBA basketball at half court, moved back, and then acted as if I were entering from the players' tunnel, wearing a shirt, sweater, sunglasses and a baseball cap—a lost tourist at the Forum. As I walked with hands in pockets, whistling and looking around, my eyes caught sight of the ball. After two quick left and right looks, I stooped down, picked up the ball, dribbled to the sideline and let go. First take, in the net. So I said to everyone, "Okay, that's it. Let's go home! Let's go get a drink."[32]

Unfortunately, Dorfman had not heard Ringo, and he was not running any film for that first sequence, but simply working out the camera track and angles. A further twenty-two takes were unsuccessful, although Nilsson reckoned he hit the rim of the basket on about eighteen occasions. Each time he would trudge back to the tunnel, put his hat, sweater and sunglasses back in place, and start over again. Ringo was heard to say nonchalantly, "Time takes time."[33] As unsuccessful take followed unsuccessful take, Dorfman was acutely aware that their three-hour window of opportunity was rapidly closing, and they still had no footage. So he urged Nilsson to a final effort:

With the help of I don't know how many grams of cocaine, he finally did it again. And we zoomed in to Ringo who by this time was asleep. So we had to wake him up and shoot his part separately. But that first time, Harry just put it right in the net. He was extraordinary, an amazing athlete.[34]

The final film was tightly edited, but the central image is a single sequence from one camera in real time, as the extraordinary arc of Nilsson's shot takes a full eight seconds to land perfectly in the net. The seconds are counted away on a superimposed scoreboard clock, and the final score is "Nilsson 1, RCA 0." There's a brief cover shot of *Duit On Mon Dei* before Nilsson tips his RCA baseball cap and the commercial is over. RCA liked the results and promised Nilsson that, as agreed, they would triple the airtime to which they had originally committed. As his personal fee, Dorfman collected the balance between the $3,800 cost and the $5,000 budget. Later, Nilsson requested figures to see if the commercial had in fact been shown more often than planned, only to discover that RCA had not kept its side of the bargain.[35]

With the making of this video, *Duit On Mon Dei* was officially completed, and so Nilsson threw a party for "intimate friends and band members."[36] They were collected by a chartered bus and taken to a restaurant with a World War I theme to celebrate finishing the album and the month-long party at the RCA studios that had accompanied its creation.

Rumors of the lavish way the album had been made reached the press. If the general reception for *Duit On Mon Dei* had been favorable, it is unlikely that anybody would have even mentioned the studio parties and the star-studded cast. But because the record is hard to categorize and strays into many different areas of stylistic territory, most rock and pop critics were bemused at best, and many of them hated what they heard. This latter group of writers seized on stories about the record's production to justify their harsh criticism. "What was this? Some kind of month long smoking and drinking bash?" asked Lon Goddard in *Disc* magazine, before going on to address his final remarks directly to Nilsson: "You used to write vividly descriptive songs, with real beauty and rare perception…once upon a time. I've had enough and can no longer defend this kind of abuse.…I refuse to believe the genius is no longer there, but if you can't do it yourself, it's time somebody else took some disciplinary action. Please get yourself together, for everybody's sake."[37] Goddard praises "Easier for Me" and Price's sensitive arrangement, but otherwise finds little to commend. Similarly, Joel Vance in *Stereo Review* pointed out that "Turn Out the Light" is vintage Nilsson, but he felt that the rest of the album was too deferential to the varied styles of his guests. Vance wrote:

> He appears to be making music not for himself (and therefore not for us), but for Ringo, Van Dyke, Dr. John and I don't know who all else. Chase all them peers out of the studio, 'Arry. It's been fun but Sunday's over and we gotta get back to work. And this time let's *duit for wei.*[38]

It was not to be until after Nilsson had made his next album *Sandman* that RCA took a firm hand and insisted that he must have an outside producer once more. Meanwhile, Nilsson briefly came very close to breaking his decision never to appear live on stage when he had the idea of presenting his backing band from the album for a single concert at Grauman's Chinese Theatre on Hollywood Boulevard. Famous for its handprints of the stars on the paved forecourt, it seemed to Nilsson to be the ideal venue at which to present a show called *God's Greatest Hits—For One Night Only! Featuring, Live on Stage: The Original Cast!* He telephoned the theater to enquire about booking it. The person he spoke to said no, so Nilsson asked who he needed to speak to in higher authority to get a decision, and the voice said, "Me!"[39] Despite trying to persuade the anonymous manager that his band would be better entertainment than the theater's regular diet of movies, it was clearly not going to happen, and after an abortive inquiry to the rival Pantages theater chain, Nilsson abandoned the idea. But just briefly he had seriously entertained the idea of going on stage with Parks, Davis, Keltner, Voormann, Starr and the others from his regular backing group. As it was, he would soon be back together with them in the studio for the next album.

Before the *Sandman* sessions began on April 15, 1975, Nilsson became involved in a project that brought one of his earlier works to life in a spectacular new way. At the end of 1974, the producer Esquire Jauchem, who ran the Boston Repertory Theatre, approached Nilsson to ask if he might be able to adapt *The Point* for the stage. Nilsson had been asked before and had never felt convinced that the quirky nature of his story would survive the transition to live performance, but Jauchem's proposal was full of unusual and original ideas, and so unexpectedly he agreed.

The Boston Repertory Theatre had been the brainchild of Jauchem and three friends who had met at Defiance College in Ohio. The designer and puppeteer Pierre Vuilleumier, Wendy Kraus, and Judy Truncer were the college contemporaries who joined forces with Jauchem to launch the company in Hyannis, Cape Cod, in 1971. Their earliest shows played to minuscule audiences, but with grit, determination, and enforced migration from one makeshift auditorium to another, the company gradually became firmly established. The inventive design and direction of unusual productions such as David Zucker's adaptation of Saint-Exupery's *Little Prince*, Cocteau's *Knights of the Round Table*, and an experimental version of Orwell's *Animal Farm*, which merged references to President Nixon with the porcine protagonist Napoleon, drew plenty of critical plaudits and as time went on quite sizable audiences.

The previews of *The Point* were to be in late February, and the show was scheduled to open on March 4, 1975, at what had been the company's home theater since 1973, the First and Second Church at the corner of Berkeley and Marlborough Streets in the Back Bay area. At the time, the building was still in use as a church every Sunday, and the company had to strike the set after the final show each Saturday and store its "stage sets, lighting board, seating risers and chairs"[40] away until reopening the following Wednesday. Members of the cast and crew spent the intervening days working to convert a former recording studio at 1 Boylston Place into a permanent theater, which eventually opened in 1976 with an adaptation of Kurt Vonnegut's *Player Piano*.

Yet even at the church, Boston Repertory Theatre was already a fully professional company, and its new stage show of Nilsson's story attracted plenty of critical attention. This was undoubtedly helped by the fact that various national television channels had repeated the original animated movie of *The Point* over the weeks leading up to Christmas 1974, the majority of previews praising it as "a welcome children's film of substance, taste and imagination."[41]

In his stage adaptation, Jauchem attempted to complement the visual invention of Wolf's animation by looking for unusual sources of inspiration. Reviewing the premiere, the Associated Press critic John L. Mullins, whose work was syndicated across the country, wrote:

> Excellently done are adaptations of a Japanese Bunraku theatre device. In one use, an actor, dressed in dark clothing and kept out of the spotlights and behind others on stage as much as possible, manipulates a life-sized puppet of the dog with two sticks. In the other, the actor, dressed the same, lifts and supports Oblio, who performs a slow motion ballet depicting the youth tumbling down a hole into the Point of No Return.[42]

To those who knew the movie, there was further delight when three giant balloons transformed into the dancing women of the "P.O.V. Waltz," or when bubbles blew across the stage during "Think About Your Troubles," as well as the moment that lights, flickering on a mirrored globe, simulated the leaves traded by the Leaf Man. To those new to the show, whether adults or children, there was plenty more to hold their attention. The character actor Gerald Berns appeared encased in a rubber "stone" suit as the Rock Man, and Boston Pops conductor Arthur Fiedler made a cameo appearance at the beginning and end of the play as the grandfather reading the tale as a bedtime story. Starring as Oblio was the young actor David Morse (billed in some accounts as eighteen years old at the time, but actually just into his twenties). He had first starred with the company as the fox in the *Little Prince* and was soon to become famous as Dr. Jack Morrison in the television series *St. Elsewhere*, but of his appearance in *The Point*, Mullins wrote that he had the "perfect face" for Oblio, and other columnists singled out his fine singing. The doyen of Bostonian critics, Elliott Norton of the *Boston Herald-American* praised the show, and its limited run was extended long into the summer, eventually transferring to the Lederer Theater in Providence, Rhode Island, for a continued season throughout August.[43]

Nilsson attended the Boston premiere with Una, and he was extremely happy about the sympathetic way his show had been adapted. The following year, he was to persuade the British actor and entrepreneur Sir Bernard Miles to present a slightly different version at the Mermaid Theatre in London, and many years later Jauchem's own adaptation would be performed again, with Nilsson's encouragement, in 1991.

Before work began on the *Sandman* album, Nilsson had another debt to discharge, which was once again to take up the fight on behalf of John Lennon and his right to remain in the United States. On February 24, Nilsson wrote a letter to the senator for California, Alan Cranston, urging him to support Lennon's case. Nilsson made an eloquent plea on the ex-Beatle's behalf, reminding the senator of Lennon's work for charity (including an occasion in Central Park the previous year where both Nilsson and Lennon had briefly appeared on stage during a fundraising "March of Dimes" concert). He concluded by saying, "I can testify the man doesn't even drink."[44] This rather suggests that the Troubadour incident had slipped his mind, but underlines the debt he owed Lennon for renegotiating his RCA contract.

With *Duit On Mon Dei* released in March, Nilsson was finally ready to return to the studio to start work on *Sandman*, and once again he elected to collaborate with Perry Botkin and Van Dyke Parks on another mixture of on-the-hoof revision of old material and spontaneously created new songs. The sessions began at RCA on April 15 with a full remake of "Jesus Christ You're Tall."

This final version of the song has a jauntier swagger than Nilsson's original demo from *Duit On Mon Dei* and is credited to the whole band as arrangers, although the bulk of the organizational work again fell on keyboard player and "maestro" Van Dyke Parks. Once more he acted as a musical secretary to Nilsson, but because the band included reed player Trevor Lawrence, who was also by this time an accomplished arranger, plus Klaus Voormann, who was nominally the contractor for the date, there were plenty of musicians in the studio who were happy to contribute material, particularly to the riffs for saxophones and brass. Parks, looking back on the album, was not in the least proprietorial about who did what:

The arrangers all played a very wonderful role with Harry in his work. He was a very collaborative man. Everyone who collaborated with him could point with pride at a tremendous service to Harry for the work they did. I'm talking on a musical level, or even within the terms of what a friend does for a friend. Because Harry drew the best out of the people around him. It was part of his gift: "See, you are somebody. Strut your stuff." He made everybody feel like a big deal, everybody, down to the last doorman.[45]

Trevor Lawrence, soon to be recruited as the producer for Nilsson's next album… *That's The Way It Is*, recalled that for those tracks credited to "the band," Nilsson came into the sessions with just one sheet of paper, rather than notated parts for the horns. "I'm sure he had it worked out in his brain," said Lawrence, "but when he got to us it was ideas…we'd make up the stuff. Which is how it was supposed to be in rock and roll, which was the music we were doing. We would get ideas and say 'How about putting this here?' He was very open to that."[46] Nilsson himself was increasingly convinced of the creative benefits of working in this cooperative way. Looking back over *Pussy Cats, Duit On Mon Dei*, and *Sandman*, he said, "Those albums were a coalition of ideas matched with songs. They were very much a group effort and there was intelligent humor involved as well—or at least we thought so—but a lot of people apparently didn't get the message or the joke."[47]

The most overtly jokey piece on the album was put together two days after "Jesus Christ You're Tall," when most of the same musicians were on hand for the final attempt (after the failures on the two previous series of sessions) to create a version of the "Flying Saucer Song" that was sufficiently coherent to be issued. Starting at six in the evening, they worked through until well after midnight, the rhythm section and horns laying down a backing track for Nilsson's mélange of barroom conversation and singing. Lawrence recalled that in contrast to some of the long periods of hanging around on the previous album, this was an intense experience and that in their short break around nine, they all "shot over the road to Martoni's"[48] for a drink. This time around, the singing—timed to fall within the first third of the track—is more prominent than on the previous versions, and the conversation is less slurred and more theatrically timed, with Nilsson taking on three distinct vocal roles as two African American barflies and the bartender. Additional voicing was by Joe Cocker. Nilsson admitted that for this comic banter to work, he had to rely less on improvisation than he had hoped to do previously, and more on conventional planning:

> "The Flying Saucer Song." I did it three times. With different bands, different people. John and I did it for *Pussy Cats*, but it didn't work out. Van Dyke and Mac [Dr. John] and I did it for *Duit On Mon Dei* and it didn't work out, and finally we managed to get it in on *Sandman*, with the same cast. The difference was, I just wrote a script out. But I didn't sort of want to resort to reading a script and singing it, you know? I wanted to just create it as we went along. That song's changed an awful lot. Well, the lyric in that one, it wasn't a question of censorship so much…but there were a couple of lines which were questionable, like a reference to hemorrhoids…. "How's your old lady?" "Oh, she's fine. Little hemorrhoidal problem now and then, but, you know." And then the guy tells this story about what happened. To me it seemed like a natural sort of a thing, in a bar, with two guys talking.[49]

In one press interview at the time, a comparison was made between his throaty-sounding voice and the even raspier backing vocals by Cocker. But Nilsson did not believe that they had a lot in common musically, saying: "I don't think there's that much of a similarity, it's just that we both can occasionally muster up a brandy tone. We're whisky throated tenors. The Orson Welles type of guy from 'Citizen Kane.'"[50] For the musicians working on the album, officially contracted for six hours up until midnight, there were some professional pitfalls during those late evening sessions when Nilsson was trying to perfect a song such as this, which had worried him for so long. "They went on forever," recalled Parks. "I mean sometimes we didn't get out of there until four a.m."[51] Everyone was aware of the fact that they were due back at RCA the following night at six, so joining Nilsson for a little social drink after work was not a good idea. The players used to try to get out and go home to bed before Nilsson rounded up the survivors for a trip to the Spotlight Bar, whose windows faced eastward to the rising sun. "It was not pretty to be up in a bar at dawn," said Parks, wearily.[52]

A few days after the "Flying Saucer Song" had finally been recorded in an acceptable version, Perry Botkin returned to work with Nilsson on the new album's big production numbers, "Something True," "The Ivy Covered Walls," and "Will She Miss Me?" Again, as he had on *Duit On Mon Dei*, Botkin was directing massed forces, starting on April 22 with a thirty-five-piece orchestra for "Something True." For this ballad, Nilsson's voice is clearer and lighter than on almost all his recent recordings, and he seems to be consciously harking back to his early association with Botkin. But the song—not helped by a slightly plodding arrangement—simply does not have the variety or invention of Nilsson's 1960s writing. Botkin himself was well aware that this was the case, saying:

> He wanted to go back to those days when we met in the early 60's and he...didn't want to be this way. He wanted to sing like he had back then. He wanted to write longer songs that were more complex, like he did back then. He wanted all of that, but he couldn't. It was out of control and he couldn't do anything about it. So, he just kept a smile on his face. And with that great personality...I think that some people may have tried to help him, but there was no way. It just wasn't going to work. So you went along with the drill and tried to make it as pleasant for him as you could.[53]

The most vocally accomplished of the Botkin/Nilsson collaborations is "The Ivy Covered Walls," which is delivered a cappella by the "Perry Botkin Jr. Singers." Back in the days of *Nilsson Sings Newman*, there is little doubt that Nilsson would have overdubbed all the vocal parts himself, but this time he was accompanied by a choir of studio singers, and the recording was done in real time with little or no overdubbing. And just as Nilsson would once have painstakingly constructed the harmonies behind his lead vocal, this time the part writing was by Botkin. The whole thing is a clever spoof of Ivy League and barber-shop glee club singing. However, the circuitous story—one of those never-ending "It was a dark and stormy night," the captain said to the mate type of tales—suggests that Nilsson had not quite worked out a proper ending, and instead of supplying one, he settled for a segue into the next track. Nevertheless, the song is an example of Botkin doing his best to try to recreate Nilsson's glory days of the previous decade.

The closing number on the album, "Will She Miss Me?" is the final Botkin collaboration and by far the grandest production on the record, with Botkin bringing the full Hollywood treatment to his orchestral setting. The somber atmosphere of a lyric about lovers unable to be honest with each other because of mutual pride is not unlike the power of "Salmon Falls," but this track is dominated by the virtuoso violin playing of the Western Swing veteran Bobby Bruce. His swooping melodic lines and elegant cadenzas become a dialogue with Nilsson's anguished voice, until it appears that all the musicians in the studio join in to applaud his extraordinary performance at the end.

The rest of the tracks are all cooperative collaborations between Nilsson and the studio band. "Pretty Soon There'll Be Nothing Left for Everybody" is a vision of future environmental disaster, with a fundamentally repetitive lyric apart from a brief contrasting section that appears in the middle and again close to the end. The swirling downward saxophone riff is a good example of working out an effective sound in the studio, but the song lacks any real sense of development. In contrast, there is a definite storyline in the lyric of "How to Write a Song," but it is likely that potential enthusiasts for the song's message were put off by the lines "Let's assume that you are just an asshole / And there's nothing in your brain." In any event, this song's really inventive moments are largely lost in a swirl of dubbed-in audience effects and general background noise.

The standout track from these impromptu sessions is "Here's Why I Did Not Go to Work Today," which is a philosophical examination of why Thursday is such a "lazy crazy day." It is the closest Nilsson ever got to writing a jazz standard, even though the tune borrows elements of its chord sequence and structure from numerous earlier pieces; for example, the final turnaround comes very close to the 1935 song "When Somebody Thinks You're Wonderful" by Harry M. Woods. On this track, Nilsson sings close to the microphone in his *A Little Touch of Schmilsson in the Night* manner, accompanied by just piano, guitar, bass, drums, and tenor saxophone. Pianist Jane Getz produces her finest of many contributions to Nilsson's albums with a delicate balance of sensitive accompaniment and assertive originality. The lyrics are vintage Nilsson, whimsical, sidelong, and witty, with the distinctly memorable line "Thursday's surreptitiously unique." The song is a glimpse that Nilsson could still create original songs of the type Perry Botkin had so valued in his 1960s work, but that Botkin felt were now largely missing from his writing. As Trevor Lawrence said, "Most people were just writing about love, it was all love songs. But Harry was pushing the envelope. You see a lot of difference and a lot of different kinds of songs, because his big thing was to be a real artist."[54]

The cover photograph of *Sandman* shows Nilsson sitting on the beach, and it was taken by Mal Evans, a former Beatles roadie. Evans (nicknamed "Mal the Pal" by Nilsson) was a Liverpudlian who had been with the Beatles from the early days. Evans and Neil Aspinall had traveled the world with the group, and he had willingly run errands and helped life go smoothly for all the band members. He had also made connections in many places with local drug dealers to supply the pills and other substances that had kept the group going on the road during the arduous schedule of the mid-1960s.[55]

Tall, bearded, and bespectacled, Evans was a likable bear of a man, described by the writer Larry Kane as having a "magnetic personality"[56] with a ready smile and plenty of charm to go with it. But when the Beatles broke up, so did Evans's reason for existence. A former telephone engineer, he had shared the highs and lows of the stadium tours and the television appearances, the mad dashes to avoid being mobbed by teenage fans, and the strange half-life that playing out their careers in public had brought to John, Paul, George, and Ringo. As Aspinall (who had gone from being Evans's fellow Liverpool roadie to become managing director of the band's Apple empire) put it, "suddenly he was an ordinary man again."[57] It was mainly Ringo who continued to find things for Evans to do, and consequently he had helped out behind the scenes for Starr's two albums produced by Richard Perry on which Nilsson had sung. By the time *Goodnight Vienna* was made, Evans had left his wife Lil in England and moved full-time to Los Angeles, where he had set up home with a new girlfriend, Fran Hughes. As Nilsson saw a lot of Ringo and was always on the lookout for social adventures, he spent plenty of hours socializing with Evans. The candid cover photograph of Nilsson on the beach holding a bottle of wine captures a happy moment around the time of the *Sandman* sessions. It was also the basis for a rather rough-and-ready photo montage on the back of the sleeve that shows a giant crab having apparently devoured Nilsson, leaving just his jeans, socks, and sneakers behind on the beach.

Within a few months of that carefree moment, Evans's life came to an abrupt end. Nilsson spent the summer of 1975 away from Los Angeles, and Ringo shuttled to and fro between America and Britain. During the fall, Evans began working on a book documenting his years with the Beatles, but he became increasingly dependent on pills, and being a big man, believed he could consume more of them than most. On January 4, 1976, his co-author John Hoernie visited Evans's West 4th Street apartment in Los Angeles to find that he had taken a sizable quantity of valium and was holding a rifle, which he was waving erratically as he spoke. Unable to persuade him to put the weapon down, Fran Hughes called the cops, and when Evans continued to brandish the gun in the face of a police warning, he was shot dead. The cover of *Sandman* marks one of the last genuinely cheerful moments in what rapidly became a tragic life.

This album's packaging was a reflection of Nilsson's life during the making of the album in more respects than just the jaunty beach photos. Its inside gatefold consisted of a line drawing in the manner of a Victorian lithograph by Klaus Voormann. For the basis of the picture, he found a print in an old book that showed steerage passengers on the deck of a steamship en route to Ellis Island.[58] They are wrapped up warmly against the chill, but in his version, the faces have been carefully adjusted to become portraits of the band and others at the sessions. A capped and bearded Nilsson sits a few paces in front of the ship's funnel, and close by, Una, in a bonnet and pinafore dress, reads from a book, with a top-hatted Van Dyke Parks peering, Toulouse-Lautrec-like, from behind the folds of her skirt. Gradually as one looks closer, most of the other musicians can be discerned in a variety of costumes and poses, scattered among the crowd onboard.

To celebrate the completion of the album in late May, after Botkin had brought the orchestra back to the studio for some final string dubs and drop-ins, Nilsson picked up the nautical theme of Voormann's drawing for a celebration party. This time instead of hiring a bus, he leased a 110-foot cruiser from the Marina del Rey and treated his musicians and friends to a two-day voyage to Santa Cruz Island, with the boat packed with "movies, stereos, and booze."[59]

Once this floating celebration was over and the album had been delivered to RCA, Nilsson and Una set off for a holiday. They arrived at Curzon Place in June and spent time in London before traveling on to Switzerland. Nilsson had become increasingly concerned about the damage he had done to his voice, and decided to undertake some alternative therapy to revive not just his vocal cords, but his whole system, which was showing signs of strain from his lifestyle. "I'd heard about sleep treatments," he wrote. "I thought it might be a nice thing to do. I was between albums, nothing to do. So, stop and get a rejuvenation treatment."[60]

He and Una drove to Montreux where Dr. Paul Niehans had set up the Clinique de Prairie. This elegant hospital, with a formal French garden linking it to a residential chalet for its thirty-five patients, had long been a destination for Hollywood stardom looking to buy back something of their youth. Niehans, a well-connected and aristocratic man who had died in 1971 at the age of 89, was known as "the father of cell therapy." His treatments principally involved injecting cells from an animal fetus into a patient's bloodstream. The theory was that the patient's body would transport the cells to the damaged areas, where they would assist in regenerating the cellular structure. Subsequent medical research has shown that Niehans's treatments were scientifically suspect at best, and there are examples of the treatment causing serious and irreversible damage. It is now banned in the United States.[61] Nevertheless, Niehans and his successor Franz Schmidt were masters of public relations, and Nilsson followed the likes of Marlene Dietrich and Miles Davis through the doors of his clinic for a week's course of cell therapy. On arrival, he was asked to stop smoking and avoid alcohol.

> Then came the day of my shots. A doctor and two nurses arrived with syringes the length and thickness of knitting needles. The doctor warned that this would hurt, and they would do it as quickly as possible. He would stick them in my ass, and the nurses would take them out. Like a toreador sticking the bull. Twelve needles.[62]

The pain was excruciating, and Nilsson had to be forcibly held down for the final shots as cells from the placenta of a newborn sheep were injected into his blood. For three days, he could only lie on his stomach, but by the end of his week's treatment (at $1,000 a night), he was just about able to get about normally and tolerate traveling. The doctors sternly advised him to give the treatment a few months to work, during which time he should avoid alcohol, smoking, and excessive exercise.

To give the therapy a chance to take effect, Nilsson did indeed quit drinking and smoking and after a relaxed trip to Amsterdam, he and Una returned to London. His original intention in Switzerland had been to undergo a course of sleep therapy, rather than sheep therapy, so he reasoned that he might as well use the next part of his summer in London to do just that. He sought out a Harley Street doctor, Peter Nixon, who offered a valium and diazepam treatment in which a patient was put into a comatose state for several days and fed intravenously. In subsequent years, somewhat like Niehans, Nixon was also to be found to be a less-than-reliable medical practitioner. He lost a £2 million U.K. libel action against the Channel Four television company, who exposed some of his articles in medical journals—and the results of treatment they described—as being "rigged."[63]

Anticipating several days of sleep, Nilsson checked into Nixon's clinic in central London with new pajamas, a bathrobe, and slippers. To help him relax on the first night, after the initial valium injection, the doctor had prescribed a small bottle of wine. Two girls visiting another patient recognized Nilsson and asked for his autograph, so he shared his wine with them. Once they had gone, he asked the nurse for another bottle to replace the one he had just given to his unexpected visitors. She refused, and Nilsson said that if she was not prepared to grant his request, he was leaving. Once again she refused. Despite having already had an injection designed to induce enforced sleep, he got dressed and walked out for good. A few blocks south of the Weymouth Street clinic was the Goat Tavern on Stafford Street, and Nilsson made his way to this regular haunt in order to call his publisher Terry Oates and to book a limo to take him home.

The barman was happy to give Nilsson drinks on credit once he had seen the hospital bracelet around his wrist, and soon the former patient was happily regaling the bar with tales of his horrific injections in Montreux and the injustice of the London clinic's wine policy, until Oates arrived to pay his tab and take him home. Quite unaware of the valium injection Nilsson had recently been given, Oates suggested they take a detour to a somewhat rough pub in London's East End where an old friend was celebrating his birthday. Soon Nilsson was seated at a battered saloon bar piano, hammering out a rather unusual version of "Happy Birthday" that included the infamous line from his own song "You're breaking my heart so fuck you!" This went down extremely well, and so Nilsson set to and provided a one-man cabaret for the birthday party as the drinks kept flowing.

When closing time arrived, he looked up to discover that both Oates and the limo had gone. The pub landlord called him a taxi, but as the shock of the outside air hit him, so too did the full force of the valium injection and an evening of drinking copiously on an empty stomach after weeks of being abstinent:

I had to sleep and at the same time I had to pee and throw up. I felt miserable. I asked the driver to stop the car. He said, "We'll be there in a few minutes."

I insisted, "No you don't understand. I've got to pee right now. I have to."

He says, "Just hold on, we'll be home in ten minutes. Just hold on."

"I haven't got ten minutes."

By that time I had my pants half unzipped and I fell asleep. I woke up in jail and wondered what the hell had happened. I went to move my head and realized my face was beaten, my arms, my legs, my back, my stomach, my kidneys. Someone had kicked the shit out of me. I called out and one of the policemen came over and asked what I wanted. So I asked him why I was in jail. He said, "You kicked a policeman in the face, didn't you?"

I honestly have no recollection of that. I only remember getting into a cab and asking him to stop so I could pee. He said, "You went pee all right, all over his cab. That's one of the reasons you're here."

"Oh my god, I'm terribly sorry. Look, I got out of the hospital and I had a lot of valium in me, some drinks.... Would you mind? Could you give me a cigarette?"

"Sure," he said. I lit it, smoked it and loved every second of it. I felt intense pain. Every movement hurt. The officer advised me that I was scheduled to appear before the magistrate at 9.00 a.m. that morning and it was now almost 6.00 a.m. He assured me I would be let out, and I asked for another cigarette. He turned to me cold as ice and said, "I gave you one."

"Ooh," I thought, "So that's what jail is like."[64]

At 6:20, Nilsson was allowed to leave the police cell to go home and prepare for his court appearance. His wallet had been emptied, and he was lost in a part of the East End of London that he had never visited before. He stole a pint of milk from a doorstep, drank it down, and set off to find a main road. Shortly, he came to a major route and to his relief a London red double-decker bus hove into sight. Except he had no money. He told his story to the conductor, who not only let him onto the bus, but arranged for him to switch to another route, on which his friend Roy would be the bus crew. "You tell Roy that Bob sent you, and tell him the story. He'll take you right round to Mayfair."[65] At seven, Nilsson staggered back to his apartment at Curzon Place. Una was horrified to find that instead of being safely asleep in a comfortable clinic, Nilsson was a disheveled wreck, covered in cuts and bruises and stained with urine.

Nilsson ranted that he wanted to leave the country immediately, but she calmed him down and called Terry Oates before starting to clean him up. Oates talked sense into him, saying, "Listen son, you've gotta get clean and go to the magistrate or they'll never let you back into England again. Now you either do or don't want that." Squeezed painfully into a suit, with the worst of his abrasions cleaned and dried, Nilsson made it to the court on time. Oates arranged a dodge with two limousines so that a decoy car drew up in front of the court to distract the posse of press reporters and photographers who had heard rumors of a star's possible appearance before the bench. Meanwhile, the second limo discreetly took Oates, Nilsson, and Una to the side door of the Bow Street Magistrates' Court.

Lining up for his turn to go before the magistrates, Nilsson had a quick word with the one Fleet Street journalist who had been canny enough to spot the car ruse and slip inside the courthouse, to whom he told a guarded account of his side of the story. He then gave his autograph to the next miscreant in the line, who recognized him before confessing to Nilsson that he was to be tried for armed robbery. Once in court, there was a moment when the presiding magistrate misheard Nilsson's guilty plea and started ordering a future trial to be held, but once he had been convinced that the singer had actually admitted his guilt, Nilsson was let off with a small fine and a caution. This helped to keep the story out of the press, although the one reporter to whom Nilsson had talked ran a short piece in the *Evening Standard* that day, which read:

American pop singer Harry Nilsson, 34, was fined £1.50 at Bow Street Court today after being arrested last night on an indecency charge.... It was stated that he had been having medical treatment and left a Harley street clinic late on Monday. He was prescribed a "hefty dose" of valium and the combined effects of this and drink were completely underestimated by Nilsson who was seen by police to urinate in a Westminster Street.[66]

After this excitement, Nilsson returned home, thanking Terry Oates and Una for doing their best to help him. He decided to give up on therapies, to lie low, and pass a quiet summer in his London apartment with Una. They finally returned to the United States in October. However, what had hitherto been a simple matter of going in and out of the country was complicated when one of the immigration officials questioned how Una would support herself. Nilsson told Derek Taylor:

He knew Una's intent was to sponge from the U.S. Government, by taking advantage of its public services—you know, like garbage collecting and freeways—without becoming a resident. As she has no visible means of support and no return ticket, the immigration authorities were concerned with the possibility of she and I having an argument and immediately going to the welfare in America. I showed the official a checkbook with my name and Una's name on it and told him I have $5 million. I pointed out that Una could write checks on my account and I further told him I was prepared to step outside and buy a first class one-way ticket to Dublin so she would have the means to get back in the event of an argument. He pointed out that because I was in customs I could not go through the door. Finally I asked him if we were doing anything illegal, to which he replied, "Not exactly, but it's a sort of a quasi thing." Then he turned to Mac at the other desk and said, "Says he's got five million bucks and they're living together. How about a fiancée status?" Mac said, "Nah, that means they've got to get married in ninety days." I told him we had no immediate intention of getting married. He told us we were living in sin. I thanked him, and eventually he gave Una permission to stay in this great country for another 90 days.[67]

Back in their rented home on Strada Vecchia Road in Bel Air that November, they settled in for the next three months in Los Angeles before Una would have to obtain a new extension to her visa. Within a day or two of their return, Nilsson and Ringo went together to see David Essex in concert and were astonished that his live show lasted for only about fifteen minutes after a huge buildup with fireworks and smoke. But Nilsson had more worrisome things to attend to than fretting about the length of concert sets.

Neither *Duit On Mon Dei* nor *Sandman* was selling well, and the management at RCA was not happy. *Sandman* had struggled to 111 on the *Billboard* album charts, and *Duit On Mon Dei* had not made it into the top 100 either. Nevertheless, Nilsson had a contract to go on making albums, and—judging by the most recent examples—at a cost that was now causing his record company real concern. It was a particular issue for Mike Berniker, the vice president responsible for A&R, who had recently joined the firm from CBS. He had made a brisk and impressive start by signing such acts as Hall and Oates to RCA, and they were beginning to make money for his division, but he perceived a general problem with artists who had been at the label for some time and whose work was not selling. He unequivocally placed Nilsson in that category. (The following year he attempted to solve some of his problems by merging the pop and R&B catalogs to make his promotional spending more efficient, but shortly thereafter he left the company and returned to Columbia, where he founded the highly successful Jazz Masterpieces series.)[68] Nilsson disliked Berniker, nicknaming him "burn-a-cur," and had more than one row with him about his status as an artist,[69] but eventually he decided the only practical strategy was to attempt to meet him halfway. He said:

> At that particular junction, I decided well maybe I'm all wet. Maybe they deserve to have their hearing. The premise is basically that you hire or buy an artist, you give him money and time in the studio and certain contractual considerations, and in return he produces to the best of his ability what he can do to benefit both the record company and himself—artistically and economically, from a business standpoint. And I had been starting off a lot of what I was doing as an artist. And I thought well maybe they're right because *Sandman* and *Duit On Mon Dei* weren't selling what I thought they could sell, so I went and ate humble pie and said "What do you want me to do?" That could range to anything. They could turn to me and say "We want you to do what you think is right" or "We want you to show up at seven o'clock." And it came out somewhere in between. Basically, what it boiled down to is they weren't too sure about me producing the albums, and they weren't too sure about the content of some of the lyrics. And so I said, "OK, I'll do other people's songs, and have an outside producer, and put some strings and horns on to make it sound like an album." And that's what we did, and that's the way it was.[70]

For some time, Nilsson had been considering making a record of songs by the New Orleans pianist, composer, and singer Allen Toussaint. He had first talked of the idea well before the *Pussy Cats* sessions, and now he reasoned that the time could be right for him to do this. He told Derek Taylor in a letter that he was "in preparation" for the Toussaint record, but in the same lengthy account of his plans, he also said, "Next week in answer to those who want to know if I'm ever going to get back together, I'm planning to cut 'Sail Away,'—Randy's wonderful wog words."[71] (This is a reference to the line in Randy Newman's song that goes "Climb aboard little wog, sail away with me." The word "wog" was offensive slang used to describe black Africans.)

In any event, unable to decide how to split his time between what seemed to be two entirely separate projects, Nilsson opted to try to include some Toussaint numbers among the collection of other people's songs he had picked out for the new album (at that point untitled, but eventually dubbed… *That's the Way It Is*). Faced with Berniker's view that he needed a producer, Nilsson brought in Trevor Lawrence, one of his long-time associates, to do the job. He was not only a versatile session saxophonist, but he had written arrangements for Richard Perry, including part of Ringo's version of "Easy for Me." In Lawrence's view, there was another reason that he had been chosen, which was that he and Nilsson had spent a considerable amount of time hanging out together during previous sessions, from *Pussy Cats* onward, and they clicked socially. Prior to getting started on the new record, they met several times at the famous Brown Derby on Vine Street in

Hollywood to talk through the choice of music and artists and to get a head start on the written arrangements. Lawrence said:

I was a person that he trusted to do the music and to bounce off of. And I was the producer. My philosophy of being a producer with Harry isn't to tell him what to do or what it ought to be, but to try and interpret what he wants, and try and get that done for him.[72]

The studio sessions started—as Nilsson had told Taylor they would—on November 12, 1975, with "Sail Away," which RCA planned to release ahead of the album as a single. Lawrence had previously arranged and recorded a version of the song for Etta James, but he came up with a completely new symphonic arrangement for Nilsson and a forty-piece orchestra. The musicians included most of Hollywood's top studio players, but as Lawrence recalled, they were nearly hijacked before a note had been played. "We walk in," he recalled, "and Harry had rented this coffee dispenser. Inside were bottles of sake, and the coffee machine was keeping the sake hot. We've got all these musicians in the studio and all this sake. Harry just kept the party on. Everybody had a great time, but everybody worked."[73]

The musicians may have been well lubricated, but they play magnificently on Newman's satirical take on a slave trader selling the American dream to a naïve African, and Nilsson's voice sounds in good fettle. He not only reaches cleanly into the highest register he had achieved on record since *A Little Touch Of Schmilsson In The Night*, but he double-tracks over his own vocal at the end of each verse and injects passion into the choruses. However, toward the end, a hoarseness sets in that is somewhat reminiscent of the timbre of Rod Stewart's voice. This is almost certainly because he had decided to record his lead vocal live with the full orchestra as he had done with Gordon Jenkins in London. Yet unlike those gentle arrangements, Lawrence's chart required great strength and volume from the players, over which any singer's instinct would be to project forcibly. Not only that, but the setup was not as ideal as it had been in London, and Nilsson was not so well-placed acoustically to balance himself against the massed strings and brass. Although Nilsson's long-term colleague Richie Schmitt was the album's main overall engineer, RCA's studio B came with its own technical crew. Lawrence recalled:

We had an engineer that everybody was so hot to use. When he came in and saw the stage with all the music, this guy broke down. People had started doing one instrument at a time and overdubbing, but he came in and here's forty people. We ended up having to get one of the older guys that worked with the studio to be the engineer because this guy just wouldn't do it. He just melted.[74]

The finished version of Nilsson's "Sail Away" has a distinct and independent character from Newman's 1972 recording of his own song, and it seemed to have the right formula for a single. However, it did not appear—as originally planned—before the album because of the need to find a suitable B-side. Eventually it was paired with "Moonshine Bandit," but that song, written by Nilsson and guitarist Danny Kortchmar, was not to be recorded until mid-February 1976.

Work on the rest of the album began on December 2, with a cover version of the old Heartbeats hit "A Thousand Miles Away," which had reached number five on the R&B charts in 1957 and was more recently heard on the soundtrack of the 1973 movie *American Graffiti*. Originally, the vocal track was cut by Nilsson alone, but after that early December session, the soul singer Tony Le Peau was drafted in to add additional vocals, thereby effectively removing much of Nilsson's characteristic stamp of personality from the track. It seems a supreme irony that a man who had once been the perfect backing singer for Ringo Starr and Carly Simon was now reduced to bringing in someone else to do that job for him.

The decision was up to Lawrence, who realized he had different responsibilities now that he was no longer a member of the regular cohort of musicians who played in the "God's Greatest Hits" band, but the man who had to deliver a finished product to RCA. His decision to bring in another vocalist was because, despite the way Nilsson's voice had sounded just three weeks earlier, when it came time to do this particular track, it was not up to the job. "His voice had gone pretty bad," recalled Lawrence. "He was going off to San Francisco to meet some doctor to help him with his throat."[75] Fortunately, this treatment seems to have worked, and Nilsson returned to reasonable voice for the remainder of the album, although, to assist his vocal recovery, it was recorded at intervals over the next three months.

Remarkably, less than one week after recording "A Thousand Miles Away," Nilsson coaxed his voice back sufficiently to make one more foray into the golden high register that had been the hallmark of all his earlier work. In a beautifully paced version of George Harrison's "That Is All" (originally out on the ex-Beatle's 1973 album *Living In The Material World*), he was briefly back in spectacular form. Compared with Harrison's own nasal falsetto, Nilsson's voice has no break between registers, and his effortless run upward at the top of his range on the phrase "That is all I'm living for" is as good as anything he ever recorded. "We didn't do that many takes," said Lawrence, "he really was an artist."[76] The same session on December 8 produced a cover of Gerry Beckley's song "I Need You." But whereas "That Is All" allowed Nilsson to display his voice at its best, this song shows signs of strain. Clearly aiming to recreate Richard Perry's winning formula for "Without You," Lawrence wrote a heavyweight orchestral backing in Paul Buckmaster style for "I Need You."

Once Nilsson has sung gently through the introductory verse and the sound of the orchestra swells up behind him, he lacks the power and control to carry the chorus effectively. It becomes a series of disconnected phrases as he works hard to articulate each line of the song, and toward the end his usually flawless tuning drifts wide of the mark on the repeated tagline "I Need You." It was probably a mistake to try to record more than one song at each session, and had Nilsson retained the sureness of vocal control he showed on "That is All," this second song of the night might well have been a very much better recording. He had, apparently, originally planned to record it in 1971 when he first met Gerry Beckley and other members of the group America during the first London sessions with Richard Perry. According to Beckley:

> He loved that song and virtually every time we got together, if there was a piano, he'd make me sit down and play that song, over and over again. And he asked me if we had plans to make it a single, which we didn't at that time. We were in between songs. There were a few different ideas floating around, but one of them was "Let's go back and record some new material," and of that, "Horse With No Name," was one of the songs, which became our new single. And it wasn't until that was a hit in the States that we needed a follow up. As a result, "I Need You" did get released, and Harry scrapped his plans.[77]

Beckley subsequently regretted that Nilsson had waited until 1975 to try recording his own version, believing that his voice would have served him much better at the start of the decade.

Almost a week after that session came Nilsson's first formal attempt to tackle the Toussaint repertoire, with the regular members of his studio backing band led from the piano by Dr. John (Mac Rebennack). Informal tapes exist from this period of Nilsson and Dr. John jamming through a wide range of ideas,[78] but this session, which focused on "Holy Cow," the song Toussaint wrote and recorded with Lee Dorsey in 1966, marks the moment that the project officially arrived at the RCA studios. That night, December 12, they also worked on "Who's Gonna Help a Brother Get Further?" by Toussaint, although the session sheets take the title from the first line of the lyric "Standing on the Corner." Neither of these songs finally made it to the finished album, but the collaboration with Dr. John continued throughout the making of the record, culminating in the powerful song "Daylight Has Caught Me," co-written by Nilsson and Rebennack, which was cut at one of the final sessions on March 19, 1976.

Intriguingly, the gestation of this song can be heard in the informal jam session tapes from the time, showing how the major part of Nilsson's lyric "Daylight has caught me, can't go nowhere" (harking back perhaps to his role as Count Downe) was originally fitted to an entirely different harmonic structure and melody. That demo version shows Dr. John playing a chord sequence with a strong downward chromatic movement from measure to measure (rather like Fats Waller's chords for "Blue Turning Grey Over You") over which Nilsson sings a ballad melody that is clearly based on the 1928 song "She's Funny That Way" by Whiting and Moret. Between a couple of attempts at that slow setting of the words, they try an uptempo treatment that is much closer to the final version of the song, with a New Orleans shuffle beat and more static chords. At one point, Nilsson is momentarily thrown as Rebennack shifts into a minor key. "I'm trying to make something different," he says, explaining that just running through the same sequence over and over again is rather dull. The final song features a simple alternation between two chords an interval of a fourth apart for its first eight measures, and the issued version is one of the strongest pieces on the album. It proves the value of experimentation and development away from the studio, compared to the more hit-and- miss methods Nilsson had used on his previous three records.

Equally intriguing from these jams are the unfinished snatches of three songs that all show comparable potential. One uses the imagery of turning off and rewinding a tape to play down emotional trouble, another explores "the four things that are important, sickness, health, wealth and death," and the final one, "I used to be a black man," examines the melding of African American culture with the mainstream. The collaboration was clearly fun on both sides, and as well as these demos of new songs, there are recordings of Nilsson and Dr. John together at the piano fumbling through duet versions of various Scott Joplin and George Gershwin tunes. Dr. John is repeatedly amazed by some of the tricky ragtime fingering Nilsson has mastered, whereas Nilsson is in awe of the speed with which Dr. John picks up chord sequences and adds his own characteristic rolling bass lines.

Although their jointly written song "Daylight Has Caught Me" is as close as Nilsson came to fulfilling his plans to release a Toussaint record, there is a further collaboration on the album. This is a duet with singer Lynda Laurence. She was actually the wife of Trevor Lawrence and used to joke that all she had to do was "change one letter in her name" when they got married.[79] She was a member of the Supremes and had known Nilsson during all the years he had worked with Trevor. Their medley of "Just One Look" and "Baby I'm Yours" shows real musical chemistry between them, but again suffers from the frailty of Nilsson's voice. "Those are live vocals," recalled Lawrence, confirming that there were no overdubs and the interaction between the voices is genuine.[80] The opening of the first song and the segue into the second shows a strong blending of tone and timbre, but on the final sections of both songs, again trying unsuccessfully to project over the orchestra, Nilsson raises his volume and arrives at a husky croak. However much he may have disliked the comparison, he presages the rasping sound of Joe Cocker in his 1982 duet with Jennifer Warnes on "Up Where We Belong."

The final pieces on the album, his and Kortchmar's co-written "Moonshine Bandit" and Conrad Mauge Jr.'s "Zombie Jamboree" both return to the Caribbean feel of *Duit On Mon Dei*.

The end result is more consistent in quality than the previous three albums, and the covers of "Sail Away" and "That Is All" plus the jaunty new song "Daylight Has Caught Me" include Nilsson's best singing since the Richard Perry days. But in terms of focus, in terms of presenting a consistent image to his fans, the strategy of singing cover songs with even as accomplished a producer as Lawrence was not to solve RCA's marketing problem. "There are so many facets, so many angles to his work, that the normal listener can't grasp them," said Klaus Voormann.[81] And Lawrence agreed, "They wanted another album like

Nilsson Schmilsson, and Harry didn't like that at all. He was fighting for his right to be an artist."[82]

The fight continued right up to the question of what to call the album. Having met Mike Berniker halfway by making what he regarded as radio-friendly songs with no scatological lyrics, Nilsson's schoolboy sense of humor prompted him to propose the title *Eldridge and Beaver Cleaver USA*. (This wording finally appeared on a poster on Nilsson's wall in the cover photograph.) In his proposition to Berniker, studiously avoiding any reference to the pubic connotations of "beaver," Nilsson reasoned that by titling his record after a Black Panther activist and a fictional naughty boy from a 1950s television series, it would represent contemporary American society and be a "nice bicentennial title."[83] RCA disagreed, and they were equally unenthusiastic about Nilsson's next, somewhat geriatric-focused idea, *The Legs Go First*. In the end, it was decided to use a cover photo of Nilsson watching the television news and to adopt veteran news anchor Walter Cronkite's signing-off phrase "…that's the way it is." Unfortunately, Cronkite refused to allow his image to be used on the cover and so too did the other occasional user of the phrase, John Chancellor, thereby rather ruining the reference. In the end, the designer superimposed the face of another well-known news broadcaster, Edward R. Murrow, who had died in 1965 and was in no position to complain. The album came out in June 1976, closely followed by the single of "Sail Away." Despite Berniker's best-laid plans, the record only reached 158 on the album charts, thereby proving to be less commercially successful than either *Duit On Mon Dei* or *Sandman*.

Ride with me, glide with me
Stay by my side with me through the night

9

PERFECT DAY

THE PRESS REACTION to ... *That's The Way It Is* was more positive than the sales figures might suggest. Critic Dave Marsh, whose "Rolling Stone" column was syndicated widely across the United States, was typical, noting, "All the best material here is written by others, and the record contains the best singing Nilsson has done in years—especially on pal Randy Newman's 'Sail Away.' "[1] This song, perhaps because of its existing reputation, tended to be the one singled out as the outstanding performance on the album, with a later reviewer saying that Nilsson was "the one singer who could bring out the song's high drama while avoiding any jingoistic temptations."[2] The greater care taken over the arrangements and well-performed familiar material amid the originals definitely signaled to industry insiders that Nilsson was still a creative force to be reckoned with, even if the fluctuations of form and content in the five albums that came after *Nilsson Schmilsson* had not allowed him to keep the big public following that once might have been expected.

Noel Coppage in *Stereo Review* mused that Nilsson was now playing at making albums the way that Marlon Brando and Orson Welles seemed to be playing with movie acting by the mid-1970s, in effect caricaturing himself. But as well as singling out the "primal scream" of "Sail Away," Coppage also identified "Daylight Has Caught Me" as the outstanding original piece on the record. His most telling observation was that on ... *That's The Way It Is* and its immediate predecessors, "we listeners have to do most of the work to make the album mean something."[3] For Nilsson, however, this was entirely deliberate. While RCA and the likes of *Stereo Review* were looking for consistency, his view of himself was exactly the opposite: "I've always thought of myself as the most diversified singer of all time, from working with Gordon Jenkins and John Lennon to *The Point* and *Nilsson Sings Newman*."[4]

Yet despite what the majority of critics clearly regarded as a return to form, once ... *That's The Way It Is* had been finished in March, the rest of 1976 saw a hiatus in Nilsson's creative energy as a recording artist. Instead, he turned to a domestic project—to build one of the most unusual houses in Los Angeles for himself and Una. He had indicated his ambition to do this in a letter to Derek Taylor late in 1975 when he wrote: "I'm meeting with architects who will build our home."[5] According to Una Nilsson, it wasn't so much a question of "architects" as a fortuitous meeting with one particular architect, who already had a tenuous connection with the site that Nilsson spontaneously decided he wanted to purchase. She said:

> I think what happened was he thought, "Wouldn't it be nice to have a house?" We started house hunting while we rented the home on Strada Vecchia Road in Bel Air, but didn't like anything we saw. One day we were standing on the deck in Strada Vecchia and we looked out, and we saw a lot, and we thought, "That would do!" So we did some research. Harry loved the idea of living in Bel Air as it was very beautiful. It was not particularly built up, because it was always laid out with only a limited number of homes allowed there. So we saw the lot, found out it was for sale, purchased it, and…the lot below it was being built on at the time. The house there had been designed by a student of an architect at UCLA, so we spoke to him [the architect]. His name was Eugene Kupper and Eugene designed our house. And as anyone who has built a house knows, it takes years. We rented a variety of homes while it was being built. But it was really fun to go through the project of building a home. That architect was in a group of maybe four architects, and they were called the Silvers, and they were considered post modernists.[6]

Kupper was an associate professor of architecture at UCLA, and he had already won a couple of prestigious awards for his buildings by the time he met Nilsson. Because he mixed academic work with projects as a working architect for a number of different Los Angeles partnerships, he had not, like the rest of the Silver group, become associated with a particular office or a particular style. Kupper was best known in architectural circles for his philosophy of design, which was that there is "a concept in every line, a theory in every wall, and a philosophy in every building."[7] The lot at 10549 Rocca Place in Bel Air presented him with a challenge. It was on a rocky hillside, so the house had to nestle on a site with little or no naturally level ground. It sat astride an outcrop that gave views in three directions, to the mountains, the city, and the ocean, and ideally all of these should be visible from the main living spaces. The house was surrounded by four acres of land, so positioning it was also a critical issue, in order to make the most of the outside space. Kupper's design solution was to work from a long central hallway running along the axis of the outcrop, with rooms and views opening out from it on both sides. Una Nilsson recalled:

> When he designed the house, he made a little cardboard model, and every aspect of it was fun. He showed this to one of his old professors, along with the floorplan. And the professor said, "Hmm, yes, yes, that's all very nice. Where did you ever find somebody who would let you build this?" But that was Harry. Because he just

loved everybody's creativity to come out, and to be in a position to work with an architect. And he was glad to find an architect who did what he wanted to do. It was just great, and if you looked at it from different directions it took on different shapes. During one of the first meetings, when the architect was asking what we were looking for, there was an album cover on the table, and on it was this little icon for Nilsson House Productions, and it's the Nilsson House. Just four windows and a chimney… that was the beginning.[8]

Kupper took the idea and developed it so that the theme would recur on every plane from which one viewed the house. "This is a house a child might draw," he said. "The entrance court tells the archetypal story of a house—a door, a window, a roof and a chimney."[9] The entrance door was (he omitted to mention) nine feet tall and five feet wide, and throughout the building, he played with dimensions. The grand corridor from the entrance ran right through the building only to peter out playfully into a bathroom. The kitchen was double height, with a shuttered window opening way above head height to let in light, as did some first-floor windows in one of the several two-story bathrooms. There were whimsical touches that Kupper said had been inspired by Nilsson songs: porches with no doors, a colonnade that opened into a variety of spaces. But overall what the house projected was a sense of merriment and adventure.

Architecture critics took notice when the house was finally completed some three years after the foundations were laid, principally because a domestic project on this scale, where an architect had been given what appeared to be free rein to try postmodern experiments, was rare. They might have disagreed with some of the finer details, but overall they followed the views of Suzanne Stephens in *Progressive Architecture*, who wrote of the almost-completed building: "It presents in effect dance notations, where some steps are nicely worked on and put into stunning combination with others. A strong choreography could emerge. The use of vernacular materials, archetypal forms, and certain Modernist principles indicates that the synthesis and development of these manipulations promise yet to take us 'beyond modernism.' "[10]

Having put the work in motion, Nilsson became a frequent visitor to the site. During the final sessions for … *That's The Way It Is* in February and March 1976, he and Trevor Lawrence would make their way over to the lot. "We'd sit on the foundations and drink and talk," recalled Lawrence,[11] who suggested that Nilsson was already thinking of it as his home, even though it had yet to be finished. When the house was completed, it eventually became the ideal place for him and Una to bring up their children. She described it as a "playpen," and in retrospect she believed that they had been extremely indulgent parents. "It had lots of soft furniture and the children used to jump from the loft into the living room," she recalled. "The hallway was something like 180 feet long, and they used to ride their bicycles up and down the hall."[12]

With Eugene Kupper firmly in control, the foundations for what was already being referred to as the Nilsson House already dug out of the hillside, and … *That's The Way It*

Is finished in late March 1976, Una and Nilsson decided to head for a break in New York during April. Their visit was to coincide with the appearance in the city of a comedy troupe from England whose members had acquired almost rock-star status. On April 14, *Monty Python Live!* opened at the City Center Theater in Manhattan. Nilsson already knew Graham Chapman from his drinking bouts with Ringo, Keith Moon, and Marc Bolan, but now he was to meet the rest of the *Flying Circus* team, whose work he already knew well from watching British television in Curzon Place and from the repeats of their programs on ABC television in the United States from 1975. These, although clumsily re-edited, had built up a huge cult following, members of which could recite most of the better-known sketches verbatim. The stage show, assembled from the funniest of the Pythons' television and movie sketches, was to be the theatrical event of the spring. As the team of Chapman, John Cleese, Terry Gilliam, Eric Idle, Terry Jones, and Michael Palin (plus their regular female co-star Carol Cleveland) ran through the "Dead Parrot" sketch, the "Ministry of Silly Walks," the "Gumbies," and "The Man Who Gives Abuse," the audience mouthed along with the well-known lines. Every night the show closed with the "Lumberjack Song" in which Idle sang the story of a Canadian lumberjack whose ambition was to put on women's clothing. The song was accompanied by a male chorus dressed as Royal Canadian Mounted Policemen.

Everyone from Leonard Bernstein to Paul Simon and from veteran songwriter Adolph Green to the Velvet Underground's John Cale was at the first-night party, along with comic actors Chevy Chase and John Belushi. The doyen of New York critics, Clive Barnes, loved the show, and its limited run was quickly sold out.[13]

Among the other Python fans in town was George Harrison. He did not go to the opening, but he subsequently came to see the show about midway through its run. He was already friends with Eric Idle, who after meeting the ex-Beatle at the Los Angeles screening of the movie *Monty Python and The Holy Grail* in 1975, had gone on to write advertising copy for Harrison's solo album *Extra Texture* and had added some Pythonesque voices to his record "This Song." When they met again at the theater, they were chatting, when Idle came up with a sudden thought:

I said, "Well, why not be on stage? Be a lumberjack?" So he said he'd like to do that. He dressed up as a lumberjack and he came on stage, and nobody ever knew. There is actually a picture of him that I have. Then the next day I think he left for his holidays and I was to join him about a week later. Then I met Harry on the street at 6th Avenue. He was with [the actor] Ed Begley Jr., who I think I knew vaguely, so he introduced us. Harry heard that George had done it, and he wanted to have his go. And of course his go…he'd had a few, Harry. He came staggering onto the stage. I think he had managed to get his hat on. His costume was all open, he had dark glasses on and he had a drink in his hand. He staggered round and everybody went, "Oh flipping heck, who brought him on?" Because the Pythons were very disciplined, and did not approve of larking about. Anyway we got through it. Normally at the end of it we would step back so the curtain could drop. And we all went, "Where's Harry?" He'd gone straight forwards into the audience, and he fell off the stage and broke his wrist, apparently. I don't remember seeing him after that.[14]

The rest of the Pythons were somewhat less forgiving toward Nilsson. Michael Palin recalled him "coked to the eyeballs and full of booze" before he "keeled over into the front row and lay helplessly astride the wooden edge of the orchestra pit." According to the songwriter and singer Neil Innes, who toured as a musician with the Python live show, Nilsson and Harrison were not the only "exalted guests" who appeared incognito as Canadian Mounties in the "Lumberjack Song," but everyone except Nilsson tried to keep their appearance among the regular chorus of scarlet-clad singers a secret. "He was the only one whose buttons were done up incorrectly and whose hat was too jaunty. Failing to stand up again after a bow and disappearing into the orchestra pit was also a bit of a giveaway."[15]

Not long afterward, Nilsson and Una returned to Los Angeles, as Nilsson waited for his wrist to heal. One diversion that he enjoyed shortly after they came back to the West Coast was to hang out on a coastal cruise organized by the owners of the Record Plant. Gary Kellgren, one of the partners in the business, had fitted out a 110-foot yacht as a floating studio and was offering musicians the chance to record at sea. Quite how the throb of the boat's motors was overcome, even by Kellgren's state-of-the-art twenty-four-track equipment, was not clear, but he persuaded Jimmy Webb to try recording afloat, and Nilsson, along with other stars such as Glen Campbell and Sly Stone, joined him as a passenger on at least one of the longer recording cruises that traveled down the coast from San Francisco to Baja in Mexico.[16]

Although Nilsson told the immigration officials that he and Una had no immediate plans to marry when they entered the country in late 1975, the reason that they could not do so was that the court had still not entered its final judgment on his divorce from Diane. The judgment eventually came through on June 23, 1976.[17] This now made it possible for them to marry and with not only a home under construction, but also the news that Una was pregnant, they decided to do so that summer. However, the decision was not quite as premeditated as this might suggest. According to Una, "We just decided on a whim. We decided on a Monday and got married on the Thursday."[18] The Thursday in question was August 12, 1976, and the ceremony was booked for the Pilot's Lounge reception suite at the Airport Marriott Hotel in Los Angeles, from where Nilsson and Una would fly to New York, traveling onward to London. (The London apartment had been occupied on a long lease from December until August, so this was their first opportunity since the previous fall to return there.) Una recalled that Van Dyke Parks suggested a priest who would conduct the ceremony and found them an accordionist and violinist to provide music at the reception. The catering was done by the former girl Friday at Apple, Chris O'Dell. She and her business partner Tina Firestone had launched an events company in Los Angeles called Brains Unlimited, which had been financed by Ringo's long-term associate Hilary Gerrard. This wedding was their first big show-business event.[19] The best man was to be Ringo Starr. Nilsson recalled:

The day prior to the wedding, he walked into Tiffany's in Beverly Hills, asking to see a handful of rings. After looking them over, Ringo said to the salesman, "I'll just take these and return the others tomorrow, okay?" As the salesman began to speak, Ringo lowered his shades and smiled. The salesman thanked him. Ringo, some others and I proceeded to get loaded, heavily loaded.

The next day, wedding day, I was like Hell with a hangover. The first order of the day was three large shots of brandy, laying the clothing out still shaking, two more shots and a nice long hot, then cold, shower. As I dressed I began to sweat like Mike Tyson, so I held off with the shirt for a while. I noticed on the nightstand an 8-track of nice coke, so I thought, "To hell with it, you only marry thrice." It didn't help the diaphoresis, but I felt I could at least walk. The limousine arrived. Ringo gave me a toot for luck and the limo driver gave me a gram for luck. I was obliged to do some more with him, and even the priest…shared another gram. By now I was shaking so much I could barely stand. Ringo reached in his pocket and displayed eight or ten rings. Within two attempts he found the right sizes. Then it was up to me to place the beautiful square gold circles on the love of my life's delicate non-shaking hand. Ringo observed, "Look, he's shaking." He must have thought it was nerves, and helped me to steady my hands and slip on the ring.[20]

Chris O'Dell led the applause, and wine was served to the guests. To keep him going, Nilsson had a flask of brandy in his pocket, and soon he and Una left the reception as a limo whisked them to the airport for their flight to New York. At Kennedy, they were met by another limo and ferried to the Pierre Hotel, their usual temporary home in Manhattan. Greeting the bellmen by name, Nilsson ordered a bottle of Remy Martin for the room and called a couple of friends. It was not long before there was a full-scale party going on in the suite. Around midnight, Una slipped off to bed, but Nilsson carried on drinking and smoking, until slivers of dawn light showed under the heavy curtains. Sending his friends home, he went into the bedroom and looked down at his bride. "What have I done?" he thought. "What an asshole. What a way to start!"[21] He took a valium and slid into a deep sleep, failing to remember that he had arranged for a visitor to call that morning before he and Una set off for Britain on the Cunard liner *Queen Elizabeth II*.

The mystery visitor had made contact with Nilsson via the New York office of RCA. There was a fan-mail secretary there who had called Nilsson a month or so earlier to say there was a letter she thought he should see. It was quite brief and came from a Drake Nilsson who said he believed they were brothers. Intrigued, Nilsson called him, and Drake asked if he recalled staying at the Stephen's Hotel in Chicago in 1952. This brief childhood visit to the Windy City was a clear memory in Nilsson's mind, and he began to take Drake seriously. Soon after the call, a large manila envelope arrived containing a birth certificate, listing Drake's place of birth as 726 Jefferson Avenue, Brooklyn. Not only was this the Martin family apartment, but the document was witnessed by Nilsson's uncle John.

So how come there was another brother—quite aside from his father's surviving son Gary[22]—about whom Nilsson knew nothing? There were obviously reasons why Bette Nilsson did not want anyone to know too much about what had happened, and so the information on the birth certificate was designed to confuse. Drake Nilsson takes up the story:

> My mother kept me a secret for many years from Harry and Michelle [Nilsson's half sister]. I was born, November 21, 1949. According to my birth certificate, I was the child of "Florence and Wolfe Nilsson." I was born in a hospital in the Bushwick section of Brooklyn. My parents' address at the time was 762 Jefferson Avenue. My birth certificate is wrong in several areas. My mother's name at the time of my birth was Elizabeth a.k.a. Bette Nilsson. My father's name was Harry E. Nilsson. The birth certificate shows Florence (my maternal grandmother's name) and Wolfe (which was the last name of my mother's best friend Margaret). I was never given up for adoption. I was left with my mother's friends or family, because during those times my mother didn't want to be a mom. Like Harry I was left with Aunt Cissy and Uncle Fred for a time, as well as the Wolfe Family. Margaret's maiden name was Merritt and her sister was Viola Lasher, who wound up with me because Charlie Wolfe threatened my life if his wife Margaret didn't give him the rent money to go drinking. I stayed with the Lashers until I was eighteen years old and then left to join the Navy during Vietnam. In 1973, I returned home from the war and met and married my childhood sweetheart Linda. I also resumed my work at a local flower shop that I wound up owning in 1980. But when Harry did the album called *Harry*, the picture on the album cover looked so much like me that a friend bought me the album and gave it to me, stating, "This guy's pretty good and has your last name." I took the album home and fell in love with the music. Something about this guy felt familiar. My wife finally pushed me into contacting RCA A&R in New York City. Harry then called me and we arranged to meet.[23]

When Drake arrived at the Pierre Hotel on Friday, August 13, 1976, and made his way up to the suite, Nilsson was in no suitable state to receive him. He had barely been asleep for a couple of hours, and it was not easy fighting off the effects of the valium on top of over forty-eight hours of brandy and cocaine. Una tried hard to shake him awake, and he groggily asked her to offer Drake coffee and give him ten minutes to pull himself together. Nilsson eventually managed to stand up, pull on a bathrobe, and down a glass of orange juice left for him by Una. "I paused," he said, "took two deep breaths, entered the living room and stood eye to eye with this complete stranger. He came forward and we embraced. He seemed very excited and I couldn't tell him what he was doing to my poor body."[24]

During the next couple of hours, over coffee and rolls as Nilsson gradually came to, he and Una heard Drake's story. He had been wounded in Vietnam before being shipped home, and it was during his convalescence that he had been given the copy of the *Harry* album. Before he contacted RCA, he had made great efforts to track down his family, using the telephone directory to contact all the Martins and Nilssons listed in New York, Brooklyn, and New Jersey without success. It was agreed that Nilsson would be in touch with Drake again on his return from London. The one person nobody could ask about Drake was Harry Nilsson Sr. He had died on November 25, 1975. On his return from Europe that month, Nilsson had made a flying visit to Gainesville to see his father just before he passed away, but that was before he was aware of Drake's existence.

However, after meeting Drake and before leaving for England, Nilsson sent a note to his mother asking for her side of the story. She had by now settled in the L.A. area and was running a little antique store. His letter to her sparked off a period when they wrote to one another more often as she gradually told him more about the past.

One of her first letters to arrive in London sidestepped the issue of Drake, but looking back at the wedding, it confirmed how delighted she was to have Una as a member of the family. "Since I too have Irish blood," she wrote, "I'll venture to say that this is one marriage that has the leprechauns dancing on the green!" She went on: "Una looked like everything in the world that was right and good and I was so happy to have her officially as a daughter."[25] In his draft of an autobiography, Nilsson noted that Bette "did eventually" tell him about Drake and that following their meeting, "she embraced Drake as her son and communicated with him."[26] However, her immediate concern in August 1976 was to recover Nilsson's Volkswagen "Thing" from his former rented home on Strada Vecchia and pass it on to his half-sister Michelle to use while he was in Europe. Also on her mind was finding a temporary home for a new Mercedes that would be delivered for him to use on his return. This was a gift from the local dealership of the Chrysler Corporation, in return for using "Me and My Arrow" on a television advertisement campaign for its new Plymouth Arrow automobile, as Van Dyke Parks explained:

> They came to Harry and said, "We've got to have that song, 'Me and My Arrow,' that's perfect." [It was the] perfect song for a big ad campaign for the Motor City. Harry's only caveat was that they give him a top of the line Mercedes, and that would seal the deal. Well, of course, when they first heard this, they were so insulted [because he wanted a competing brand] that they were going to pass, but they eventually used it.[27]

Bette's biggest disappointment in her letters to Nilsson was that the proposed date for a British version of *The Point* stage show had been postponed from October, when she had hoped to come to London to see it. Plans were well in hand for the show, however, and she was eventually to arrive in late December in time for the preview performances at Sir

Bernard Miles's Mermaid Theatre. A rather bleak modernist building at Puddle Dock, this was the City of London's newest theater, built on the site of a warehouse that had been bombed in World War II on the banks of the Thames at Blackfriars.

Perhaps it is fortunate that the opening of the play was delayed beyond October, because the new Nilsson baby was due in November and eventually arrived on the 14th. Una recalled:

> Our first son Beau was born at St Teresa's in Wimbledon. There was a particular doctor we wanted to use, an obstetrician there. He had his rooms on Harley Street, but Wimbledon was where he worked. You know how it feels when you're expecting your first child. You're so idealistic. We'd come across a book, a French book, about gentle childbirth, and the idea was that the delivery room should be quiet, the lights not too bright and not too traumatic an experience, so we were interested in that, and that's how we got to that doctor. We were looking for someone who would go along with that.[28]

After Beau was born, the family moved back to Curzon Place, which was to be the family home until he was old enough to travel back to the United States. For the next month, Nilsson divided his time between being home with Una and their son and working at the Mermaid Theatre to get the British production of *The Point* underway. When Bette arrived from America to see her new grandson and the play, Nilsson accommodated her in lavish style at the prestigious Inn on the Park hotel, a short distance from his apartment. However, she complained that he had been "so busy I have barely seen him." She did, on the other hand, spend plenty of time with Una and her grandson and reported: "Beau is fat and handsome and completely indifferent to his American relatives."[29]

The delay in the opening of the production, and consequently the unexpectedly large amount of time Nilsson spent at the theater, was the result of his unhappiness about the musical side of the British version of the show. There was something not quite right, but he could not put his finger on it. He had attended the auditions for all the principal roles, and he recalled that the accompanist to David Delve, who was cast as the Leaf Man, played with the kind of flair that he felt was missing from the show itself. That accompanist was Mike McNaught, who was already quite well known in London for leading a group at Ronnie Scott's club in the early 1970s called the London Jazz Four. This quartet had recorded sophisticated jazz versions of a number of Beatles songs. More recently, he and Delve had been writing music for children's albums featuring such well-known British characters as the little wooden toy Noddy, the glove puppet Sooty, and Rupert the Bear. It was one of these songs for young people that he and Delve had played at the audition. McNaught remembered:

> I used to play for a lot of actor friends' auditions and for *The Point* instead of the usual cattle-market, each of the actors was given half an hour to audition. David read for the Leaf Man (got the part and was brilliant) and sang our song, and suddenly

Harry appeared. I never expected him to be at the auditions for some reason, but he asked who wrote the song, said he loved it, and did we have any more?

"Drawers-full," I said.

"We must have lunch," he said.

"Great," I said, and that was that.

About a month later the director, Ron Pember, invited me to lunch. He said they were in the middle of rehearsals and they seemed to have a bit of a problem musically, so could I come and have a look? They had a young MD [Musical Director] who was excellent but for some reason had the "feel" all wrong, so I explained this to the director. He said, "You'd better talk to Harry."

Harry said, "Where can we get a drink?" And then asked me to take over.[30]

McNaught did so and looked after both the arrangements of Nilsson's original music and any new material that was needed. The British press announced that the first previews would begin on December 16, 1976,[31] and the show officially opened immediately after Christmas to become that year's children's play at the Mermaid.

In keeping with its reputation as a company outside the main area of London's theater world that presented new and unusual work, the Mermaid had built part of its popular success on mounting seasonal plays that took a novel view of the traditional pantomime, more orthodox versions of which were on offer in the West End, as was the annual presentation of J. M. Barrie's *Peter Pan*.

The Mermaid Theatre's founder, Sir Bernard Miles, had become well known as the fearsome pirate Long John Silver in the venue's most famous children's entertainment, an adaptation of Robert Louis Stevenson's *Treasure Island*. This was a role he first played in 1959. Most years since then had involved a reprise of the performance, although on one occasion in 1968, Silver was played by Barry Humphries, and over the years the show was stolen regularly by the comedian Spike Milligan, who played the castaway Ben Gunn with what one reviewer called "a new dimension of insanity."[32] So for the theater to present a different show when there was still demand for its regular annual installment of pirates was a big vote of confidence in Nilsson, who told the press, "Although it's opening at Christmas, it won't be a pantomime. We're trying to get away from that. It's funny how the British always seem to associate anything light or animated with Christmas. It's different in America."[33] Instead of using Esquire Jauchem's Boston adaptation, the Mermaid opted for a new script by the British director Ron Pember and Sir Bernard Miles.

In the production, Miles played the grandfather reading the tale at the start and end, appearing—as Arthur Fiedler had done during the main part of the run in Boston—on film. But he was also very much a stage presence in the role of the King. "I like to use music and song and dance and jokes and television and film, all at the same time," explained Nilsson.[34] Colin Bennett was the Count and Oscar Jones the Rock Man. The role of Oblio was played by the charismatic principal dancer from the Royal Ballet company, Wayne Sleep. To make the most of his talent, the press reported that he "has choreographed himself a number of twirling, spinning numbers to Nilsson's expanded music."[35]

These "show-off" numbers, as he called them, were written by McNaught, who felt that this incarnation of the stage show, with strong performances from all the ensemble and Sleep's lighter-than-air portrayal of Oblio, came "close to the magic of the original." Indeed, McNaught had been such a fan of the movie since it first appeared that he often used Nilsson's soundtrack album to demonstrate to record and radio producers how to write effective contemporary material for children.[36]

Most critics loved the show, and it did brisk enough business for the Mermaid immediately to book it again for the following Christmas season. However, there were those who disliked it, principal among whom was the influential theater critic of *Punch* magazine, Sheridan Morley. Attacking the show's "sickening winsomeness," he worked up a head of splenetic steam, going on to lambast "an evening about as theatrically exciting and inventive as an exhibition of old socks." He lavished faint praise on Oscar Jones as the Rock Man, notably for his singing in what Morley rather inaccurately characterized as "some splendid Louis Armstrong imitations" and on the puppeteer Paul Aylett, who operated the fluffy and somewhat un-pointed dog Arrow. But then it was back to critical invective, as he summed up:

> The whole mishmash must be a laborious plea for tolerance. What kind of tolerance, though? Racial? Sexual? Political? Economic? Probably all four—it's not the kind of show inclined to concentrate on essentials, or explain itself in more detail than could be grasped by the average two-year-old foreigner.[37]

The following year when the show returned for an eleven-week run, he advised his readers that "going finally mad, the Mermaid management have brought back the musical *The Point*. It was terrible last year...." According to Morley, not even "the addition of a couple of ex-Monkees, Micky Dolenz and Davy Jones" could save it.[38] But he was in a minority of one. For example, *The Listener* qualified its only note of caution, "*The Point* at the Mermaid is very moral indeed, but do not be deterred from going on that account." And *Plays and Players* also endorsed the show.[39]

For the 1977/8 revival, the show underwent some big changes, not least of which was the addition of several other Nilsson songs to the music originally written for *The Point*. "Gotta Get Up" was incorporated from *Nilsson Schmilsson* and "Remember" from *Son of Schmilsson*. (At the same time, "Here's Why I Did Not Go to Work Today" from *Sandman*, which had been a solo turn for Oscar Jones as the Rock Man, was dropped.) A new song, "Blanket for a Sail," which had been added to the 1976 production was retained and turned into a feature for Jones. The reason for the reshaping of the show was that, having cast Davy Jones as Oblio when Wayne Sleep announced he was not available for the revival, Jones persuaded Nilsson to bring in Dolenz as well.

Nilsson had remained firm friends with Dolenz since their Laurel Canyon days, but although he had written two songs for the Monkees that had featured Jones as principal singer, he and Jones had never been particularly close. That had changed when the two of them briefly visited Japan together in the summer of 1977 to add the backing vocals to a bizarre series of television commercials that Ringo Starr was making for a Japanese leisurewear company. Starr reprised his role as the flying saucer pilot from the Dorfman video, and Jones and Nilsson came up with some inventive harmonies as they oohed and aahed together behind Ringo's lead vocal on "I Love My Suit." When Jones suggested Dolenz join the cast of *The Point*, Nilsson was only too happy to agree.

Nevertheless, although he was cast as both the Leaf Man and the son of the Count, Dolenz was effectively a bit-part player. Prior to coming to London, he and Jones had been doing a series of concert appearances singing their former Monkees hits as "Dolenz and Jones," and so the additional songs were intended to give them a chance to capitalize on this established double act. "Gotta Get Up" was inserted toward the end of the show as a song and dance number featuring the pair of them and choreographed by Gillian Gregory, who had recently helped to stage *Tommy* by the Who.

Their routine is preserved for posterity because a few days before the play opened, the two former Monkees appeared on the London Weekend Television program *Our Show* on Saturday, December 17, 1977. Interviewed by the ten-year-old Susan Tully (a child actress who went on to star in the BBC soap opera *East Enders*), they then performed the song in the studio accompanied by Mike McNaught. There were interruptions from the dog Arrow, now a very bright shade of blue and an extremely pointed puppet, operated for this edition of the show by David Claridge, who later achieved considerable fame as the manipulator of another famous British puppet character, Roland Rat.[40]

On screen, everything about the two youthful stars is affable, and they diplomatically field questions about their ex-bandmates despite having barely been in communication with them for some time. There is obvious chemistry between the pair, and everything augured well for the show. Dolenz moved into Nilsson's Curzon Place apartment as 1978 began and looked forward to a new lease on life as a stage actor, having recently separated from Samantha and come through a period of depression. He wrote: "The atmosphere on *The Point*... started out clean and clear, but it gradually got thick and clouded with emotional pollution."[41] Within a week or two, he and Jones were not on speaking terms, had a huge backstage fistfight, and when the run finished, they did not talk to one another again for nine years. Their stormy relationship may have been one factor that prevented the show from transferring to a West End theater for an extended run, which had been Bernard Miles's plan for this revival, but even so, the fully sold-out musical raised sufficient money for the Mermaid to close for a period of refurbishment as soon as the play that followed *The Point* was over.[42]

In retrospect, Dolenz, who became a seasoned television and stage director in Britain in the years following his appearance in *The Point*, felt that the show was flawed as a stage musical. He believed it might not have fared well with a transfer to a larger, less intimate theater than the Mermaid. Several songs that had worked brilliantly on film to feed the visual invention of Fred Wolf did not have the importance to the plot that is usually essential in the theater. "The dramatic moments in the play did not turn on the songs," he said, "and there weren't nearly enough songs to make it a musical. I think Wayne Sleep got away with it because he turned it into a ballet."[43]

Mike McNaught, who worked on both productions of the show, agreed. To him, the Dolenz/Jones version, although it is preserved on an original cast album and therefore became much better known was not as satisfying as the 1976/7 production. He wrote: "The show with Davy and Micky didn't actually become the 'Davy and Micky Show' but a lot of the innocence of the original disappeared. They both worked hard at it, but it never ever felt that they were part of the story."[44]

McNaught himself, however, became a central part of the Nilsson story in early 1977 when it was decided to make the next RCA album in London, before the family returned to Los Angeles in April. He said:

> During the first run of the show Harry said he really liked the string things I had written for Wayne, and that he was going to record a new album in London in the Spring. He said he wanted to do it with strings and a rhythm section, and that he'd already asked another arranger to do it, but the guy was finding it hard to commit. Early in the New Year, Harry asked me to arrange the new album.[45]

Choosing a completely unknown British arranger for this album apparently caused some consternation at RCA's offices, not least because ... *That's The Way It Is* had not succeeded in selling more strongly than its predecessors, and this looked like an even greater risk. However, Nilsson could now argue that doing cover versions of other people's material was less commercially successful for him than singing his own compositions. Furthermore, he decided to use Robin Geoffrey Cable as both engineer and co-producer, thereby returning to the man who had so successfully worked on his two albums with Richard Perry. And with time on his hands in London to work on new songs while *The Point* was running and Beau was getting bigger and stronger, Nilsson applied himself to more advance preparation than for any album since the George Tipton days. According to McNaught:

> We routined the songs during the run of the show. We'd find some corner or other and Harry would get the guitar and I'd get the Walkman and he'd play me the song. If we got to a bit in the song where the chord he wanted "wasn't on the instrument," he'd say, "You'll suss it Mike!" and carry on. Except for a couple of occasions, he let me arrange the shape of each song on my own, so much so that when I first ran through "All I Think About Is You" with the band, he didn't recognize it![46]

A string orchestra was assembled at Audio International Studios in London during February, and with what had now become Nilsson's standard approach, he sang every song live with the musicians. They aimed to get two songs done each night in sessions that ran from 7 p.m. until 10 p.m., and in order to preserve Nilsson's voice, these were spread out over the course of two weeks. As with every Nilsson recording, there was something of a party atmosphere, with celebrity friends and members of the cast of *The Point* dropping in, but the whole enterprise was more focused and less frenetic than the previous Los Angeles sessions. One night, Graham Chapman came by and suggested the album should be called *Prick Up Your Ears*, which RCA did not find amusing.[47] (The following year, John Lahr's biography of the London playwright Joe Orton immortalized the title.)

Much as some of the *Pussy Cats* sessions had been documented with Polaroid camera shots of the proceedings, Nilsson encouraged every musician to take photographs of what was going on each night, with the intention of creating a collage of pictures as he had done for the inside sleeve of *Duit On Mon Dei*. There were candid photographs of the guitarists Foggy Lyttle and Paul Keogh, bassists Chris Laurence and Dave Olney, percussionists Tony Carr and Ray Cooper, plus drummers Barry DeSouza and Barry Morgan, as well as the string section led by Laurie Lewis. Both Lewis and McNaught were in the band at the Mermaid that played for *The Point*, so on the nights of recording sessions, both men had to find stand-ins for the stage show. There were to have been six sessions in all, but the album went so smoothly that it was finished in five. However, Nilsson asked McNaught to bring the band back for the final recording date anyway. Mike recalled:

When everybody arrived the next evening the studio was decked out for a party. Food, drink, you name it. The guys were really chuffed. As was Harry. The album had gone really well. I remember Tony Carr, who played percussion, coming up to me mid-way through the evening saying, "Mike, I feel really bad." Thinking he'd had two or three too many, I asked why. "Well, Harry throws us this lovely party, and I have to charge him porterage!"[48]

The opening track, "All I Think About Is You," sets the tone for the album: a sophisticated figure from Dave Olney's fretless electric bass underpins a string introduction, and there are long sustained high notes from the boys' choir of St. Paul's Cathedral, London. Originally, the boys were only to have appeared on the closing track, "Perfect Day," but they made such an impression that Nilsson and McNaught added them to this opener as well. When Nilsson's voice comes in, it is deliberately set in a baritone register. There is no straining for high notes and no "soulful" grate. It is a return to the mellifluous instrument of his earlier days, albeit half an octave lower, and the strings and boys' voices swoop and cascade around it. When the orchestra takes over the theme, Chris Laurence's double bass improvises beneath it, providing a delicate and subtle contrast to Olney's sound at the beginning. "I wanted the bottom end to make the whole thing flow," recalled McNaught, "and so I just told them to help themselves."[49] The first reviews picked this up, Richard S. Ginell saying of McNaught's string arrangements, "He writes with imagination and taking full advantage of the orchestra's sonic possibilities." The benefit, according to this review, was that "Nilsson is free to explore his considerable melodic gift once again."[50]

This is the key to appreciating this whole record. It is not a rock and roll album in the vein of *Pussy Cats* or parts of *Son of Schmilsson*. Instead, it is a curious cross between the lyricism of *A Little Touch of Schmilsson in the Night* and the whimsical early work of *Pandemonium Shadow Show* and *Aerial Ballet*.

The second track "I Never Thought I'd Get This Lonely" picked up ideas from a song Nilsson had first sketched out in 1973.[51] It has a brief foray into the falsetto register, and a small amount of vocal double-tracking, as well as some Nilsson whistling. The end even has him chanting a rather approximate cross between scat singing and Indian carnatic syllabic rhythms, but the overall bouncy rhythmic atmosphere is created by the infectious percussion of Ray Cooper enjoying a joyous reunion with Nilsson after their work on the Richard Perry albums. Just as had been the case with Perry, the majority of Cooper's most inventive ideas were added later. McNaught again:

> After the orchestra had gone each evening, Harry and Ray Cooper would overdub more percussion from Ray's myriad collection of toys. Harry's specialty was his wedding ring on a brandy bottle and as the night wore on the level in the bottle would drop, leading Robin Cable to complain, "Harry, the note keeps changing!"

On "Who Done It?" a patter song conflating the whole tradition of country-house murder mysteries with strong overtones of Nilsson's favorite film comedians in the plot of *The Laurel and Hardy Murder Case*, Cooper and McNaught combine to drop in a whole range of passing musical jokes and allusions. After liberally quoting Beethoven, they gently send up the long tradition of string writing for movie suspense scenes by punctuating it with gunshots, clock chimes, and running footsteps, all artfully dropped in between the vocals.

"Lean On Me," another piece that had its gestation earlier in the 1970s, again settles into Nilsson's baritone register for the main vocal, but there is some overdubbing in his normal tenor range and some forays even higher toward the end of the song. What McNaught has done is to create a setting that allows Nilsson's voice to flourish by careful pitching, so that again there is no forcing, even when the orchestra gets highly agitated during the backing to the second section of the song.

"Goin' Down" had been tried out as a demo during the *Duit On Mon Dei* sessions, and now it was equipped with some Slim Whitman-style yodeling. It is not a great song and does not fit well with the warm, romantic atmosphere of "All I Think About Is You," "Lean On Me," "Sweet Surrender," and "Perfect Day," which form the core of the album. Strangely, the rather depressing lyric of "Old Bones," which is an anticipation of old age, fits the mood of the album much better. This is at least in part because of the inventive arrangement, which begins with the violinists using their bows to hit the strings of their instruments in an effect known as spiccato, thus creating a brittle, boney texture. Some scratchy guiro playing from Cooper and some fragmentary vocal overdubbing that has moments in common with "Jump Into the Fire" keep the level of novelty and invention high throughout the piece.

Nilsson's favorite song from the album (which he recorded again in later life and also added to *The Point*) was "Blanket for a Sail." It is a return to the innocent songs of childhood that pervaded his early albums, although without the bittersweet overtones of absentee fathers. It is tempting to see this as a lullaby for three-month-old Beau, as Nilsson urges him to "Rest your head on a pillow / and I'll tell you a tale." Equally, the "Laughin' Man" who banishes gloom through humor is a song aimed directly at children. Finally, "Perfect Day" with the return of the boys' choir and some discreet backing vocals by Mara Gibb, is the song of a recently married man who exudes happiness and contentment. This is the first Nilsson album since *The Point* that is without anger and torment wrapped up in at least some of the songs. Even "Goin' Down," about a man drowning in emotion, seems infused with some form of positive outlook, if only in its musical setting.

Nilsson was pleased with the sound and feel of the album, believing it to be his best work in many years,[52] and in March, he and Cable worked on the final mix at Air Studios in London. When it came time to send everything to RCA, the problems began. Mike McNaught remembers:

I don't know what the title of the album was to be but I'm pretty sure it wasn't *Knnillssonn*. People had been constantly taking photographs of everyone in the band as Harry wanted a gate-sleeve with all the musicians' names and pictures included. I don't know what stage any artwork had got to. All I know is that it was all put together, all the photographs, everything, and sent to RCA in the States and lost.[53]

To get a replacement cover design underway quickly, Klaus Voormann was called in to help. Taking his cue from the inside gatefold photograph of John Lennon's *Walls and Bridges*, which has a three-layered portrait of Lennon spliced together, in which he wears four pairs of spectacles, Voormann had the idea of superimposing two pairs of eyes on a similar full-face portrait photo of Nilsson, and for the inside fold, adding facing portraits with two mouths and beards as well. "You see yourself…as I really am," ran the somewhat confusing caption. This design played on the pun of Nilsson's name being spelled with doubled consonants, and he would joke that since it had been consistently misspelled throughout his career, it was time for him to do so himself.

"I didn't take the sleeve photo," said Voormann, "but it was my idea to do that. Once we had the photos taken, I worked on the design."[54] Instead of the busy, active gatefold that Nilsson had originally envisaged showing all his musicians, *Knnillssonn* acquired a clinical monochrome look focused on his face alone. Indeed, RCA launched a promotional facemask with an extra set of eyeholes cut into it and the legend "You won't believe your ears."

The album was released in July, and the first reviews were extremely favorable. "If Nilsson is your thing, and many find his music delightfully romantic, then this album will satisfy, for it is one of his best,"[55] was typical. So too was the observation that "Harry Nilsson has finally put out an album which can hold its own with the *Schmilsson* period

LPs."[56] One long-term critic of Nilsson, the syndicated columnist Dave Marsh, who, while praising the singing, had already expressed his reservations about… *That's The Way It Is*, and did not enthuse over this album. His most positive comment was that "the overt elements of crooner parody are belied by the totality of commitment."[57] Overall, critics disagreed with Marsh, and most sided with *Billboard*, which said: "Harry Nilsson's beautiful soft tenor voice makes all these new songs seem so smooth and easy, the vocals coming amid the lush razor-precise orchestrations this writer-singer is generally associated with."[58] Others felt that some of the songs had an element of superficiality about them compared to the weighty topics covered in Randy Newman's lyrics, for instance. But the most perceptive review was from Noel Coppage in *Stereo Review*, who observed astutely that "the old Nilsson studio magic is what's really going on in *Knnillsson*."[59] He went on to praise this "blatantly individualistic" album for its "intelligent use of strings" and also noted how Nilsson had used the stereo image to enhance his vocals (and the accompanying percussion effects) on several tracks and that his interaction with the orchestra was delightfully and rhythmically complex.

There were many more reviews and features on this album than there had been for anything Nilsson had done since *Pussy Cats*, and the marketing campaign that reproduced Voormann's album design on packs of cards, facemasks, and press advertisements was as copious as the *Pandemonium Shadow Show* "True One" promotion from a decade before. A limited-edition single of "Lean On Me" backed by "Goin' Down" was sent out to the press in June by RCA as a "sneak preview of an album we believe will be one of the finest to be released in 1977." Within a few weeks of the album release, singles of "All I Think About Is You" backed by "Old Bones" and "Who Done It" backed by "Perfect Day" had been released with artwork that again picked up on Voormann's multi-eyed theme.

Even more bizarrely, there was a filmed version of "All I Think About Is You" that consisted of a four-minute close-up of Nilsson singing the words with his eyes closed, and a second pair of eyes rather eerily superimposed lower down on his face open and look around as he sings. This was offered to those television companies (such as the BBC in London) that had taken to showing short movies during their chart shows, if the musicians in question could not be brought in to lip-synch or play live to their single. When the album was released, Nilsson was pleased with the attention it got from his record company—until, that is, Elvis Presley died on August 16. Then, it seemed to him, RCA focused so completely on its best-selling dead artist that it conveniently forgot its one-time best-selling living singer. In many interviews, Nilsson was to say that it was the death of Elvis that precipitated the end of his relationship with his record company, three albums before the end of his agreement.

It is undeniably true that RCA used Presley's death to mount an impressive sales campaign for his back catalog and to give priority in manufacturing to repressing his singles and LPs. But it is not entirely the case that the company gave up on Nilsson. Press advertisements continued, and there was even a promotional Christmas card for the 1977 holiday season showing the album cover and the legend "Christmas won't be Christmas without Harry." The reality was that despite far more consistent and targeted marketing than the three previous albums, *Knnillssonn* just did not grab sufficient public attention, and although it reached 108 on the album charts and stayed there for ten weeks, it failed to climb into the top 100 as *Pussy Cats* had done. Nilsson's deliberate desire to be, at best, wide-ranging and unclassifiable and, at worst, radically inconsistent, had cost him his audience.

At the end of 1977, for the opening of the second British production of *The Point*, Nilsson, Una, and Beau paid a brief visit to London and then returned to Los Angeles, mother and son taking a few days' detour via Dublin. Their new home in Bel Air was not ready, so they would spend 1978 in rented houses. Although Nilsson's dissatisfaction with RCA was growing, the Christmas campaign for *Knnillssonn* was still underway, and there was a recording session to take place in RCA's studios as soon as the New Year began.

On January 3, Nilsson recorded a single version of "Ain't It Kinda Wonderful,"[60] which was written by the actor Gene Wilder to be used on the closing credits of the soundtrack to his movie *The World's Greatest Lover*. The picture is set in the era of Hollywood just before the talkies, and so the backing for Nilsson's voice is modeled on 1920s jazz, with a banjolele strumming the chords plus a chalumeau clarinet and a muted trumpet playing behind the vocal. The singing is a magical return to his youthful form by Nilsson. His voice sounds as clear, transparent and young as on his 1960s discs, and the atmosphere resembles that of "Nobody Cares About the Railroads Any More." Just one verse was used in the movie, but the single released to support the film has an extra section of vocal at the end. It was his last recording at RCA studios. Ironically, Nilsson's voice was not heard on the movie trailer, as he had not returned to Los Angeles in time to dub in his vocal, and so in the months leading up to the release of the film, cinemagoers heard Gene Wilder doing an impression of how he thought Nilsson would sing the song.

It is a sad twist of fate that just as Nilsson's voice can truly be said to have returned to something very close to the beauty and flexibility of his early years, his contract with RCA was abruptly ended. In time, he might well have accepted that the company had actually tried hard with *Knnillsson* had he dispassionately reviewed the degree of promotion that had been put into the record. But before that was possible, RCA went behind his back to do something that made him incandescent with anger.

Without consulting him, the company compiled a *Nilsson: Greatest Hits* album. For someone who cared not just about each of his albums as an entity, but also about the sequence and placing of every track much as Richard Perry did, to pull a random collection of his material together was tantamount to desecration. No matter that to RCA, it was a way of recouping some of the advance money that had been paid to Nilsson, he firmly believed that a *Greatest Hits* compilation should only appear after he died or left RCA.

To add insult to injury, the cover featured a photo montage. In it, Ken Luppens, a messenger with a passing resemblance to Nilsson, who had been spotted delivering to RCA, was dressed as the singer and photographed from behind holding a mirror. He appeared to be looking at an image of himself, but it was a reversed print of the hatted Nilsson superimposed from the *Pussy Cats* sleeve. "How about that for trash?" asked Nilsson of Dawn Eden, when she interviewed him many years later.[61] So in February 1978, Nilsson negotiated a release from his contract. Had he gone on to make the remaining three albums agreed in April 1974, he would have been paid a total of $562,500 for each one, less the cost of the recording sessions. He walked away with a termination payment of $1,500,000.[62] His eleven years with RCA were over.

10

IT'S SO EASY

IN THE IMMEDIATE aftermath of his departure from RCA, Nilsson talked about the possibilities of moving to another label. Pressed by British journalist Colin Richardson during an April 1978 interview just six weeks after the split as to which companies he might be contemplating, he mentioned Warner Brothers, A&M, and Columbia. He also reiterated that he felt he had the capacity to make several albums in the future. His long association with Derek Taylor (who was still running Warner's London special projects division) made that company an obvious possibility, but Nilsson was not under any illusions about the likely odds of being signed to a far larger firm than RCA. He said:

> Warner Brothers represents sixty percent of all records sold in the United States, and there are twelve hundred record companies in America, and there are six thousand, two hundred singles released every year. It's a big company, and they control sixty percent of the music. And, plus, they just signed Paul Simon, so...it's a very big bite for them to take, 'cause I'm cold, I haven't had a hit in years...and they have to take *me* on and I've gotta deal with that and get a hit there.[1]

This showed remarkable self-awareness and in all probability revisited some of the arguments that had resonated around RCA during the discussions of the *Greatest Hits* compilation (which after all the fuss only managed to reach number 140 on the album charts). It is also highly probable that when he was in the process of leaving RCA, Nilsson had talked things over with Derek Taylor. He had been in the enviable position of not having to produce *A Little Touch of Schmilsson in the Night* for his own company, and so therefore had never really taken a commercial risk on Nilsson himself. Looking back at this moment in Nilsson's life, Taylor reflected:

> By then, Harry had so confused his audience, by these switches and changes, that they'd lost interest in him. They couldn't follow him. He did have a plot. The plot was to do what he wanted to do with the people with whom he wanted to do it, when he wanted to do it, and how. And this is a lot to ask of a block of people, and a lot to ask of the broadcasting outlets, with their formats and so on.[2]

The upshot of this was that Nilsson did not sign a new record contract immediately, but he was already working on other ideas that would bear fruit. At the time of the first London run of *The Point*, he mentioned to journalists that he had been writing songs for two more prospective stage shows, *Zapata* and *Barnum*.[3] Of these two ideas, *Barnum* never made it beyond the page, although some sketches exist in Nilsson's papers, but *Zapata* would eventually see the light of day in 1980.

Equally, another long-term project was already simmering on the back burner. In mid-1977, during the time when Nilsson was back in Los Angeles from London, he had been invited to the home of the film producer Robert Evans, who had persuaded Paramount to buy the movie rights to the cartoon character Popeye. Evans had originally interested Dustin Hoffman in the role, but Hoffman did not get along with the satirist, cartoonist, and playwright Jules Feiffer, whom Evans had hired to do the screenplay, and so Hoffman had withdrawn. This almost led to the collapse of the project, but Evans managed to retain the studio's interest by signing up the young Robin Williams, who was just beginning to make his name in the television series *Mork and Mindy*. Nilsson was flattered to be asked but not sure he really wanted to write the songs for a musical film in which a real-life actor played a cartoon sailor.

"We shared two or three vodkas," Nilsson said, "and then I told him I didn't think it was such a good idea to do *Popeye*."[4] Nilsson made a few jokey suggestions of better projects in which Evans might invest his studio's money, and left, assuming he would hear no more about it. But several months later, when Evans had provisionally appointed Robert Altman as his director, the idea of Nilsson writing in his whimsical children's songbook vein still appealed to both men, and so they remained in contact with him. Things would not take off until 1979, but Nilsson already knew that movies and stage musicals do not happen overnight.

In the meantime, he had made some other decisions about how he would use the next year or so. Instead of dividing his time between London and Los Angeles, from the start of 1978, he intended to spend virtually all his time in America. He had a long-term dislike of flying, notwithstanding the extremely short journey times offered by Concorde, which took only three hours from New York to London. And much as he and Una had enjoyed sailing on the *QE2*, it was not the most efficient means of getting to and fro.

So he decided to lend his London apartment to Keith Moon as soon as Micky Dolenz had finished his run in *The Point*. Nilsson and Moon had shared some extraordinarily debauched adventures over the years, but he was confident that his flat would be well cared for, not least because Moon had been a short-term tenant before. He told Colin Richardson:

> Keith was perfect with the place. I mean, Keith is known to be a madman, but, I'm telling you straight, he's a gentleman and a good man. Fine man. And he's got a heart bigger than this room. He took care of it because he respected it and understood. He took care. That's why I'm leasing it to Keith Moon now.[5]

During the spring of 1978, Nilsson settled into a relatively stable life in Los Angeles. Mostly he was at home in his rented house with Una and Beau. But from time to time he would turn up out of the blue on a friend's doorstep and invite them to join him for a drink or dinner. Friends treated these invitations with caution. Jimmy Webb, for example, said:

> It was fun. It's just that you never knew when you were going to be coming home, when you left the house. That was the down side. You'd say, "Hi honey, I'm going out with Harry," and my wife would go, "Oh, no! When are you coming home?"[6]

Van Dyke Parks was another pal who found himself being whisked off to lose a day or two of his life with Nilsson:

> We had a real good time. We had a real rowdy time, and I think that he suffered my arguments real well and was influenced by them. But…he started out almost bordering antagonism with people who tried to pull rank with him. That's because he couldn't suffer stupidity. He just hated to be with fools. And so he had a short fuse. But we had great mutual respect, and, I think, a very eventful relationship. But I was honest with him in all regards. I would tell him when it was time to go home; and then he'd say, "Take the car." It was pretty simple. He'd get another car.[7]

These outings were known among his friends as "the Harry ride." Nobody knew, according to his attorney Lee Blackman, who was often picked up from his office by Nilsson in a limo for a late afternoon "lunch," where or when these adventures were going to end.[8] But with Nilsson's quick wit, intellect, and capacity for getting on with a wide cross-section of people, they inevitably involved having plenty of fun. Even his own family got caught up in Nilsson's taste for such events. His son Zak, from his first marriage to Diane, remembers that it was about this time when he and his mother were living in Northern California that he received an invitation from his father:

Harry asked if I wanted to go stay at Disneyland with him for a few days, which of course was like asking me if I was interested in being happy. So it was arranged, and I flew down to meet Harry and we went to Disneyland. We arrived at the Disneyland Hotel and checked in. We brought our things up to the room, which was a very nice double room, and then we went downstairs. First stop? The bar. I happily followed him there and hung out in the lounge area and watched "The Harry Show" begin. He couldn't help himself. He loved talking with people, and he loved his fans. When people started to recognize him in the bar, he became the main attraction and soon he had swarms of people sitting around him. Everybody loved him, and I was honestly just happy to be in the room with him at that point. After a couple hours though, I became bored and interrupted him to let him know I was going up to the room. He said okay, kissed me on the forehead and said good-night. I gave him a hug. As I left the bar, he had moved over to the piano and had begun playing and singing for the crowd.

I was fast asleep at around 3 a.m. when I heard knocking on the door and a sort of half-whispered, half-mumbled "Zak? Zak? Let me in. I don't have my room key. Zak?" After a few moments I blearily realized what was going on, and let him in. "Oh thank you," he slurred, as he stumbled to his bed and got in. I made sure he was all right, then I went back to sleep.

The next day, I remember walking through Disneyland, and I remember very clearly that I wanted to ride Space Mountain, and I wanted him to go with me. I realize now that he was probably very hungover, because he was squinting in the sun and moving slowly. He gently encouraged me to go ahead on my own and tried to excuse himself from participating, but I pleaded with him to go with me. And my dad was such a kind and gentle person at heart, he couldn't bring himself to deny me. So we both went on Space Mountain together, and I'm sure it was hell for him. He did his best not to let it show though, and he made me happy.[9]

Much of the time from early 1978 onward, Nilsson regularly installed himself in the bar at the Bel Air Hotel, to the extent that he came to refer to it as his "office." Klaus Voormann remembered that Nilsson would get up and leave his house around lunchtime, saying he was "going to get the papers," before making his way to the bar at the Bel Air and ordering the first Brandy Alexander of the day.[10] The hotel nestled in the hills on Stone Canyon Road, and although it has since been extensively modernized, in the 1970s, it had a very distinctive atmosphere. It was still possible to see areas of the building that had been sensitively converted from a very beautiful nineteenth-century stone stable block, giving it a timeless quality. It was and remains today secluded and private, yet extremely close to Sunset Boulevard.

During one period in the 1970s, Nilsson was frequently still holding court there late in the evening when the bar closed for the night, so he was given a set of keys to lock up after the staff had gone home.[11] It was the main place where he entertained—in particular during the months before he was able to move into the Nilsson house—and it was where his social circle consistently went for lively conversation or spirited argument. Eric Idle, who had now become a good friend of Nilsson's, was living permanently in Los Angeles by this time. He said:

> I had millions of evenings with him. Down at the bar at the Bel Air, his local. He was a *kamikaze* arguer. He was like an Irish fighter. He'd come at you and you didn't know where the fuck you were going to get kicked next. There weren't any rules of disputation. He'd challenge you to repeat the arguments having had four shots. It's brass. It's Yorkshire brass.... But enchanting, totally enchanting.... You just wanted to go off with him and get as drunk as you possibly could. And often did.[12]

If he was not at the Bel Air Hotel, Nilsson had other regular haunts in and around the city, and when Ringo Starr was in town, it was more often than not the Beverly Wilshire Hotel, where Starr usually stayed. On September 7, 1978, Nilsson was hanging out in Ringo's suite there with Derek Taylor and a few other friends, when—once again—it was Hilary Gerrard who took a phone call for Nilsson with bad news. Nilsson recalled:

> He ran to me and said, "Harry, Keith Moon is dead. He died in your bed and the police are there looking for drugs." Later Pete Townshend called and said something about Keith wanting to pay me for all the time he stayed there when we were in America. He was always talking about it but it made no sense to me at the time. But it was Pete taking the load off. He bought the flat, insisting on it, bless him. I'd had enough, besides Una and I were expecting and we wanted to build [our house] in America. The flat at number 9 had been the scene of outrageous laughter and fun, and sorrow... it was no longer a place for joy.[13]

Moon's death reminded Nilsson of the many adventures they had together in London. At one point, around the time of their attempt to stay sober for a weekend, Moon had actually shared the Curzon Place apartment with Nilsson for a few weeks. He recalled their attempts to cook, mixing brown and green ingredients so that they came out grey, with each pretending to the other that the results were delicious. On another occasion when nobody could find the errant drummer, Moon was found sound asleep, snoring under Nilsson's dining room table. That time, Mal Evans "picked him up like a doll" and carried him downstairs, whereupon Moon fluffed up his mink coat and swayed across the road to his pink Rolls Royce, in which his personal assistant Dougal Butler then drove him home.[14] There were extravagant London parties, such as the week-long event at the Londonderry Hotel in Park Lane, where Moon smashed a hole in the wall while showing Peter Sellers how to open a champagne bottle without touching the cork. There was the evening he and Nilsson turned up at the Speakeasy Club with humorist Vivian Stanshall and sabotaged the house band by surreptitiously intoxicating the bassist (an ex-colleague of Stanshall's in the Bonzo Dog Doo-Dah Band) to the point where he could no longer play.[15] When *The Point* opened in London, Moon's new minder, Richard Dorse, successfully demonstrated to the packed bar at the Mermaid Theatre how he could kick a lighted cigarette out of Nilsson's mouth. "You would have missed the action in half an eye-blink," wrote an impressed Graham Chapman, who was looking on.[16]

In America, there had been the debauched stay at the beach house in Santa Monica during the making of *Pussy Cats*. There were many evenings at the Rainbow Bar and Grill with the Hollywood Vampires drinking club. There had been long sessions at the Record Plant in the fall of 1974 in which Nilsson had joined in with Moon's vocals for a demo version of "Together" during the making of Keith's solo album *Two Sides of the Moon*. And more recently, there had been many afternoons sitting around a table with Graham Chapman, drinking and planning the pirate movie that some years later would become *Yellowbeard*. Overall, Nilsson mourned a friend who "was extremely bright and quick with a word or deed."[17]

Although Nilsson never lost his fondness for London, once the apartment was sold, his future visits would always involve staying in hotels. But as 1979 dawned, he and Una finally moved into the Nilsson house on Rocca Place. Their second son, Ben, was born there on June 2. It was a perfect moment for Nilsson to have a stable and permanent home base in Los Angeles, because this was to be the year in which he began recording his next album, and he also composed the first songs for the score of *Popeye*. Within a very short time of moving in, he transferred much of his social life to his house. Lee Blackman recalled:

> He wouldn't have to go out for the parties any more, because they were at the house in Bel Air. He used to have Friday night parties, and whoever was on the list for that week would come up there. Una would cook food, he had a bartender to serve drinks, and no-one drank to excess. There would be brilliant and stimulating conversations with some of the most creative people in Los Angeles, which would go on for hours, and then at a certain point it would be movie time.[18]

Una Nilsson continues the story:

> One very nice feature of the house was it had a 16 mm. screen, which came down. It was very well designed. And then a nice projection room with a couple of 16 mm. projectors and we had a service you would call up, with a directory of titles and they would mail them to you. It's a bit like renting a DVD today. Back then, the idea of having any kind of screen in a place in your house was a nice thing. It wasn't 35 mm.—that's a whole other story. You'd have to have a projectionist, because of the unions and so on, because in those days there were a lot of restrictions. But this worked fine, and the screen was beautiful. This big screen used to drop down and we had lots of movie nights.[19]

The house also had a pool room, and as well as various guests demonstrating their prowess at the table on Friday nights, Una's parents, the O'Keeffes, used to enjoy a game of pool most evenings during their visits to see the family.

Against this stable domestic background, Nilsson began work on a new album. The process took most of 1979, because this record was not made in a single burst of creative energy spread over a few weeks. Instead, Nilsson would go from time to time to Cherokee Studios, which was run by guitarist Bruce Robb in the impressive building that had formerly been the MGM recording studio. With Robb as engineer and his business partner, the guitarist Steve Cropper, as producer, Nilsson would put down whatever song was ready. The resulting album, *Flash Harry*, was ultimately bought by the British arm of Mercury Records, which was then a division of PolyGram (and has more recently become part of the Universal Music Group). The record would be released in 1980, but its long gestation period meant that in this instance almost all Nilsson's eclectic styles and tastes were shoehorned into one album, thereby consolidating the very image problem that Derek Taylor perceived had worked against the commercial success of the previous releases.

Before he turned to production, Cropper was already one of the world's leading guitarists, having played in the Stax Records house band, Booker T and the MGs. He contributed memorable solos to albums by Otis Redding and Sam and Dave. His partnership with Robb had led to Cherokee becoming one of the most sought-after studios in late 1970s Los Angeles, and Nilsson liked the idea of working with fellow musicians as producers. The resulting cast list of the album is largely a reunion of many members of Nilsson's former RCA house band, including Perry Botkin Jr., Van Dyke Parks, Dr. John, Jim Keltner, and Danny Kortchmar, but it also shows that this was the first chance for Nilsson to sing alongside Cropper and his regular colleagues, such as the bassist Donald "Duck" Dunn.

To give some indication of the stylistic breadth of *Flash Harry*, one track on the record, "Best Move," harks right back to Nilsson's earliest RCA sessions in the 1960s. The vocal delivery (and verse structure) is similar to "The Puppy Song," and Nilsson also provides plenty of the "doo-doo" and "ooh ooh" type of wordless syllables that he used on the Tipton arrangements. Instead of overdubbing his own backing vocals, however, some female singers have been added in by Cropper. Yet nobody familiar with early Nilsson would have any doubt that the song was by him. According to the studio's senior engineer Larold Rehbun, who worked on this session, the rather strange "swooshing" sound on the "How can it take so long" chorus was made by Steve Cropper setting off a fire extinguisher into a metal umbrella stand. It was, according to Rehbun, a remarkable feat because "in those days there was no Pro Tools to edit the sounds digitally, so Steve had to fire it exactly on the beat."[20]

The song Nilsson had co-written with Botkin, "I've Got It," has all the atmosphere of the heavily arranged Botkin "party" sound, not unlike "What's Your Sign?" with a jaunty baritone sax lead introducing a reed section led by Bobby Keys, and some neatly arranged backing singers. So, a fan of *Duit On Mon Dei* would also feel on home ground. The subject matter, of a gigolo offering what he has "got" in his trousers to a female client, only to discover that the client is a transvestite with something even bigger in "her" trousers, is delivered as a patter song, very much like "Who Done It?" from *Knnillssonn*. The street slang is at least partly autobiographical, recalling Nilsson's encounter with the prostitute he tried to pay by check, way back at the time when he had just started at the bank.

"Cheek to Cheek" is not the Irving Berlin standard of the same name, but a new piece written by Van Dyke Parks with Little Feat guitarist Lowell George (who played on some tracks of the album before his death in mid-1979) and Fred Martin (George's regular songwriting partner, who used the nom de plume "Martin Kibbee"). Perhaps because of this multiple authorship, the song seems to have several different cultural influences going on at the same time, with the Caribbean flavor of steel pans and rhythm, Nilsson demonstrating Swiss yodeling in the style of "Goin' Down" before he adds some doo-wop-style close harmony, and then a curious Mexican passage that suggests he may also have been thinking about the music for *Zapata*.

Far more cohesive is Nilsson's original "Rain," which alternates a spacey, slightly psychedelic verse with a reggae-influenced chorus. But the strongest performances are a somber, passionate version of Rick L. Christian's song "I Don't Need You," a powerful remake of "Old Dirt Road," which Nilsson and Lennon had written for *Walls and Bridges*, and a new impromptu jam in the studio that produced the atmospheric "It's So Easy." Nilsson's gritty version of "I Don't Need You" is far more emotionally punchy than Kenny Rogers's hit with the same song the following year from his album *Share Your Love*. Unfortunately, none of the tracks from *Flash Harry* was ever released as a single, because this song would have been a clear winner for Nilsson. So too would have been "Old Dirt Road," which makes a virtue of his husky post-*Pussy Cats* sound.

Perhaps the most likely hit of all would have been his distinctly psychedelic song "It's So Easy," delivered in a laconic half-spoken manner reminiscent of Lou Reed. There are references in the original, unedited studio tapes to the fact that two members of the backing band in the studio were trying out magic mushrooms (a specialty of Nilsson's Laurel Canyon friend Timothy Leary, who was often present at the sessions). But when this track was cut, Nilsson himself was experimenting with a different form of psychedelic stimulus. The session in December 1979 had started at midday on the 11th and ran right through the night, with the musicians working on some other parts of the album. Nilsson was drinking solidly right through the proceedings, and at one point he burned a hole in the pocket of his white suit with a lighted cigarette. Everyone left at 9 a.m. on the 12th, and most of the band went home, as Larold Rebhun recalls:

> At 7 p.m., everyone came back...but a small group had gone into a restaurant/bar on Sunset Boulevard for the day. Harry hadn't slept and he was still in the rather tattered white suit with the pocket burned off. The music began with the lights very low. It was a long and slow dreamy song. Harry was trying to read the lyrics that he

had scribbled on a tattered napkin from his dinner, and I ran to the copy machine to try to make a better copy for everyone. At the bottom was "Harry Nilsson, Dec 12." The song went on and Harry stated to everyone that he had never done Mescaline before this session. I thought, "Great! Now we're in for a ride!"

When he got to the last verse, he sang his name and the date as the lyric. I was laughing very hard by then, but it was a magic, crazy moment. I thought of all the talent in the room, and the fact that it was on the verge of insanity, but, that's how it's done sometimes.[21]

The track is built over a strong bass line by co-composer Paul Stallworth, with two contrasting guitars and low-key drum accompaniment. Cropper later overdubbed some backing singers and synthesizer fills, but the energy and strength of the track comes from the way Nilsson's slightly fuzzy voice interacts with the plangent solo blues guitar, and how both of these elements contrast with the minimal bass part and sustained harmonies from the second guitar. The unedited session tape shows how the whole track unfurled as a low-key, relaxed jam. It points to a direction Nilsson might well have followed had he gone on to make any further albums.

The most distinctive aspect of *Flash Harry*, however, was that it was bookended by two songs by Eric Idle. The grand finale was "Always Look On the Bright Side of Life," a remake of the closing song from the movie *Life of Brian*. According to Idle, it was the Hollywood premiere in August 1979 of the Monty Python film (which starred Graham Chapman as Brian Cohen in a life that ran parallel to that of Jesus Christ) that prompted Nilsson to make his own version of the tune. This was at least partly because of the moral outrage that the Python team's satirical take on a quasi-Biblical story had caused worldwide. Taking "a whack at the biblical world," as one California paper put it, the movie combined "careful planning with outrageous sacrilege."[22] Nilsson was intrigued by both the satirical story itself and the extraordinary reaction to the film. "Thousands have signed petitions deploring the arrival of 'Life of Brian,'" ran one report. "Because of its alleged ridiculing of Christ, many Christians have denounced the movie sight unseen."[23] To Nilsson, including a song on his album that communicated the aura of controversy attached to the movie was an excellent idea, as Idle recalled:

He loved the movie. Him and Timothy Leary were going, "Brian, Brian. Brian, Brian...." And he loved the song. And so he *must* record it. That was the thing. He *had* to record it. So, "Okay." And then he got this huge studio, he got Donald "Duck" Dunn, some really proper musicians, and he started to make a record. And it seemed to go on for weeks, this process, for just the one track. I get bored very, very quickly in a studio situation. I'm done in two hours or I'm going home. Anyway it took forever and it was a perfectly fine version. It was sadly apparent his voice was not the same thing it had once been. He got all his mates to come and sing on the chorus of it. So we had a nice evening where everybody was drinking and doing the usual things, and then being recorded singing: "Always look on the bright side...."[24]

Despite Idle's dislike of the lengthy process involved, Nilsson's version of the song is one of the tightest pieces of production on the record. It totally avoids the cockney cheeriness of Idle's character in the movie as he sings to the crucified Brian, and instrumentally it takes a very different tack from co-composer John Altman's movie score, which has some clever counterpoint between the soaring strings and a somber French horn section. Instead, it is the epitome of a well-produced pop song, with a strong arrangement growing gradually from Nilsson singing with a spare piano accompaniment to the sound of full orchestra and chorus, anchored by a tuba that gives just a hint of the British music-hall atmosphere of the movie vocal. Nilsson no doubt enjoyed telling his listeners that life was "a piece of shit," a phrase guaranteed not to help the song get any airplay, but it was a first-rate closing track for the album.

Opening the record was a short, whimsical song about Nilsson, played and sung by Idle and fellow vocalist Charlie Dore, the only example from any Nilsson record in which he does not appear anywhere on the track. It was mainly inspired by Idle's experience as a friend and drinking companion of Nilsson's—"he's a pretty nifty guy, always looks you in the eye." But it also poked fun at what seemed to Idle to be the interminable process of recording in Los Angeles, compared to the brisk habits honed by years of working on tight BBC budgets to get the most music out of the least studio time:

He kept saying, "Always look on the bright side...." And I'd say "Yeah!" But I couldn't make up my mind whether I was supposed to go, "Yes, Thank you!" Or whatever. There was no kind of adequate response I seemed to be able to make to Harry doing this song. So I wrote this little song. I think I wrote it in California, and then when I got back to London I recorded it. It was a sweet little ditty. I was playing with Ricky Fataar in those days, who was one of the Rutles. We recorded it, and we have Charlie Dore who was a wonderful singer on it. And it sort of expressed what I felt:

Here's a little gentle song, a sort of sentimental song,
At least it didn't take us very long, Harry....

Derek Taylor took a tape of it down to Malta where Harry had started work on *Popeye*. And I think it just knocked him out. It was just so unexpected. And he put it as the opening track.[25]

Flash Harry was not released until mid-1980 when Nilsson's work on the *Popeye* movie was over. For reasons known only to the company, Mercury released the album solely in the United Kingdom and Japan, so it failed to get any exposure in the United States and effectively brought down the curtain on Nilsson's recording career. With three potential hits, the Python song, and a whistle-stop tour through Nilsson's entire stylistic range, it was tragic that this first post-RCA album never gave him the opportunity to rebuild his audience in America and prove to the fans who had bought into *Knnillssonn* that as the 1980s began he still had plenty to say.[26]

Meanwhile *Popeye* offered Nilsson, at least in principle, the chance to do with his own music what *Midnight Cowboy* had done for Fred Neil's. However, unlike a regular Hollywood film, a Robert Altman production was different. Instead of using Hollywood's studio facilities, he had decided to create a town from scratch on the coast of Malta as the setting for his retelling of the Popeye story. Never mind that it was only accessible by steep footpath or in a Land Rover, or that he had to sink an old ferryboat in the mouth of the chosen cove to prevent the waves from washing away the actors and set, Altman wanted to create an entirely consistent atmosphere for his fictional harbor of Sweethaven. After months of preparation, Altman flew the entire cast and crew of *Popeye* to Malta on January 3, 1980, where they stayed for almost five months. In a radical departure from normal practice, he included Nilsson and the soundtrack musicians among the Maltese contingent.

Nilsson, however, had been caught up in the groundwork for the movie long before this, and for much of 1979, he worked in parallel on making the *Flash Harry* album and on writing the first songs for *Popeye*. After his inconclusive conversation with Robert Evans in 1977, little had happened, apart from the occasional friendly telephone call. But in early 1979, Altman, who had been finally confirmed by Paramount as their preferred director after some months of indecision, summoned Nilsson to his Lion's Gate production offices to start discussing the details of the film. Over the previous months, the studio bosses had tried to discourage Altman from his choice of composer, saying that Nilsson was washed up and would get drunk. Altman realized that during his own long process of being contracted to make the movie, some of the same criticism had been leveled at him. "So I called Harry Nilsson, although I had never met him in my life, and we got along terrifically."[27]

This was slightly economical with the truth. In 1969, when Nilsson was very much an up-and-coming talent, Altman had sounded him out about providing the music for *That Cold Day In The Park*, a psychosexual movie starring Sandy Dennis that was eventually given a minimalist score by Johnny Mandel. Altman saw a connection between Nilsson's songs of fatherless childhood and his young protagonist, played by Michael Burns. Nilsson had turned that idea down, but the two had remained aware of one another and their respective bodies of work ever since.[28]

In 1977, when Nilsson met Robert Evans and expressed his reservations about *Popeye*, he still had a record contract with RCA and he did not need to do the movie. Now, even though he had been paid as much as if he had actually made the final albums from his original RCA agreement and was already at work on *Flash Harry*, he was interested in any new creative project. He liked Altman from the moment they met face to face at Lion's Gate, and so he decided to do a sales pitch. He told the director that Leonard Cohen would "cry the film to death," that John Lennon "firstly wouldn't" and "secondly he can't" do the job, and that he did not think Randy Newman would do it. He suggested Paul Williams (knowing that he was currently writing the music for the first *Muppet Movie*), saying, "next to me he's the nicest brightest guy, most cheerful guy, to do *Popeye*."[29] Altman needed little persuading. At the beginning of May 1979, Paramount called and asked Nilsson to deliver three songs in three weeks. It was a test to see if their reservations about Nilsson were justified, or if they could go along with what was now Altman's preferred choice of composer.

By the end of the month, he had written "Sweethaven," "I'm Mean," "He Needs Me," and "Swee' Pea's Lullaby," in the process commandeering his lawyer Lee Blackman's sailboat to play his demo tapes at sea to see if the tunes had the right nautical flavor.[30] When he delivered the results on time, he was confirmed as the film's songwriter. In the glacial pace of a movie development schedule, nothing then appeared to happen between the end of May and late August, when he got a call from Altman about the difficulty he was having persuading the studio to cast the actress Shelley Duvall as Olive Oyl. Nilsson's solution was simple. He would take Duvall to Cherokee Studios and record her feature song "He Needs Me," which was already written and waiting to be used.[31] Nilsson originally did this in secret, to surprise Altman, but when he eventually played his demo to the director, they hatched a plan together to impress the studio executives. On August 27, chairman Barry Diller, president Michael Eisner, and members of the parent board at Gulf and Western who owned the company came to Lion's Gate to see a progress report. During the evening, Altman showed scenes of Duvall on screen, accompanied by her version of the Nilsson song as the soundtrack. Her willowy figure looked the part of Olive Oyl, and her tremulous, untrained singing voice seemed to reinforce her credentials. There was no further discussion. She had the part.[32]

The next contact Nilsson had with the movie was a workshop that Altman organized during September in the Venice Beach area to test out some of his actors and singers. Nilsson (together with Una and baby Ben)[33] came along with the nine songs he had written by this time, and to play them, he invited Van Dyke Parks, Klaus Voormann, and banjoist Doug Dillard. To their surprise, Altman cast the musicians as actors in the movie, along with the clowns, dancers, and singers he was putting through their paces at the workshop.

Although Nilsson had by this time written several songs, none of them actually corresponded with the places in the story or subjects for lyrics that had been indicated in the screenplay by Jules Feiffer. "I had placed songs that Harry just would not write," he said, and before long a tetchy atmosphere developed, until he, Altman, and Nilsson stopped communicating directly with one another and began using Evans as go-between.[34] Consequently, Evans decided to send them to Malta together to see the set firsthand and settle their differences. So in early November, the three men traveled to the location for a few days and miraculously managed to bury the hatchet and plan a way forward. Nilsson returned to the United States ready to write another five songs. However, just as he was getting into his stride, his mother Bette died. No more songs were to be written before Nilsson, Una, the children, and his musicians arrived in Malta.

Nilsson had never really approved of his mother working in her little antique shop when he was prepared to pay for her to live a life of leisure, but it gave her a purpose and she was more settled and secure in her last years than she had ever been. She was on good terms with him and Michelle, and—after the surprise of his reappearance—with Drake. In one of her last letters to him she wrote:

> My life is mostly over and I can truthfully say that the only happiness I've ever had has been in knowing that I have good children, who have been wonderfully kind to me and have loved me in spite of all my failings.[35]

Shortly after the funeral, the Nilsson family set off for Malta. It was far from the ideal winter break in the sun that had been envisaged. Storms damaged the set, its inaccessibility was a constant problem, and for much of the time, Una and the children were holed up in what Derek Taylor described as "a bleak apartment house"[36] several miles from the fictional Sweethaven. Meanwhile, Nilsson, Van Dyke Parks, Ray Cooper, Klaus Voormann, and Douglas Dillard struggled both to record the music and (with the exception of Nilsson) act their roles, vacillating between the rickety village constructed by the film's carpenters and a makeshift recording studio.

After the luxury of Cherokee Studios in Los Angeles, what Nilsson found on Malta was about as different as it was possible to be. In a temporary building, instead of what had now become the industry standard of a twenty-four-track recording machine, there were two primitive eight-track tape recorders hooked up together. For most practical purposes, they used just one of them, and only seven tracks of that, because the eighth track would generally be used as a click track or to synchronize dialogue to the film. Although Tom Pearson would eventually provide additional music for the narrative scenes in postproduction, Nilsson was working with Parks on doing some segments of underscoring for the musical sections of the film as they went along, as well as finishing the missing songs. His main job was then to record basic tracks of all the vocal numbers with the cast. Consequently, there was a constant flow of work. He wrote:

> The actual [studio] interior is made out of egg crates, and it is also a projection room for the dailies (rushes) during the day. And this control room doubles as the transfer room for the dialogue that they shoot at night or the day before, so we can't use it in the mornings. We have to use it after 1:30 p.m., and then when someone from Walt Disney or Bob Evans is looking at film, then we can't use it 'til the evening which means work begins at 7:30 p.m. We tear down the seats from the dailies and start working around nine. We finish at four in the morning, whatever it is, and nights when we weren't doing that I'd work here myself, because there's no noise 'til

five, five thirty. But rats! Big rats are round here. They set a trap one day and killed nine in fifteen minutes. One night I peed on one. It looked up at me, surprised.[37]

The intensity with which the musicians worked in these far-from-ideal conditions was something that everyone involved in shooting the movie appreciated. The band turned Nilsson's rough demos of songs from Los Angeles and his new compositions into virtually finished numbers, so that for the final mix, Nilsson and Parks would be able to take the tapes to Evergreen Studios in Burbank, where they needed only to add some final strings and woodwind. "It was almost like the Nilsson club on set," recalled Ray Cooper. "The young actors and actresses would come and they'd just sit around listening to us make music. They would come in tired, and they would go out uplifted, ready for the next day's shoot."[38]

Nevertheless, what amounted to almost five months of filming took its toll on everyone, despite the "uplifting" qualities of the music. Nilsson, separated from Una and his sons for part of the time, sneaking away to see them when possible, and otherwise using whatever stimulants were available to keep him going through the night or on set for daytime filming, was under pressure. To relieve this a little, he organized his band into a "gang," the Falcons (named for the 1941 John Huston movie with Humphrey Bogart, the *Maltese Falcon*), and Shelley Duvall countered by organizing a female gang, the Falconettes. There were some high jinks and horseplay, with some of the more amusing pranks noted in Duvall's photocopied "newspaper" that her gang circulated among the cast. But the musicians were fretting. Van Dyke Parks's wife Sally gave birth to their daughter on the island during February, and both wanted to get home as quickly as possible. Doug Dillard fell on some stone stairs and hurt himself badly. But they were sustained by belief in the project. Parks, who arranged all the music for Nilsson's Falcons to play, reflected:

> Altman gave Harry an incredible carte blanche for the music, for the songs, and that was wonderful for Altman to do. Altman and Harry shared a lot of things, for example, a deep understanding about the abstraction of the process, the creative process, [both] able to understand that a concept might be revealed, rather than planned. They both had that skill, that extemporaneous flair. So that went very well. I think Altman was afraid of being engulfed by a large romantic score, but he got it in the action, in the underscoring, which I didn't do. But I had thought somehow that just the opposite would happen—that the songs would appear larger than life, and that the score would be a minimalist score. I thought that would be better.[39]

Altman's original idea had been that Nilsson would "supply simplicity,"[40] and that was what he was briefed to do. As a result, most of the songs he wrote were pared down to the basic essentials. Popeye's "I Yam What I Yam" is a simple repetitive phrase that barely develops, shifting between three basic chords with few of the unexpected harmonic twists that Nilsson was still producing in his other songs from that time. Olive Oyl's "He Needs Me" has an equally simple melody, but again, in comic-book style, the song is based on a lot of repetition. When Shelley Duvall ventures into a characteristic Nilsson wordless "dah-de-dum" chorus, she immediately proves the *New York Times* film critic Vincent Canby's point that "there's not one member of the cast who can really sing."[41]

His was among the kindest of the major reviews. Canby noted that "the score with lyrics and music by Harry Nilsson has some very nice things in it," but he went on to say, "You keep expecting the film to erupt with the kind of boisterousness that is only possible in a musical. It never ever does."[42]

Because Altman had Tom Pearson write a much lusher score for the incidental music, it consistently overshadowed the spare, simple songs that should have been the musical heart of the movie. And because Nilsson had followed Jules Feiffer's vision of a film that captured the linear economy of E. C. Segar's original Popeye cartoons from *Thimble Theater*, they would only ever have seemed suitably extravagant if the rest of the musical texture of the film, as Parks suggested, was so low key as to throw them into sharp relief. Instead, their ability to deliver the dash of simplistic cartoon flavor that Nilsson intended was compromised by their overall sonic setting.

"He's Large," for example, makes much of just repeating the word "large" for comic effect, rather like a standup comedian's catchphrase. The repetition of the word first by Duvall and then by the female chorus builds on the premise that repeating a single word can eventually become funny in its own right. Here the melody and accompanying texture are vintage Nilsson, with a memorable tune and some inventive bass playing from Voormann, but the vocal is deliberately unsophisticated. Equally, Bluto's "I'm Mean" is a well-constructed patter song, but against the more naturally flowing score for the rest of the movie, this is typical of the musical numbers that seemed even more two dimensional than they were intended to be.

"Harry Nilsson's music and lyrics are the dregs," wrote Dan Gire in the *Chicago Daily Herald*. "Dull, unimaginative and listless, [they] pull the eyelids down even faster than Altman's lethargic direction."[43] He went on to suggest that what the movie needed most was a can of spinach. Syndicated columnist Debra Kurtz told her readers that Robin Williams was a true delight, but "the musical score by Harry Nilsson unfortunately detracts from the film."[44] Meanwhile, one of Canada's most-read film critics, Leonard Klady, wrote of this "bold unconventional entertainment" that "the only weak link is the uneven musical score."[45]

Despite the extraordinary amount of effort that went into the movie, the relocation to Malta, and the creation of one of the most elaborate sets in film history, *Popeye* was a turkey. If Nilsson's songs had been sung by trained singers, they would have sounded better. If he had allowed the lyrics to develop with the same freedom as some of his melodies, rather than retain cartoon-like repetition and simple delivery, they could have worked in their own right. But as Dan Gire pointed out, the best song in the score was the closing "Popeye the Sailor Man," written years before by Sam Lerner and equipped with the only tune in the movie that the audience might be humming as they left the theater. In time, *Popeye* was to gross in excess of $60 million, but its initial critical reception was so damning that Altman ended up selling his Lion's Gate production company and starting his career again from scratch. Nilsson had now devoted much of 1979 and 1980 to making an album that nobody in America could hear and a movie that was heavily criticized for his score. So in the second half of 1980, he made a total change of direction.

The months after his return from Malta were devoted to completing and presenting *Zapata,* the stage musical he had been contemplating for some years. The idea had come from the actor and game-show host Bert Convy, who had recently won an Emmy for his nationally broadcast program *Tattletales.* Convy first approached Perry Botkin Jr., whom he had known since the days of the Cheers. The idea was to dramatize the life of the Mexican revolutionary Emiliano Zapata, who had led the land rights revolution in 1910. Botkin immediately turned the idea down, with the suggestion that what was really needed was a Mexican songwriter. But a couple of days later, Convy suddenly had the idea of approaching Nilsson. Botkin's telephone rang again:

> Bert called me and said, "Harry wants to do it, but he won't do it without you."
> And I thought, "I'll do this with Harry. We obviously can work together. And it might be good for me, just in terms of doing what I do." So I said, "Okay. I'll do it."[46]

The idea was first floated to the two men by Convy in 1976, when Nilsson mentioned it to the press just as *The Point* was opening in London. But apart from a few hastily jotted-down ideas, nothing really happened until he got back from Malta in the summer of 1980. After finishing the postproduction work on the music for *Popeye* with Van Dyke Parks, Nilsson turned his full attention to the new musical. Convy had apparently wanted to produce a show about Zapata for years even before he first mentioned it to Nilsson, but despite the long gestation period, he still had only quite vague notions of the plot and characters. So, much as he had begun work on *Popeye* by virtually ignoring Feiffer's script, Nilsson decided the thing to do was just to start writing songs and see what happened. Botkin recalled:

> He would come over to my house, and we would usually start to work on it, right after lunch.... He would come over with lyrics, and he would start singing. He'd just sing, and I'd sit down at the piano, and I would play. I realized that my job was going to be the janitor. I'd sweep up these pieces that Harry was spewing out here, and then I'd turn them into something that had some theatrical positioning. But I didn't mess with his words, I didn't mess with the melodies that he was singing, I might have changed a note here or there, and I fiddled with the harmonies, and made them a little more sophisticated than he would have done, because we were hopefully doing a Broadway show. So that's how we would go to work. He had a bottle of brandy that I had put his name on, and he would start with a brandy. We

usually got an hour, an hour and a half maybe, sometimes two. But pretty soon he'd be rambling. And the working day was over.[47]

Work had not long started on the songs when the screenwriter Allan Katz was brought in to develop the book for the show. Rather than base his script on the 1952 John Steinbeck movie *Viva Zapata!* that had starred Marlon Brando, he opted to adapt a somewhat obscure Spanish play on the same subject by Rafael Buñuel, the son of the filmmaker Luis Buñuel. Rafael had been running a small theater company in Mexico and had recently arrived to set up something similar in Los Angeles. The homespun scale of Buñuel's script for his Mexican repertory company seemed to Katz and Convy an ideal vehicle to which music and lyrics could be added or, in the case of the songs already written, adapted.

Katz was by this time a good friend of Nilsson's. They met frequently at the house of the British screenwriter Ian La Frenais—"the one with the orange shag carpet," as Eric Idle, another regular guest there, recalled.[48] Katz was naturally humorous, described by Idle as a "very funny comedian,"[49] and he had been one of the writers on the *M*A*S*H* television series and on the long-running comedy show *All In The Family*. He later went on to write the award-winning musical *Song of Singapore* in 1993.

However, being a comic writer with most of his experience in television was not necessarily going to guarantee that Katz would create a strong stage show at his first attempt. Convy, a man who also worked almost exclusively in television, was equally unlikely to gauge the different demands of the musical theater. When the first reviews of the production at the Goodspeed Opera House in East Haddam, Connecticut, appeared, its shortcomings were clinically laid bare:

It could have been a probing, trenchant, dramatic, insightful story of an ignorant farmer of high ideals leading men in the fight for land rights.

Instead, we get an old-fashioned Hollywood-cliché sort of red-white-and-green Mexico where intelligence is banished, where the natives sing Ay-ay-ay, where decisions are made with the snap of a finger, the hint of a song. It's TV-land, where each episode must fit neatly into 10-minute sequences (as if to allow for commercials). Glibness reigns unrestrained, people are reduced to ciphers and stooges.[50]

If this seems unnecessarily harsh, it is because the Goodspeed house had a well-established reputation for spotting and developing prime musical theater productions that went on to run on Broadway and elsewhere around the world, and so expectations were high. The 1965 hit musical *Man of La Mancha* had started there, and so too had *Annie* which, in 1980, was three years into its record-breaking six-year run at the Alvin Theater in New York. During the summer of 1980, the Goodspeed was presenting a revival of George M. Cohan's *Little Johnny Jones*, but advance sales were showing signs of falling off, and the company was looking for a new production for the fall. In June, Nilsson and

Botkin went into the studio to make some preliminary demos of their *Zapata* songs, starting with a long expository narrative called "This Means War." Botkin said:

> The Goodspeed Opera House is the top of the line of regional theater, and we got there on the basis of that demo. It was a song telling the audience what the show was about. Which was Harry singing. And it was an interesting circumstance. The drink had really finally taken its toll on his voice, and he was doing a lot of screaming. Rock stuff, because that was really all he could do. And just prior to our doing the demo for this show, he went to a doctor's appointment, where the doctor said, "Harry, if you don't sober up, you're going to die. Any moment." He really laid into him. And he made a deal with Harry that if he would quit for three months—just stop drinking for three months—that would be very helpful. So he talked Harry into giving up booze. And during that time, we did the demo. And he sounded just like the old Harry. He got his voice back, and it was the last time on that demo, that he ever sounded that way.[51]

Nilsson adopts a rich, somewhat nicotine-stained Hispanic accent for the song that tells how Zapata and his villagers "made war on all those fools who would not let them grow their own beans." He uses the metaphor of a tortilla full of refried beans as a symbol of culinary independence in a land where "not even freeholders are free." It is a strong, catchy introductory piece, and the production team at Goodspeed was duly impressed by this and a couple of the other finished demos. Among them, "These Are the Brave" is a classic Nilsson performance with double-tracked vocals, some falsetto singing that eloquently demonstrates Botkin's point about his voice having recovered, and some "aye, aye, aye" wordless singing that immediately conjures up the atmosphere of "Everybody's Talkin'." With a villainous song for the character Bufalo Pepe called "Big White Horse" that mirrors Bluto's "I'm Mean" from *Popeye*, it looked as if Nilsson was about to produce his best writing in years.

However, at the end of the three months of sobriety, Nilsson began drinking again. Botkin recalled that he went on a week's bender, ending up in Seattle, before joining Ringo Starr, who had just announced that he would marry the former James Bond girl, Barbara Bach. As a result, when Convy was rehearsing the show at the Goodpseed before the opening night in September, Nilsson was nowhere to be found. This caused a nightmare for Botkin who, because of his television work writing the music for *Mork and Mindy*, could not go to Connecticut to work with the theater company. He recalled:

> We opened and the shows kept getting shorter. Bert would cut things out. And the whole time the show was going on, Harry was…with Ringo, because Ringo was getting married. And I'm sitting there in Los Angeles with Allan Katz, and we had to write an extra couple of songs, because we only had nine tunes. There were more reprises in this show than ever in the history of musical theater. Allan and I wrote

one transitional piece, and then when Harry came back, he and I sat down and wrote another song doing the Sam the explainer business, called "Mexico!" It was a big Broadway kind of show number and we opened the show with that.[52]

Nilsson and Starr attended the premiere of *Zapata* together on September 18, 1980. Playbills from the early part of the run contained the printed warning "Program subject to change," and the reviews were qualified by noting that "changes are said to be going in before *Zapata* closes its run at Goodspeed."[53] Songs and dances came and went, but the plot remained unaltered, which was that Zapata begins the show convinced he can lead a revolution to give the land back to the people. He meets the former singer Maggie, whom his men capture, and they fall in love. Through their revolutionary acts, he and his friend Pancho Villa achieve a change in the presidency, but this does not restore the land to the people. So they need to continue with their struggle, in which Zapata's idealism is matched by his love for Maggie. A narrative song at the end tells of his subsequent assassination.

Among the surviving demo recordings for the score are some instrumental interludes by a mariachi band that played rather appealingly out of tune. But this was no band of Los Angeles studio professionals aiming at ethnic authenticity. Larold Rehbun remembered that Nilsson had run into a genuine Mexican band playing in the Olvera Street district of Los Angeles near Union Station and had brought them into Cherokee Studios to run a few tunes. "Harry spoke a little Spanish," he recalled, "and asked them to come along." The biggest challenge for the studio was to balance the guitarrón (an acoustic bass guitar) and the strident trumpets.[54] Alongside this distinctly Mexican-flavored material, Nilsson also recorded a couple of potential hit songs for the heroine Maggie. The first of these, "Why Don't You Let Me Go Free?" is an emotional appeal to Zapata: "Why don't you lay down your arms and I will open mine," while "Bedsprings"—a song that charts Maggie's fall from being a singer whom men stood in line to hear to becoming a madam outside whose property men again stand in line to hear the squeaking of bedsprings—was sufficiently memorable to have been recorded as a fully finished single, although it was never released.

Ironically, Convy cut the one song from the show that ended up being an independent hit, which was the "Wedding Song." Nilsson's own demo is a beautifully sung version with the singer Andrea Robinson working beside him as their two voices weave elaborate countermelodies together. She recalled that he told her, "I'm on the wagon," and related to her the difficulty it was causing him to abstain from alcohol. Yet, she remembered, because of the temporary recovery of his full vocal faculties, it gave her the chance to work with one of the greatest voices of the time:

I was very lucky to experience the real Harry. And as he was co producing, he was kind, very supportive, very impressed with my singing, and very open with his compliments. He made me feel very appreciated. I could never forget that either. Also I looked down at his shoes. He was wearing wing tips. One black and one brown.

He just strutted them around a bit, and said, "Like them? I just felt like it." So we started our session in the best way, laughing.[55]

It is one of Nilsson's finest late recordings, and he was so pleased with it that, shortly after it was made, he played it to the Egyptian-born Greek singer Demis Roussos when he visited Los Angeles. Within weeks, Roussos had recorded it as a duet with Linda Taylor for his album *Man of the World*, and before the end of 1980, his record company released it as a single that went on to chart success in both Italy and France.[56] Back in the United States, *Zapata* only ran for sixteen weeks and never made the transfer to Broadway, as a result of which, none of Nilsson's other songs from it were ever released. The lukewarm critical reception for *Zapata* was comparable to that for *Popeye*. "Nilsson is a pop writer of a certain facile appeal as seen in his *The Point* a few seasons back. But he seems out of his depth here. Not only are the lyrics trite, unpoetic, without resonances or overtones, but the melodies boast mere vigor, not memorability."[57]

Having had a somewhat checkered year, at the end of 1980, Nilsson agreed to try his hand at record production. His first project was to co-write and produce a pair of tracks for Ringo Starr's forthcoming album, which was provisionally titled *Can't Fight Lightning*. These were "Drumming Is My Madness" and "Stop and Take Time To Smell The Roses." Nilsson also oversaw the production of a remake of Starr's own "Back Off Boogaloo" for the same album. All three tracks were cut with Starr (for the most part speaking rather than singing) backed by a boisterous horn section at Chris Blackwell's Compass Point Studios at Nassau in the Bahamas between December 1 and December 5, 1980. The album would eventually take its title from the song Nilsson and Starr had written together and would be known as *Stop and Smell the Roses*. Once these tracks were in the can, Starr stayed on with his wife-to-be for a holiday in the Bahamas. He and Nilsson planned to reconvene in January, when two new songs newly written for the album by John Lennon would be recorded. Lennon himself had promised to join the sessions.

As Starr stayed on for his vacation, Nilsson returned to Los Angeles to continue his new role as producer, having agreed to spend the next few days on some tracks for a new record being made by the singer Frank Stallone. He was the younger brother of the film actor Sylvester Stallone, whose home was next door to the Nilsson house in Bel Air. Because Frank was also living there in 1980, he had become a good friend of the Nilsson family. Frank had first met Nilsson at RCA a few years before when he was signed to the label during the *Sandman* period. They had kept in touch ever since by letter, signing off to one another as "Schmil" and "Stalloneoni," and now they renewed their acquaintance as neighbors. Over a drink, Stallone rather tentatively asked Nilsson to produce his next disc and was delighted when his proposal was accepted.

For these sessions, which were being made for the Scotti Brothers label, Nilsson assembled Van Dyke Parks, Jesse Ed Davis, Klaus Voormann, and Jim Keltner. The engineer was Robin Geoffrey Cable. They were to record Joni Mitchell's "Case of You," Bing Crosby's "Blue of the Night," and an original by Frank called "The Sea Song." Nilsson contributed some discreet backing vocals to "Case of You" and some unorthodox percussion for "The Sea Song" by slapping his knees as Parks played a somewhat nautical accompaniment on the accordion. Nilsson also double- tracked some characteristic close-harmony backing vocals on the chorus of this song, and it probably comes close to the sound of Nilsson's "Falcons" as they sounded when they entertained the *Popeye* actors in their makeshift studio on Malta. Next they began work on a fourth tune. Stallone recalled:

We were recording a song called "Take It From the Boys," and Harry was behind the glass. Mark Hudson, who was a friend of mine and a great admirer of Harry's was also there. Harry had been drinking, and on this song he was driving me crazy. He was a Gemini, and seemed to be almost like two people. At this point he just got so anal about certain things on the record. I was singing a line that went something like: "If you want me I'll be in the bar." He would come on the talkback and say "No, Stalloneoni, 'be in the ba-ar,' OK?"

I'd say, "Stop interrupting me!"

After several attempts I finally got it, and I looked up through the glass. Now, earlier, even when Harry was criticizing me, there was a lot of movement back there, jiving around and having fun. This time I looked up and "Bump!" no movement. So I ask, "What's going on?" And one of them comes on the talkback and says, "John's been shot." And I say, "John who?" Harry said, "Lennon." The call had come to Una and she had called the studio. I walked into the booth and I knew the session was finished. They weren't exactly crying, but the mood was deep sadness. Harry had been drinking whisky, but now the coke comes out. And this event was the trigger, even for people who had been clean for ages like Jesse Ed Davis, to start using again. Harry always had coke on him in his front pocket, and they started putting lines out. So now it's the drinking and the coke. It just went on and on. And then Harry tried to get us back in the studio, but after that, nothing was going to work. The next day the Scotti brothers wanted to hear what we'd done, and it was unusable. It was a nightmare, because the session had gone on way into the night and nothing could be salvaged. They were not happy. Harry just said, "Fuck it." He was used to doing things his way in the studio and he was Harry Nilsson. He wasn't into discipline, despite the fact we were using double- or triple-scale musicians. And it must have cost a fortune. But he really loved John, and he and several of the guys who had been in the Plastic Ono Band just happened to be in the studio together with me. That's why they were all so affected.[58]

Lennon's shooting on December 8, 1980, brought to an abrupt end a year in which Nilsson had been busier than at any time since his early days when he had been working in the bank by night and selling songs by day. After the movie, stage show, *Flash Harry* album, and production work, Nilsson's professional life came to a complete stop.

There would be no recordings in January with John and Ringo together in the studio. He would never make another completed studio album of his own. And as the tragic horror of Lennon's death sank in, his life would gradually be taken over by a passionate desire to see handguns banned in the United States.

11

LAY DOWN YOUR ARMS

THE MURDER OF John Lennon was a turning point in Nilsson's life. Up until the events of December 8, 1980, he had not been a particularly politically motivated person. Even the violent death of his friend Mal Evans had not prompted him into action, beyond writing a check to one of the organizations that lobbied for stricter licensing of firearms. But when Lennon was killed, Nilsson immediately took up the cause for control of handguns, and espoused it with a level of passion and commitment that never left him for the rest of his life. It was not just that he felt he owed Lennon gratitude for the generous terms of his RCA contract, or that they had enjoyed outrageous times together on both sides of the country during the *Pussy Cats* era. It was that Lennon represented something close to his musical soul, as Jimmy Webb explained:

> Harry was primarily a Beatles man. He was the number one Beatles fan in the whole world. He and I would argue, and he'd say, "I don't know why anybody else makes music. The only people who make any music that's worth listening to are the Beatles. And there will never be another band like the Beatles." And I'd say, "Bullshit!" And we would argue about that for a while. He was adamant, "No. There is nothing in the world but the Beatles, it's the Father, Son, the Holy Ghost, and the Beatles. And I'm trying to impress this upon you. This is the truth." So when Harry got to make records with John Lennon and got to be friends with Ringo Starr, and sort of got to be in a way "the fifth Beatle," his life was complete. That's all he ever wanted. He wanted to know those people. He wanted to be admired by them. That's all there was to it. Everything else was the small print, like a P.S.[1]

So, feeling that part of his soul had been extinguished along with Lennon's life, Nilsson put his own musical career on hold and called the headquarters of the National Coalition to Ban Handguns in Washington D.C. to ask what he could do to help. This organization was the larger of two national groups, the other being HCI (Handgun Control Inc.), that were campaigning for greater control of weapons and licensing schemes. Born out of an initiative from the United Methodist Board of Church and Society, the Coalition was made up of thirty member societies that had independently started local activities to grapple with gun laws that differed widely from state to state. Lennon's murder galvanized many Beatles fans into action on the Coalition's behalf, and the gun problem was to become even more of a national issue with the attempt on President Reagan's life in March 1981 by John Hinckley Jr. By that time, Nilsson was already an effective full-time anti-handgun campaigner.

After talking to various members of the organization, he realized that his show business contacts could give the campaign a level of visibility and profile that it had not previously achieved, and he undertook to set up a Hollywood branch. "They needed opinion-makers," he said. "I Rolodexed my way through my friends."[2]

Nilsson hired Mel Brooks's former personal assistant Sherry to deal with what would become a sizable correspondence with influential acquaintances and contacts, and, as he told Derek Taylor in an account of the start of his campaign, he returned to the state of sobriety that he had last experienced during the writing of *Zapata*. He wrote:

> I've started the Pretty-again diet.... Fifteen years of debauchery, [and now it's] eight days no sugar, no fat, no booze, no regrets and isn't it wonderful, no real horror show. My aim is to be as thin as a homeopathic soup made from a pigeon's shadow. Pretty young men and women will clamor for me and I will say, "No." Then again, "No thank you, I've had enough." I knew there were two ten o'clocks, but didn't realize how nice the early one is.[3]

His immediate goal was to find high-visibility sponsors to form a committee to promote the Los Angeles program for a nationally coordinated week of action and events in the fall of 1981. By a combination of begging letters, telephone calls, and personal encouragement, his committee eventually included Senator Edward Kennedy, actress Carol Burnett, comic actor Steve Martin, former football player Joe Namath, the members of rock band Sha Na Na, and the former attorney general and veteran campaigner Ramsey Clark. For radio and TV advertisements, Nilsson asked for Ringo Starr's help, and—equally motivated by the desire to change the status quo following Lennon's murder—Starr obliged with a soundtrack that not only personally greeted Harry, Una, Ben, and Beau, but carried the clear message: "Hi, Ringo here, announcing that National End Handgun Violence Week, October 25th to the 31st, is having a rally in *your* city. Will you please join us? Thank you!"

This particular date had been chosen by the Coalition's founder, Jerry S. Fortinsky, because it coincided with Congress beginning to consider relaxing the revisions to gun control that had been introduced in 1968. Equally, a new revision of the McClure-Volkmer Act that was shortly to come before the Senate would, according to Fortinsky, potentially make it quite legal for someone such as the notorious ex-member of the Charles Manson community, Squeaky Fromme, to buy another weapon without restriction, even though she had attempted to assassinate President Johnson in 1975. Such lax legislation would, argued the Coalition, make events such as Lennon's killing more frequent and more likely.[4]

Immediately after the October 1981 week of activities across the United States, Nilsson was elected chairman of the National Committee of the Coalition. His first year of involvement, he told journalists, had cost him a fortune, but he was in the fortunate position to be able to afford to spend his time on the cause. "What good is [being] wealthy if someone shoots you in the head?" he asked. "John Lennon had all the money in the world. It's easy to make people angry, but how do you make them less apathetic?"[5] His answer to this was to begin traveling widely to join rallies and protest movements wherever and whenever there was pressure on a state legislature to ban handguns or restrict their use. His long-term goal with the Coalition, he said, was to make it bigger, wealthier, and more powerful than the National Rifle Association. In 1981, the NRA, which argued for the lifting of all restrictions on gun ownership, had two million members and an annual income of $35 million, which was largely spent on lobbying. Nilsson told one interviewer:

> We want to have that kind of clout, so that we can approach a congressman and ask, "Are you for sale? We'll buy you." And if they're not for sale, we'll do everything in our power to see they're not re-elected.[6]

At the end of 1981, a year after Lennon's murder, and having worked tirelessly throughout that time to make an impression on the campaign against handguns, Nilsson finally summoned up the nerve to write to Yoko Ono about her husband's death. In the letter, he said:

> Dear Bag O'Laughs, Now that we're both in our 40s, I guess it's OK to talk straight. John and I once had a great Yoko vs. Una debate. He said you were the blues and I said what I could.... [Then] I got to thinking about Nilsson's 4th law, which clearly states that the brighter the light, the more likely it is to be extinguished.[7]

This highly personal letter, emphasizing Lennon's shining qualities, is a genuine insight into what drove Nilsson forward in his campaign. Journalists who, on meeting him, first expected to find someone who personified the whimsical wit of his early records, the rebel who sang the risqué words of "You're Breakin' My Heart," or the hell-raiser of tabloid press fame, were nonplussed to meet someone very earnest and focused, who reeled off numerical statistics about gun ownership and the proliferation of weaponry in chilling detail. There was no doubting that in putting his musical career aside to pursue the national campaign against handguns, Nilsson was utterly serious.

In early 1982, as well as attending several conventions and rallies, he organized a reception in Los Angeles for "Californians Against Street Crime and Concealed Weapons," and his invitation listed the high-profile donors whom he had cajoled into funding the event, including Gene Wilder with a gift of $1,575, Leonard Nimoy with $1,975, and Art Garfunkel with $2,200. It is doubtful that any of the stars of music and movies whom he listed as patrons would have been involved at all were it not for Nilsson's constant advocacy of the anti-gun cause.[8] At every opportunity, he was photographed with politicians or stars to get across his message. Far from being the retiring musician who never appeared live, Nilsson's face started to become well-known in the press, and he also began occasionally singing in public to promote the cause. In Hawaii that same spring, he sang "Give Peace a Chance" to a large rally and was photographed with Mike Keller, who ran the Schutter Foundation, a charitable concern set up the previous year by the lawyer David Schutter to attempt to impose a comprehensive handgun ban on the island.[9]

After fourteen months or so of almost full-time involvement in the Coalition, Nilsson gradually allowed himself a few very small-scale musical projects. Gone was the level of activity that had produced a movie score, a stage musical, an album, and production work for Ringo and Frank Stallone in 1980. Instead, in 1982, he largely recycled earlier ideas. So, for example, when Perry Botkin was commissioned to provide the music for a children's Christmas animation based on the popular cartoon character Ziggy drawn by Tom Wilson, he invited Nilsson to write a song for the main titles. The result was a reworking of "Love Is the Answer" from Zapata. With a children's choir intoning "Give! Give! Give!" Nilsson interpolated a mixture of sung and spoken lines such as "Give with all your heart." The resulting song, "Give, Love, Joy!" created a thematic backdrop for the short Emmy-winning movie Ziggy's Gift, the melody being brilliantly picked up in the rest of Botkin's score. As the diminutive Ziggy and his dog Fuzz accidentally disrupt the criminal activities of a gang of crooked Santas, Botkin inventively employs virtually every film score cliché, one after another, from a walking bass accompanying sneak thieves to tipsily sung carols, and from jazzily speeding trucks to a final fireside Christmas celebration with pastoral woodwind, strings, and harp. Yet Nilsson's theme runs right through it all, giving the film a melodic backbone. Just as his music for The Point struck the right note of innocence for a children's animation, so did this charmingly revised version of the song from Zapata.

His other musical venture of the year was more directly linked to the campaign against handguns. From the spring until the fall of 1982, in various parts of the United States, there was a series of annual conventions for Beatles fans, known as "Beatlefests." These meetings—which in several cases had been running regularly since the group broke up in the 1960s—drew together those most likely to support his cause. Consequently, Nilsson recorded a single to be sold at the events to raise awareness for the handgun campaign, entitled "With a Bullet." It was a conversation piece, rather like the "Flying Saucer Song," only in this case, the victim of an armed attack tries to talk sense into a gun-toting criminal. To make it, Nilsson gatecrashed a Los Angeles record session by the rock vibraphonist Buzzy Linhart on June 28, 1982. There he sat at the piano and recorded the song, plus several different versions of the introduction. Each of these was tailored to one of the various Beatlefest events around the country, the next of which was to kick off on July 9 in Los Angeles. The season would finally come to a close at Seacaucus, New Jersey, in late October.

The song was issued back to back with a low-budget recording of another new piece called "Judy," which Nilsson had written at the March Beatles fans' meeting in New York in return for a $500 donation to the National Coalition to Ban Handguns. These cheaply produced singles pressed on bright red vinyl became rare collectors' items. Nilsson himself attended most of the conventions, signing autographs, selling the singles, and generally trying to move Beatles enthusiasts from passive anger over Lennon's death to active involvement, in order to prevent such a thing from happening again. The tribute band Liverpool often appeared at Beatlefests, and in future years, Nilsson would further break his taboo about live performance and appear with them onstage to try yet another means of getting the anti-handgun message across.

In December 1982, Nilsson took time off from the campaign to travel with Una and the children to Mexico, where Graham Chapman was filming his post-Python comedy movie *Yellowbeard*. This was the culmination of the discussions Chapman had had years earlier over many a drink with Keith Moon and Nilsson, and it is clear from his letters and notes that he intended to commission Nilsson to write a score. However, the producers of the film thought otherwise, perhaps shuddering at the memory of *Popeye*'s critical reception, and so although Nilsson drafted several songs and even recorded demos of one called "Men at Sea," to the accompaniment of his own Casio keyboard, none of his work made it into the movie. Apparently once filming was complete and Nilsson had returned to Los Angeles, he invited Chapman and the actor Martin Hewitt (who played the Jim Hawkins-inspired character Dan in the picture) to the Nilsson house to hear more demo versions of what amounted to a fairly fully sketched-out soundtrack.[10]

The film was not a success. Chaotic rewriting, last-minute recasting, production delays, and copious amounts of alcohol did not make for a disciplined, well-run set or for the consistently humorous end product promised by its glittering cast of comedy stars. Eric Idle, who played Commander Clement in the movie, invited another of his rock-star friends, who even played an uncredited walk-on part, to come to Mexico and see what was happening. He recalled: "I took Bowie down there and he got really blitzed."

Nilsson made up for not being asked to contribute music on the soundtrack by creating a rather different musical backdrop—paying a local mariachi band to wander about, playing raucously, at the hotel where most of the cast were staying. But a cloud fell over the whole affair when one of the film's principal actors, Marty Feldman, the British comedian and another of Nilsson's drinking buddies, suddenly died of a heart attack shortly before filming ended. When the movie eventually appeared in the summer of 1983, most reviewers agreed with the apt judgment of the well-known Canadian film critic Leonard Klady that it was "a long string of gags in search of a well-structured story."[11]

In 1983, Nilsson revamped another of the songs from *Zapata* for a film score. In this case it was a contribution to the British director Tony Garnett's anti-weapon movie *Handgun* (eventually released under the title *Deep in the Heart*). The plot involved a young woman who moves to Texas to teach, dates a lawyer who rapes her at gunpoint, and then—after training herself to be proficient with firearms—seeks her violent revenge. The anti-gun theme of the picture appealed to Nilsson, and his song "Lay Down Your Arms" was a reworking of "Why Don't You Let Me Go Free?" building a hypnotically repetitive rhythm out of the original couplet "Lay down your arms, and I will open mine." His fully finished studio recording (which suffered from some clumsy edits in the version used on the movie soundtrack) picks up the Caribbean mood of *Duit On Mon Dei*, featuring a reggae rhythm, a slick ska-influenced horn section (that sounds very much as if an uncredited Bobby Keys was leading the saxophones), and Nilsson's own overdubbed vocals in various registers and accents. At this point, despite one of his longest periods away from regular work in the studio, Nilsson could still match any of his earlier recordings for invention and vocal style.

This was to be readily apparent when in 1983 he contributed three pieces to an album of songs by Yoko Ono called *Every Man Has a Woman*. Originally conceived as her fiftieth birthday record to come out in February that year, it took somewhat longer to make than planned and eventually appeared in 1984. Even after his letter to Ono in 1981, Nilsson did not speak to her face to face for another year, on the grounds that he "just didn't have anything to say."[12] However, when they met again, they fell into each other's arms, and this was when "the most fascinating woman he had ever met" persuaded him to record some songs for her album.[13] The disc that eventually emerged contained newly finished versions of some 1970s recordings by John Lennon, together with new covers of Ono's work, not just by Nilsson, but also by Rosanne Cash, Elvis Costello, Roberta Flack, Sean Lennon, and Eddie Money. In the three songs eventually selected as Nilsson's contribution to the disc (he actually recorded close to an additional album's worth of Ono material),[14] some very different sides of his personality are on display. "Silver Horse" is a beautifully sung ballad, showcasing the "young" Nilsson voice, with a clear upper register and some deft vocal arabesques. "Dream Love" is closer to the slightly rougher "rock" voice of *Son of Schmilsson*, whereas "Loneliness" is more contemporary. Nilsson half speaks, half sings the vocal line over an insistent disco beat, with a trio of female backing singers. Ono's record company, PolyGram, decided that once the album had appeared, they would release this track from the album as a new Nilsson single, and so, planning the promotion in advance, they called once again on Stanley Dorfman to make a short film based on the song. He recalled:

We took "Loneliness," one of the songs, and by then Harry was living in Bel Air, in that lovely big house and we shot it in his home. Harry was a sort of insane Laurel and Hardy fan. He knew everything about them and everything they ever did. And there was a comedian who did impressions of Laurel and Hardy. A fat comedian.

So we booked him for no reason at all. And we made up this sort of surreal music video, where Harry walks into his own house and there's Oliver Hardy watering his garden, just incidentally. As it turned out, Harry had had a big fight with Una the night before, and she'd walked out. He persuaded her to come back just to do the music video. She had three kids. They were all walking, one very small and the others a little larger. So she played the loving wife, although they'd had a screaming fight the night before. We also had Timothy Leary in it. But he was so bad as an actor we had to cut him out. We had all sorts of people who came in and out. Some were left in and some were cut out. But we ended up with this nice music video.[15]

Although the fictional plot of the promotional film is that Nilsson returns to an empty home, which his wife and children, Beau, Ben, and Annie, appear to have deserted, they all reappear happy and smiling at the end. Along the way, Dorfman references the *Duit On Mon Dei* video, as Nilsson, clad in leather coat and shades, gets out of his silver Mercedes and picks up a basketball, which he shoots immediately through a hoop on his garage. The Oliver Hardy character looks on. In subsequent sequences, for those in the know, both *Son of Dracula* and *Ziggy's Gift* are referred to visually, and in a series of dream episodes, the short movie then tours the Nilsson house room by room. It is the best surviving record on film of Nilsson and his family at home—even if the circumstances on the day were a little strained.

Aside from this very unusual spat with Una, Nilsson's home life with his family was every bit as idyllic as Dorfman presented it in the closing segment of the film. It was particularly appealing to Nilsson's older son Zak, who said:

[I had a number of] short term visits with him, and then my inevitable departure to go back to live with my mother. I never wanted to leave. I wanted to live with Harry, along with my half brothers and sisters. I wanted to be a part of that family, not the family I lived with. Like Harry, I didn't get along with my mother very well, and I always understood why they separated. My mother was a hard person to live with. So going to visit with Harry was, for me, a splinter of paradise. A week or two of blissful fantasy in which I forgot all about my normal life, punctuated by that last limo ride to the airport when reality began to set in again.[16]

"Loneliness" was the last commercially released single of Nilsson's career. The promotional film was finally edited by Dorfman for release during July 1984. However, by that time, Nilsson was no longer living in Bel Air, but close to New York City, where he had moved the family in late 1983. The East Coast was to become Nilsson's base for the next few years.

Ostensibly, the reason for this was that on July 28, 1984, the Olympic Games were to open in Los Angeles. With all the fuss surrounding the games, Nilsson decided not only to quit town for the duration of the event, which finished on August 12, but to move lock, stock, and barrel to the East Coast well before Olympic fever gripped the city. This plan had been one of the reasons for the tension remembered by Stanley Dorfman between Nilsson and Una, who recalled:

> We were living in Bel Air, and we had lived there for quite a long time. By then we had three children, and we were expecting a fourth. And the Olympics were coming to Los Angeles. I think Harry wanted a change. I think he wanted to spend some time in New York. I really didn't want to go, but he persuaded me that we should go, because he thought the city here would be very crowded and we shouldn't be in L.A. for the Olympics. So we set out for New York. We stayed in several different places. In due course, we rented a house in Mamaroneck, which is just north of New York City. I enjoyed that house very much, and Olivia was born there.[17]

At the start of July 1984, the month in which the Olympics began, Nilsson was in New York City, hanging out with Terry Southern. The co-author of *Candy*, creator of the screenplay for *Magic Christian*, and co-writer of the movies *Dr. Strangelove* and *Easy Rider*, among other films, Southern was discussing with Nilsson the idea that the two of them should form a movie production company. More than that, they had become regular drinking and social buddies. Southern had recently been a member of the *Saturday Night Live* writing team and during his time on that television show, with its high-pressure demands on the writers to be consistently funny, his drug and alcohol intake had rivaled that of Nilsson. When they hooked up in New York, Southern was working on a possible film biography of Jim Morrison, and his early novel *Flash and Filigree* had been newly republished with an introduction by William Burroughs, which reinforced his credentials as one of the hippest of hip writers.

Around the beginning of July, the pair bumped into the singer Jimmy Buffett in a Manhattan bar, who invited them to go up to Boston where he was to appear in a huge free concert. For various reasons, Nilsson and Southern arrived late and missed the show, only catching up with Buffett when it was over. Nilsson takes up the story:

> I said, "Well we're gonna go now, goodbye."
> And I said to Terry, "Let's go!"
> "Where?"
> "Washington. We'll catch Ringo playing the drums for the Beach Boys."
> "Um, right."
> So, we got a plane from Boston to Washington. It was the largest concert, I think, ever, in history. There were a million plus people who showed up at this street concert.[18] It was very, very hot, 102 degrees hot. I was wearing a black leather jacket and shades, just for a look, and I didn't care. Terry was looking like a youthful

man of indeterminate age who had just found the secret of looking rumpled and acceptable. We went to what was presumably the back entrance, where there's this poor guard and we gave him a double act.

I said, "Look, obviously we're not kids looking for autographs."

He said, "But you don't have any passes."

I said, "Can't you just call Ringo in his trailer and he'll okay it?"

He said, "I can't leave my post."

I said, "You can't leave your post?"

And he said, "No."

I said, "Good. Watch my father for me, I'll leave him as collateral and I'll be back in ten minutes. Thank you."

And I walked right past him. He couldn't come after me, because he'd be leaving his post. Meanwhile, Terry's sitting there pissed because I called him my father. Inside, I leaned up against one of the two hundred trailers.

"Do you happen to know where Ringo Starr's dressing room is?" This guy says, "You're leaning on it."

I open the door and there were all the Boys, Beach. And they were singing a song, and, they're all trying to tell Ringo how to play the drums at this one special part. He saw me walk in with a look of relief and disbelief that there I was and there he was. So he stopped everything, we embraced and he explained who I was to everyone. I said, "There's one other problem. Terry's being held hostage, right now, at the back gate. Can we send somebody to bring him in?"

Just then, someone said, "Showtime!" And everybody runs out of the trailer. I'm caught up with the crowd, saying, "We gotta find somebody to send back to the gate! I don't want to go back there, I'll never get back in."

The next thing you know, a few steps later, we're standing on the stage, and there are the Beach Boys playing to a million people, and I'm standing on the stage looking at my dear friend Ringo.[19]

There is a film of this event, released as the closing climax to the documentary *The Beach Boys—An American Band*, which came out in January 1985.[20] On both sides of the stage, there is a crowd of onlookers, and Nilsson can clearly be seen among them in three scenes, wearing his shades and a black leather jacket, with his hair dark with sweat.

At this Washington, D.C., concert, which took place at the mall, Starr played three numbers in all during his guest spot with the band: "Back In The U.S.S.R.," "You Can't Do That," and "Day Tripper."[21] Nilsson was invited to travel down to Florida for the next Beach Boys show at which Ringo would again be guesting in place of the band's original drummer Dennis Wilson (who had drowned the previous December). But Nilsson and Southern (who finally talked his way in) were too exhausted after their trip to Boston to accept and so they returned to New York. It was with some relief that Nilsson came home to Mamaroneck. However, shortly after this jaunt with Southern, Nilsson decided to make his stay in the East permanent, as Una recalled:

> We thought, well, maybe we should buy a house. So we ended up buying 409 North Broadway, [Nyack,] in Rockland County, on the other side of the Hudson River. It was also a lovely location, right on the Hudson River. Lovely views. Victorian.[22]

While their home in Nyack was being renovated and before the family could move in, the Nilssons lived briefly in another house belonging to the cartoonist who had drawn Ziggy, Tom Wilson. It was situated in Westchester County just north of New York City. The contrast to Los Angeles weather was perhaps the most significant change from their former lifestyle, because in winter, the temperatures plummeted. Una recalled it being extremely cold during their first winter on the East Coast, and she remembered the older members of her young family exploring the snowy landscape on a double sled at about the time of Olivia's birth in on January 22, 1984. Despite the chill, it was overall a surprisingly successful move, given how settled the family had been in Bel Air. Nilsson had access to New York and its social life, and the family quickly adjusted into a new and slightly different rhythm from before. Una said:

> We still traveled. I went to Ireland every year and my parents came to me every year. We'd go to London, and I remember a particularly lovely vacation in Switzerland. We were in Wengen, which was gorgeous. I think we were in the East four or five years over all. Beau and Ben went to Rockland County day school, and Annie went to a little pre-school called Playgarten. That was the thinking.[23]

Their third son Kief was also born while they were in the New York area in June 1985. But, as Una suggested, there were frequent trips away. Sometimes they traveled as a family; other times it was just Nilsson and Una, or occasionally Nilsson on his own, either continuing his crusade against handguns or taking a vacation with an old buddy, such as Ringo. Recalling one of the latter adventures, Nilsson wrote:

> One time, we actually went to Bermuda on one passport. Ringo had his, but mine had expired, as we found out on the way to the airport. "Holy shit, it's expired!" Well, we'll wriggle out of it. So when it was our turn up, Ringo started to go to the desk and I said, "Excuse me." I put my passport down, and then Ringo put his next to it. So the guy looked at me and then he glances up, he looks at Ringo and he realizes he's got Ringo Starr's passport. And he's looking at the pages and I say, "Excuse me, I'm running a little late," and he says, "Yeah, sure." He just took my passport book up, stamped it and gave it back to me, and then went back to Ringo and stamped his. And then, "Thank you very much." Now I was clear, I could get into

Bermuda. Getting out was another story. That required going to the consulate. That took many more hours than I would have liked it to have. But, in the end, I flew out with a new passport with an accordion folder inside. Because I had filled that one up, and the new one said "Passport issued, Bermuda."[24]

Bermuda was a frequent holiday destination for Nilsson and Ringo. On another occasion, Ringo rented a house on the island, ideally placed for his wife Barbara to swim every day. Nilsson and Una flew out via Florida to join them but had a disastrous journey with a mix-up over tickets and lost luggage. In due course, they settled in to the house, but on the first afternoon, the power failed. Apparently there was a strike, so the entire island was blacked out, and despite the heat, there was no air conditioning or refrigeration in the villa. To eat that night, the four went off to a local restaurant that was functioning by candlelight, and in due course they returned home. Nilsson had a very particular reason to remember what happened next:

We decided to say goodnight after the second bottle of brandy. But it's hard to say goodnight, especially when you're sweating and you don't even want to go in the room because of the heat and the bugs. But we gave it a try and eventually, unable to sleep, I went to another room, separate from Una. I just said, "This looks like a nice tightly closed room, I don't see any insects, it's cool, and I've gotta little spray here." But then I began to feel them, one bite, two bites, three bites—that was all, it wasn't too bad, I'd slap occasionally. It doesn't seem too bad. All I have to do is keep my eyes closed, and think of sleep. After about twenty minutes I couldn't take it anymore. I was ready to scream out loud for someone to get me 911 and a gun. I eventually decided to let the little bastards climb all over me, then I'd jump off a nearby cliff. Anyway, come the next day, it was a horror show. They had eaten me alive. We counted something like 800 bites on my legs. Unbelievable. It was just like having a terrible rash right up and down both legs. Not to mention soft parts of your anatomy and your face and arms. I was sick, they put so much poison in me, and had taken out so much blood. I just wanted to go home to New York. Ringo drove us back. I said, "I got bitten." And he says, "Oh yeah, well look at all these." He showed me his arm, and so I dropped my pants, by the beach, to show Hilary and Ringo, and said, "Look at all these." He was shocked, my legs were swollen and I was full of poison. It took a long time to get rid of them, but it provides me with a wonderful memory of that trip. Losing the luggage, getting the wrong priced tickets, eaten alive by animals, power failure. Thanks for the wonderful vacation.[25]

With the move to New York State, the pace of Nilsson's lobbying against gun laws relaxed somewhat. He still traveled to Beatlefest conventions and took opportunities to be photographed with politicians and media personalities to spread the message. However, in terms of his future life, perhaps the most significant of his travels had nothing to do with handguns and took place in the summer, a few months after his move east. He went off to Australia to promote his tracks from the Yoko Ono album. On August 14, 1984, Nilsson settled into a waterfront luxury apartment in Sydney, and he not only undertook a punishing schedule of interviews and radio shows to promote the single of "Loneliness" (complete with Dorfman's now-finished film), but he also threw himself into an energetic social whirl. By sheer chance, Gerry Beckley and America were on tour at the same time that Nilsson was there, and they arrived in Sydney just after he did. Beckley recalled:

> We were staying at the Sebel Townhouse, and the man at the front desk said, "Mr. Beckley, there's five telegrams for you, here." I never receive any telegrams. This is the time before e-mail, but five telegrams? So I open up the first one, and it has one word on it, and it says, "You." And I open up the second, and it says, "Welcome." And so I, of course, then rip open the remaining three. You had to assemble it and it said, "Welcome to Sydney, you assholes." And it was from Harry who was staying in Sydney.... One of the unique things about the Sebel Townhouse is that it had no qualms about announcing who was staying there... and it also had those little movable letters to announce the events in the hotel. And for one of the rooms, it said, "Harry Welcomes America." Harry had arranged a catered event to welcome us to Sydney. This was a fantastic thing... and Harry's there with one of his friends. They had a full bar set up with appetizers and hors d'oeuvres, and everything. And it was just fantastic.[26]

Nilsson went along to hear Beckley's first concert in the Sydney suburb of Balmain, and after the show officially finished, it was Nilsson who went onstage—supposedly to introduce an encore, which was intended to be a rousing version of "Horse With No Name." But before the band got a chance to come back, he sat at the piano, banged out some C major chords, and launched into a version of "Give Peace a Chance," which got the entire audience singing. It was, recalled Beckley, "a hand-holding five-minute-long rendition," with people "leaping up on stage to be a part of it."[27] Just as Stanley Dorfman had been surprised to witness Nilsson warming up the audience for BBC television shows in the early 70s, Beckley was astonished that this man, who famously did not appear live, had a natural talent for working a crowd. But for Nilsson, it was a not-to-be-missed opportunity to get the anti-gun message across to a new public, and he seized the opportunity with alacrity.

He went back with the group to their hotel and was still drinking and partying hard at three in the morning. Yet when America arrived at the ABC studio to appear on breakfast television the next day, there was a sober, coherent Nilsson already on the set, holding forth eloquently on the Yoko Ono album.

Such social events aside (and among his other friends who happened to be in Sydney at the time were Graham Chapman, his ward John Tomiczek, and the Hollywood actors Robert DeNiro and Harvey Keitel), the reason that this visit to Australia was so significant in Nilsson's life was because he used the trip to invest in some real estate. He acquired a tract of land in the Hunter Valley wine-growing area. Compared to its ubiquity in the world market in the twenty-first century, in the mid-1980s, the Australian wine industry had yet to make its international breakthrough, although the conditions were right for remarkable growth. With considerable acuity, Nilsson spotted its potential. Una observed:

> Harry had lovely ideas. In this case, his idea was we'll buy this land in Australia, and it'll be good for the children. We would never use it, but it would grow in value, just in the way that Bob Hope and all these people bought ranches around Los Angeles and then ended up doing well by them. So that was Harry's long-term idea. He had this idea of Australia as the next frontier.[28]

It would be some years before the wisdom of this investment became apparent, but Nilsson carefully negotiated the complex laws for non-Australians to buy in the country and invested in partnership with OXPA Property Pty. Ltd.

In due course, Nilsson returned to his new home in New York. But in the fall of 1984, he visited London, catching up again with some old friends for the kind of behavior that had brought him the "raising hell with Harry" reputation. One of the first people he met with for a night out was Eric Idle:

> We ended up in Tramp. I was with George. Harry was there and Ringo was there. And it got really quite late. And for some reason we challenged the Italian waiters to a "Volare" sing-off. We all climbed on a table and they all climbed on another table. And we tried to sing "Volare" louder than they could. It was really funny. And then everybody got down, and we sat down again, and the manager says: "Thanks chaps," and then Ringo says, "Just another bottle of brandy!" There was just a moment's pause, and then everybody scattered.[29]

Such events in nightclubs were one thing, but on an evening out with Bobby Keys, Nilsson managed almost to eclipse the events of his return from the valium sleep treatment a few years before. The two of them had been at Mick Jagger's house until three in the morning, after which they got a cab and went looking for somewhere to get a hamburger. Nilsson headed for his usual late-night haunt, the Pelican Café at the Londonderry Hotel on Park Lane, near his former flat in Curzon Place, but it was closed. So their driver took them to a cabbie's diner on the Thames embankment, strictly for the use of London taxi staff, where he thought their celebrity status might get them a meal. But before being served, they managed to get into an altercation. Consequently, Nilsson and Keys took on twelve irate drivers, and although they were badly beaten themselves, during the fisticuffs, one cabbie suffered a broken jaw and another had a heart attack. The police were incredulous that anyone would be foolish enough to get into a fight against such odds, and mainly for that reason, Nilsson narrowly avoided another night in jail.[30]

Around this time, Jimmy Webb was staying at the Inn on the Park in London, and Nilsson went to see him on his way back to his own hotel after a night of carousing. It was quite early in the morning, and Webb was in his bathrobe. Nilsson suggested they go onto the balcony for a smoke, and the door clicked shut behind them. It was November and not the warmest time to be locked outside on the ninth floor of a hotel. Nilsson realized that the next room's balcony was only a few feet away and slightly lower, and reckoned he could jump across. He recalled: "I was drunk enough to fear nothing. I managed to get on top of the thin rod iron railing…as I am about to make my jump, Jim, fearing me falling, couldn't help himself. He caught hold of my leg, forcing me to shout, 'Let go of my goddamn leg, Jim. For Christ's sake, I'm okay!' I made my jump, landed on my feet and promptly went to my hands and knees. I moved the door handle, which clicked. I pulled it open and stepped inside."[31] Webb takes up the story:

> He walked into the room where newlyweds were consummating their relationship, and said, "Excuse me, never mind, just coming through, carry on!" He went through, closed the door. Now he's *very* happy because he has me on a fire escape, locked out in this November weather, and he's perfectly okay. So he goes down to the lobby and collects Bruce Grakal, my attorney and says, "Let's go see Jimmy." They get back on the elevator. They come up the elevator. They come up to my room. Somehow or other they get into my room and they come over to the window. Now they look at me like I'm a monkey in a cage and they're rapping on the glass going, "How is it?" "Is it getting any warmer out there?" And so they tortured me for a while, and I think I had to promise to let him introduce me at the Royal Albert Hall, or something like that, and he finally relented and let me back into the hotel room."[32]

A year or two earlier, Nilsson had received an abject apology from the house manager of the Britannia Hotel in Grosvenor Square, where he often stayed in London after giving up his apartment. "One of the staff's main duties," wrote the hotel's Mr. Wright, "is to protect the guests, and therefore we stringently discourage any 'ladies of the night' on the premises. With this in mind, the Night Porter tackled Mr. Nilsson's guests.…"[33] Staying up all night, drinking copiously at Tramp, bringing what appeared to be ladies of "ill repute" to his hotel room, jumping between ninth floor balconies, and getting into fistfights, Nilsson seemed to be doing his best to keep his hell-raising reputation going. And yet, compared with the depressed character he presented to his friends after his split from Diane, he was now grounded and happy, a secure family man. Given his behavior, it might be reasonable to suspect that occasionally it had put undue strain on his relationship with Una. But she adamantly disagreed:

> People forget we're both actually Irish Catholics. I'm an Irish Catholic, and he's a third generation Irish Catholic on the Martin side. And in those days, growing up in Ireland, divorce was actually against the constitution of the country. It was

against the law of the land, anyway. So I didn't have any problems with commitment. I can remember people advising me to leave Harry. They'd think they were doing me a favor: "Oh you should leave him because he's drinking, and so on." But it just wouldn't occur to me.

I'm very sensitive to that because people criticize him, but they don't really understand. I think it's all about love. When you meet the person you love and you're going to marry, and you're going to live with, I think you have a little vision. I think everybody does this, of how it's going to be. And our little vision was that we would have this sacred family life, separate from his life. He was in the entertainment business, which has a tremendous amount of stresses, and this was our little oasis. That's what we did. We loved having the family.[34]

Nilsson's family was now the bedrock of his existence. Indeed, as he said in a live National Public Radio interview on the *Flo & Eddie* show in 1990, he got rid of his piano and guitar in the early 1980s to focus on raising his family.[35] Building his house and spending time with his children were—along with the handgun crusade—the most important things in his life. And as Una recalled, after the years of debauchery, he was anxious to make up for lost time: "Every time that we had a baby—and we had four babies born at home—he'd be lying there in bed with this little tiny newborn a couple of hours old, and get very emotional about it, because he loved the babies. Then he'd say 'Let's have another one!' "[36]

Not long after they moved to New York, the family went boating on Lake Champlain up north near the Canadian border. Annie Nilsson, age three, fell off the dock into the water, and Nilsson, fully dressed, jumped in to save her. It was an event vividly etched in the young girl's imagination, as no sooner had he grasped her and pulled her to the surface than the dockside ladder he tried to climb fell away, and they were plunged back into the water. But Nilsson prevailed and rescued her. In her view, this was dramatic proof that his first thought was always for the children's wellbeing. As she grew up, Annie realized how strongly he was focused on his family. She said: "He loved being a father. It was so clear that he was so excited by us, and there were so many of us! He became very involved in wanting to know what was going on with us and wanting to impart his wisdom on to us. He was so loving and generous and sweet."[37]

Looking back, his sons Ben and Beau both felt they had a strong and positive relationship with their father. In contrast to the patchwork quilt of his own upbringing, he focused on providing a stable family home as a basis for his children to grow up in, but one that nevertheless allowed them to be themselves. Beau recalled:

There was no pressure to be any certain way. There was an emphasis on doing well in school, which I had trouble with. There was an emphasis on being nice to anyone that's around, on using your mouth to get out of a bad situation instead of your fists. He said, "Feel life out. See what happens. See what road it takes you down. You'll

figure out soon enough that with all the bad things, there is a reason they are bad."
I felt great about that advice. The communication with him was always so open,
there was nothing I couldn't say.[38]

Ben confirmed this, saying:

> He encouraged whatever you were doing. He never tried to push anyone in the
> family in any direction. It wasn't like you're going to be the singer, the musician,
> the dancer....If you came home with something you did, he was happy to see it.
> He was very encouraging about it, which was a good attitude, a good policy to have
> with your kids.[39]

There is no clearer example of how Nilsson viewed his relationship with his children
than the frequent letters he wrote home during his travels on behalf of the anti-handgun
campaign. In one note, his writing made a little jumpy by mid-air turbulence as he jotted
down his thoughts on a flight from Honolulu, he said to Ben and Beau, "I look forward
to all the problems you both share with Mom and I—I mean that—if you have the need
and the balls to. And I and Mom both want you to be normally miserable at school and
heroes at home."[40]

Given the focus on his children and the fact that he cut down his drinking considerably when he was at home in Nyack, there was nevertheless one member of his family who provoked a very different set of reactions in Nilsson, and that was his son Zak.
Notwithstanding that his own emotions about his father were what he described as
"multifaceted," Zak was well aware that he was a direct link to Nilsson's unhappy past.
Although that past had inspired some of his best songs, it was still uncomfortable for him
to be reminded of it. Zak observed:

> He always felt guilty about splitting up with my mother and leaving me without a
> father, because that's exactly what happened to him as a kid. It even happened in
> the way he sang about it in "1941." You could substitute "1971" and it would be my
> story. Harry made it clear that he cared about me, and even I could sense the waves
> of guilt on his part when we were together. He never wanted it to be this way for
> me, and I've never blamed him for it. I hope, and I believe, that he knew that. When
> he was living in Nyack, NY, I once went to visit him, and we went out and he got
> drunk at a bar again. This was different though, because he had been trying very
> hard to stay off drinking, he had been having health problems and, thank God, Una
> had been helping him stay clean.
>
> He told me, "I can't help it. When you come to visit me, I can't control my
> drinking, son. I see you, and I have to drink." He was nearly in tears when he said
> that to me. I understood what he meant. He never fully got over the shame he
> felt for doing to me what, in his mind, was done to him as a child. I was never

old enough to form the words necessary to alleviate his guilt, to assure him that he hadn't done anything wrong by me, and that I loved him, no matter what. So these visits always had this chain reaction of guilt where he felt guilty about how he had left me, and I felt guilty that he felt that way, and every time it ended with me crying into his shoulder as I left for the airport, which I'm sure only made it worse.[41]

Although Nilsson's other children recall that he was still writing songs at this period in the 1980s, jotting down lyrics on napkins, menus, or odd scraps of paper, and although he was prone to singing in his automobile as he drove them around, music was no longer the center of his career. Away from the handgun crusade, Nilsson was taking an increasing interest in the business of the media. He had invested some of his money from the severance of his RCA contract in film and television companies, and indeed in July 1983, well before the move east, he had been named as a possible chairman of Cinnamon Broadcasting in Utah when that group of businesses was reorganized. As a major stockholder, the press saw him as a logical choice.[42]

The following year, in between bouts of carousing, Nilsson's plans to form a movie production company with Terry Southern began to move forward, and by the fall of 1985, they came to fruition. Hawkeye Entertainment was incorporated on October 23 that year. The firm took office space in Studio City, Los Angeles, at 11330 Ventura Boulevard (buying the building itself a couple of years later). But although the logic of this was that any movie production business needed to be located close to the center of the film industry, it meant that from the outset Nilsson was usually absent from the day-to-day running of the company, and this remained the case for its first few years by virtue of him living on the East Coast. Equally, Southern, whose time was divided between active screenwriting on various movies and thinking up ideas over drinks with Nilsson, was also not present regularly.

The man recruited to look after the company, James Hock Jr., also originally lived on the East Coast, and he retained a permanent home on Long Island while living in a Hollywood hotel for much of his time in charge of Hawkeye as president and chief executive officer.[43] Hock was a former high-flying investment banker who had been a Wall Street mergers-and-acquisitions specialist within the capital markets division of Citicorp before assisting in the setup of Hawkeye.[44] Hock believed in acquiring other businesses to make the firm grow, whereas Nilsson and Southern believed in developing their own creative ideas. Aware of this, but convinced of the need to establish a strong capital base for their activities, Hock set about building up income and assets so that he could take the company public in 1987. He expanded the firm's capital base by acquiring other companies, including graphic design and advertising agencies, which were not directly related to Hawkeye's core business. Fourteen million shares were released on March 25, 1987, at twenty-five cents apiece, being what was known as "penny stock." Nilsson bought a substantial number of them—several million—himself. Later that year, however, it would become apparent that Nilsson and Southern were fundamentally incompatible with the man they had recruited to run the firm.[45]

Nilsson and Southern were not short of ideas. Numerous treatments, synopses, and sections of screenplays that they developed together survive in Nilsson's files. Yet in his sober, reflective moments, even Southern recognized that beneath the veneer of being a competitive production company, Hawkeye was something of a vanity project for Nilsson. He said:

> Nilsson was a very creative guy. He had this story about a reporter who works for tabloids like the *Enquirer* or the *Star*, writing outlandish stories like "Headless Man Seen in Topless Bar." So we wrote a script called *Obits*. Harry was able to finance the writing.[46]

Obits, *Silk City*, *Lost Highway*, and *We The Jury* were all screen treatments that Nilsson financed through Hawkeye and which their New York agents, Oscard Associates, offered to a selection of producers and studios. They were not successful. One reader described *Obits* (originally a story by Roger Watkins in which a newspaper reporter discovers two identical obituaries written ten years apart, and who lives in a partial fantasy world) as "vague, puerile and offensive."[47] That reviewer took most objection to the character of the reporter Harry being brought into the orbit of a ghastly family called the Stoats, among whom public masturbation, incontinence, and nudity were commonplace. Despite the liberal climate of the late 1980s, this script seemed to those producers who got as far as actually reading it to have no redeeming features whatever.

A fantasy world was also at the center of the only screenplay that Southern and Nilsson did fully develop into a finished movie. This was *The Telephone*, set in a claustrophobic apartment in which an actor delivers a monologue into a phone, adopting the voices of various characters in the process, and gradually letting the audience realize that they are witnessing a personal battle against unemployment and mounting debt. Ultimately it becomes clear to the audience that the telephone has actually been cut off for months, and the conversations—even the answering machine messages that are replayed—all exist solely in the character's head. The telephone engineer who conveys to the actor that this is the case is beaten to death with the telephone. It was intended to be a tour-de-force role for Robin Williams. "We wrote it with him in mind," said Southern. "We made this strenuous effort to get the script to him or at least talk to him on the phone…[but] we found out his manager didn't want him to do the film at all."[48]

The days of Williams's amicable association with Nilsson on *Popeye* were long past, and at the time *The Telephone* was being pitched to his manager, he was already working on what would become one of his most acclaimed roles, as Adrian Cronauer in *Good Morning Vietnam*. Then fate took a hand, and one evening in the basement garage of the Chateau Marmont in Hollywood, Nilsson and Southern happened to pull up next to Whoopi Goldberg's car. They struck up a conversation and explained their idea for *The Telephone* to her. She quickly became interested, and instead of going upstairs for their planned meeting with former Monty Python star Terry Gilliam, who was waiting patiently in the hotel, they fell into a deep conversation with Goldberg.[49] Her previous three movies, *Jumping Jack Flash*, *Burglar*, and *Fatal Beauty*, had not been able to recreate her success in 1985 with *The Color Purple*, and she was on the lookout for a suitable vehicle to demonstrate her credentials as a serious actress, to win back both the critics and her audience.

She signed a letter of intent saying that she would make the movie if financing could be found, and eventually New World Pictures agreed to underwrite the project on a budget of $2 million. Southern and Nilsson each received $100,000 on signing the agreement, although Nilsson's share went straight back into Hawkeye Entertainment and represented virtually the company's entire above-the-line income for 1987.[50] Amid the excitement of having the company's first script turned into a movie, with Southern attending the filming in San Francisco, the question of generating long-term revenue for Hawkeye was put to one side. Instead, finishing *The Telephone*, in a way that came even close to the original script became a struggle for artistic integrity.

The director was the well-known character actor Rip Torn, who was well established in theater, but not particularly experienced or well known in movies. He did, however, share the experience with Goldberg of having lived in the 22nd Street neighborhood of Manhattan at the time when she was a young, unknown actress, and this common ground led to them agreeing to work together. However, New World tilted the playing field by effectively giving Goldberg carte blanche in her contract to introduce changes to the screenplay. She was able to overrule Torn at almost every step. Her husband was recruited to replace the cinematographer he had intended to use, and as Southern recalled, she just rode roughshod over his words:

> She was able to ignore the script and just wing it. She's a very creative woman, and her improvisations were often good, but she had gotten involved because she really loved the script, and now she was suddenly making all these changes. So any time she and Rip would get into an argument about a scene, she had this upper hand. After she did her improvisations, Rip would say, "OK, let's do one for the writer."[51]

When the movie was finished, there was an entirely predictable battle between Goldberg, Hawkeye, and New World over the final cut, with each of the three parties wanting control. In the end, money talked, and the production company whose finances had underwritten the project released a film consisting of Goldberg's largely improvised scenes, even though she had lost her lawsuits against both New World and Hawkeye to prevent it from being issued in this form. Among the compromises made in the released version was the excision of some of Southern's best pieces of writing, including a scene in which an actor dressed as a hot dog has a somewhat surreal dialog with Goldberg through the window of her apartment.[52] Unhappy with the officially edited movie, Torn and Southern consequently made their own "director's cut," based on the "one for the writer" takes of each scene, which they brought to the Sundance Film Festival in January 1988.[53] By all accounts, this was a passable art-house movie. But the commercially released version was savaged by the press.

The *New York Times* laid into what it described as "a cheap, labor-intensive idea for a movie," going on to say that "no amount of manic invention could have saved it."[54] Pointing out that the idea was derivative of Jean Cocteau's *Human Voice*, the review goes on to quote audience members who catcalled, "I want my money back." Most unkindly, the reviewer, who no doubt knew something of Nilsson's and Southern's social habits, said that the idea "might have seemed great at around three in the morning after a long night out." But this critic was not alone. Michael Sragow in the *San Francisco Examiner* wrote, "The movie represents the worst kind of vanity filmmaking, the kind that makes the star look horrid."[55] He went on to denigrate this "limp pretentious drama" and to declare that "the movie dies from a bad case of the morbid cutes."

However, both Nilsson and Southern failed to see the writing on the wall for their production venture. Buoyed up by having one of their screenplays filmed, they were sure that their philosophy for the company was right and that they could function as an "entertainment boutique,"[56] working on projects they both liked. In early August 1987, they parted company with James Hock Jr. over what Nilsson called "divergent philosophies with regard to business and creative decisions."[57] Nilsson appointed himself CEO and hired an executive recruitment agency to find a replacement for Hock. But by January 1988, no suitable candidates had been found, so Nilsson decided to take on the job permanently, and in due course he moved his family back again to Los Angeles. During the calendar year 1987, despite the income from Nilsson's advance for *The Telephone*, Hawkeye Entertainment lost over $240,000.[58] When these results were announced, the press reported that Hock was bitter about the experience of being fired. He pointed out in interviews that when he left the company, the shares were trading at thirty-eight cents each and revenue was growing, but by January, with the first reviews of *The Telephone* published, they had dropped to six cents and there was no sales growth whatever.[59]

As the new CEO, Nilsson threw his energy into trying to get a film studio and distributor interested in *Obits*. Undeterred by the poor script-reader reports from Hollywood, he traveled to London in April 1988 to drum up financing, and the innovative production designer Pablo Ferro briefly lent his name to the project. But in the end, nobody was prepared to take the risk on a screenplay of such dubious taste. The experienced producer Si Litvinoff (who had backed Stanley Kubrick's controversial 1971 film *A Clockwork Orange*) was brought in to see if he could help Hawkeye develop some of Nilsson and Southern's other ideas, but he soon got cold feet, saying, "Harry seemed to change his mind every day. He wouldn't show up for meetings. I saw the ship sinking."[60]

Yet the ship remained resolutely afloat after Litvinoff's departure, although it was losing even more alarming quantities of money, reporting a loss in July 1988 of $637,595 and no revenue in the preceding nine months. Eventually, a small amount of income arrived from the production of talking books. Within a couple of years, a modest but distinguished list of these would include Timothy Leary's reading of his autobiography

Flashback and Davy Jones's *They Made a Monkee Out of Me*, but this activity contributed insignificant revenue compared to the amounts that could be derived from film budgets. Yet it seemed that nobody in the movie industry on either side of the Atlantic was prepared to take the risk of backing another Hawkeye script.[61]

Nilsson talked to the press about his frugality in terms of the company's management,[62] but the reality was different. Having become used to his somewhat profligate methods of making records, Nilsson did not balk at hiring public relations companies for simple announcements from Hawkeye, and the firm appears to have employed a considerable number of staff on its nonexistent income. Furthermore, although Nilsson was generally putting his own money into the company, Southern was constantly taking it out in the form of a regular monthly retainer. A Philadelphia lawyer and shareholder in the firm, Eric P. Lipman, who sat on Hawkeye's advisory board, cautioned that Nilsson and Southern were "using the company to finance their pet projects, regardless of whether they would benefit shareholders"[63] The financial manager hired to look after the business was Cindy L. Sims. She effectively also controlled Nilsson's personal finances because she managed his income from recording and publishing royalties, as well as directing the finances of Hawkeye.

Sims had Nilsson's complete confidence, and he was content, as Una Nilsson explained, to hand over all of his financial affairs to her, drawing only small amounts in cash to take care of his and his family's daily needs. Una said:

> Harry trusted his attorney and he trusted his accountant. And he always said to them, "I never want to end up back on Alvorado Street and be poor again. I've been poor. Manage my investments, manage my property." He didn't get involved at all. He said, "You do that."[64]

Sims exuded an air of confident control, and it appeared to insider and outsider alike that she was somehow capable of maintaining financial discipline at Hawkeye despite its inexorable slide into unprofitability. In any case, Nilsson and his family were otherwise preoccupied. Soon after their return to California, they moved to a different house from Eugene Kupper's modernist masterpiece. Una Nilsson recalled:

> First we went back to Bel Air, but the reason we moved to Hidden Hills was that we now had five children and we were sort of bursting at the seams. I wanted them to be in a more traditional home, and to be near the schools and the parks. I always loved to walk. That was the thinking. It wasn't a financial decision to go. So we bought a house on Long Valley Road in Hidden Hills. It was a lovely place to live, a lovely spacious feeling.[65]

Now he was back in Los Angeles full-time after his years on the East Coast, and despite the demands of Hawkeye or of moving to another house, Nilsson made plans to resume his musical career. He began writing a new collection of songs, and far from denying the autobiographical element in his work on which he had always drawn, he now told journalists that he was—and always had been—writing for himself. Consequently, he planned to call the projected new album *Myself*. It was to include a humorous take on what had now become his somewhat heavy personal appearance, "The 245-Pound Man." He also mentioned a song called "U.C.L.A." and another that attempted to combine hip hop with psychoanalysis called "Shrink Rap."[66] He commented that his voice was now lower and huskier than ever before, but he felt that he could use it differently from his younger "choirboy" sound.

Before he managed to advance plans to record his own album, he was invited to Australia to take part in a rock musical based on the Trojan wars called *Paris*, after the prince of Troy who died on the battlefield. Much of the background music, with the London Symphony Orchestra and a band of top British session musicians, had already been recorded in London, but the authors of the show, Jon English and David Mackay, brought most of the singing stars to Australia to overdub the vocal parts. Some of the sessions were done at Sydney Opera House. Nilsson arrived in Sydney on August 19, 1989, and stayed until early September.[67] The cast included Francis Rossi of Status Quo, Demis Roussos, the "Dame Edna Everidge" actor Barry Humphries, and British singer/songwriter Joe Fagin, as well as Nilsson. On his return, he joked to his daughter Olivia "I'm just back from Sydney, the city not the man, where I played Paris, the man not the city."[68] In fact, Nilsson sang the part of Ulysses, and although it is a relatively minor role, his "Prayer" is a remarkable example of what a fine musical theater singer Nilsson might have been. Despite its lower, huskier quality, his voice still has much of its old flexibility, and he sings movingly of life and death before changing gears into his "Jump Into The Fire" rasp for the lines "This war is a tragic folly, we must end it somehow." Despite the best part of ten years spent mainly away from music, Nilsson still had the ability to communicate forcefully in song.

Soon after Nilsson returned from Australia, Graham Chapman died from cancer in England on October 4, 1989. As a tribute to his friend, Nilsson organized an American memorial event, at which Chapman's many California friends could pay their respects. This finally took place in January 1990 at the St. James Club in Los Angeles in association with the local chapter of BAFTA (the British Academy of Film and Television Arts). It was evident from photographs and reports of this event that Nilsson was trying to get his weight under control, as he appeared slimmer than in other recent pictures and told reporters he was "drinking only Coca-Cola."[69] Yet a few months later in the year, he had gone back to drinking alcohol copiously, and he quickly regained the weight he had lost. Around this time he was reunited with another former Python, Eric Idle, who had remained a Los Angeles resident during Nilsson's year on the East Coast. Idle recalled:

> I think at a certain point he became the overweight sweaty Harry and it didn't take
> much to work out that he was trouble. And you'd take the exit. I mean my wife was

heavily pregnant, but he offered her about four lines of blow, and we said, "Hello, Harry! Have you seen this bulge here?" And he went, "Oh I'm so sorry, so sorry...." But he was still very generous and he was very funny.[70]

It was another former Monty Python member whom Nilsson met again in mid-1990 who offered him the chance to make what turned out to be his last commercially issued recording. This was Terry Gilliam, who had gone on from being the animator and cartoonist with *Monty Python's Flying Circus* to become an experienced and versatile film director. He invited Nilsson to sing on the closing credits of *The Fisher King*, which was released in 1991. The song was "How About You," written in 1941 by Ralph Freed and Burton Lane for the soundtrack of the Judy Garland/Mickey Rooney film *Babes on Broadway*. It was a perfect vehicle for Nilsson's mature worldly-wise voice, but in the recording for the soundtrack, he simultaneously managed to summon up the same lightweight nonchalance that had underpinned his work with Gordon Jenkins nearly twenty years earlier. The choice of song was almost accidental, as Gilliam recalled:

> I was shooting in L.A. and had dinner with Harry, somewhere up in Laurel Canyon. There's an Italian restaurant towards the top. I was saying, "I need a song for the end of this film." There had been a song mentioned in the script, but it wasn't right, and he and I just started throwing ideas around. That's how it was, working with Python or anyone really talented. I want to take credit, because I think I was the one that came up with this one, but I won't swear to that. It was a flurry of ideas [until I said] "That's it!" Those things don't happen alone. They happen because two people get together and the ideas come. The idea came, and Harry had to sing it. Ray Cooper, who's been on every film I've done, was involved in the music, and he knew Harry from way back. And we got Harry over [to London]. I remember sitting on the floor at George Fenton's apartment—George wrote the music for the film—just the four of us, trying to get the tempo right. Harry was on the tape recorder. We worked it all out and went into the session. Ray got some really good musicians in and just did it. It was very simple. Just a couple of takes.[71]

This recording took place at C.T.S. Studios in London in February 1991. In the movie, as Jeff Bridges and Robin Williams lie on their backs naked in Central Park, looking up at the sky and the silhouettes of the New York skyscrapers, they begin to sing the song. For the accompanying score, Fenton supplied a symphonic introduction that picks up from the voices of the stars and kicks off the final title sequence. Swirling strings accompany a fireworks display in the sky above Manhattan, but as Nilsson comes in and the credits roll, the performance narrows down to nothing more than his voice accompanied by a rhythm section of organ, bass, and Cooper's subtle percussion. There is a beautiful balance between Nilsson's singing or whistling and some truly exceptional bass playing by Nathan East. Ray Cooper found making the recording an emotional experience:

> We could not finish the film without Harry being in it, there's no question, in the end credits sequence. The whole thing needed wrapping up. It had to be Harry—his heart, his breath, his whistle, and his wonderful voice. So *I Like New York in June*, [*How About You?*] what better song could you get? It just so happened that the Eric Clapton band happened to be in town with Nathan East, so we grabbed him and Harry was here of course. And it was a magical, magical day, with Harry physically struggling. I remember this happening so many times to great artists. You forget they're physically challenged in some way, yet when they get on the platform, they become seventeen, they get rosy cheeks, they become young, naughty men or young wonderful people. As soon as he sat down on his stool in the booth with the headphones on, it was young Harry. He was like his oldest son or his youngest son all wrapped up in one. And the voice was absolutely appropriate for the piece, and I do believe, because I can't walk out of that film until the very last vestige of the final note disappears, that it kept everyone in their seats. They stayed there because of Harry's voice, which is great. And Terry was so overjoyed and relieved because it wouldn't have been the same without Harry.[72]

Cooper's point about the physical challenge Nilsson faced was significant. By this point in early 1991, Nilsson's weight, his drinking, and the years of cocaine intake had seriously taken their toll on his wellbeing. In late August 1990, he had to enter the St. Luke's rehabilitation clinic near Pasadena as a result of a drunk-driving conviction. He had been stopped by officers on July 9 with 0.23 percent alcohol in his blood, three times the legal limit, and he agreed to get treatment, as was reported to the court when the case was finally heard some months later.[73] In a candid letter to the management of the clinic, written during his stay, he confesses that he came in with "resentments and a lot of denial," which, following a bout of flu, made his start uneasy and difficult. But he believed he had made progress with the "third step" and by early September was desperate to be allowed to go home, saying "I am very needed now by my wife and family (not to mention by business)."[74] He was eventually able to leave and return to Una and his children. But even after forsaking brandy for wine and reducing his habitual drug intake, he now moved more slowly and sometimes painfully, and the athletic man who had plucked Annie from a lake or who could shoot a basketball into the hoop from nearly fifty feet away was gone for good.

When he went to London at the very beginning of 1991 for *The Fisher King*, Una was only a few weeks away from giving birth to their fourth son Oscar, who was born on February 23. It was impossible for her to travel with him, not least because there were five other young children still at home. So, because his poor health meant it was a good idea for someone to be with him, his traveling companion was his eldest son Zak. In addition to the various visits he had made to Bel Air or Nyack, Zak had occasionally traveled with his father to other destinations a little farther flung than the childhood visit to Disneyland. A trip to Washington State in the mid-1980s had involved a typical range of Nilsson adventures from being locked out of the hotel to getting drunk with a hitchhiker they picked up on the way, not to mention crashing their rental car into a telephone pole.[75]

When Nilsson was traveling extensively for the anti-handgun crusade in the early 1980s, Zak was among the recipients of his copious letters, written while flying and packed with little jokes and observations. He had also sent Zak a copy of Richard Adams's novel *Watership Down*, which was bought in London and adorned with little drawings and captions by Nilsson. Yet Zak recalled that the trip he made to London at age twenty was the only time that the two of them ever spent a significant amount of time together as adults:

I ended up flying out to London to do the *Fisher King* sessions with him in '91. That turned out to be a really good decision, and I really enjoyed that. He was very comfortable in the studio, that's one setting where he was definitely in his element, and he just did what had to be done. It went pretty smoothly. But for me it was about spending the time with him. I remember at the last night before I had to leave, I had to get up at something like five in the morning to go back to Heathrow [for my flight] and so I decided to stay up all night, because that's sort of what I'd gotten into, staying up all night. I knew Harry did too, so we agreed to stay up all night, just the two of us in the hotel room, talking about whatever. But around four in the morning, he got too tired, and he had to go to sleep, so I left after that.[76]

Nilsson's days of staying up carousing until dawn were over. In mid-February, he returned to the family in Hidden Hills, in time for the birth of Oscar and intending to focus his attention back on the business of Hawkeye. His immediate task was to follow up on the fortunes of a new script he had written called *500 Santas*, in which two homeless men contrive to receive lavish Christmas gifts by sending what appear to be generous presents in stolen Tiffany's bags to the presidents of Fortune 500 companies. They figure that such exalted businessmen simply send reciprocal presents to anyone who sends them something, and the men could then split the proceeds between themselves and their homeless friends. Only Donald Trump sees through the ruse, but is so impressed by it as a business plan that he does not give their game away. The treatment was sent out to commissioning vice presidents at all the main television networks during the time Nilsson was in Britain, along with a draft outline of a sequel to *The Point*.[77]

Cindy Sims was active in all the efforts to get this and other Hawkeye projects bought by network television or film producers. As well as organizing the distribution of scripts and outlines, she reported to Nilsson regularly by memo and telephone, and he felt fully briefed on his company's activities. But unbeknown to him, by April 1991, she had systematically embezzled virtually all his money in a vain attempt to keep the business afloat. Far from being the competent manager he had trusted, for some years she had concealed from Nilsson that the business was in dire trouble and that she had been using his assets, one by one, to keep creditors from his door. "We went to bed one night a financially secure family of eight and woke up the next morning with $300 in our checking account," wrote Nilsson to the court when he was forced to file for bankruptcy.[78] It was a tremendous personal and emotional shock to Nilsson, who had trusted Sims completely. Una Nilsson observed:

> We only found out when Oscar was two months old. And that was really, really hard. But you know, it's not death. Death is much harder than financial setbacks. It's a shock. The biggest shock is knowing that you've been lied to. You're being lied to because you're not being told the truth, even though you're not asking the questions. That really came from the way Harry had set it up, but we completely trusted that person.[79]

According to his attorney Lee Blackman, Nilsson told him that the financial problems were finally discovered when a foreclosure notice was served on the family's new house.[80] The mortgage payments had apparently not been made for some time, and it then emerged that Sims had been hiding previous such notices.[81] With advice from a specialist attorney, Nilsson filed for Chapter Eleven bankruptcy, which offered a degree of protection and gave him time to realize cash from his remaining assets and reorganize his finances in order to meet his obligations to his creditors. There were approximately seventy-five creditors, in addition to the mortgage company who had issued the foreclosure notice, claiming virtually the full $500,000 value of the property.[82] The highest claim came from the IRS, demanding back taxes that Sims had left unpaid, some of which dated from 1979. In addition, there were claims for wrongful dismissal against Hawkeye by a former employee for $650,000; fees for various lawyers handling the bankruptcy and tax arrears amounting to over $50,000; another $50,000 in unpaid alimony to Diane; and—most extraordinarily of all—a claim from Cindy Sims herself for back pay amounting to $350,000.[83] Although his close friends and family were aware of his predicament, the Chapter Eleven arrangement allowed Nilsson to keep his disastrous financial problems private, and the press did not pick up the story. In due course, court proceedings were brought against Sims, and she eventually served two years in jail for grand theft.[84] But when the news first broke, it was kept as quiet as possible. Perry Botkin was one of the few friends to be told, and he was amazed, saying:

> It was the first time with all the drugs and the booze that somebody screwed him. Because she was that way, that accountant, she took advantage of him. She knew she could rob Peter to pay Paul, and do all of that manipulation, because Harry didn't know.... He was hanging out with Terry Southern.[85]

The discovery of Sims's deception, not only of Nilsson, but also of other clients from whom she had stolen to bolster up Hawkeye Entertainment, led to the immediate collapse of the company and the end of Nilsson's association with Southern.[86] Nilsson now needed to demonstrate to the court that in addition to his remaining assets, he had sufficient money coming in from royalties to cover his debts in the long term. His intention, according to Blackman, was to make satisfactory payment arrangements with every legitimate creditor.[87] He also began actively looking for work, going "through my Rolodex 'til the corners are all bent," as he put it in a letter to the court.[88] The house in Bel Air (which Nilsson had not sold when the family moved) was put on the market at $3,995,000, advertised by the Fred Sands Estates agency as an "Architectural Showplace." Nilsson later observed ruefully that "we finally sold the house at half price thanks to bad timing in the market. It was on for a long time and went through four brokers."[89] The Hidden Hills house also had to go in order to meet the foreclosure demands.

But Nilsson was not without friends. Many of those who had been recipients of his generosity in the past now returned the favor. Small gifts and loans eased the passing days as Nilsson and Una anxiously looked for somewhere else to live. In the end, Ringo Starr bought a modest house for the family to live in. It was in Agoura, about ten miles west of their former home in Hidden Hills. They were able to move there, ultimately buying it from him when the situation improved. According to the court documents, Ringo also loaned the family $25,000 in ready cash. Meanwhile, Yoko Ono sent a sizable check to provide what she called "seed money" for his next project, with a very sympathetic letter, saying: "I know you are an exceptionally clever man, and pretty soon you'll hit the goldmine again, be your cocky self, and become obnoxious to all us mortals! Get Going!"[90] But such kindnesses and small royalty checks apart, ultimately it was Nilsson himself who had unwittingly provided the financial security that helped them through the first stages of being penniless. Una Nilsson recalled:

> It was Australia that saved us, because a little while later the land in Australia was sold, and divided between the Australian investors and us, and it came to about $130,000 and that's what we lived on. Because otherwise there just was no money.[91]

Small royalty checks arrived from RCA and his publishers, but these were usually dwarfed by the sheer cost of the bankruptcy proceedings themselves. The shock of sudden bankruptcy, however, tipped Nilsson from indifferent health into becoming a seriously ill man. He became clinically depressed, but in the year 1991/2, he also suffered increasingly from restricted movement caused by neuropathy, developed a painful hiatal hernia, was diagnosed with blood clots in his legs and, more seriously, his lungs (which threatened fatal strokes or heart attacks), as well as developing full-blown diabetes. By the fall of 1992, he had been rushed into the intensive care unit at the hospital three times, twice for blood clots and once for suspected rectal cancer. He felt suicidal, at times just wanting to hide under the bedcovers "hoping that somebody will cover one of my old songs" and suffering wakeful nights and "crying jags." He saw a psychiatrist (whom he'd met because she counseled his childhood friend Jerry Smith for depression, who nevertheless hanged himself in February 1990). She prescribed Prozac for Nilsson, and he was able to function only by taking heavy doses of the drug.[92] While some friends proffered money, others offered company and support. Perry Botkin recalled:

> He ended up in the Valley. I used to go and pick him up there and take him to lunch. And he was in bad shape. He was diabetic. Which I am too, so I knew something about it. He didn't pay any attention to it. He had neuropathy. We would go to a restaurant and I would have to drop him off at the door, and then go park. 'Cos he couldn't make the journey from the car to the restaurant. It was sad. And I saw a lot of him during that time. He always had this plan or that plan.[93]

Yet, maybe not in the way that either he or Botkin envisaged, Nilsson's various plans ultimately saved him and allowed him to settle his debts. He decided he needed a personal manager to rebuild his music career. So he signed up with David Spero, who had been very well known as a radio DJ but had recently turned to artist management after a spell as a senior executive with Columbia Pictures. Spero had just started handling the career of ex-Eagle Joe Walsh, whose solo album *Ordinary Average Guy* was released during 1991, and he was working hard to bring Walsh back together with his fellow former Eagle Glenn Frey, with the intention of getting them back on a lucrative touring circuit. His earlier experience of managing singer and guitarist Michael Stanley in the 1970s meant that Spero was well aware of the way that live concerts could be used to make considerable income for stars with sufficient name recognition. He convinced Nilsson that the only way to bring in the kind of money he so obviously needed was to break his taboo about performing live and go out on the road, singing his hit songs, with the added cachet that he had never done it before. There are letters from Spero written during the course of the summer of 1991 setting up a tour for Nilsson, but this ultimately came to nothing as a result of his acute health problems.[94] Instead, apart from managing to sell a couple of film ideas as short stories, the first tangible project to make a difference to Nilsson's fortunes was a revival of the stage version of *The Point* in Los Angeles.

The show opened at the Chapel Court Theatre on September 21, 1991. Once again, like the first stage version, it was directed by Esquire Jauchem, and coincidentally his new West Coast company was located in a converted church—this time the Hollywood United Methodist Church—just as his earlier Boston company had been. Jauchem had hoped to restage the show well before this, but in the wake of the London productions, there had been some controversy as to who owned the rights. He told the *Los Angeles Times* that this issue had taken "ten years to get resolved,"[95] but for obvious reasons Nilsson was now very anxious to see the play staged, and he helped cut through the forest of red tape that had held Jauchem back. Again, Pierre Vuillemier was the designer, and he produced a new and inventive fluffy, blue Arrow puppet, as well as planning a staging that would involve the cast working around three sides of the audience, thereby inverting the concept of theater in the round by effectively putting the audience in the center of things. The new production was very much a 1990s version of the show, featuring new choreography by Janet Eilber, a live band that veered toward the rock end of the stylistic spectrum, and very ambitious puppets and effects. The bees attacked the audience from above; the three sisters flew over the crowd and were then transformed into an eight-foot-high puppet. There was plenty of foam, bubbles, and colored lighting. According to Nilsson, this production was the outcome of long discussions with Jauchem, and he was "going ahead and staging it as we'd agreed to over the years"⁹⁶

Singer Lee Newman, initially an understudy and then, as the run went on, the actor playing Oblio, traveled back specially from New York to audition when he heard the show was to be presented in Los Angeles. He recalled:

> Harry would come to the rehearsals and oversee it. In fact he would bring Oscar with him on some days. This show, for Los Angeles, was a big deal, because L.A. is not really a theater town. But it ran for six months because it was extended. Of course that's what Harry wanted. He was so delighted to see it on stage—he wanted it to go to Broadway.⁹⁷

The play did not make the transfer to Broadway, but having a professional stage production running for several months in Los Angeles was immensely beneficial to Nilsson as he tried to revive his fortunes, not least because it helped to rekindle interest in the original television film and the RCA soundtrack album. In January 1992, *The Point* was the subject of a special showing at an animation festival in Santa Fe, demonstrating, as the organizers put it, that "animation can often stimulate the imagination in ways that dramatic films can't."⁹⁸

The live production of *The Point* increased interest in the original album, and Nilsson was assisted in the quest to earn income from his back catalog by the release of two other records.

First, a few weeks before he had known of his bankruptcy, he cut a new version of the song "Blanket for a Sail" (originally recorded for *Knnillssonn* and then shoehorned into *The Point*) for the compilation album *For Our Children*, which Walt Disney distributed on behalf of the Pediatric AIDS Foundation. Bob Dylan, Paul McCartney, Brian Wilson, Little Richard, and several other stars donated songs to this album, which was well reviewed, the Associated Press critic noting that Nilsson had "returned from utter obscurity" to contribute.⁹⁹ Although all proceeds of this record went to the Foundation, it nevertheless had the effect of reviving interest in *Knnillssonn*.

Second, Nilsson was helped by the march of technology. Since 1985, the CD revolution had been gathering momentum, and many artists were finding that their old LP records were getting a new lease on life as collectors replaced their vinyl with CDs. In the fall of 1991, although it had been an album Nilsson hated and had precipitated his split from the label, his *All Time Greatest Hits* compilation from RCA was reissued on CD. From the point of view of his finances, the timing could hardly have been better for an anthology of all his best-known songs to appear in the new format.[100] The CD became a convenient calling card for Nilsson himself as he tried to drum up new business, and it triggered a long-running debate between him and RCA over the production of a more comprehensive collection of his earlier work. From the outset of these talks, Nilsson planned a three-CD boxed set, whereas RCA's producer Paul Williams (not the singer/songwriter of the same name) was adamant that it should be no more than a double-CD package, which he estimated would sell many, many more units.

The debate would go on for the best part of two years, but the completion of the anthology was eventually set for early 1994. Nilsson devised a sequence of tracks covering three CDs, picked by musical content and "feel" rather than chronology "to explain who I am to the listening public."[101] He only withdrew his objections and finally gave in to the label's plans for the smaller package at the very start of 1994, when it was clear they would not go along with his ideas. Meanwhile, RCA went to some lengths to restore the original masters into acceptable digital quality for its own selection.

In the interim, Nilsson decided that he had to record a new album. He had toyed with the idea in 1990, as he explained to journalists at the time, but by mid-1991, there was a real imperative to get a new disc made before his health deteriorated further. Yet he had no label deal and no obvious home for a new project. *Flash Harry* (after being issued by Mercury in the U.K.) had more or less disappeared without a trace, and with it any contacts with that firm. In his earlier years, Nilsson had the ear of the most senior executives at RCA. Now, well over a decade after his last new album for that company, and regarded only as a back-catalog artist, he had no leverage to get a new record issued by his main label. Terry Gilliam met him after the release of *The Fisher King* and observed:

> The thing about film and music industries is they have no memory. If you drop off the system for a couple of years, you've vanished. You don't exist anymore. And I think Harry dropped off longer than he ought to have, so it was hard to get back in. He was selling off his library of music, trying to get money. There was a point that really made me sad, when he had all these CDs and was going around to ad agencies trying to sell his songs for commercials, just to get some money. And it went on and on.[102]

In 1990, when Nilsson appeared on the *Flo & Eddie* public radio show and explained that he had sold his piano and guitar, he was driven to their temporary studio on the Universal City Studios lot by Andy Cahan, an ex-member of the Turtles. They immediately struck up an acquaintanceship. When Cahan subsequently built a home studio, he renewed the friendship, so he and Nilsson would meet sporadically during 1991 to 1993 at that studio to record demos of songs. One or two of them, such as "Me, Myself and I," eventually found their way onto movie, television, or commercial soundtracks, whereas others were refinements of the ideas that Nilsson had talked about in his press interviews in 1990, such as "Shrink Rap" and "The 245-Pound Man."

But as 1991 gave way to 1992, as well as the informal projects with Cahan, Nilsson started working on a complete, professionally finished album produced by musician Mark Hudson, who had recently gone through a divorce and was living and working in his own studio. The two had first met in 1969 when Mark's family band, the Hudson Brothers, recorded "I Guess The Lord Must Be In New York City" for Decca, and they had stayed in contact ever since. During the years when Nilsson had been primarily concerned with handgun control, Hudson had repeatedly urged him to return to the studio, but now the impetus of needing to earn money finally propelled him into action.

Nilsson would turn up regularly at Hudson's studio with cassette tapes of new songs that he had been working on at home. Some pieces, according to Hudson, would be broken off for conversations with Ben and Beau; others might be recorded with the television playing in the background.[103] Starting with the lyric to a new song called "Try, Try, Try," Nilsson and Hudson began extracting finished items from the tapes and compiling them into the repertoire for the album. One of the completed songs was "U.C.L.A." This was ultimately brought out by the Nilsson estate's publishing administrator, Warner/Chappell Music, on a limited-edition CD for the industry only called *Perfect Day*. Nilsson had discussed the song in earlier interviews, but in its finished form, it became a complex web of Beatles references, including the lines:

There's no more *Penny Lane*
There's no more *Yesterday*
But something in the way she moves
Keeps me hanging on from Day To Day
There's no more Oyster Bar
There's no more Ringo Starr....

As this song was being written, Mark Hudson was genuinely amazed how, years after his earlier work with Richard Perry or Van Dyke Parks, Nilsson still seemed to be able to conjure up well-turned lyrics such as these almost instantly:

I'd be sitting there writing words with him and he'd do this stuff. And I'd be so envious, going green, I'd say, "Where does this stuff come from?" And he'd say, "I don't know Marky, it just comes out." And he'd be sitting in this haze of cigarette smoke with ashes falling all over the place.[104]

Hudson knew Nilsson's body of work well enough to cajole him into using some of his devices from earlier songs on the new recordings, so that "U.C.L.A." has a vocal leap into the falsetto range and finishes on an overdubbed chorus of "oohs" and "aahs." The other track that Warner/Chappell used from the final (but at the time of writing unreleased) album they worked on together is "Animal Farm," which has a somewhat McCartney-like two-beat accompaniment but is prefaced by some adept Nilsson whistling, much like the beginning of "How About You?" from *The Fisher King*.

With this new music being written and recorded, despite his ongoing health problems, Nilsson believed he could revive his career and—as David Spero had suggested—gradually move into live performing. His work with Hudson and Cahan had given him confidence that his vocal skill was returning, so plans were made to mount a national series of concerts in early 1993. As the time approached, Nilsson became almost cavalier about his health problems. His last spell in the intensive care unit in the fall of 1992 came to an end when he called Van Dyke Parks to "rescue" him. Parks said:

> He decided to leave, so I came, and it was time for me to take him home. I remember
> the nurse running down the hall, "You can't do that! You can't leave." He could leave,
> you know. So we got out of there, he asked me for a cigarette, and I took him home.[105]

With Nilsson back at home, rested, and apparently recovered, memos began flying between the booking agent Wayne Forte at the International Talent Group in New York City and the Los Angeles attorney Candice Hanson, who was representing Nilsson's interests as a live performer. In turn, she was liaising with Paul Williams at RCA to ensure that the repertoire for the tour would be consistent with the tracks planned for inclusion on the Nilsson retrospective two-CD set. On February 12, 1993, Forte wrote, suggesting that Nilsson appear in a range of U.S. and Canadian cities, including Toronto, Vancouver, Boston, New York, Philadelphia, Washington, and Detroit. By the time Hanson replied two days later, unknown to her, Nilsson had already suffered a massive heart attack, which occurred on February 14.[106]

Nilsson was rushed to the Cedars-Sinai Medical Center, and his life was saved. By the following weekend, the papers reported that he was "in fair condition,"[107] and he was eventually well enough for Parks, once again, to rescue him and take him home. But any possibility of a series of live concerts was now out of the question. For the remaining eleven months of his life, Nilsson was a seriously sick man. Una Nilsson faced the future philosophically:

> I think we did know the end was coming. But somewhat for the children and some-
> what for ourselves, we just decided to live every day as if we were going to live on
> together. But it was a limited life because he was very tired. And it was very hard for
> him to walk. When you have a compromised heart, it's hard to walk. He used to love
> to walk when he was younger. I remember, in London, he used to walk at night and he
> would do things like count the trees in the squares, and then show off the next day, ask-
> ing, "How many trees are in Berkeley Square?" And the answer would be "Thirty-three
> and a sapling." He loved to do things like that. Something nobody else would do.[108]

In the months following his release from the hospital, Nilsson continued to meet Mark Hudson and slowly, painfully, carry on working on the new album. He gave several interviews in which he looked back over his life, and he began dictating an autobiography, which he never finished. Between times, he would still get together with old friends such as Van Dyke Parks, Perry Botkin, and Jimmy Webb, but he was no longer drinking even wine or taking the drugs that had been such a regular part of his life for so long. The dramatic transformation in his physical appearance was noticed by everyone who knew him, but it was most shocking to his children. Annie Nilsson said:

> I think being eleven, I had a sense of what was going on, and I avoided him. I was very scared. He had an oxygen tank in his room, and hundreds of pills that he had to swallow on the hour. It was such a strange image to contrast with this hero figure that I had known, my strong amazing father. His hair was getting gray. It was just this awful image, and so I think I really hid from him for the last few months. I don't have strong memories of it, except just fear, and watching him deteriorate, which I couldn't handle.[109]

His second daughter Olivia also recalled the last months, when the vital, funny father she had known was gradually slipping away. She said:

> I remember him being in bed a lot and sick, and us kids would bring him a big glass of water. He was the only person I ever met who liked to drink milk with ice and he'd ask for that. And his feet were always hurting because he had neuropathy. And, so I remember him just being weakened, and when he did walk, he had to have a cane.[110]

At Christmas in 1993, Nilsson and his family were invited to spend the holidays with the artist E. J. Gold, who had photographed Nilsson in the 1960s and later produced a series of paintings inspired by "The Moonbeam Song." Gold lived near Grass Valley in Northern California, some twenty miles or so northeast of Sacramento. Una was concerned about the effect of a flight on Nilsson's health, but in the end, she and Nilsson felt that the children might enjoy spending Christmas in a log cabin in the foothills of the mountains, so they agreed that the family would go. Some home movies exist of a tired-looking Nilsson sitting around the dining table and talking to Gold and other members of his artists' community. The subject often turned to Nilsson's own mortality. He also listened to some of his old records, commenting on them as he looked back at the past.

A few days after his return to Los Angeles at the very start of 1994, Nilsson was interviewed by the writer Dawn Eden. She had been commissioned to write the liner notes to his RCA retrospective collection. In the tapes of her conversations with him, Nilsson began by reading some of the finished segments of his autobiography to her and then answered her questions, in effect authoring a short version of his life story that would become the extensive booklet for his *Personal Best* album. Eden went on to transcribe more of the interview for a long article in *Goldmine* magazine. Pallid, still overweight, moving slowly, and with a throaty wheeze, Nilsson recounted his recollections because he seemed to have a premonition that the chances of doing so were diminishing fast.

A day or two after Eden interviewed Nilsson, he and Una met Jimmy Webb and his wife for dinner at The Ivy in Santa Monica. At this point, Nilsson had more or less given up his battle with RCA to release his own three-CD selection of his work. It seems that with this very personal anthology in mind, Nilsson persuaded Webb to join him in his car afterward, as the women made their own way home. Webb recalled:

> He drove me over in front of the Loew's Hotel and he said, "I just want you to listen to this with me." He had two or three tapes, and he took them out and put them in the sound system. We started to listen to Harry's songs, and we must have listened for a couple of hours. He played them one after the other: new ones, old ones, some that I had heard before, some that I knew that he had written that hadn't gotten recorded that he had wanted to record, some that he hadn't finished. But they were all wry and tender and funny, and vulnerable and sweet and sour at the same time. It got to the end and the tape player clicked, and it was silent in the car, and we looked around, and Santa Monica was quiet. There were no cars on the street, and it was just me and Harry in the car. He said, "Well, that's my life's work. Thanks for listening." And that's the last time I saw him.[111]

Nilsson went home and resumed his low-key life, resting and working on the anthology and more future plans, including short stories. He had a tale accepted for publication by *Galaxy* magazine that he had written for his sons, "The Boy That Always Said 'No,' "[112] and he had roughed out further stories. But on Saturday January 15, he told Una he felt unwell. She said:

> He had a toothache that afternoon, and he needed a dentist. He should have gone to our regular dentist, or he should have gone to a hospital to have the tooth removed. But he used the service, 1-800-DENTIST, because it was Saturday and his regular dentist wasn't working that day. They sent him to an oral surgeon, who took the tooth out. And he came home.
>
> That Saturday night, there was a movie I wanted to see on TV, and we were in bed watching it. And then I started to fall asleep and I said to Harry, "Oh, I can't stay awake for the end of the movie, goodnight."
>
> And that's when he rolled over to say goodnight and he said, "I want you to know I love you so much, so much." And that was the last thing he ever said.[113]

12

EPILOGUE

TWO DAYS AFTER Nilsson's death, at 4:10 a.m. on January 17, 1994, Los Angeles was struck by a massive earthquake. The epicenter was in the Resada district in the San Fernando Valley, but areas in a range of over eighty miles were badly affected. As well as buildings collapsing, many of the freeways were so severely damaged that most of the major roads had to be closed down, bringing the normally traffic-heavy city to a virtual standstill. Nilsson's funeral took place against a backdrop of destruction on a vast scale, with estimated damage running into billions of dollars. Yet by some quirk, the freeway to the Valley Oaks Memorial Park near Nilsson's home in Agoura remained largely undamaged, and so it was possible for mourners to get to his funeral.

Those who made the journey found it a slightly eerie experience, with so much devastation along the route to the cemetery. Micky Dolenz remembered the funeral itself starting as a very quiet, sober affair, and quite a contrast to the riotous times he had enjoyed with Nilsson during his life.[1] Jimmy Webb gave the main eulogy, a particularly painful task for him as apparently Nilsson had been intending to hear him perform at the Roxy on Friday the 14th, but had begged off with the toothache, so what would have been their final meeting never happened. Yet despite the intensity of his grief, Webb dug deep into his store of memories of his long-term best friend and recalled many a hilarious event, soon bringing a touch of gaiety and laughter to the proceedings. "We laughed a lot," recalled Perry Botkin, "because there are so many memories about Harry that were so funny, and so off the wall."[2] As the speeches were made, earth tremors could still be felt, as Gerry Beckley recalled:

Throughout the whole ceremony, Harry was lying there in the open casket. There's all of these aftershocks, and the ground was shaking and Jimmy talking. . . . I'd never been to a funeral before in my life, so that tells you what Harry meant to me. But I suppose people are very sad at funerals, all sorts of different emotions come out.

I was actually happy that I was there. It just seemed so fitting. It was a nice variety of people that I knew to be very close with Harry. But the ground was shaking as we laid him to rest.[3]

When Perry Botkin looked at Nilsson in the open casket before the interment, he felt that the one thing missing was the trademark pair of dark glasses that Nilsson had habitually worn for many years. More than one mourner at the graveside joked that the earthquake and its aftershocks were the consequence of Nilsson getting to heaven and finding the bars closed.

The more intrepid of his friends were not deterred from coming by a mere natural disaster. Nilsson's long-term publisher Terry Oates and his wife Mandy actually made the trip from Britain, although they were slightly concerned as they left London that they might find it impossible to land in Los Angeles. Overall, most of Nilsson's closest friends and family members made it to the cemetery. But among those who did not, his home having been seriously affected by the earthquake, was Eric Idle. Remarkably, the funeral came to him:

I thought, "Well, he won't be there. What's the point?"

And then there was a ring at the door, and it was George Harrison and all the guys that had been to the funeral, and they wanted me to cheer them up, because that's what comedians do, is cheer people up in the face of death. And we had a bit of a drink to him. It was fun to see everybody, and they told me one or two of the jokes at the funeral, such as Allan Katz, just as they were lowering the coffin, said, "Oh, Harry did mention to me that he wanted me to have his royalties."[4]

The gathering finally broke up, rather sadly summed up by Perry Botkin as "a lot of people that hadn't seen each other in a long time, who got together and said, 'Oh, we must get together,' and never did."[5]

By the end of January, Nilsson's permanent legacy was already being established. His death created widespread interest in his earlier work in a way that the flurry of press reports following his 1993 heart attack had not. RCA immediately re-promoted the *All Time Greatest Hits* CD, so that new reviews of it appeared nationally, and it was viewed by the marketing team as a stepping stone to the forthcoming appearance of the *Personal Best* anthology. Most reviewers endorsed the sentiment expressed by the *Los Angeles Times*: "It's doubly sad that Harry Nilsson died last week, before he had a chance to reclaim the reputation he established two decades ago as one of the finest singer-songwriters of the pop-music era."[6]

At the American Music Awards on February 7, three weeks after his death, Nilsson was seen in a public service video he had shot in early January with Ringo Starr, driving a sporty-looking Dodge Viper. Featuring the two of them singing the Beatles' song "Drive My Car," the promotion was part of a national campaign called Rockers Against Drunk

Driving, or RADD.[7] Despite his death, the Nilsson family decided that the campaign should continue, and full-page press advertisements showing Nilsson and Ringo together appeared in newspapers across the country during February, sponsored by the Chrysler Corporation.[8]

Although rumors were rife that Mark Hudson would imminently release Nilsson's final recording under the title *Harry's Got a Brown New Robe*, not least because Nilsson had telephoned David Spero on January 12 sounding very "up and excited"[9] that he had just finished recording the songs, nothing appeared. With the exception of the two songs released by Warner/Chappell, nothing has come out since. But in April 1994, the RCA *Personal Best* anthology was released, and it was immediately heavily promoted. Some critics remained bemused by the sheer variety and range of Nilsson's work. But whereas this had once made him impossible to categorize and hard to sell, the very breadth of his output was now seen as a selling point in itself, as the *Los Angeles Times* reviewer Dennis Hunt put it:

> His wildly eclectic musical tastes ranged from basic rock to folk-rock to flowery pop and even to quirky ditties. Fluent in many styles, he can sound Beatle-esque, slip into a soulful mode or even mimic a crooner of the '20s.[10]

Dawn Eden's liner notes and her extended version of them in *Goldmine* were the start of a lengthy process of re-evaluating Nilsson's work, culminating in a reissue series from RCA that, by the end of the decade, saw almost all his original albums re-released, often with additional tracks and ephemera. Hand in glove with this came journalistic reappraisals with a series of occasional articles in the music press surveying his career, starting in May 1995 with a lengthy assessment in the record collectors' magazine *Discoveries*.[11]

The RCA series of reissues dealt with the majority of Nilsson's own recordings, but another project, intended to focus on Nilsson's gifts as a songwriter, had just gotten started when he died. This was the brainchild of Al Kooper, who had covered "Without Her" back in 1967 with Blood, Sweat and Tears, and later made his own version of "Mournin' Glory Story." Kooper visited Nilsson shortly after the 1993 heart attack and learned of his desperate financial plight. He got together with the seasoned producer Danny Kapilian with the idea of persuading Nilsson's friends and colleagues to record a collection of his finest songs. With some trepidation, Kooper approached Nilsson to seek his blessing for the project. "I dialed Harry and had one of the most heartwarming conversations of this half-century," he recalled. "He was thrilled! He was flattered! He suggested a favorite band of his, Jellyfish, be included."[12]

Four months into the project, Nilsson died. Consequently, Kapilian and Kooper slightly raised their sights and approached Ringo Starr, Randy Newman, Jimmy Webb, Gerry Beckley, and Brian Wilson, among others, to create what would, in effect, be a memorial album to Nilsson. At Una's suggestion, they agreed to donate all royalties from the project to the Coalition to Stop Gun Violence. The resulting album, *For the Love of*

Harry, appeared in 1995 and did an effective job of reminding the world of what Derek Taylor referred to as the "capacity to endure" of the songs Nilsson had written.[13] The album is bookended by Randy Newman's very personal version of "Remember (Christmas)" and Jimmy Webb's "Lifeline." Brian Wilson sings his favorite Nilsson song "This Could Be The Night" and Kooper himself bravely tackles "Salmon Falls." The twenty-three tracks receive performances of such stature that they belie Perry Botkin's observation that only Nilsson could effectively interpret his own songs. Yet the continued use of his own recordings in films and television commercials shows that the individual vision he brought to all his work still has a place in the contemporary musical landscape.

The renewal of interest in his work and the sales of the *Personal Best* anthology led to a revival in Nilsson's fortunes in the months after his death. On August 26, 1994, the Bankruptcy Court of the Central District of California formally closed the Chapter Eleven bankruptcy case. Nilsson's debts were discharged.[14]

In most of the obituaries that appeared at the time, Nilsson's career was summed up by mentioning his two Grammy-winning records, with the suggestion that thereafter he went into an inexorable downturn of self-destruction and failed to capitalize on his potential. In many interviews, Nilsson himself appeared to take a similar view, telling the BBC in London:

I've fulfilled most of my expectations, I've been disappointed at certain times, I mean, being relegated to having sung "Everybody's Talkin'" and "Without You" ain't exactly what I set out to do. In a lot of people's minds, that's where it's gonna end up.[15]

The process of revaluing his output begun by Dawn Eden has changed that. Derek Taylor's perceptive observation that "1941" was genuinely something new has thrown attention back to the emotional and lyrical depths of his early work. The subject matter exploring personal loss, early love, and absentee fathers is balanced by one of the most glorious voices in pop music. The Newman record stretched studio technique to its limits, trying overdubbing experiments that went beyond anything else of the period. The Richard Perry albums broke new ground in everything from recording technology to the stylistic range of their content.

The later RCA albums never gave up on experimentation, and whether it was a case of drawing three generations of music-makers together under the baton of Gordon Jenkins and beginning the—now very fashionable—return to the great American songbook, or trying new fusions of Caribbean sounds with Van Dyke Parks and Robert Greenidge, Nilsson now seems to have been in on the ground floor of two of the most enduring movements in pop, namely heritage and world music. His stage and screen work broke new ground too, fusing lively animation with guileless musical invention. His RCA albums have not been out of print since his death.

Yet the paradox that was Nilsson remains: Pop artist or recluse? Family man or hell-raiser? Dazzling singer or profound songwriter? Comedian or tragedian?

Nilsson was all those things and more, and he packed as much into his fifty two and a half years than most musicians could hope to manage in a far longer lifespan. Many listeners will still recognize his name only from his two great hits. But his body of work is far more substantial than that. Until the collapse of Hawkeye Entertainment, which broke him in every sense, Nilsson proved that he could live the rock and roll lifestyle and yet remain a private family man. By refusing to appear live, yet competing on level terms with the greatest recording artists of the 1960s and '70s, he also proved that it was possible to have a successful pop career on one's own terms, to avoid being dictated to by the industry, to challenge convention, and to leave a legacy that stands proudly as one of the most individual and creative collections of work in the second half of the twentieth century.

Albums

AS A GUIDE to the music discussed in this book, this lists the original album issues of Nilsson's work, the tracks they originally contained, and the year of release.

SPOTLIGHT ON NILSSON (TOWER) 1966

The Path That Leads to Trouble
Good Times
So You Think You've Got Troubles
I'm Gonna Lose My Mind
She's Yours
Sixteen Tons
Born in Grenada
You Can't Take Your Love (Away from Me)
Growin' Up
Do You Believe

PANDEMONIUM SHADOW SHOW (RCA) 1967

Ten Little Indians
1941

Cuddly Toy
She Sang Hymns Out of Tune
You Can't Do That
Sleep Late My Lady Friend
She's Leaving Home
There Will Never Be
Without Her
Freckles
It's Been So Long
River Deep—Mountain High

AERIAL BALLET (RCA) 1968

Daddy's Song (deleted from LP after first release)
Good Old Desk
Don't Leave Me, Baby
Mr. Richland's Favorite Song
Little Cowboy
Together
Everybody's Talkin'
I Said Goodbye to Me
Little Cowboy (ii)
Mr. Tinker
One
The Wailing of the Willow
Bath

SKIDOO (RCA) 1968 (SOUNDTRACK ALBUM)

The Cast and Crew
I Will Take You There
Skidoo/Commercials
Goodnight Mr. Banks/Let's Get the Hardware/Murder in the Carwash
Angie's Suite
The Tree
Garbage Can Ballet
Tony's Trip
Escape: Impossible/Green Bay Packers' March
Man Wasn't Meant to Fly

Escape: Possible
Skidoo/Goodnight Mr. Banks

HARRY (RCA) 1969

The Puppy Song
Nobody Cares About the Railroads Any More
Open Your Window
Mother Nature's Son
Fairfax Rag
City Life
Mournin' Glory Story
Maybe
Marchin' Down Broadway
I Guess the Lord Must Be in New York City
Rainmaker
Mr. Bojangles
Simon Smith and the Amazing Dancing Bear

NILSSON SINGS NEWMAN (RCA) 1970

Vine St.
Love Story
Yellow Man
Caroline
Cowboy
The Beehive State
I'll Be Home
Living Without You
Dayton Ohio 1903
So Long Dad

THE POINT (RCA) 1971

Everything's Got 'Em
The Town (narration)
Me and My Arrow
The Game (narration)
Poli High

The Trial and Banishment (narration)
Think About Your Troubles
The Pointed Man (narration)
Life Line
The Birds (narration)
P.O.V. Waltz
The Clearing in the Woods (narration)
Are You Sleeping?
Oblio's Return (narration)

AERIAL PANDEMONIUM BALLET (RCA) 1971 (EDITED AND REMIXED VERSION OF
PANDEMONIUM SHADOW SHOW AND AERIAL BALLET)

Introduction
1941
Daddy's Song
Mr. Richland's Favorite Song
Good Old Desk
Everybody's Talkin'
Bath
Fill
River Deep—Mountain High
Sleep Late My Lady Friend
Don't Leave Me, Baby
Without Her
Together
One
Closing

NILSSON SCHMILSSON (RCA) 1971

Gotta Get Up
Driving Along
Early In The Morning
The Moonbeam Song
Down
Without You
Coconut
Let the Good Times Roll
Jump Into the Fire

I'll Never Leave You

SON OF SCHMILSSON (RCA) 1972

Take 54
Remember (Christmas)
Turn On Your Radio
You're Breaking My Heart
Spaceman
The Lottery Song
At My Front Door
Ambush
I'd Rather Be Dead
The Most Beautiful World in the World

A LITTLE TOUCH OF SCHMILSSON IN THE NIGHT (RCA) 1973

Lazy Moon
For Me and My Gal
It Had to Be You
Always
Makin' Whoopee!
You Made Me Love You
Lullaby in Ragtime
I Wonder Who's Kissing Her Now
What'll I Do?
Nevertheless (I'm In Love With You)
This Is All I Ask
As Time Goes By

SON OF DRACULA (RAPPLE) 1974

It Is He Who Will Be King
Daybreak
At My Front Door
Count Downe Meets Merlin and Amber
The Moonbeam Song
Perhaps This Is All a Dream
Remember (Christmas)

Intro/Without You
The Count's Vulnerability
Down
Frankenstein, Merlin and the Operation
Jump Into the Fire
The Abduction of Count Downe
The End (Moonbeam)

PUSSY CATS (RCA) 1974

Many Rivers to Cross
Subterranean Homesick Blues
Don't Forget Me
All My Life
Old Forgotten Soldier
Save the Last Dance for Me
Mucho Mungo/Mt. Elga
Loop de Loop
Black Sails
Rock Around the Clock

DUIT ON MON DEI (RCA) 1975

Jesus Christ You're Tall
It's a Jungle Out There
Down By the Sea
Kojak Columbo
Easier for Me
Turn Out the Light
Salmon Falls
Puget Sound
What's Your Sign?
Home
Good for God

SANDMAN (RCA) 1976

I'll Take a Tango
Something True

Pretty Soon There'll Be Nothing Left for Everybody
The Ivy Covered Walls
(Thursday) Here's Why I Did Not Go to Work Today
The Flying Saucer Song
How to Write a Song
Jesus Christ You're Tall
Will She Miss Me

…THAT'S THE WAY IT IS (RCA) 1976

That Is All
Just One Look/Baby I'm Yours
Moonshine Bandit
I Need You
A Thousand Miles Away
Sail Away
She Sits Down On Me
Daylight Has Caught Me
Zombie Jamboree
That Is All (Reprise)

KNNILLSSONN (RCA) 1977

All I Think About Is You
I Never Thought I'd Get This Lonely
Who Done It?
Lean On Me
Goin' Down
Old Bones
Sweet Surrender
Blanket for a Sail
Laughin' Man
Perfect Day

POPEYE (BOARDWALK) 1980 (SOUNDTRACK ALBUM)

I Yam What I Yam
He Needs Me
Swee' Pea's Lullaby
Din' We

Sweethaven
Blow Me Down
Sailin'
It's Not Easy Bein' Me
He's Large
I'm Mean
Kids
I'm Popeye the Sailor Man

FLASH HARRY (MERCURY) 1980

Harry (sung by Eric Idle and Charlie Dore)
Cheek to Cheek
Best Move
Old Dirt Road
I Don't Need To
Rain
I've Got It
It's So Easy
How Long Can Disco On
Bright Side of Life

A TOUCH MORE SCHMILSSON IN THE NIGHT (RCA) RECORDED 1973,
RELEASED 1988

I'm Always Chasing Rainbows
Make Believe
You Made Me Love You (alternate take)
Trust In Me
Lullaby in Ragtime (alternate take)
All I Think About Is You (from Knnillssonn)
Perfect Day (from Knnillssonn)
Always (alternate take)
It's Only a Paper Moon
It Had to Be You (alternate take)
Thanks for the Memory
Over the Rainbow

Notes

PREFACE

1. Author's interview with Richard Perry for BBC Radio, 2005.

2. Joyce Haber, "Harry Nilsson—A Square in Hip Circles," *Los Angeles Times* [undated clipping from July 1968 in Nilsson scrapbooks].

3. *High Fidelity*, November 1968.

4. Barrett Hansen, "Aerial Ballet," *Rolling Stone*, September 14, 1968.

5. Derek Taylor, *Nilsson Aerial Ballet* [liner notes to RCA SF 7973, 1968].

6. Robert Kimball and Abigail Kuflik, "Harry Nilsson," *Stereo Review*, September 1973, p. 66.

7. Ibid.

8. Zak Nilsson interviewed by John Scheinfeld for LSL Productions, 2006.

CHAPTER I

1. Harry Nilsson Sr. was born on January 20, 1917. Harry Edward Nilsson III's birth certificate lists his father's age as twenty-five, but this is a year off. In various sources, Nilsson's name has been spelled as "Nelson," but this has no basis in fact.

2. Nilsson draft autobiography, p. 18.

3. Author's interview with Gary Nilsson, July 10, 2011. This confirmed Harry Nilsson Sr.'s occupation in the merchant marines, a fact that is noted on his gravestone in Palatka, Florida, where he died on November 25, 1975.

4. Craig Steven Wilder, *A Covenant with Color—Race and Social Power in Brooklyn*, p. 196.

5. *The Oral Autobiography of Harry Nilsson*, p. 63.

6. Nilsson draft autobiography, p. 19.

7. Letter from Gary Nilsson to the author, July 12, 2011.

8. Van Dyke Parks interviewed by John Scheinfeld for LSL Productions, 2003.

9. Jimmy Webb interviewed by John Scheinfeld for LSL Productions, 2003.

10. Harry Nilsson interviewed by Stuart Grundy for BBC Radio, 1977.

11. Dawn Eden, "One Last Touch of Nilsson," *Goldmine*, vol. 20, no. 9, issue 359, April 29, 1994.

12. Nilsson draft autobiography, p. 10.

13. Ibid., p. 21.

14. Diane Nilsson interviewed by David Leaf for LSL Productions, 2005.

15. Nilsson draft autobiography, p. 20.

16. Van Dyke Parks interviewed by Stuart Grundy for BBC Radio 2, broadcast February 8, 1997; Parks/Scheinfeld, 2003.

17. Nilsson draft autobiography, p. 62.

18. *The Oral Autobiography of Harry Nilsson*, p. 63.

19. Nilsson/Grundy, 1997.

20. Zak Nilsson interviewed by John Scheinfeld, 2004.

21. Mr. Bonzai, "Adventures of Harry Nilsson," *Mix*, vol. 7, no. 5, May 1983, p. 74.

22. Nilsson draft autobiography, p. 63.

23. Ibid., p. 64.

24. *The Oral Autobiography of Harry Nilsson*, p. 63.

25. Ibid.

26. Ibid.

27. Ibid.

28. Nilsson draft autobiography, p. 4.

29. Joyce Haber, "Harry Nilsson—A Square in Hip Circles," *Los Angeles Times* [undated clipping from July 1968 in Nilsson scrapbooks].

30. Nilsson/Grundy, 1977.

31. Nilsson draft autobiography, p. 2.

32. Ibid., p. 7

33. Ibid., p. 8.

34. Ibid., p. 5.

35. Ibid., p. 6.

36. Joyce Haber, op. cit.

37. *The Oral Autobiography of Harry Nilsson*, p. 83.

38. Nilsson draft autobiography, p. 12.

39. Dawn Eden, "The Harry Nilsson Anthology" [liner note to RCA 66354-2/4, 1994].

40. Robert Kimball and Abigail Kuflik, "Harry Nilsson," *Stereo Review*, September 1973, p. 63.

41. Joyce Haber, op. cit.

42. Nilsson draft autobiography, p. 11.

43. Ibid., p. 11.

44. Ibid., p. 12.

45. Ibid., p. 13.

46. Ibid., p. 16.

47. Kurt Lassen, "A Banker Cashes In On Music," *Palatka Daily News*, March 6, 1969.

48. Dawn Eden, "One Last Touch of Nilsson."

49. Nilsson draft autobiography, p. 16.

50. Ibid., p. 17.

51. Webb/Scheinfeld, 2003.

52. Stephen E. Kercher, *Revel with a Cause: Liberal Satire in Postwar America*, p. 409.

53. Joyce Haber, op. cit.

54. Robert Kimball and Abigail Kuflik, op. cit.

55. Eugene N. White, *The Comptroller and the Transformation of American Banking 1960–1990*, p. 20.

56. David Sanjek, "Leeds Music Corporation," in Shepherd, Horn, et al., *Continuum Encyclopedia of Popular Music of the World, Vol. 1: Media, industry and society*, p. 558.

57. Turner quoted in Peter Doggett, "Harry Nilsson: the Debut Sessions" [liner note to *Nilsson '62*, Retro 804, 1995].

58. Doggett (ibid.) says American Studios, but the online obituary of Turner by Ian McFarlane [http://launch.groups.yahoo.com/group/spectropop/message/45224, accessed July 2010] suggests Gold Star. The acoustic of some tracks—notably "There's Gotta Be a Girl"—suggests that Gold Star is more likely.

CHAPTER 2

1. Diane Nilsson interviewed by David Leaf for LSL Productions, 2005.

2. Michelle Stralibing, "Nilsson Speaks," *TeenSet* [undated clipping circa 1968 in Nilsson files].

3. Nilsson draft autobiography, p. 75.

4. Lewis Segal, "Everybody's Talking About Harry Nilsson: Can a successful writer-composer-performer-producer remain in, but not of, the music business?" *Entertainment World*, December 5, 1969, p. 7.

5. Michelle Stralibing, op. cit.

6. Turner quoted in Peter Doggett, "Harry Nilsson: the Debut Sessions" [liner note to *Nilsson '62*, Retro 804, 1995].

7. Tom Nolan, "Nilsson, Randy Newman, Gordon Alexander: Bittersweet Romantics in a Hard Rock Candyland," *Eye*, December 1968, p. 44.

8. Peter Doggett, op. cit.

9. "I remember getting a check for $5 as an advance for a song I co-wrote that appeared on a Randy Sparks album." Nilsson quoted in Barry Alfonso, "The slightly warped Popeye of Harry Nilsson," *Songwriter*, March 1981, p. 24. Check from New Christy Minstrel Publishing Co. dated August 16, 1966, in Nilsson's business files.

10. http://fortheloveofharry.blogspot.com/2010/12/new-christy-minstrels-travelin-man-1963.html [accessed July 11, 2011].

11. Copyright dates for this and all Nilsson songs up to 1973 are from a letter to Nilsson's lawyers, Segel, Rubinstein and Gordon, from the Copyright Office of the Library of Congress, dated October 4, 1973.

12. Mr. Bonzai, "Adventures of Harry Nilsson," *Mix*, Vol. 7, No. 5, May 1983, p. 74; Tom Nolan, op. cit., p. 44.

13. Dawn Eden, "The Harry Nilsson Anthology."

14. Buddy Lewis, "Country Music has lost a great talent," obituary post for Buddy Lewis at http://buddylewismusic.com/news.html from April 17, 2007.

15. Dawn Eden, "The Harry Nilsson Anthology."

16. Harry Nilsson interviewed by Stuart Grundy for BBC Radio, 1977.

17. Jacoba Atlas, "An Underground Artist Surfaces," *Beat*, January 27, 1968; Barry Alfonso, op. cit.

18. Mr. Bonzai, op. cit., p. 74.

19. A. J. Morgan, "Nilsson—Dracula Meets the Sandman," *Circus*, October 1975, no. 120, p. 50.

20. Dawn Eden, "One Last Touch of Nilsson."

21. David Litchfield, "Harry Nilsson and Litchfield," *Ritz*, March 1985, no. 97, p. 28.

22. "It Just Ain't Right," "Learning From You," "Oh Caroline," "Take This Heart," "There's Gotta Be a Girl," and "Building Me Up."

23. "Marascalco: Atlantic Deal," *Billboard*, June 5, 1965, p. 6.

24. Dawn Eden, "One Last Touch of Nilsson."

25. "(All For The Beatles) Stand Up and Holler" was copyrighted on May 20, 1964.

26. Ibid.

27. "D'You Wanna (Have Some Fun)?" copyrighted August 3, 1964. It was copyrighted in Nilsson's sole name, but registered at BMI as a joint composition with Marascalco. "Groovy Little Susie" (spelled with an "s" and not the "z" of Bo Pete's record label) was registered under Marascalco's sole name, although Nilsson told Dawn Eden (op. cit.) that it was a joint composition.

28. Dawn Eden, "The Harry Nilsson Anthology."

29. Dawn Eden, "One Last Touch of Nilsson."

30. *The Oral Autobiography of Harry Nilsson*, p. 78. The book referred to is McCabe, *Mr. Laurel and Mr. Hardy*.

31. Marriage date confirmed in a letter from Nilsson's lawyer, Lee Blackman, July 30, 2010.

32. *The Oral Autobiography of Harry Nilsson*.

33. Ibid.

34. Doug Hoefer interviewed by John Scheinfeld for LSL Productions, 2005.

35. "Pop special merit: Jan Berry in Jan and Dean's Pop Symphony No. 1," *Billboard*, September 25, 1965, p. 42.

36. "Cavalier of the month: Nilsson," *Cavalier,* May 1969, p. 69.

37. Perry Botkin Jr., interviewed by the author, February 21, 2011; and interviewed by Stuart Grundy for BBC Radio, February 1997. In a 2003 interview with John Scheinfeld, Botkin suggests Nilsson was paid $50 per week, but I have gone with the $25 of the earlier interview as it was closer in time to the events described.

38. Perry Botkin Jr. interviewed by John Scheinfeld and Lee Blackman for LSL Productions, 2003.

39. Barry Alfonso, op. cit.

40. Dawn Eden, "One Last Touch of Nilsson."

41. Letter to the author from Perry Botkin Jr., August 6, 2010.

42. Botkin/Scheinfeld/Blackman, 2003.

43. Author's interview with Lee Blackman, March 1, 2011.

44. Letter to the author from Perry Botkin Jr., August 6, 2010.

45. Dawn Eden, "The Harry Nilsson Anthology."

46. Ibid.; author's interview with Perry Botkin Jr., February 21, 2011.

47. Barry Alfonso, op. cit.

48. Ibid.; Dawn Eden, "One Last Touch of Nilsson."

49. Online obituary of Turner by Ian McFarlane [http://launch.groups.yahoo.com/group/spectropop/message/45224, accessed July 2010].

50. Tom Wolfe, "The First Tycoon of Teen," *New York Herald Tribune*, January 3, 1965.

51. Ribowsky, *He's a Rebel—Phil Spector: Rock and Roll's Legendary Producer*, p. 34.

52. Ibid., p. 205.

53. Ibid.; Brown, *Tearing Down The Wall of Sound—The Rise and Fall of Phil Spector*, p. 193.

54. Brian Wilson interviewed by John Scheinfeld for LSL Productions, 2004.

55. Brown, op. cit.; http://fortheloveofharry.blogspot.com/2008/04/this-could-be-night-acetate-1964-65.html (accessed August 6, 2010).

56. Author's interview with Perry Botkin, February 21, 2011.

57. This is discussed in the Nilsson chapter in Courrier, *Randy Newman's American Dreams*, p. 115. See also Dawn Eden, op. cit.

58. Dawn Eden, "One Last Touch of Nilsson."

59. Rich Du Brow, "Nilsson—Quiet Man with a Big Talent," *Palatka, Fla. Daily News*, December 18, 1968, 11.

60. Botkin/Scheinfeld/Blackman, 2003.

61. Ibid.

62. Jackson, *Garcia: An American Life*, p. 116.

63. Rick Jarrard interviewed by John Scheinfeld for LSL Productions, 2003.

64. Ibid.

65. Nilsson/Grundy, 1977.

66. Contract examined by Lee Blackman, March 3, 2011.

67. Nilsson/Grundy, 1977.

68. Kubernik, Calamar, Diltz, and Adler, *Canyon of Dreams: The Magic and the Music of Laurel Canyon*, p. 161.

69. Dawn Eden, "The Harry Nilsson Anthology."

70. Micky Dolenz interviewed by John Scheinfeld for LSL Productions, 2003.

71. "Colgems maps total expansion," *Billboard*, December 9, 1967, p. 3.

72. Joyce Haber, op. cit.

73. *The Oral Autobiography of Harry Nilsson*, p. 88.

CHAPTER 3

1. Rick Jarrard interviewed by John Scheinfeld for LSL Productions, 2003.

2. *The Horn Call* (International Horn Society Journal), vols. 1–3, 1971, p. 39.

3. RCA Press Release, October 1967.

4. Jarrard/Scheinfeld, 2003.

5. Jacoba Atlas, "An Underground Artist Surfaces," *The Beat*, January 27, 1968, p. 8.

6. Id.

7. "Link Nilsson as Dunbar Writer," *Billboard*, August 19, 1967, p. 6.

8. "Ten Little Indians," *Billboard*, October 21, 1967; Rawlings, *Then, Now and Rare British Beat 1960-69*, p. 204; Lewis, *Led Zeppelin—The 'Tight But Loose' Files: Celebration II*, p. 24.

9. Taylor, *Fifty Years Adrift (In an Open-Necked Shirt)*, p. 333.

10. Nilsson draft autobiography, p. 78.

11. Jacoba Atlas, "An Underground Artist Surfaces," *The Beat*, January 27, 1968, p. 8.

12. Taylor, op. cit., p. 332. Taylor also suggests that it was Weiss who invited Nilsson to the event, but this disagrees with Nilsson's own memoir, which I have relied on here.

13. Nilsson draft autobiography, p. 77.

14. Letter to the author from Tim Blackmore, October 10, 2010.

15. "Nilsson The True One," *Billboard*, October 21, 1967.

16. Andrea T. Sheridan, "Aerial Pandemonium Ballet Show" [notes to RCA Victor 74321 757422, 1999].

17. Jarrard/Scheinfeld, 2003.

18. Author's interview with Gary Nilsson, July 10, 2011.

19. "1941" registered "unpublished" on November 2, 1967, E 22540; recording date from RCA recording ledger, UPA3-5568.

20. From Nilsson's interview tapes with Dawn Eden, January 1994.

21. *High Fidelity*, vol. 18 (issues 1–6) 1968 (page reference not on clipping in Nilsson archive).

22. "Under the album covers: Pandemonium Shadow Show," *Appleton Post-Crescent* (Wisconsin), November 12, 1967.

23. Jarrard/Scheinfeld, 2003.

24. RCA Press Release, October 1967.

25. William D. Laffler, "Hi-fi & Low," *Statesville Record and Landmark* (North Carolina), November 18, 1967.

26. Carl La Fong, "Notes from the Underground," *Record World*, August 31, 1968.

27. "Nilsson Originals," in "Show Time" *Gazette-Mail* (Charleston, VA), March 10, 1968.

28. "Sunbury/Dunbar's First Year—'Ahead of Sked,' " *Cashbox*, August 31, 1968.

29. Jacoba Atlas, op. cit.

30. Jarrard/Scheinfeld, 2003.

31. Ed Ochs, "Nilson High-Rated Writer," *Billboard*, November 30, 1968.

32. *Nilsson v. Jefferson et al.*, Circuit Court, N.D. California, December 31, 1896, no. 12.296, *Federal Reporter*, vol. 78, F. 366.

33. Dawn Eden, "The Harry Nilsson Anthology."

34. Cresswell, *1001 Songs: The Great Songs of All Time and the Artists, Stories and Secrets*, p. 38.

35. Diane Nilsson interviewed by David Leaf for LSL Productions, 2005.

36. Jarrard/Scheinfeld, 2003.

37. Eliot, *Paul Simon—A Life*, p. 93. Eliot confirms that Simon turned down Schlesinger's request and suggests that Newman's song "Cowboy" was written for the film.

38. Harry Nilsson interviewed by Stuart Grundy for BBC Radio, 1977.

39. Spencer, *Film and television scores, 1950-1979: a critical survey by genre*, p. 99.

40. "Otto Preminger Signs Singer for 'Skidoo,' " *Joplin Globe* (Missouri) April 7, 1968, p. 4.

41. Nilsson's intentions regarding this lyric confirmed by Lee Blackman, who had talked about it with him; interviewed by the author, March 1, 2011.

42. Nilsson/Grundy, 1977.

43. "Anatomy of a Three Dog Night," *Billboard*, March 9, 1974, p. 35.

44. Barry Robinson, "Today's music has shades of meaning and philosophy" [interview with Nilsson], *Lowell Sun*, September 11, 1969, p. 36.

45. Examples include Ellison, *Loneliness, the Search for Intimacy*; Phillips, *Diversity and Groups*; Scevak and Cantwell, *Stepping Stones*.

46. Stephen Holden, "Patti Page was first to overdub voice," *Chicago Tribune*, July 21, 1988.

47. "Cavalier of the Month: Nilsson," *Cavalier*, May 1969, p. 70.

48. Bill Yaryan, "Getting Better all the time," *Independent Star-News* (Pasadena, CA), July 27, 1968, p. 6.

49. M.A., "Nilsson: Aerial Ballet," *High Fidelity*, November 1968 [no page reference in Nilsson clippings file].

50. Dawn Eden, "The Harry Nilsson Anthology."

51. "Palatkan to make TV debut," Daytona paper (name unknown), June 19, 1968. "Record artist Nilsson…will make his television debut in Miami today. He will appear on the *Woody Woodbury Show*, singing '1941,' a cut from his first record LP *Pandemonium Shadow Show*. A debut May 22 was in Los Angeles and New York. The show was aired in Boston, Chicago and Detroit last week."

52. "Otto Preminger Signs Singer for 'Skidoo,' " *Joplin Globe* (Missouri), April 7, 1968, p. 4.

53. "My Love Song to You" was performed by Gleason and Art Carney on the television show *The Honeymooners* in an episode called "The Songwriters," first aired on December 11, 1954. It is possible that Nilsson's own "Garbage Can Ballet" triggered this memory, because Gleason's song begins "The garbage cans go clang.…"

54. Nilsson draft autobiography, p. 59.

55. Roger Ebert, "On The 'Skidoo' Set with Otto Preminger," *Chicago Sun-Times*, June 16, 1968 [no page reference in Nilsson clippings file].

56. Derek Taylor, *Nilsson Aerial Ballet* [liner notes to RCA SF 7973, 1968].

57. *The Oral Autobiography of Harry Nilsson*, p. 61.

58. Dawn Eden, "The Harry Nilsson Anthology."

59. DVD of interview in Kane, *Lennon Revealed*.

60. *The Oral Autobiography of Harry Nilsson*, p. 62.

61. O'Dell, with Ketcham, *Miss O'Dell*, p. 47.

62. Ibid. The company moved to 3 Savile Row in July 1968, just a few weeks after Nilsson's visit.

63. Blackmore, October 10, 2010.

64. Everett's opening comments on "It's Been So Long," MGM 1421.

65. Dates and sequence of events from Coleman, *Lennon, the Definitive Biography*, 463ff; and from BBC 2 "Release," an arts television program aired on June 22, 1968.

66. *The Oral Autobiography of Harry Nilsson*, p. 63.

67. Ibid.

68. Ibid. Nilsson recalled McCartney's then-girlfriend as Linda, although other accounts from the time suggest this might have been just prior to the time when they became a couple.

69. Ibid.

70. Derek Taylor interviewed by Stuart Grundy for BBC Radio 2, broadcast February 8, 1997.

71. Jarrard/Scheinfeld, 2003.

72. Dates from RCA recording ledgers. "Rainmaker" and a group of other potential songs for *Harry* had been cut at an earlier session on July 24.

73. Photograph of billboard by M. Newton, July 25, 1968, in RCA archives.

74. Gary Nilsson interviewed by Lee Blackman, March 1, 2011.

75. "Harry Nilssons See Son, Premiere of 'Skidoo,'" *Daytona Beach Morning Journal*, December 19, 1968.

CHAPTER 4

1. Sandi had filed for divorce from Nilsson on November 22, 1967. Nilsson filed a cross-complaint against Sandi on June 11, 1968. Final judgment was entered on May 26, 1969. Marriage to Diane Nilsson, December 31, 1969, in Las Vegas. Dates confirmed by Nilsson's lawyer Lee Blackman in a letter dated July 30, 2010.

2. Segarini quoted on the Whistletaste music blog: http://whistletaste.blogspot. co.uk/2011/01/segarini-sings-nilsson.html [accessed August 20, 2012].

3. Diane Nilsson interviewed by David Leaf for LSL Productions, 2005.

4. Ibid.

5. Ibid.

6. Author's interview with Samantha Juste, February 20, 2011.

7. Dolenz and Bego, *I'm a Believer, my Life of Monkees, Music and Madness*, p. 161.

8. Ibid., pp. 162–163.

9. Ibid.

10. Ibid.

11. Juste, 2011.

12. Ed Ochs, "Nilsson High-Rated Writer," *Billboard*, November 30, 1968.

13. Details from Smithsonian website (which also includes Wright's correspondence) [http:// siarchives.si.edu/history/exhibits/documents/wright.htm] accessed July 20, 2011.

14. *Orville and Wilbur, A Play with Music in Two Acts*, words and music by Harry Nilsson; manuscript outline in Nilsson personal files.

15. Joyce Haber, "Harry Nilsson—A Square in Hip Circles," *Los Angeles Times* [undated clipping from July 1968 in Nilsson scrapbooks].

16. Ochs, op. cit.

17. Nilsson/Leaf, 2005.

18. Dates and song details from RCA archives.

19. "Harry Nilsson to make debut on TV Series," *Joplin Globe* (Missouri), February 16, 1969.

20. Tom Mackin, "Between a Ghost and Hope Lange," *Brief Encounters from Einstein to Elvis*, p. 238.

21. Ochs, op. cit.

22. "[It] bears a close resemblance to Lennon-McCartney's 'For No One' and is probably about the dismal future of their girl who no longer needed her boyfriend." Bill Yaryan, "Getting Better All the Time," *Star News* (Pasadena, CA), August 9, 1969, p. 6.

23. Michael Ross, "His songs swing gracefully between compassion and observation: Harry Nilsson," *Los Angeles Herald Examiner*, section E1, January 25, 1970.

24. McDougal, *Five Easy Decades—How Jack Nicholson Became the Biggest Movie Star in Modern Times*, p. 85.

25. Lecowicz, *The Monkees Tale*, p. 53.

26. Juste, 2011.

27. James Goodfriend, "Stereo Review's Records of the Year Awards for 1969," *Stereo Review*, October 1969.

28. Peter Reilly, "Make Room For Harry," *Stereo Review*, February 1970, p. 108; Bill Yaryan, op. cit. Joan Crosby, "Singer Harry Nilsson Is Being Discovered," *Corpus Christi Caller-Times* (Texas), October 26, 1969.

29. Bill Yaryan, op. cit.

30. Mary Campbell, "Neil Song is Nilsson Hit," *Janesville Gazette* (Wisconsin), October 24, 1969, p. 18.

31. Ibid.

32. "Cavalier of the Month: Nilsson," *Cavalier,* May 1969, p. 71.

33. Bill Martin interviewed by John Scheinfeld, 2004.

34. Warner Brothers 1856, released in 1970, and co-produced by Hank Cicalo.

35. Richard Robinson, "Harry Nilsson's Talkin'," *Hit Parader*, June 1970, p. 12.

36. Martin/Scheinfeld, 2004.

37. Courrier, *Randy Newman's American Dreams*, p. 116.

38. Robert Windeler, "Randy Newman: If You're An American Composer, You're Blues-Oriented," *Stereo Review*, October 1971, p. 74.

39. Harry Nilsson interviewed by Stuart Grundy for BBC Radio, 1977.

40. Ibid.

41. Randy Newman interviewed by Stuart Grundy for BBC Radio 2, broadcast February 8, 1997.

42. Roger Smith, *Nilsson Sings Newman* [liner notes to RCA 74321 757442, 2000].

43. August 20, 7–10 p.m.: "Vine St.," "Cowboy," "Snow." August 27, 7–10 p.m.: "Linda," "Living Without You." September 22, 2–5 p.m.: "So Long Dad," "Love Story." September 23, 2–5 p.m.: "Beehive State." September 24, 2–5 p.m.: "I'll Be Home." September 25, 2–5 p.m.: "Dayton Ohio 1903," "Yellow Man," "Caroline." Details from RCA archives.

44. Roger Smith, op cit.

45. Nilsson/Leaf, 2005.

46. Ibid.

47. Jacoba Atlas, "Nilsson Sings Randy Newman," *Melody Maker*, December 27, 1969, p. 14.

48. Roger Smith, op. cit.

49. Newman/Grundy, 1997.

50. Roger Smith, op. cit.

51. N.C., "Nilsson Sings Newman," *Stereo Review*, August 1970, p. 105.

52. "Cavalier of the Month: Nilsson," *Cavalier*, May 1969, p. 71.

53. http://fortheloveofharry.blogspot.com/2008/02/marry-me-little-unreleased-1969.html [accessed July 24, 2011].

54. Recorded December 16, 1969, according to RCA ledgers.

55. Joan Crosby, op. cit. Other interviews about the wedding include, for example, Ritchie Yorke, "Everybody's Talkin' About Harry Nilsson," *Fusion*, December 12, 1969.

56. Crosby, op. cit.

57. Nilsson/Leaf, 2005.

58. Juste, 2011.

59. Jimmy Webb interviewed by David Leaf for LSL productions, 2003.

60. Betty Martin, "Nilsson will film feature," *Los Angeles Times*, January 8, 1970, part IV, p. 12.

61. Jacoba Atlas, op. cit.

62. Martin/Scheinfeld, 2004.

63. "The unpublished interview" with Colin Richardson, April 10, 1978, http://fortheloveofharry.blogspot.com/2010/04/harry-nilsson-unpublished-interview.html [accessed August 6, 2011].

64. Timothy Leary, "She Comes in Colors," *The Politics of Ecstasy*, p. 132 (originally published by *Playboy*, September 1966).

65. Turner, *The Fab Four—The Gospel According to the Beatles*, 2006; Ian Herbert, "Revealed: Dentist who introduced Beatles to LSD," *Independent*, September 9, 2006.

66. Dolenz and Bego, *I'm a Believer, My Life of Monkees Music and Madness*, p. 160.

67. Juste, 2011.

68. Author's interview with Fred Wolf, October 8, 2011.

69. Nilsson/Grundy, 1977.

70. Author's interview with Wolf, 2011.

71. Fred Wolf interviewed by John Scheinfeld for LSL Productions, 2004.

72. In Susan F. Schnelzer, "The Point" [liner note to RCA7423 757432, 1999], the executive's name is given as Marty Starger, although Fred Wolf in an interview with the author on October 8, 2011, suggested that it was Diller whom Nilsson pursued. Wolf subsequently discussed details of the movie with Diller, but a letter from Nilsson to Starger survives from March 11, 1971, confirming that it was they who "flew East together."

73. Nilsson/Grundy, 1977. In Richardson, op. cit., Nilsson says Hoffman was paid $20,000 and that ABC had to approve this additional budget, http://fortheloveofharry.blogspot.com/2010/04/harry-nilsson-unpublished-interview.html [accessed August 6, 2011]. In terms of Hoffman's usual fee, this equates in Nilsson's terms to him doing the movie "for nothing."

74. Lenburg, *Dustin Hoffman—Hollywood's Antihero*, p. 70. John Scheinfeld's 2010 film biography of Nilsson, *Who Is Harry Nilsson (And Why Is Everybody Talkin' About Him)*, took its title from wordplay on the name of the *Harry Kellerman* movie.

75. Wolf/Scheinfeld, 2004.

76. "Palatkan's Son Wins Grammy," *Daytona Beach Morning Journal*, May 6, 1970.

77. Richard Robinson, "Harry Nilsson's Talkin'," *Hit Parader*, June 1970, p. 12.

78. Wolf/Scheinfeld, 2004.

79. Ibid.

80. "Harry Makes his Point," *Rock*, March 15, 1971, p. 26.

81. In a letter to Derek Taylor from September 1970, Nilsson refers to Dorfman's visit. Reproduced in Taylor, *Fifty Years Adrift (In an Open-Necked Shirt)*, p. 420.

82. Author's interview with Stanley Dorfman, February 21, 2011.

CHAPTER 5

1. Zak Nilsson interviewed by John Scheinfeld for LSL Productions, 2004.

2. Diane Nilsson interviewed by David Leaf for LSL Productions, 2005.

3. Nilsson/Scheinfeld, 2004. Quoted by permission of the Harry Nilsson estate.

4. "Harry Nilsson Makes a Point," *Pasadena Star-News*, January 31, 1971, p. 82.

5. Letter from Nilsson to Starger, March 11, 1971, from Nilsson personal files.

6. Jeanne Harrison, "Under Twenty," *San Mateo Times*, July 15, 1971, p. 27.

7. "One of the Best," *Albuquerque Tribune*, July 1, 1971.

8. Taylor, *Fifty Years Adrift (In an Open-Necked Shirt)*, p. 420.

9. Jeff Sherwood, "Tiny Tim at Troubadour," *The Valley News*, January 16, 1970, p. 24.

10. Bronson, *Billboard's Hottest Hot 100 Hits*, 68; Clayson, *Ringo Starr, Straight Man or Joker*, p. 117.

11. Richard Perry interviewed by John Scheinfeld for LSL Productions, 2003.

12. Dawn Eden, "The Harry Nilsson Anthology."

13. "Record Reviews," *Twin Falls Times-News*, June 23, 1970, p. 13.

14. Nilsson/Leaf, 2005.

15. Tipton letter to Lee Newman, February 10, 2002.

16. Alan Rich, "Some Definitions Redefined," *New York*, March 13, 1972, p. 68.

17. Author's interview with Richard Perry, February 11, 2005.

18. Ibid. Perry says it was Rolling Stones producer Glyn Johns who tipped him off.

19. Background information in a letter to the author from Chris Spedding, August 8, 2011.

20. Curtis Armstrong, *Nilsson Schmilsson* [notes to RCA 74321 757452, 1999].

21. Perry/Scheinfeld, 2003.

22. Richard Perry, in an interview with the author on August 8, 2011, said: "I asked Paul to do the strings after we had cut the basic track. I don't remember precisely, but I think Harry had put some sort of rough vocal down, which Paul used to write the string parts. I think he did the vocal again after the strings were in place. I only recall him doing the final version of the vocal once."

23. Perry/Scheinfeld, 2003.

24. Derek Taylor interviewed by Stuart Grundy for BBC Radio 2, broadcast February 8, 1997.

25. Curtis Armstrong, *Nilsson Schmilsson* [notes to RCA 74321 757452, 1999].

26. E-mail to the author from Chris Spedding, August 8, 2011.

27. Perry, 2005.

28. Author's interview with Richard Perry, August 8, 2011.

29. Chris Spedding interviewed by Stuart Grundy for BBC Radio 2, 1997.

30. E-mail to the author from Chris Spedding, August 6, 2011.

31. Perry, 2005.

32. E-mail to the author from Herbie Flowers, August 10, 2011.

33. Spedding, August 6, 2011.

34. Flowers, 2011.

35. Spedding, August 6, 2011.

36. Dawn Eden, op. cit.

37. Perry, 2005.

38. Spedding, August 6, 2011.

39. Perry, 2011.

40. Dawn Eden, op. cit.

41. Manuscript in Harry Nilsson papers, Los Angeles.

42. Flowers, 2011.

43. Chapman and Gilber, *Rock to Riches*, p. 42.

44. Perry/Scheinfeld, 2003.

45. Perry, 2005.

46. David Proctor, "Nilsson Schmilsson," *Salt Lake Tribune*, March 17, 1972, p. 2C.

47. Perry, 2005.

48. Bud Scoppa, "Records," *Rolling Stone*, February 17, 1972, p. 48.

49. For example, "Jump Into The Fire," *Billboard*, March 18, 1972, p. 17.

50. Nilsson/Leaf, 2005.

51. Spedding, August 6, 2011.

52. Flowers, 2011.

53. http://www.themarqueeclub.net/1971 [accessed August 4, 2011].

54. Nilsson/Leaf, 2005.

55. Author's interview with Samantha Juste, February 20, 2011.

56. *The Oral Autobiography of Harry Nilsson.*

57. Author's interview with Stanley Dorfman, February 21, 2011.

58. Ibid.

59. Ibid.

60. Tape LLVT990P, transmission date confirmed by BBC Libraries and Archives, August 2, 2011.

61. Stanley Dorfman interviewed by John Scheinfeld for LSL Productions, 2004.

62. "Firms Prime Big LPs for Xmas," *Billboard*, November 27, 1971, p. 1.

63. Perry/Scheinfeld, 2003.

64. Ibid.

65. "Top Sixty Pop Spotlight," *Billboard*, December 4, 1971, p. 52.

66. Perry/Scheinfeld, 2003.

67. Nilsson/Leaf, 2005.

68. Keith Altham, "Come out Harry, the time is right," *New Musical Express,* March 25, 1972, p. 12.

69. Dates confirmed in a letter from Nilsson's lawyer, Lee Blackman, July 30, 2010.

70. Perry/Scheinfeld, 2003.

71. Ibid.

72. Stephen Holden, "Records," *Rolling Stone*, August 17, 1972.

73. Keith Altham, op. cit.

74. E-mail to the author, August 9, 2011.

75. Dawn Eden, op. cit.

76. E-mail to the author, August 9, 2011.

77. RCA "sweetening" session, April 28, 1972, at RCA. This also added horns (mainly unused on the final cut) to "I'd Rather Be Dead" and to "What's Your Sign," which did not get included in the album.

78. Nilsson's soundtrack commentary on *Did Somebody Drop His Mouse?*

79. Ray Cooper interviewed by John Scheinfeld for LSL Productions, 2004.

80. Perry/Scheinfeld, 2003.

81. Ibid.

82. Newman, *A Touch From God—It's Only Rock and Roll*, p. 79.

83. David Proctor, " 'Son of Schmilsson' better than Dad," *Salt Lake Tribune*, July 21, 1972, p. C2.

84. Photo caption in *Record Mirror,* March 25, 1972.

85. The RCA session log lists Herbie Flowers on bass, but he confirms he was not on this session, and the movie clearly shows Voormann.

86. Lon Goddard, "Nilsson's New Album," *Record Mirror*, April 8, 1972, p. 15.

87. Ibid.

88. Keith Altham, op. cit.

CHAPTER 6

1. Joan Taylor interviewed by John Scheinfeld for LSL Productions, 2004.

2. Ray Cooper interviewed by John Scheinfeld for LSL Productions, 2004.

3. Nilsson draft autobiography, p. 90.

4. Nilsson draft autobiography, p. 28.

5. *The Oral Autobiography of Harry Nilsson.*

6. "Youth Beat," *The Daily News* (Salisbury, MD), September 3, 1972.

7. Harry, *The Ringo Starr Encyclopedia*, p. 317.

8. Ibid., p. 316.

9. *Rolling Stone*, April 30, 1981, quoted in Clayson, *Ringo Starr—A Life*, p. 238.

10. O'Dell with Ketcham, *Miss O'Dell*, p. 234.

11. Author's interview with Samantha Juste, February 20, 2011.

12. Author's interview with Richard Perry, February 11, 2005.

13. Simpson, *The Rough Guide to Cult Pop*, 282.

14. Clayson, *Ringo Starr—A Life*, p. 238; Fletcher, *Dear Boy—The Life of Keith Moon*, p. 324.

15. Nilsson draft autobiography, p. 33.

16. Ibid, p. 35.

17. Richard Perry interviewed by John Scheinfeld for LSL Productions, 2003.

18. Perry, 2005.

19. Jenkins, *Goodbye—In Search of Gordon Jenkins*, p. 266.

20. Ibid., p. 255.

21. Derek Taylor interviewed by Stuart Grundy for BBC Radio 2, broadcast February 8, 1997.

22. Danny Holloway, "Nilsson Schmaltzon?" *New Musical Express*, April 7, 1973.

23. Rick Sanders, "A Little Touch of Harry," *Record Mirror*, April 7, 1973.

24. Taylor/Grundy, 1997.

25. Bruce Jenkins, op. cit.

26. Derek Taylor and Harry Nilsson interviewed by Alison Steele (on the radio show "Nightbird and Co.") in 1973, from For the Love of Harry website [http://fortheloveofharry.blogspot.com/2008/12/nightbird-company-cosmic-connections.html] accessed October 10, 2011.

27. Author's interview with Stanley Dorfman, February 21, 2011.

28. Jim Conley, "Recordings," *Albilene Reporter-News*, December 2, 1973, p. 130.

29. Bruce Jenkins, op. cit.

30. Dorfman, 2011.

31. Jimmy Webb interviewed by John Scheinfeld for LSL Productions, 2003.

32. Nilsson draft autobiography, p. 49.

33. Dorfman, 2011.

34. Nilsson draft autobiography, p. 49.

35. Nilsson draft autobiography, p. 51.

36. Dorfman, 2011.

37. Ibid.

38. Webb/Scheinfeld, 2003.

39. Una Nilsson interviewed by John Scheinfeld, 2005.

40. Nilsson draft autobiography, p. 54.

41. Ibid., p. 55.

CHAPTER 7

1. Author's interview with Una Nilsson, February 23, 2011.

2. Nilsson draft autobiography, p. 56.

3. Jon Landau, "Mind Games," *Rolling Stone*, January 3, 1974.

4. Thompson, *Phil Spector—Wall of Pain*.

5. Urish and Bielen, *The Words and Music of John Lennon*, p. 65.

6. L. Kane, *Lennon Revealed*, p. 99.

7. Author's interview with May Pang, February 2005, with additional material from Pang, September 5, 2012.

8. Adam Block, "Drunk with John, George, Ringo, and…," *Creem*, July 1975, p. 40.

9. Dave Thompson, op. cit.

10. Pang, 2005.

11. Chuck Berry's "You Can't Catch Me" and "Sweet Little Sixteen," Lloyd Price's "Just Because," and Larry Williams's "Bony Moronie." Three further tracks were issued on CD in 2004.

12. Cooper and Zimmerman, *Golf Monster*, p. 125.

13. *Billboard*, December 8, 1973; *Billboard*, December 15, 1973.

14. Nilsson draft autobiography, p. 90.

15. Melly, *Mellymobile*, p. 143.

16. Author's interview with Samantha Juste, February 20, 2011.

17. Letters from Nilsson to Una O'Keeffe postmarked October 1973.

18. Una Nilsson, 2011.

19. Juste, 2011.

20. Bianculli, *Dangerously Funny, The Uncensored Story of the Smothers Brothers Comedy Hour*, p. 333.

21. Kane, op. cit., p. 100.

22. "Beatle Bops Photog: Woman files police charge," *Star-News* (Pasadena, CA), March 14, 1974, p. 61.

23. Jimmy Webb interviewed by Stuart Grundy for BBC Radio 2.

24. "Joyce Haber on Hollywood," *Salt Lake Tribune*, March 26, 1974, p. 9.

25. "Trouble at the Troubadour: Lennon's Hard Day's Night," *Rolling Stone*, April 25, 1974.

26. Harry Nilsson interviewed by Stuart Grundy for BBC Radio, 1977.

27. Adam Block, "Drunk with John, George, Ringo, and…," *Creem*, July 1975, p. 40.

28. Pang, 2005; 2012.

29. Ibid.

30. Mr. Bonzai, "The Adventures of Harry Nilsson," *Mix*, vol. 7, no. 5, May 1980, p. 78.

31. Fletcher, *Dear Boy—The Life of Keith Moon*, p. 386.

32. John Swenson, "Do You Want to Know a Secret," *Crawdaddy*, September 1974, p. 34.

33. Ibid.

34. May Pang interviewed by Stuart Grundy for BBC Radio 2.

35. O'Dell with Ketchum, *Miss O'Dell*, p. 268.

36. Author's interview with Richard Perry, February 2005.

37. Author's interview with Klaus Voormann, February 24, 2012.

38. Pang, 2005; 2012.

39. Dawson, *And on piano…Nicky Hopkins*, p. 167.

40. Blaney, *John Lennon—Listen to this Book*, p. 142.

41. "Lennon," *Rolling Stone*, June 5, 1975 [no page number on clipping in Nilsson scrapbook].

42. Tom Dupree, "Dracula Schmacula," *Zoo World*, June 6, 1974, p. 12.

43. Ibid.

44. Weaver, "Suzanna Leigh," *I Was A Monster Movie Maker*, p. 139.

45. "Pride Exits UA for Atlantic in Distrib Pact," *Billboard*, May 4, 1974, p. 3.

46. "Glancy job turnaround," *Billboard*, December 15, 1973, p. 3.

47. Dawn Eden, "One Last Touch of Nilsson."

48. Confirmed by Lee Blackman, Nilsson's lawyer, in letters of December 5 and December 15, 2011.

49. Curtis Armstrong, "Duit on Mon Dei" [liner note to RCA 7432 1950242, 2002], suggests that the recording costs were picked up by RCA, but Lee Blackman confirms that even though they were initially paid by RCA, the sums were deducted from Nilsson's $562,500 advance when the album was finally delivered.

50. John Swenson, op. cit., p. 34.

51. Nilsson draft autobiography, p. 88.

52. Ibid., p. 86.

53. Ibid.

54. Derek Taylor, "Pussy Cats" [liner note to RCA BVCM 35124, 1974].

55. Coleman, *Lennon: The Definitive Biography*, p. 618.

56. Dates confirmed by Una Nilsson, December 12, 2011.

57. Pang, 2005; 2012.

58. Ringo Starr interviewed by Michael Wale for BBC Radio 1 "Rock Speak," November 1974.

59. Ibid.

60. Author's interview with Stanley Dorfman, February 21, 2011.

61. Nilsson draft autobiography, p. 46.

CHAPTER 8

1. Nilsson draft autobiography, p. 38.

2. "Cass Elliot, top singer dead at 33," A.P. report in *Vallejo Times-Herald* (California), July 30, 1974, p. 4.

3. Ibid.

4. Ibid.

5. "Pathologist raises query on 'Mama' Cass death," *The Times*, July 31, 1974.

6. "Inquest told obesity led to 'Mama' Cass death," *The Times*, August 6, 1974. Death certificate posted at http://www.findadeath.com/Deceased/e/Cass%20Elliot/DC.JPG, (accessed January 19, 2012).

7. Perry Botkin Jr. interviewed by John Scheinfeld for LSL Productions, 2003.

8. Una Nilsson interviewed by John Scheinfeld for LSL Productions, 2005.

9. Botkin/Scheinfeld, 2003.

10. Ibid.

11. A. J. Morgan, "Nilsson—Dracula meets the Sandman," *Circus*, no. 120, October 1975, p. 50.

12. Ibid., p. 52.

13. Robin Welles, "Nilsson in pain: Back at work," *Anderson Herald* (Indiana), May 25, 1975, p. 29.

14. A. J. Morgan, op. cit.

15. Ibid.

16. E-mail to the author from Van Dyke Parks, December 8, 2011.

17. Jimmy Webb interviewed by Stuart Grundy for BBC Radio 2, broadcast February 8, 1997.

18. Author's interview with Klaus Voormann, February 24, 2012.

19. Author's interview with Van Dyke Parks, February 22, 2011.

20. Van Dyke Parks interviewed by Stuart Grundy for BBC Radio 2, broadcast February 8, 1997.

21. Brian Wilson finally re-recorded and issued a version of *Smile* in 2003/4. The original sessions were reassembled and released as *The Smile Sessions* by Capitol in 2011, but at the time Parks worked with Nilsson, they had officially been abandoned.

22. Parks, 2011.

23. Una Nilsson/Scheinfeld, 2005.

24. Van Dyke Parks interviewed by John Scheinfeld for LSL Productions, 2003.

25. Voorman, 2012.

26. Parks/Scheinfeld, 2003.

27. Ibid.

28. Harry Nilsson interviewed by Stuart Grundy for BBC Radio, 1977.

29. Ibid.

30. Nilsson draft autobiography, p. 47.

31. Parks/Scheinfeld, 2003.

32. Nilsson draft autobiography, p. 47.

33. Ibid.

34. Author's interview with Stanley Dorfman, February 21, 2011.

35. Nilsson draft autobiography, p. 48.

36. A. J. Morgan, op. cit.

37. Lon Goddard, "Rock Bottom Harry," *Disc,* April 12, 1975, p. 21.

38. Joel Vance, "'Arry Nilsson's Peers," *Stereo Review*, vol. 36, 1976 (no page number on clipping in Nilsson's files).

39. Colin Richardson, "The Unpublished Interview" [http://fortheloveofharry.blogspot.com/2007/01/harry-nilsson-unpublished-interview_01.html] accessed February 24, 2012.

40. David Zucker, "Boston Repertory Theatre, 1971-1978" Part III (online at http://www.theatermirror.com/brt3.htm—accessed February 19, 2012).

41. Syndicated television column in *News Journal* (Mansfield, OH), December 7, 1974, p. 14.

42. John L. Mullins, " 'The Point,' once cartoon, comes to life on Hub stage," *Newport Daily News* (Rhode Island), March 10, 1975, p. 7.

43. "The Stage," *Harvard Crimson*, August 12, 1975.

44. Letter to Cranston, February 24, 1975, in Nilsson's personal files.

45. Parks/Scheinfeld, 2003.

46. Trevor Lawrence interviewed by John Scheinfeld for LSL Productions, 2005.

47. Timothy White, "Harry Nilsson—Leave it to Beaver," *Crawdaddy*, August 1976, p. 21.

48. Lawrence/Scheinfeld, 2005.

49. Nilsson/Grundy, 1977.

50. A. J. Morgan, op. cit.

51. Parks/Scheinfeld, 2003.

52. Ibid.

53. Botkin/Scheinfeld, 2003.

54. Lawrence/Scheinfeld, 2005.

55. Brown and Gaines, *The Love You Make—An Insider's Story of the Beatles*, p. 139.

56. Kane, *Lennon Revealed*, p. 199.

57. Brown and Gaines, op. cit., p. 359.

58. Voorman, 2012.

59. A. J. Morgan, op. cit.

60. Nilsson draft autobiography, p. 65.

61. J. Tierney, "Buying Time," *In Health*, vol. 4, no. 1, 1990, p. 35; the negative aspects of the theory are summed up in Stephen Barrett, M.D., "Cellular Therapy" at http://www.quackwatch.org/01QuackeryRelatedTopics/Cancer/cellular.html [accessed February 23, 2012]. A more positive report is Carol Kahn, "Cell Therapy, an Exclusive Report from Europe," *Life Extension Magazine*, November 1997.

62. Nilsson draft autobiography, p. 67.

63. "Doctor loses C4 libel case," *Independent*, May 16, 1997, p. 2.

64. Nilsson draft autobiography, p. 71.

65. Ibid., p. 72.

66. "Harry Nilsson fined," *Evening Standard*, July 8, 1975.

67. Letter from Nilsson to Derek Taylor, November 6, 1975.

68. "RCA in merger of A and R," *Billboard*, November 6, 1976; Stephen Holden, "Michael Berniker, 73, record producer, dies," *New York Times*, July 29, 2008.

69. Lawrence/Scheinfeld, 2005.

70. Nilsson/Grundy, 1977.

71. Letter from Nilsson to Derek Taylor, November 6, 1975.

72. Lawrence/Scheinfeld, 2005.

73. Ibid.

74. Ibid.

75. Ibid.

76. Ibid.

77. Gerry Beckley interviewed by John Scheinfeld for LSL productions.

78. Thanks to Kief O. Nilsson for the opportunity to hear Nilsson's cassette tapes of this material.

79. "Cindy Birdsong to make brief return to the Supremes," *Jet*, November 1, 1973, p. 84.

80. Lawrence/Scheinfeld, 2005.

81. Voorman, 2012.

82. Lawrence/Scheinfeld, 2005.

83. Curtis Armstrong, "… That's The Way It Is" (liner notes to RCA 74321950262, 2002).

CHAPTER 9

1. Dave Marsh, "Rolling Stone," *Corpus Christi Times*, August 20, 1976.

2. Rush Evans, "We're Just Wild About Harry," *Discoveries*, May 1995, p. 35.

3. Neil Coppage, "Nilsson: Still Workin' On It," *Stereo Review*, September 1976, p. 108.

4. Barry Alfonso, "The Slightly Warped Popeye of Harry Nilsson," *Songwriter*, March 1981, p. 24.

5. Letter from Nilsson to Derek Taylor, November 6, 1975.

6. Author's interview with Una Nilsson, February 2011.

7. "The Nilsson House," *Skyline*, September 1979 [no page no. on clipping in Nilsson files].

8. Una Nilsson, 2011.

9. Paul Goldberger, "Nilsson House," *Architectural Digest*, November, 1979, p. 132.

10. Suzanne Stephens, "Nilsson House," *Progressive Architecture*, December 1979 [no folio numbers].

11. Trevor Lawrence interviewed by John Scheinfeld for LSL Productions, 2005.

12. Una Nilsson, 2011.

13. Idle, ed., *Monty Python Live*, p. 26.

14. Author's interview with Eric Idle, February 2011.

15. Author's conversation with Michael Palin, November 23, 2011; Idle, op. cit., p. 31.

16. Rich Wiseman, "Rolling Stone," *The Advocate* (Ohio), May 28, 1976.

17. Date confirmed in a letter from Nilsson's attorney, Lee Blackman, on July 30, 2010.

18. Una Nilsson interviewed by John Scheinfeld for LSL Productions, 2005.

19. O'Dell with Ketchum, *Miss O'Dell*, p. 344.

20. Nilsson draft autobiography, p. 22.

21. Ibid., p. 23.

22. His father's other son by his second marriage, Keith, died in infancy. Letter to the author from Gary Nilsson, July 12, 2011.

23. Letter to the author from Drake E. Nilsson, March 18, 2011. Harry Nilsson accepted that he and Drake shared the same mother, although he had different theories about Drake's paternity.

24. Nilsson draft autobiography, p. 24.

25. Letter from Bette Nilsson to Nilsson, August 29, 1976.

26. Nilsson draft autobiography, p. 27.

27. Van Dyke Parks interviewed by John Scheinfeld for LSL Productions, 2003.

28. Una Nilsson, 2011.

29. Letter from Bette Nilsson to Drake Nilsson, December 24, 1976.

30. Letter to the author from Mike McNaught, February 27, 2012.

31. David Wigg, "That Nilsson Touch Is Pointing to New Success," *Daily Telegraph*, November 1976 [no date and page in Nilsson clippings file].

32. Carpenter, *Spike Milligan*, p. 221.

33. Sheila Prophet, "Hasn't Anyone Ever Told Harry Nilsson It's Rude To Point?" *Record Mirror*, November 13, 1976.

34. "World's Longest Pun Now On London Stage," UPI report in *Greely Daily Tribune* (Colorado), January 27, 1977, p. 35.

35. Ibid.

36. McNaught, February 27, 2012.

37. Sheridan Morley, "Miss the Point," *Punch*, January 19, 1977 [no page number on clipping in Nilsson's files].

38. *Punch*, January 1978 [no date or page number in Nilsson clippings file].

39. *Listener*, January 1978 [no date or folio number]; *Plays and Players*, issue 25, December 1977, p. 4.

40. http://www.youtube.com/watch?v=IsLC5D4Iy9Y [accessed February 29, 2012].

41. Dolenz and Bego, *I'm a Believer*, p. 182.

42. A short season featuring the actor Tom Conti in *Whose Life Is It Anyway?*
43. Micky Dolenz interviewed by John Scheinfeld for LSL Productions, 2003.
44. McNaught, February 27, 2012.
45. Ibid.
46. Letter to the author from Mike McNaught, February 28, 2012.
47. Ibid.
48. Ibid. "Porterage" was an extra fee that the British Musicians' Union allowed those who played bulky or awkwardly shaped instruments to charge over and above their scale payments for a recording session.
49. Letter to the author from Mike McNaught, March 1, 2012.
50. Richard S. Ginell, "State," *Valley News* (Van Nuys, California), August 12, 1977, p. 56.
51. Curtis Armstrong, *Knnillssonn* [liner note to RCA 7432 1 950262, 2002].
52. Dawn Eden, *The Harry Nilsson Anthology.*
53. McNaught, March 1, 2012.
54. Author's interview with Klaus Voormann, February 24, 2012.
55. "Knnillssonn," *Valley Morning Star* (Harlington, Texas), September 11, 1977, p. 34.
56. Richard S. Ginell, op. cit.
57. Dave Marsh, "Nilsson: 'Knnillssonn,'" *Courier News* (Blytheville, Arkansas), August 11, 1977, p. 9.
58. Billboard review from July 1977 at http://www.billboard.com/news/knnillssonn-905492.story#/news/knnillssonn-905492.story [accessed March 4 2012].
59. Noel Coppage, "Knnillssonn," *Stereo Review*, September 1977, p. 205.
60. Date from session records in RCA archives.
61. Dawn Eden, "One Last Touch of Nilsson."
62. Confirmed by Nilsson's attorney, Lee Blackman, in a letter to the author, December 15, 2011.

CHAPTER 10

1. Colin Richardson, "The Unpublished Interview," April 10, 1978 [http://fortheloveof-harry.blogspot.com/2010/04/harry-nilsson-unpublished-interview.html] accessed March 2, 2012.
2. Derek Taylor interviewed by Stuart Grundy for BBC Radio 2, broadcast February 8, 1997.
3. Sheila Prophet, "Hasn't Anyone Ever Told Harry Nilsson It's Rude To Point?" *Record Mirror*, November 13, 1976.
4. Terry, *The Popeye Story*, p. 26.
5. Colin Richardson, op. cit. Nilsson used the word "leasing" in the interview, but it is clear from his memoirs and other interviews that he lent the apartment to Moon without charging him.
6. Jimmy Webb interviewed by John Scheinfeld for LSL Productions, 2003.
7. Van Dyke Parks interviewed by John Scheinfeld for LSL Productions, 2003.
8. Author's interview with Lee Blackman, February 2011.
9. E-mail from Zak Nilsson, October 15, 2012.
10. Author's interview with Klaus Voormann, February 24, 2012.

11. Blackman, 2011.

12. Author's interview with Eric Idle, February 2011.

13. Nilsson draft autobiography, p. 37.

14. Ibid. p. 31.

15. Author's interview with John Altman, March 17, 2011.

16. Chapman, *A Liar's Autobiography*, p. 160.

17. Ibid.

18. Author's interview with Lee Blackman, February 2012.

19. Author's interview with Una Nilsson, February 2012.

20. Author's interview with Larold Rebhun, March 10, 2012.

21. http://www.larold.com/ [accessed March 3, 2012].

22. C. P. Smith, " 'Life of Brian' packs Monty Python Whack," *Santa Ana Register*, August 21, 1979.

23. Jerry Elsea, "Interesting satirical material in righteous ban of unread book," *Cedar Rapids Gazette*, February 24, 1980, p. 9.

24. Idle, 2011.

25. Ibid. The Rutles were Idle's television comedy group parodying the Beatles.

26. At the time of writing, a new CD edition of the album is scheduled to appear in the United States in the summer of 2013, including four previously unissued Nilsson songs from the period: "Old Dirt Road" (alternative version), "Feet," "Leave The Rest To Molly," and "She Drifted Away."

27. Terry, op. cit., p. 27.

28. Letter from Derek Taylor to Barbara Downey at *Rolling Stone*, September 26, 1980.

29. Ibid.

30. Blackman, 2011.

31. Larold Rehbun confirms that he recorded the sessions with Duvall at Cherokee; letter to the author, March 3, 2012.

32. Terry, op. cit., p. 60.

33. Ibid. A photo caption suggests it was Beau who came with the Nilssons to Venice, but it is clearly Ben, not his older brother.

34. Ibid., p. 85.

35. Letter from Bette Nilsson to Drake Nilsson, written November 18, 1976, mailed on March 2, 1977.

36. Taylor, op. cit.

37. Ibid.

38. Ray Cooper interviewed by John Scheinfeld for LSL Productions, 2004.

39. Parks/Scheinfeld, 2003.

40. Taylor, op. cit.

41. Vincent Canby, "Live action *Popeye* on the big screen," *Stars and Stripes*, January 4, 1981, p. 12 (reprinted from *New York Times*).

42. Ibid.

43. Dan Gire, "*Popeye* is what it is, disappointing," *Chicago Daily Herald*, December 13, 1980, p. 12.

44. Debra Kurtz, " 'Popeye' special treat," *Waterloo Courier* (Iowa), December 19, 1980, p. 54.

45. Dan Klady, "*Popeye* true to comic strip," *Winnipeg Free Press*, December 15, 1980, p. 44.
46. Author's interview with Perry Botkin, February 2011.
47. Ibid.
48. Idle, 2012.
49. Ibid.
50. Thor Eckert Jr., "Mexico's Zapata cut down by Goodspeed's production clichés," *Christian Science Monitor*, November 10, 1980.
51. Botkin, 2011.
52. Ibid. Starr finally married Barbara Bach on April 27, 1981, but they spent the summer of 1980 in London and France before returning to Los Angeles.
53. Thor Eckert Jr., "Mexico's Zapata cut down by Goodspeed's production clichés," *Christian Science Monitor*, November 10, 1980.
54. Rehbun, 2012.
55. E-mail from Andrea Robinson, May 14, 2012.
56. Roussos also recorded "Love Is the Answer" from *Zapata*, but it was not released for several years until it became a CD bonus track.
57. Thor Eckert Jr., "Mexico's Zapata cut down by Goodspeed's production clichés," *Christian Science Monitor*, November 10, 1980.
58. Author's interview with Frank Stallone, February 2010.

CHAPTER 11

1. Jimmy Webb interviewed by Stuart Grundy for BBC Radio 2.
2. Pierre Bowman, "Nilsson," *Honolulu Advertiser*, February 11, 1982, p. C1.
3. Letter from Nilsson to Derek Taylor, March 17, 1981.
4. "Coalition for Handgun Control Plans Full Week of Activities," *Harvard Crimson*, October 26, 1981.
5. Pierre Bowman, op. cit.
6. Ibid.
7. Copy of letter from Nilsson to Yoko Ono, December 1981, in Nilsson's files.
8. Invitation to reception, March 5, 1982.
9. John Christensen, "Nilsson Sings a New Song," *Honolulu Star Bulletin*, February 11, 1982; *Honolulu Advertiser*, March 13, 1982.
10. Chapman, *Yellowbeard*, p. 24.
11. Leonard Klady, "Yellowbeard Film: Jokes Run Aground," *Winnipeg Free Press*, June 27, 1983, p. 50.
12. D. D. McNicoll, "A Drinking Violet but Never in Public," *The Australian*, August 21, 1984, p. 3.
13. Ibid.
14. An album called *Harry Does Yoko* was announced for release in 1985 but never appeared. Ed St. John, "Harry's Just Wild About Yoko," *National Times*, August 24, 1984, arts section, p. 29
15. Author's interview with Stanley Dorfman, February 2011.
16. E-mail from Zak Nilsson, October 15, 2012.
17. Author's interview with Una Nilsson, February 2011.

18. Estimates for the attendance very, but most agree with Warner (*American Singing Groups*, p. 330) that the crowd was "upwards of 500,000" not least because the group had been banned from playing in the mall the previous year, and the public responded by turning up in droves. Rolfe, "Washington Economy" in the *Crowell-Collier Yearbook 1984*, p. 585, estimated the crowd at "more than a million," hence Nilsson's conjecture of crowd numbers has a basis in contemporary reporting.

19. Nilsson draft autobiography, p. 94; with additions from *The Oral Autobiography of Harry Nilsson*.

20. Faye Zuckerman, "Movie Review," *Billboard*, February 9, 1985, p. 32.

21. Harry, *The Ringo Starr Encyclopedia*, p. 20.

22. Una Nilsson, 2011.

23. Ibid.

24. Nilsson draft autobiography, p. 90.

25. Ibid, p. 91; with additions from *The Oral Autobiography of Harry Nilsson*.

26. Gerry Beckley interviewed by John Scheinfeld for LSL Productions, 2003.

27. Ibid.

28. Una Nilsson, 2011.

29. Author's interview with Eric Idle, February 2011.

30. Nilsson draft autobiography, p. 76.

31. Ibid. p. 41.

32. Jimmy Webb interviewed by David Leaf for LSL Productions, 2003.

33. Letter from the Britannia Hotel, May 1, 1981, to Nilsson's travel agent, D. M. Belger.

34. Una Nilsson, 2011.

35. "The Eddie and Flo Show" from 1990, posted on http://fortheloveofharry.blogspot.co.uk/search/label/1990, accessed April 2, 2012.

36. Una Nilsson, 2011.

37. Annie Nilsson interviewed by John Scheinfeld for LSL Productions, 2005.

38. Beau Nilsson interviewed by John Scheinfeld for LSL Productions, 2004.

39. Ben Nilsson interviewed by John Scheinfeld for LSL Productions, 2004.

40. Letter from Nilsson to Ben and Beau Nilsson, August 9, 1989.

41. E-mail from Zak Nilsson, October 15, 2012.

42. "Cinnamon Broadcasting, Utah's Cortex to merge," *Deseret News*, July 1, 1983 [no page number on clipping in Nilsson's files].

43. Keith Bradsher, "Hawkeye ousts its CEO," *Los Angeles Times*, August 5, 1987. This article gives Hock's address as the Bel Age Hotel in West Hollywood.

44. Ibid.

45. Ibid.

46. McGilligan, "Terry Southern," in *Backstory 3: Interviews with Screenwriters of the 1960s*, p. 399.

47. Hill, *A Grand Guy, The Life and Art of Terry Southern* [no page ref.].

48. Patrick McGilligan, op. cit., p. 399.

49. Terry Gilliam interviewed by John Scheinfeld for LSL Productions, 2004.

50. Bradsher, op. cit., reported income of $112,000 in the six months to April 1987, with a net operating profit of $21,294.

51. Patrick McGilligan, op. cit., p. 399.

52. Gerber with Lisanti, *Trippin' With Terry Southern—What I think I remember*, p. 199.

53. Hill, *A Grand Guy, The Life and Art of Terry Southern* [no page ref.].

54. Caryn James, "Whoopi Goldberg in 'Telephone,' " *New York Times*, February 14, 1988.

55. Michael Sragow, "Whoopi stars in 'The Telephone,' " *San Francisco Examiner*, reprinted in *The News* (Frederick, Maryland), January 30, 1988, p. E7.

56. James Bates, "Once-famous songwriter now struggles in obscurity," *Winnipeg Free Press*, January 16, 1988.

57. "People," *The Hawk Eye* (Burlington, Iowa), August 6, 1987, p. 8A.

58. Bates, op. cit.

59. Ibid.

60. Lee Hill, op. cit.

61. Michael Szymanski, "Comeback Schmumback, The Return of Son of Schmilsson," *Los Angeles Magazine*, October, 1990, p. 73.

62. "Nilsson Talkin," *Los Angeles Times*, January 12, 1988.

63. Ibid.

64. Una Nilsson, 2011.

65. Ibid.

66. Szymanski: Op. cit.; Paul Zollo, "Harry Nilsson is alive and well and living in L.A." [undated clipping from *Los Angeles Times* in Nilsson's personal files, circa October 1990]. Szymanski spells the song title "You See L.A."

67. Press release in Nilsson's files for release of *Paris* album, February 27, 1990.

68. E-mail from Una Nilsson, February 2010.

69. Bill Higgins, "Offbeat Memorial for a Comedian," *Los Angeles Times*, January 25, 1990, p. E3.

70. Idle, 2011.

71. Terry Gilliam interviewed by John Scheinfeld for LSL Productions, 2004.

72. Ray Cooper interviewed by John Scheinfeld for LSL Productions, 2004.

73. "Singer Enters Plea In Charge," *Aiken Standard* (South Carolina), April 11, 1991, p. 13.

74. Letter from Nilsson to the staff of St. Luke's, September 15, 1990.

75. E-mail from Zak Nilsson, October 15, 2012.

76. Zak Nilsson interviewed by John Scheinfeld for LSL Productions, 2004.

77. Letter from Cindy L. Sims to Nilsson, January 3, 1991.

78. James Bates, "In the end, only creditors talked to Nilsson," *Los Angeles Times*, November 4, 1994.

79. Una Nilsson, 2011.

80. Author's interview with Lee Blackman, February 2011.

81. Bates, op. cit.

82. Ibid.

83. Letter from Nilsson to his creditors, November 26, 1992.

84. Bates, op. cit.

85. Author's interview with Perry Botkin Jr., February 2011.

86. "Nilsson was blindsided when he and other clients of business manager Cindy Sims discovered in 1991 that she had been taking their money." Bates, op. cit.

87. Blackman, 2011.

88. Bates, op. cit.

89. Letter from Nilsson to his creditors, November 26, 1992.

90. Letter to Nilsson from Yoko Ono (undated) in Nilsson's files for 1991.

91. Una Nilsson, 2011.

92. Letter from Nilsson to his creditors, November 26, 1992.

93. Botkin, 2011.

94. Letters from Spero in Nilsson's personal files for 1991.

95. Lynne Heffley, "Nilsson able to make his 'Point' again," *Los Angeles Times*, September 19, 1991.

96. Ibid.

97. Lee Newman interviewed by John Scheinfeld for LSL Productions, 2004.

98. "Animation Festival," *Santa Fe New Mexican*, January 24, 1992, p. 63.

99. *Daily Herald* (Chicago), May 22, 1991, p. 15.

100. "All Time Greatest" CD issue advertised in *Cedar Rapids Gazette*, November 17, 1991, p. 357.

101. Dawn Eden, "One Last Touch of Nilsson." Dawn Eden, "Nilsson's 'involvement' in compilation a figment of label's imagination," *Goldmine*, February 2, 1996.

102. Terry Gilliam interviewed by John Scheinfeld for LSL Productions, 2004.

103. Mark Hudson interviewed by John Scheinfeld for LSL Productions, 2005.

104. Ibid.

105. Van Dyke Parks interviewed by John Scheinfeld for LSL Productions, 2003.

106. Memos from Forte and Hanson copied to Paul Williams in RCA archives.

107. "Harry Nilsson," *Pacific Stars and Stripes*, February 23, 1993, p. 9.

108. Una Nilsson interviewed by John Scheinfeld for LSL Productions, 2005.

109. Annie Nilsson interviewed by John Scheinfeld for LSL Productions, 2005.

110. Olivia Nilsson interviewed by John Scheinfeld for LSL Productions, 2005.

111. Jimmy Webb interviewed by David Leaf for LSL Productions, 2003.

112. Published in *Galaxy*, March/April 1994, p. 92.

113. Una Nilsson/Scheinfeld, 2005.

CHAPTER 12

1. Micky Dolenz interviewed by John Scheinfeld for LSL Productions, 2005.

2. Perry Botkin Jr. interviewed by John Scheinfeld and Lee Blackman for LSL Productions, 2003.

3. Gerry Beckley interviewed by Stuart Grundy for BBC Radio 2, broadcast February 8, 1997.

4. Eric Idle interviewed by John Scheinfeld for LSL Productions, 2005.

5. Botkin/Scheinfeld/Blackman, 2005.

6. Randy Lewis, "Harry Nilsson *All Time Greatest Hits*, RCA," *Los Angeles Times*, January 27, 1994.

7. Carlos V. Lozano, "Grammy Winner Harry Nilsson Dies," *Los Angeles Times*, January 16, 1994.

8. "Chrysler Corp. is sponsoring the non-profit group Recording Artists Against Drunk Driving," *Daily News*, February 21, 1994.

9. Lozano, op. cit.

10. Dennis Hunt, "Harry Nilsson: A Welcome Retrospective," *Los Angeles Times*, March 21, 1995.

11. Rush Evans, "We're Just Wild About Harry," *Discoveries*, May 1995, p. 35.

12. Al Kooper, "For the Love of Harry," liner note to Music Masters 13254, 1995.

13. Derek Taylor, "Thoughts of Harry," liner note to Music Masters 13254, 1995.

14. Notice of Entry of Judgment, August 26, 1994.

15. Nilsson/Grundy, 1977.

Bibliography

Bianculli, David. *Dangerously Funny, The Uncensored Story of the Smothers Brothers Comedy Hour.* New York: Simon and Schuster, 2009.

Blaney, John. *John Lennon—Listen to this Book.* London: Paperjukebox, 2005.

Bronson, Fred. *Billboard's Hottest Hot 100 Hits.* New York: Billboard Books, 1991.

Brown, Mick. *Tearing Down The Wall of Sound—The Rise and Fall of Phil Spector.* London: Bloomsbury, 2007.

Brown, Peter, and Steven Gaines. *The Love You Make—An Insider's Story of the Beatles.* New York: Signet, 1983.

Carpenter, Humphrey. *Spike Milligan.* London: Coronet, 2003.

Chapman, Andrew, and Lee Gilber. *Rock to Riches.* Dulles, VA: Capital, 2008.

Chapman, Graham. *A Liar's Autobiography.* London: Methuen, 1990.

Chapman, Graham. *Yellowbeard—High Jinks on the High Seas.* New York: Carroll and Graf, 2005.

Clayson, Alan. *Ringo Starr, Straight Man or Joker.* St. Paul, MN: Paragon House, 1992.

Clayson, Alan. *Ringo Starr—A Life,* 2nd edition. London: Sanctuary, 2001.

Coleman, Ray. *Lennon, the Definitive Biography.* London: Pan, 2000.

Cooper, Alice, and Kent Zimmerman. *Golf Monster.* New York: Crown, 2007.

Courrier, Kevin. *Randy Newman's American Dreams.* Toronto: ECW, 2005.

Cresswell, Toby. *1001 Songs: The Great Songs of All Time and the Artists, Stories and Secrets.* New York: Da Capo, 2006.

Dawson, Julian. *And on piano ... Nicky Hopkins.* London: Desert Hearts, 2011.

Dolenz, Micky, and Mark Bego. *I'm a Believer, my Life of Monkees, Music and Madness.* New York: Hyperion, 1993.

Eliot, Marc. *Paul Simon—A Life.* Hoboken, NJ: Wiley, 2010.

Ellison, Craig W. *Loneliness, the Search for Intimacy*. Texarkana, TX: Christian Herald Books, 1980.

Fletcher, Tony. *Dear Boy—The Life of Keith Moon*. London: Omnibus, 2005.

Gerber, Gail, with Tom Lisanti. *Trippin' With Terry Southern—What I think I remember*. Jefferson, NC: McFarland, 2009.

Harry, Bill. *The Ringo Starr Encyclopedia*. London: Virgin, 2004.

Hill, Lee. *A Grand Guy, The Life and Art of Terry Southern*. New York: HarperCollins, 2001.

Idle, Eric, ed. *Monty Python Live*. London: Simon and Schuster, 2009.

Jackson, Blair. *Garcia: An American Life*. New York: Penguin, 2000.

Jenkins, Bruce. *Goodbye—In Search of Gordon Jenkins*. Berkeley, CA: Frog Ltd., 2005.

Kane, Larry. *Lennon Revealed*. Philadelphia: Running Press, 2005.

Kercher, Stephen E. *Revel With a Cause: Liberal Satire in Postwar America*. Chicago: University of Chicago Press, 2006.

Kubernik, Harvey, Scott Calamar, Henry Diltz, and Lou Adler. *Canyon of Dreams: The Magic and the Music of Laurel Canyon*. New York: Sterling, 2009.

Leary, Timothy. *The Politics of Ecstasy*. Berkeley, CA: Ronin, 1998.

Lecowicz, Eric. *The Monkees Tale*. Berkeley, CA: Last Gasp, 1985.

Lenburg, Jeff. *Dustin Hoffman—Hollywood's Antihero*. Bloomington, IN: iUniverse, 2001.

Lewis, Dave. *Led Zeppelin—The 'Tight But Loose' Files: Celebration II*, London: Omnibus, 2004.

Mackin, Tom. *Brief Encounters from Einstein to Elvis*, Bloomington, IN: Author House, 2008.

McCabe, John. *Mr. Laurel and Mr. Hardy*. New York: Doubleday, 1961.

McDougal, Dennis. *Five Easy Decades—How Jack Nicholson Became the Biggest Movie Star in Modern Times*. Chichester, UK: Wiley, 2007.

McGilligan, Patrick. *Backstory 3: Interviews with Screenwriters of the 1960s*. Berkeley, CA: University of California Press, 1997

Melly, George. *Mellymobile*. London: Robson, 1982.

Newman, Del. *A Touch From God—It's Only Rock and Roll*. Clacton-on-Sea, UK: Apex, 2010.

O'Dell, Chris, with Katherine Ketcham. *Miss O'Dell*. New York: Touchstone, 2009.

Phillips, Katherine W. *Diversity and Groups*. Bingley, UK: Emerald, 2008.

Rawlings, Terry. *Then, Now and Rare British Beat 1960–69*. London: Omnibus, 2002.

Ribowsky, Mark. *He's a Rebel—Phil Spector: Rock and Roll's Legendary Producer*, 2nd edition. New York: Da Capo, 2006.

Scevak, Jill, and Robert Cantwell. *Stepping Stones*. Camberwell, AU: ACER, 2007.

Shepherd, John, David Horn et al., eds. *Continuum Encyclopedia of Popular Music of the World, Vol. 1: Media, industry and society*. New York: Continuum, 2003.

Simpson, Paul. *The Rough Guide to Cult Pop*. London: DK Pub./Rough Guides, 2003.

Spencer, Kristopher, *Film and television scores, 1950–1979: a critical survey by genre*. Jefferson, NC: McFarland, 2008.

Taylor, Derek. *Fifty Years Adrift (In an Open-Necked Shirt)*. London: Genesis, 1984.

Terry, Bridget. *The Popeye Story*. New York: Tom Doherty Associates, 1980.

Thompson, Dave. *Phil Spector—Wall of Pain*. London: Music Sales, 2010.

Turner, Steve. *The Fab Four—The Gospel According to the Beatles*. London: WJK, 2006.

Urish, Ben, and Kenneth J. Bielen. *The Words and Music of John Lennon.* Westport, CT: Praeger, 2005.

Warner, Jay. *American Singing Groups: A History from the 1940s to Today.* New York: Hal Leonard, 2006.

Weaver, Tom. *I Was A Monster Movie Maker.* Jefferson, NC: McFarland, 2001.

White, Eugene N. *The Comptroller and the Transformation of American Banking, 1960–1990.* Darby, PA: Diane, 1992.

Wilder, Craig Steven. *A Covenant with Color—Race and Social Power in Brooklyn.* New York: Columbia University Press, 2001.

Index

Garcia, Jerry, 46
Garfield, Gil, 37, 38, 40, 43, 45, 47
Garfunkel, Art, 256
"Gayla," 105
Geffen, David, 104
George, Lowell, 238
Gerber, Joan, 111
Gerrard, Hilary, 171, 184, 217, 235
Getz, Jane, 188, 200
Ghost and Mrs. Muir, The, 90–91, 133
Gibb, Mara, 227
Gilberto, Astrud
    covers "Without Her," 61
Gilliam, Terry, 275, 282
Ginell, Richard S., 225
Gire, Dan, 245
"Girlfriend," 90
"Give! Love! Joy!" 256
"Give Peace a Chance," 256, 264
Glancy, Kenneth, 178
Gleason, Jackie, 71–74, 76, 83
God's Greatest Hits. See Duit On Mon Dei
Goddard, Lon, 142, 194
"Goin' Down," 226, 227, 228, 238
Gold, E.J., 285
Goldberg, Whoopi, 270–272
Goldmine, xi, 20, 31, 178, 286, 289
"Good Day Sunshine," 53
"Good For God," 191
"Good Golly Miss Molly," 31, 33
"Good Old Desk," 25, 64
"Good Times," 38, 49
Goodnight Vienna (Starr album) 180–182, 185, 200
Goodspeed Opera House (Connecticut), 247–248
Gordon, Jim, 94, 120, 125, 127, 128
Gordon, Larry, 105
Gordy, Jr., Berry, 28
"Gotta Get Up," 115, 123, 129, 133, 175, 222, 223
Grakal, Bruce, 48, 158, 266
Grammy Awards, 24, 27, 67, 110, 122, 134, 152, 154
Grauman, Sid, 19, 21, 194
Great Escape, The, 53
Greatest Hits, 229, 231, 282, 288
"Green Green," 27
Greenidge, Robert, 187
Greenburg, Anthony, 185

"Groovy Little Suzie," 33, 34
"Growin' Up," 45, 64, 137
Grundy, Stuart, 48, 192

Haber, Joyce, 12, 50
"Ha Ha Said the Clown," 54
Ham, Pete, 121, 122, 123
Handgun (movie), 258
"Happy Together," 48
"Hard Day's Night, A," 53
Harrison, George, 55–56, 75, 81, 82, 134, 138, 139, 144, 208, 215, 288
    and movies, 146
    plays on *Son of Schmilsson*, 136
    Harry, 7, 81, 83, 88, 90, 94–95, 96, 102, 116, 123, 218
    cover design, 98, 129
"Harry" (by Eric Idle), 240
Harry and Ringo's Night Out (movie), 177
Hawkeye Entertainment, 269–273
    collapse, 277
    Nilsson as CEO, 272
Hay, Alexandra, 72
Hayes, Johnny, 54
"He Ain't Gonna Get My Girl," 23
Head (movie), 69–70, 87
    soundtrack album, 93–94
"Headlines," 38
Hefner, Hugh, 64
Heider, Wally, 101
Hells Angels, 8–9, 35
"He Needs Me," 242, 245
"Here I Sit," 44
"Here's Why I Did Not Go to Work Today," 200, 222
"He's Large," 245
Hewitt, Martin, 257
"Hey Little Girl," 49
Hidden Hills, (Nilsson home), 273, 277
High Fidelity, 60, 71
Hock, Jr., James, 269, 272
Hoefer, Doug, 36
Hoefer, Fred, 3, 6, 11, 12–13, 108, 218
Hoefer, Steve, 5
Hoernie, John, 201
Hoffman, Dustin, 66, 109, 111, 116, 232
Holden, Stephen, 136
Holland, Milton, 53
Holloway, Danny, 155